A MIGHTY
BAPTISM

A MIGHTY BAPTISM

Race, Gender, and the Creation of American Protestantism

Edited by
Susan Juster
and
Lisa MacFarlane

CORNELL UNIVERSITY PRESS   Ithaca and London

First published 1996 by Cornell University Press.

Library of Congress Cataloging-in-Publication Data
A mighty baptism : race, gender, and the creation of American
   Protestantism / edited by Susan Juster and Lisa MacFarlane.
       p.   cm.
   Includes bibliographical references and index.
   ISBN 0-8014-3024-0 (alk. paper).—ISBN 0-8014-8212-7 (pbk. :
alk. paper)
     1. Protestant churches—United States—History.   2. United States—
Church history.   3. Sex role—Religious aspects—Christianity—
History.   4. United States—Race relations.   5. Afro-Americans—
Religion.   I. Juster, Susan.   II. MacFarlane, Lisa.
BR515.M53   1996
280'.4'0973—dc20   95-49743

Printed in the United States of America

To Jane and Matt, Emma and Lydia

Contents

PART III
BLACK AND WHITE IN THE SPIRITUAL BORDERLANDS

Acknowledgments

This book grew out of a friendship and an intellectual commitment to studying religious experience as a powerful source of personal and social identity. We rediscovered both at a 1990 conference honoring the teaching and scholarship of John Owen King III, with whom we had been privileged to work at the University of Michigan. The book took shape over several years of conversations, where we explored the fertile terrain of American religion as well as the tangled disciplinary traditions of literature and history. We worked, at times struggled, to find a common language in which to talk about the relationship between text and context in the lives of Protestant believers. In the process we have learned as much about our own distinctive ways of reading and writing the past—our own leaps of faith, in a sense—as about theirs. Our deepest debt is to each other, then—as scholars and friends.

We would like to pay the highest tribute to our contributors, most of whom we did not know before we began this project. They bore patiently the inevitable delays that accompany a collaborative effort of this scope, never wavering in their commitment. We think the essays collected here represent some of the most exciting and innovative work being done in American religious studies today, and we thank the authors for making their work available to us and to our readers.

Our home institutions provided invaluable support during the course of the project, both financially and intellectually. We thank the staffs of the Department of History, University of Michigan, and the Department of English, University of New Hampshire, for helping in all the small ways that make academic life easier. Lisa MacFarlane also thanks the Center for the Humanities, the College of Liberal Arts, and the Graduate School at the University of New Hampshire, and, most especially, the Louisville Institute for the Study of Protestantism and Culture, for providing crucial financial support along the way.

Several colleagues and friends read earlier drafts of our introductory essay and helped us think about the volume as a whole. Our thanks to Ann Braude, Elsa Barkley Brown, Susan Curtis, Laura Lee Downs, Richard Fox, Melody Graulich, Jean Humez, and Colleen McDannell. Peter Agree of Cornell University Press was our patron saint, helping shepherd this volume along when it threatened to collapse under its own weight. From the beginning he was confident that we could do this, despite our own doubts, and he was—as we have come to know and trust—right. And in the final stages, Molly Doyle provided fresh eyes and great good sense in helping with proofs and indexing.

David Mayfield and David Watt cooked meals, cared for children, listened patiently to rambling monologues, endured endless long-distance telephone conversations. We thank them for these, and more important, for everything. And to our children, Jane and Matt, Emma and Lydia (who arrived in the midst of the final draft of our introduction), we dedicate this book. They did nothing to help things along, except by their presence to recall us to the miracles that attend daily life. They make our lives richer—if messier—than we ever could have hoped.

S. J. and L. M.

A MIGHTY BAPTISM

INTRODUCTION

"A Sperit in de Body"

SUSAN JUSTER AND LISA MACFARLANE

I dreamed I see Jim Marvyn a sinkin' in de water, an' stretchin' up his hands. An' den I dreamed I see the Lord Jesus come a-walkin' on the water an' take hold ob his hand, an' says he, "O thou of little faith, wherefore didst thou doubt?" An' den he lifted him right out . . . De [minister], he don't like to hab us talk much 'bout dese ver tings, 'cause he tinks it's kind of heathenish. But den, folks as is used to seein' sech tings knows de look ob a sperit *out* o' de body from de look of a sperit *in* de body.[1]

The above passage from Harriet Beecher Stowe's 1859 novel *The Minister's Wooing* calls us to think about the relationship between body and soul in America's "Protestant Age." This passage succinctly illustrates the themes of this volume: how American Protestants, male and female, black and white, came to understand and express their spiritual beliefs in an era of intense religious renewal. Stowe was not alone in recognizing how the different spiritual experiences of women and blacks undermined the religious authority of her New England forefathers. But she was uniquely positioned to appreciate personally both the threats to the old orthodoxies and the opportunities for a revitalized Christian experience. Her family connections placed her squarely in the middle of Protestantism's response to a fractured and rapidly transforming nation: she was daughter to Lyman Beecher, a pugnacious evangelical minister; wife to Calvin Ellis Stowe, an improvident theological scholar; sister to Henry Ward Beecher, a flamboyant pastor of a fashionable urban congregation. And she herself was the author of the hugely successful, sentimental abolitionist novel, *Uncle Tom's Cabin*, which urged Christian mothers to "feel right." A Stowe or a Beecher was involved in many of the central challenges facing nineteenth-century Protestant religion: the feminization of mainstream denominations, the introduction of racial politics into religious communities, the decline in the professional status of the ministry, and the clash between charismatic sectarian voices and the corpse-cold theology of orthodox thinkers.

Within the relative safety of a historical romance, *The Minister's Wooing* alludes to all of these, and nowhere more compactly than in the figure of the

---

1. Harriet Beecher Stowe, *The Minister's Wooing* (New York, 1982), p. 797.

speaker in the opening passage. She is Candace, a black house servant to the Marvyn family, who believes that their son—the novel's dashing hero James—has been drowned at sea without having experienced a saving grace. To the grieving family, Candace offers a rich and complicated vision of the "resurrected" James (who in fact is not dead at all but merely missing at sea), a vision at once spiritually uplifting and socially subversive. Her speech shows the gendered and racialized nature of some of the central debates in nineteenth-century Protestantism, between a "feminized" spiritual life and a male-dominated church, between white Christianity and African tradition, between an empowering if idiosyncratic individual faith and a supporting if restricting community.

Candace acknowledges that, by dreaming, she is defying her minister—a fictional rendition of the famous Calvinist theologian Samuel Hopkins, who is portrayed elsewhere in the novel as morally courageous but emotionally distant. But she refuses to erase her African spiritual legacy; she cannot control her dreams, which are in fact prophetic. Nor will she disavow them by the light of day—"to folks as is used to seein' sech tings," dreams reinforce Christian faith. Her dream centers on Christ himself, who interrupts Candace's black dialect with King James lyricism, and her ventriloquy echoes the syncretic marriage of African American spiritual beliefs with Christian narrative. He appears to her walking across the water to save an unconverted soul. His action and words provide a text for Candace's New Testament belief in love and inclusiveness, in contrast to Hopkins' strict doctrine of election. When the minister's theology, with its rigid economy of salvation, fails to comfort the bereaved family, Candace's ministry succeeds across racial, gender, and class lines with what Stowe saw as a woman-centered gospel of feeling.[2] Candace justifies her reliance on dreams and on feeling by claiming a natural and superior wisdom of the heart that Stowe bases on her racial heritage and her gender. The minister may know the letter of the law, Stowe argues, but Candace sounds the depths of its spirit; he may champion an orthodox creed, but she celebrates an ecstatic and evangelical practice. But if Candace represents a revisioned Christianity, it is limited in its power, manifested in private exchanges among individuals rather than in official documents or policies. Despite the rebellions of her dreams and her subversive woman's gospel, she daily submits to an institution founded and governed by white men.

Black and white, male and female, clergy and laity, institutional structures and individual intuition, bodily presence and spiritual power, the intellectual practice of theology and the emotional experience of faith: these themes, so richly suggested in Stowe's work, echo throughout this collec-

---

2. Joan Hedrick, "'Peaceable Fruits': The Ministry of Harriet Beecher Stowe," *American Quarterly* 40 (Sept. 1988): 307–32.

tion. As a literary scholar and historian, we wanted to bring together other Americanists who, like us, were interested in the relationships and tensions of race and gender within American Protestantism during the pivotal years from 1780 to 1920. The scholars whose essays appear here all share a commitment to seeing religion as both lived experience and textual representation, to seeing spirituality revealed equally in material cultural practices, in written and visual texts, and in individual lives.

Religion is not a simple thing to study, or even to define. In some of the essays that follow, for example, religion appears as a thing in itself: it is an historical actor with its own resources and motivations, an institution that prescribes both options for and limits to historical change. We believe that examining the interplay of gender and race is central to understanding the often turbulent role religion has played in our national past, from early missionary encounters in the seventeenth century to the rise of fundamentalist politics in the twentieth. No matter how interested we are in the experiential dimension of faith, we cannot lose sight of the institutional power of religion in churches, voluntary associations, and political bodies. Some of us have emphasized this institutional power, arguing that individuals negotiate their religious beliefs within the contexts provided by church structures and theological forums.

But of perhaps greater concern to many of the authors in this volume is the way religion is a means by which individuals construct a sense of identity. For many believers, the institutional aspects of faith are secondary to the intensely personal experience of knowing and worshiping God. In seeking to describe this encounter between the human and the divine, race and gender are best understood as dialogic and evolving social vocabularies, as multiple voices or discourses in an ongoing cultural conversation. These voices have the power to construct our identities as social and spiritual beings, to shape not just how others see us but how we see ourselves. But more important, our identities also derive from our active responses to our changing needs and desires, responses which in turn serve to reconstruct the categories into which we are placed. We see race and gender, then, as both socially constructed and individually malleable, as shaped both by institutions and by real human beings living real lives. To put it more simply, we all want, in Robert Orsi's words, to understand "how people live in, with, and against, the discourses they inherit."[3]

The essays that follow comprise a series of conversations about this process, not a set of conclusions. Although in this introduction we suggest some ways in which these excursions into the religious landscape of

3. Robert Orsi, "'He Keeps Me Going': Women's Devotion to Saint Jude Thaddeus and the Dialectic of Gender in American Catholicism, 1929–1965," in *Belief in History: Innovative Approaches to European and American Religion*, ed. Thomas Kselman (South Bend, Ind., 1991), p. 155.

nineteenth-century America can be read against one another, we hope that our readers will find different ways to compare them. We hope, too, that these essays will stimulate a revival in the study of religion—a continually controversial subject at the center of American experience.

While several volumes of essays on the role of women in American religion have appeared, no collection addresses the question of gender: how religious beliefs and practices have been coded as "masculine" or "feminine" and with what consequences for American believers.[4] As the new scholarship on masculinity has amply demonstrated, gender is a fluid analytical tool that illuminates how women and men together confront culturally conditioned and institutionally structured definitions of "real" manhood and "true" womanhood.[5] Similarly, no studies of the cultural coding of race in American religion have appeared. The experiences of white and black Protestants are rarely discussed in comparative context, except to show the debilitating influence of the former over the latter, especially during the formative period of African American Christianity in the years between the Revolution and the Civil War. Important questions of origins (of how *African* African American religion is) have deflected us from recognizing the degree to which American Protestant traditions are embedded in a racialized discourse with profound social consequences for whites as well as blacks. African American religious practices not only responded to those of white Christianity, they permeated and transformed them.[6]

The essays in this volume focus primarily on the Protestant tradition in America, defined in its broadest sense. Although some of us examine mainstream denominations like Methodists and Episcopalians, others look at sectarian offshoots like the Shakers and the Garveyites, and still others explore the interplay of Protestant beliefs with quasi-religious practices like magic and the occult, which lie outside organized Christianity altogether. Protestantism was, of course, never a monolithic structure. Rather, it was a

4. Janet Wilson James, ed., *Women in American Religion* (Philadelphia, 1976); Rosemary Skinner Keller and Rosemary Reuther, eds., *Women and Religion in America* (San Francisco, 1981). A collection of essays edited by Carolyn Walker Bynum, *Gender and Religion: On the Complexity of Symbols* (Boston, 1986), provides a model for the kind of volume that is needed.
5. See, for example, scholars as distinct as Eve Kosofsky Sedgwick, *Between Men: English Literature and Male Homosocial Desire* (New York, 1985); Mark Carnes, *Secret Ritual and Manhood in Victorian America* (New Haven, 1989); and David Leverenz, *Manhood and the American Renaissance* (Ithaca, 1989).
6. See, for example, Mechal Sobel, *The World They Made Together: Black and White Values in Eighteenth-Century Virginia* (Princeton, 1987). Literary scholars have also seen intertextual relations between African American and white American traditions; see, for example, Shelley Fisher Fishkin, *Was Huck Black? Mark Twain and African-American Voices* (Oxford, 1993); and Eric J. Sundquist, *To Wake the Nations: Race in the Making of American Literature* (Cambridge, Mass., 1993).

mosaic of many cultural, racial, and ethnic strands, with beliefs and practices flexible enough to make room for prophets, upstart sectarians, and
unconventional believers. When we compare Etta Madden's Shakers, with
their feminized images of God and traditions of sexual egalitarianism, to
Gail Bederman's "muscular" Christians, with their frank championing of
patriarchal authority, we glimpse the great diversity of religious cultures
within American Protestantism.

The dominance of Protestantism as a "national religion," particularly
after the disintegration of state churches in the early nineteenth century,
was in fact secured by a constant process of fragmentation and reintegra-
tion. Mainstream Protestant churches faced a number of unique challenges
in this period. Successive revivals swelled the attendance at old churches,
and massive immigration (both voluntary and involuntary) created new
churches and new faiths at an unprecedented rate.[7] The sectarian nature of
American Protestantism has been a persistent source of conflict from the
colonial period to the present day, but it has also been a vital source of
political innovation and cultural regeneration. Oppositional sects like the
Shakers and the Garveyites have shaped American political culture just as
profoundly as mainstream denominations like the Methodists and the Baptists, and sometimes in disquieting ways.[8]

Revisiting the familiar terrain of the nineteenth century helps clarify the
relationship between this diverse religious tradition and larger social and
political events. The period from the Revolutionary War to the end of the
First World War, which was the formative era of organized political movements to enfranchise women and emancipate blacks, occupies a central
place in the literature on race and gender in American history. Americans
began seriously to question the ideological and political assumptions that
excluded women and blacks from the body politic. At the same time, social
divisions of race and gender came to seem more "natural," more rooted in
biological destiny, and hence more immutable.[9] This fundamental paradox

7. For discussions of the impact of revivalism on nineteenth-century Protestantism, see
George M. Thomas, *Revivalism and Cultural Change: Christianity, Nation Building, and the
Market in the Nineteenth-Century United States* (Chicago, 1989); William McLoughlin, *Reviv-
als, Awakenings, and Reform: An Essay on Religion and Social Change in America, 1607–1977*
(Chicago, 1978); Donald G. Mathews, "The Second Great Awakening as an Organizing
Process, 1780–1830," *American Quarterly* 21 (1969): 23–43; and Timothy L. Smith, *Revival-
ism and Social Reform: American Protestantism on the Eve of the Civil War*, rev. ed. (Baltimore,
1980).

8. See R. Laurence Moore, *Religious Outsiders and the Making of Americans* (New York,
1986) for a succinct exposition on the role of religious sects in the making of American
political culture.

9. Thomas Lacqueur, *Making Sex: Body and Gender from the Greeks to Freud* (Cambridge,
Mass., 1990); Henry Louis Gates, Jr., "Introduction: Writing 'Race' and the Difference it
Makes," in *"Race," Writing, and Difference*, ed. Henry Louis Gates, Jr. (Chicago, 1986), pp.
1–20.

has generated enormous scholarly interest in nineteenth-century America as the seedbed of contemporary dilemmas about the intractability of racial and sexual inequities in a democratic society. Literary scholars, too, see this period as encompassing dramatic shifts in the history of American letters. After the Revolution the desire for cultural independence compelled authors, most of them white and male, to define what it meant to be an American, a citizen of this new and unique political entity. By the postbellum period, the rise of realism as a political and literary aesthetic encouraged a generation of women and African American writers to record their experiences as well. Their efforts challenged readers to rethink the nature of the national experience; yet, shaped as these works were by established literary conventions and the demands of the market, they often reinscribed prevailing assumptions about gender and race.

For whites and blacks alike, the disintegration of Protestant hegemony at the turn of the twentieth century coincided with a renewed sense of declension in the community of religious believers. As church pews were filled increasingly with women and as the clergy seemed to be losing their moral and political authority in a secularizing nation, concern over the future of religion was pervasive. The trope of declension was not unique to the early twentieth century, of course. From the earliest colonists to the voices of today crying out for a return to values, American believers have constantly lamented what they perceived as a falling away from faith. Declension and revivalism have long coexisted as organizing metaphors for structuring religious experience in America.[10] What looks like decline from one perspective is, of course, an opportunity for religious innovation from another perspective—innovations which include not only new communities but even new religious rituals, symbols, and stories. Revivalism and declension manifest themselves in an uneasy tension between building a community of saints and celebrating the individual's personal experience—a tension at the center of the broader political and cultural life of the nation as well.

We begin, then, with a pair of essays that frame this critical period: Susan Juster's discussion of female prophecy in the post-Revolutionary years in Chapter 1 and Barbara Bair's cautionary tale about a charismatic black woman preacher in the Garveyite movement of the 1920s in Chapter 2. Juster's Jemima Wilkinson, founder of the distinctly quirky Society of the Universal Friend, and Bair's Laura Kofey, a rebel from the Universal Negro Improvement Association, both found their public voices where a call to exercise spiritual authority met an incendiary political message. Issues of

---

10. For a study of the jeremiad's effect on literary and cultural forms of expression, see Sacvan Bercovich, *The American Jeremiad* (Madison, 1978). For an example of the way in which contemporary scholars continue to find themselves speaking in these terms, see Robert Bellah et al., *Habits of the Heart: Individualism and Commitment in American Life* (Berkeley, 1985).

spiritual identity—who is chosen by God for public ministry and why?—are at the heart of these tales of racial and gender transgressions. Juster argues that Wilkinson needed to appropriate a male voice in order to claim power, going so far as to erase her own identity completely and proclaim herself the reborn Christ, a move which predictably isolated her from mainstream groups. Laura Kofey spoke as a black woman in a community that venerated the legacy of an African "Motherland" but relegated women to auxiliary roles in the nationalist movement. When her voice broke the bounds of racial patriarchy, she was silenced by an assassin's bullet.

The stories of Wilkinson and Kofey remind us of the continued exclusion of those whose political and spiritual views fail to conform to accepted religious paradigms. Both women were lay preachers who spoke outside the institutional structures that defined spiritual experience. They raised their individual prophetic voices against the choruses of tradition and established teachings, and they championed an emotional spiritual life against a rational theology. Moreover, each woman illustrates the relationship between religious belief and political agenda. Wilkinson sought to define and contain her vision of America as a Christian nation in the turbulent years following the Revolution, and Kofey found herself straining against the gender restrictions of Marcus Garvey's political crusade for African Americans. In different ways and in very different contexts, the lives of Wilkinson and Kofey illustrate the intricate connections between spiritual strength, ecclesiastical authority, and political status. If America was indeed a Christian nation, as its founders insisted even while formally separating church and state, then those who would claim a political inheritance would find it implicated in a Christian tradition.

The content of one's political and spiritual inheritance, of course, depends upon gender. In a nation under God, how does one reconcile citizenship—originally the prerogative of white men—with piety—the special province of women? The second set of essays takes up the question of how the gendering of various social values affected the practice of belief, especially from the vantage point of the ecclesiastical center. Lisa MacFarlane, Patricia Cline Cohen, Gail Bederman, and Mary De Jong all write about the white male ministers who dominated the religious hierarchy and who embodied the power against which rebellious church members had to struggle. Each of these essays is set against the implicit backdrop of the much-contested concept of separate spheres, which had its clearest articulation and its fiercest test in the gender wars that we associate with the "Woman Question" in late Victorian culture. The separate spheres paradigm aptly captures a discursive tradition central to the lives of many middle-class Americans in the nineteenth century; but as a description of gender relations, it belies the permeability of the line separating the private and the familial from the extradomestic.[11] As the history of antebellum social reform movements amply demonstrates, white middle-class women based their entry into the public, traditionally male domain on prescribed female virtues of piety and morality. Middle-class men, like their wives and daughters, found themselves caught in the contradictions of a gendered morality. Crossing the moral boundaries of prescriptive masculinity, bourgeois men employed feminine modes of self-presentation in pursuit of a transcendent faith.[12] Just as we recognize that "true womanhood" was only one prescriptive model among many for middle-class women, we have come to see that there were many "styles of manhood" for Victorian men as well.[13] The prototypical figure of evangelical Protestantism, the Methodist circuit rider, was distinguished as much by his ability to weep freely with his brethren as he was by his public demeanor of manly austerity.[14]

Prominent ministers such as Henry Ward Beecher embodied in their very person and position both Christian manhood and female affections, a volatile mix that often led to confused relationships between ministers and their female parishioners. Lisa MacFarlane argues in Chapter 3 that this confusion reigned in the breasts, as well as the souls, of ministers themselves. Her essay on the convention of the feminized minister in the late nineteenth-century novel *The Damnation of Theron Ware* highlights the psychological instability that attended the construction of masculinity for ministers who wielded masculine privilege and yet were dependent upon the "feminine" art of influence to maintain their livelihoods.[15] A more

11. For the best introduction to the genesis of the separate spheres paradigm in the early nineteenth century, see Nancy F. Cott, *The Bonds of Womanhood: "Woman's Sphere" in New England, 1780–1835* (New Haven, 1977). On the testing of this paradigm in the late Victorian period see Nancy Cott, *The Grounding of American Feminism* (New Haven, 1987); Rosalind Rosenberg, *Beyond Separate Spheres: The Intellectual Roots of Modern Feminism* (New Haven, 1982); Janette Hassey, *No Time for Silence: Evangelical Women in Public Ministry around the Turn of the Century* (Grand Rapids, Mich., 1986); Betty DeBerg, *Ungodly Women: Gender and the First Wave of American Fundamentalism* (Minneapolis, 1990); and Barbara J. Harris, *Beyond Her Sphere: Women and the Professions in American History* (Westport, Conn., 1978). For a critique of the separate spheres paradigm, see Linda Kerber, "Separate Spheres, Female Worlds, Woman's Place: The Rhetoric of Women's History," *Journal of American History* 75 (June 1988): 9–39.

12. On changing notions of masculinity in the nineteenth century, see E. Anthony Rotundo, *American Manhood: Transformations in Masculinity from the Revolution to the Modern Era* (New York, 1993); J. A. Mangan and James Walvin, eds., *Manliness and Morality: Middle-Class Masculinity in Britain and America 1800–1940* (New York, 1987).

13. Clyde Griffen, "Reconstructing Masculinity from the Evangelical Revival to the Waning of Progressivism: A Speculative Synthesis," in *Meanings for Manhood: Constructions of Masculinity in Victorian America*, ed. Mark Carnes and Clyde Griffen (Chicago, 1990), p. 183. For a literary study of the relationship between sexual identity and spiritual identity, see Ann-Janine Morey, *Religion and Sexuality in American Literature* (Cambridge, 1992).

14. Russell Richey, *Early American Methodism* (Bloomington, Ind., 1991).

15. Ann Douglas' *The Feminization of American Culture* (New York, 1977) began the discussion of the role of the female (rather than women) in American religion and letters; for more recent inquiries on gender and literature, see Elaine Showalter, ed., *Speaking of Gender*

solidly constructed man could also fall to the carnal temptations offered by spiritually intimate relations between a "brother in Christ" and his perhaps attractive and admiring "sisters." The celebrated trial of the Bishop Benjamin Onderdonk in the 1840s for what we would today describe as sexual harassment, narrated by Patricia Cline Cohen in Chapter 4, exposed the gender ambiguities of clerical life to the harsh light of public scrutiny. Both those who supported the philandering bishop and those who condemned his behavior were engaged in an important cultural debate over the meaning and parameters of sexuality in American religious life.

The blurring of the distinction between public and private, manliness and femininity, in the religious activities of women and men of the middle class—the very class responsible for the creation of the ideology of separate spheres in the first place—created an identity crisis in the last decades of the nineteenth and the first decades of the twentieth centuries, which Protestant leaders tried to resolve by a vigorous assertion of "muscular Christianity." The drive to re-masculinize the churches, described in Gail Bederman's article on the Men and Religion Forward Movement of 1911–1912 (Chapter 5), brought thousands of American men back into the fold and signaled the retreat of American women from active leadership roles in organized religious life. Mary De Jong's essay on female hymnists focuses on one popular forum for women to express themselves spiritually (Chapter 6). But hymns were meant to be performed and shared, to circulate in the public arena. In this process, hymns, and the women who wrote them, became subject to male compilers, editors, and ministers, who retained control both over the content and the reception of a powerful source of spiritual communion. Just as MacFarlane argues that Theron Ware is reborn as a culturally correct and psychologically unified middle-class man, and Cohen stresses Onderdonk's continued assertion of male privilege in spite of the New York courts, Bederman and De Jong show how men retained firm control of religious institutions. Although these essays emphasize the challenges the clergyman might face, they also conclude that he was usually able to defend against them.

Scholars of African American religion have transposed the dialectic between public and private, which has so dominated women's history, into a tension between assimilation and separation, between the accommodating public face of black religion and its defiant private expression. In the eighteenth and nineteenth centuries slave religion inhabited the boundaries between the private and public. The "hidden" church of the slave commu-

---

(New York, 1989); Joseph A. Boone and Michael Cadden, eds., *Engendering Men: The Question of Male Feminist Criticism* (New York, 1990); and Laura Claridge and Elizabeth Langland, eds., *Out of Bounds: Male Writers and Gender(ed) Criticism* (Amherst, Mass., 1990).

nity coexisted with the formal religious societies formed by black and white evangelicals. Slaves heard one version of the Christian story of sin and redemption in the public meetinghouse and quite another in the "hush harbors" of their private worship.[16] Despite their egalitarian rhetoric and abolitionist sympathies, the early evangelical churches continued to subordinate blacks to whites. In order, then, to preserve a separate identity as a people, some historians have argued that African Americans had to form independent religious communities grounded in indigenous African religious practices and belief systems.[17]

In Chapter 7 Yvonne Chireau suggests that slave women were instrumental in preserving traditional forms of supernatural practice such as conjuring which represented an underground religious economy in the antebellum South. Magic and religion remained intertwined in slave life in ways that both affirmed and subverted the power of whites over blacks and of men over women. Sharla Fett's essay on female faith healers explores the contradictions immanent in African American religious practice in the context of the "peculiar institution" (Chapter 8). As healers, slave women helped maintain a healthy and productive labor force for their masters while simultaneously providing spiritual comfort to the enslaved. Faith healers may have been tolerated by slaveowners because of their curative powers, but they also represented a defiant rejection of Christian models of spiritual empowerment and healing that was surely troubling to more observant masters. The line between resistance and submission was a porous one in slave culture, and never more so than in the contested realm of faith.

While mainstream Protestant denominations struggled with the specter of interracial worship in their own congregations, sectarian offshoots like the Shakers embraced a more racially inclusive ecclesiology. In Chapter 9 Etta Madden argues that Shaker theology offered black women a radical opportunity to shape the symbolic and textual life of their communities. The figure of the "Mother in Israel," personified first by Ann Lee and later by female followers such as Rebecca Jackson, blended the sexual and the

16. Jacqueline Jones, *Labor of Love, Labor of Sorrow: Black Women, Work, and the Family from Slavery to the Present* (New York, 1985); Hazel Carby, *Reconstructing Womanhood: The Emergence of the Afro-American Woman Novelist* (New York, 1987); Deborah Gray White, *Ar'n't I a Woman? Female Slaves in the Plantation South* (New York, 1985); Margaret Creel Washington, *"A Peculiar People": Slave Religion and Community-Culture Among the Gullahs* (New York, 1988).

17. For examples of the syncretism between African and European religious systems, see Mechal Sobel, *Trabelin' On: The Slave Journey to an Afro-Baptist Faith* (Westport, Conn., 1979); Sobel, *The World They Made Together*; and Albert Raboteau, *Slave Religion: The "Invisible" Institution in the Antebellum South* (New York, 1978). For an alternative view that stresses the defiant nature of slave religion, see Sylvia Frey, *Water From the Rock: Black Resistance in a Revolutionary Age* (Princeton, 1991). For a recent discussion of the institution of the black church, see C. Eric Lincoln and Lawrence H. Mamiya, *The Black Church in the African American Experience* (Durham, N.C., 1990).

spiritual into a vision of female agency so powerful that male Shakers like Alonzo Hollister tried to capture its symbolic potency for themselves. Although the maternal power of women was an icon of fear and repression in the slaveholding South, where slave nannies had access to conjure and other forms of spiritual vengeance, it was transformed by white male Shakers into an emblem of spiritual authority.

This cultural appropriation of white and black forms of Christianity went both ways. A deep ambivalence toward what Frederick Douglass called the "Christianity of this land" is evident in the literary productions of black Protestants in the nineteenth century. In Chapter 10 Stephen Hum reads the hymns collected by Richard Allen for use in the African Methodist Episcopal Church as embodying a narrative of liberation for the embattled black population of postrevolutionary Philadelphia, a narrative that sought to transcend the secular disabilities imposed on African Americans by the new political order while still "speaking" reconciliation to the white Protestant establishment. In similar fashion, John Ernest argues in Chapter 11 that antebellum black writers like William Wells Brown and Harriet Jacobs attempted to exploit the language of Christian communion to establish for African Americans a literary claim to the moral and religious patrimony of the American nation. Questioning the practice of Christianity even as they relied upon its symbols and hermeneutics, African American writers— much like the slave healers and the conjure women—were inextricably bound to the very culture they opposed.

After emancipation, the black church became an even more important force in the religious and political aspirations of African Americans. The considerable moral authority of slave women in their faith communities was not easily replicated in the formal institutional structures of black religious life after the Civil War. The "righteous discontent" of black women with regard to their exclusion from positions of leadership and public authority in the Baptist church that Evelyn Brooks Higginbotham documents in the period 1880 to 1920 was part of a much larger struggle within the African American community over gender norms and gender roles in the late Victorian era, a period described as the nadir of American race relations.[18] Like white women of the antebellum reform movements, black women in the late nineteenth century—who likewise constituted a majority of church members—found themselves marginalized as their religious communities resorted to the "politics of respectability" in order to stake out a place for themselves in mainstream American culture. As Bair's dramatic story of the assassination of Laura Kofey so vividly demonstrates, spiritual empowerment and gender subordination were fatefully (even fa-

18. Evelyn Brooks Higginbotham, *Righteous Discontent: The Women's Movement in the Black Baptist Church, 1880–1920* (Cambridge, Mass., 1993).

tally) intertwined in the history of the black church as it entered the twentieth century.

We have organized these essays into a series of concentric circles, widening from the ecclesiastical center outward into the spiritual borderlands. Our organization thus emphasizes the pervasive and often contentious relationship between established traditions and sectarian impulses in American history. There are, of course, other ways to make sense of the essays collected here. The theme of the prophetic voice and its role in Protestant soteriology connects figures as diverse as Jemima Wilkinson, Rebecca Jackson, and Laura Kofey. Both De Jong and Hum explore the place of hymnody in Protestant life, asking how those normally excluded from exegetical discourse have used this very traditional form of worship to construct an alternative model of the sacred community. Important and timely questions about the relationship between sexuality and religious authority are raised in Chireau's discussion of the intimate connection between "black" magic and sexual competition in the slave community, in Madden's reading of male Shakers' ambivalent embrace of female roles, and in MacFarlane's and Cohen's essays on the sexual tensions implicit in clerical-lay relations. Bederman's emphasis on the organizational structure of a faith community nicely counterpoints Ernest's concern with the textual construction of faith. Both Fett and De Jong argue that religious experiences, far from being otherworldly, are very much a part of the material world of economic calculation.

Uniting all the essays in this volume is a common concern for the power of faith. We mean power in two different but related senses: the power conferred by religion upon those who believe, and the power invested in religion by American culture. Power is always notoriously difficult to identify and measure. Religious communities empower their members individually and collectively in ways that range from the mundane to the transcendent, and secular institutions and spiritual authority are both tightly woven into the fabric of our national identity. Opportunities for spiritual empowerment often set in motion a delicate interplay between individual conscience and group norms.

As individuals, some believers gain a private feeling of comfort and worth from their religion, while others feel more isolated, coerced into conforming to alien ways of worship. Often, the personal, idiosyncratic nature of private belief converges with the collective message of the church, as in the case of black Shakers like Rebecca Jackson. At other times the institutional authority of a religious community undermines the private practice of faith, as in the case of African American diviners and healers on the slave plantation. If, for some men and women, religion has been an emancipatory force, for others it has been a rationale for obedience. Nor should we oppose spirituality to institutional religious expression. People have discovered spiritual transcendence through both established rituals and idiosyncratic variations. In all cases the true measure of belief remains buried in the heart, inaccessible to the contemporary scholar save through the imperfect art of historical imagination—another act of faith.

Believers also respond collectively to the spiritual energy fostered in religious communities in ways that are more visible and hence knowable. In this sense, religion can be a social force in its own right. It offers legitimacy and cultural resources to subordinate groups as well as those at the ecclesiastical center. The black church was a place for men and women both to accommodate white demands and to forge a distinctive racial identity. Women, too, black and white, used their spiritual energies to stake a claim to moral authority, which some of them would translate into a call for political rights in the abolitionist and suffrage movements. Scholars have rightly celebrated these heroic movements in the history of American Protestantism as powerful testimony to the transformative nature of religious experience. Protestantism, after all, was born and flourished in a climate of spiritual dissent and social activism.

The story of the tension between established powers and radical rebirths can, however, be overly romanticized. In our eagerness to document the religious sources of social and political discontent, we must be careful not to underestimate the enormous cultural and political power of the religious establishment. Reading these essays against each other reveals some sobering limitations. Hum reminds us that Richard Allen's hymns of liberation could not free his African American listeners from the shackles of racial or class oppression; Fett's faith healers remained enslaved despite their valuable medical services; and Chireau's conjure women retreated into folktales. Masculine power reasserted itself both for Bederman's real-life Christian soldiers and for MacFarlane's fictional one. Both Cohen and De Jong describe the power ecclesiastical men had, even over the very women in their congregations upon whom their authority depended: Benjamin Onderdonk retained most of the economic and social privileges of his office despite being found guilty of sexually molesting his female parishioners, and female hymnists saw their offerings transformed and their talents unacknowledged. Madden and Bair compellingly illustrate how the spiritual experiences of African American women were safely contained: Rebecca Jackson became "mother" to Alonzo Hollister after he appropriated the power of her maternal persona, and Laura Kofey paid the ultimate price—death—for challenging the patriarchal structure of the Garvey movement. Juster and Ernest remind us that efforts to claim rhetorical control over the sacred founding documents of the nation were deeply contradictory: even while Jemima Wilkinson was surrendering the uniqueness of her own identity to the "Universal," nineteenth-century African

American writers were struggling to incorporate "blackness" into definitions of America. Whether spiritual elevation was a sufficient recompense for the daily humiliations and deprivations of life on the margins, we cannot know.

Although we must be careful not to romanticize struggles along the margins, we must also be careful not to dismiss the religiosity of established elites. Too often, the piety of those in power—ministers included—has been derided as lacking authentic conviction. But just as the disenfranchised found their beliefs to be a source of inner strength, so too did those in positions of authority find genuine release and guidance in their faith. Bederman's Christian Soldiers, after all, sincerely believed they were strengthening their churches by returning men to positions of authority. And it would be a serious mistake to underestimate the anguished soul-searching that interracial squabbles caused white Protestant leaders, who saw their black brethren deserting the spiritual fold to set up independent congregations. As a whole, this volume tries to steer a middle course between naïveté and cynicism about the power of religion—not an easy feat.

Nineteenth-century Americans, too, tried to reconcile the personal demands of faith with its public consequences. It was indeed a "mighty baptism," in Harriet Beecher Stowe's phrase, that swept American Protestantism in the century after independence. The might of the Protestant tradition lay precisely in its ability to baptize a future born of the past's oppressive weight with the hope and the possibility of new beginnings. A baptism is, of course, a ritual that welcomes the convert into the community of the faithful. It implies that the initiate renew publicly her private commitment to God. As such, baptism, like the other metaphors for human relationships we have discussed, exists at the interstices of community responsibility and individual conscience. Then as now, baptism gives rise to a new way of seeing one's relationship to the world. Contradiction and paradox inhere in this: obedience to churchly authority might collide with commitment to conscience, and rebellion against a prevailing social order might grow out of privately held convictions. Stowe's phrase captures, then, the potentially explosive power that American Protestants tried to harness and, at times, defuse.

This volatile mix of consent and coercion within American Protestantism created Harriet Beecher Stowe's Candace—a fitting, if fictional, symbol of healing and reconciliation. Indebted to the Reverend Hopkins for her freedom, she remained critical of his theology. But in spite of her dissent, she genuinely loved Hopkins. Candace's subversive African spiritual practices coexisted easily with her respect for her minister, the very symbol of orthodox power. While this may seem paradoxical to secular readers, nineteenth-century American Protestants well understood that love and rebel-

lion often go hand in hand. For many of them, as for Candace, Protestantism was a capacious theology, sheltering a variety of believers under its
wing. As Candace herself says, "I'm clar dar's consid'able more o' de [e]lect
dan people think."[19]

19. Stowe, *Minister's Wooing*, p. 737.

PART I
Prophetic Voices
in Protestant
America

CHAPTER 1

To Slay the Beast:
Visionary Women
in the Early Republic

SUSAN JUSTER

In a recent article on women and the Enlightenment, Phyllis Mack compares the opportunities for female self-expression in the seventeenth and eighteenth centuries. "Who was better off," she asks, "the eighteenth-century intellectual whose writing and behavior were constrained by 'modern' notions of rational adulthood but who was also immune from accusations of witchcraft, or the seventeenth-century visionary who was constrained to behave in an eccentric manner in order to convince her audience that she was a true prophet?" She concludes tentatively that "the earlier period may have been a more habitable time for some women, in terms of the possible range of self-expression and public esteem available to them, than the Enlightenment."[1] The question I wish to explore in this chapter is whether a similar conclusion might be drawn about female prophets in postrevolutionary America.

What role could female religious visionaries play in an enlightened society? The question itself seems an oxymoron, juxtaposing religion with secularism, mysticism with rationalism, and the feminine world of private ecstatic experience with the male world of the public sphere. But we know that enlightened societies often accommodated a wide range of mystical and spiritual behaviors without undue cultural dissonance; magic and science were not so neatly divorced as they have become in the modern world. Apocalyptic and millennial rhetoric was an important idiom through which American revolutionaries made sense of such secular concepts as tyranny, virtue, and liberty. The American republic was truly "a visionary republic," in Ruth Bloch's apt phrase.[2] The flourishing of religious mysticism after the American Revolution (for many scholars the culminating act of the Enlightenment) had deep roots in the democratic aspirations and anxieties unleashed by the rebellion, despite the manifest distaste on the part of

1. Phyllis Mack, "Women and the Enlightenment: Introduction," *Women and History* 9 (Spring 1984): 9.
2. Ruth Bloch, *The Visionary Republic: Millennial Themes in American Thought, 1756–1800* (New York, 1985).

the revolutionary leadership for the "enthusiastical" excesses of revealed religion.[3]

No doubt religious visionaries found early republican America a hospitable place. This was the age, after all, of "crazy" Lorenzo Dow, the charismatic Methodist itinerant who spoke to God in his dreams, and Joseph Smith, who discovered the fifth gospel, the book of Mormon, in which the drama of revelation was enacted on American soil.[4] But what about women visionaries? Was there a place in the religious hothouse of the early republican period for women who saw God in visions and spoke the language of biblical revelation? Did the revolutionary upheaval unleash a host of female prophets on the scale that England witnessed during the Civil War years, when radical mystics like Eleanor Davies and Mary Cary preached the imminent and violent end of the world to large audiences of both sexes?[5] The answer is a qualified "no." In the panorama of populist visionary religion in postrevolutionary America, there are few female faces, and fewer female voices. This essay is an attempt to understand the ministry of one woman who did join the apocalyptic chorus of the American Revolution, albeit in ways that denied rather than reaffirmed her identity as a woman.

The career of Jemima Wilkinson, the charismatic ex-Quaker who preached throughout southeastern New England and western New York in the last decades of the eighteenth century and first decades of the nineteenth, is a story of paradoxes. Her militant rhetoric and apocalyptic message were encased in an apolitical language that denied any connection between the spiritual travails of the American people and the political travails of the new nation. Yet the very path that her ministry followed belied this severing of religious and political purposes, for she preached in the wake of the war campaigns that had devastated her native Rhode Island in the late 1770s and 1780s. Her appeals for radical reformation would invariably have resonated with contemporaneous appeals on the part of the revolutionary leadership for renewed civic virtue, however much she wished to distance herself from the political struggle for independence. More important, however, than the paradoxical nature of her message was the paradox of her ministry. Jemima Wilkinson did not preach as a female visionary in the tradition of those Civil War prophets and early Quaker prophetesses described so vividly by Phyllis Mack.[6] Rather, she claimed to

3. Jon Butler, *Awash in a Sea of Faith: Christianizing the American People* (Cambridge, Mass., 1990).

4. Nathan O. Hatch, *The Democratization of American Christianity* (New Haven, 1989).

5. Phyllis Mack, "Women as Prophets during the English Civil War," *Feminist Studies* 8 (Spring 1982): 19–45.

6. Mack, *Visionary Women: Ecstatic Prophecy in Seventeeth-Century England* (Berkeley, 1992).

be the reincarnation of Christ himself, the second coming of the Messiah. Her dress, comportment, and mannerisms all conveyed the central message of her ministry: that she was no longer a woman but the spirit of God. In this regard she conforms to the pattern suggested by Mack: women who claimed social or intellectual authority in the age of Enlightenment could only do so by "divest[ing] themselves of 'deviant' feminine character traits." Like early modern Jews who could assimilate only by stripping themselves of their ethnicity, women like Wilkinson could assume authoritative roles only by assimilating to masculinity.[7] Why this was so is the subject of this chapter.

From Revolution to Revival

There is no question that America in the early 1800s witnessed an evangelical revival of unprecedented proportions. Blasting the fears of conservative revolutionaries that there would be no room for God in the new republic, Americans turned to revived religion with a vengeance in the first decades of the nineteenth century. The overturning of the imperial structure of church and state was a rallying point for those who, like the Baptists of New England, valued "soul liberty" as much as political liberty.[8] Beginning in the 1780s and 1790s in New England and continuing unabated through the first three decades of the nineteenth century, the great revival left its imprint on every aspect of American religious culture. The expansiveness of evangelical Protestantism was matched only by the ambitions of its leaders, men who, like Elias Smith, saw themselves as the vanguard of a vast populist upswelling of religious fervor that would sweep away the last vestiges of establishmentarianism.

While united in their appreciation of the scope and historical importance of this Second Great Awakening, historians are divided over its larger significance in the shaping of antebellum religion. For some, the revivals were fundamentally conservative in import if not intent, serving ultimately to reaffirm the values and cultural habits upon which a mature capitalist society depended. The affinities between the revivalist call for a disciplined spiritual life and the needs of the new economic order for a disciplined labor force have not gone unnoticed, and if few scholars have gone so far as to posit a direct relationship between economic imperatives and religious practice, the suggestion that evangelical religion facilitated the spread of

---

7. Mack, "Women and the Enlightenment," pp. 6–7.
8. William McLoughlin has been the foremost authority on the Baptists of New England and their search to place religious liberty on the agenda of the American Revolution. See his collection of essays, *Soul Liberty: The Baptists' Struggle in New England, 1630–1833* (Hanover, N.H., 1991), and his monumental *New England Dissent: The Baptists and the Separation of Church and State, 1633–1833* (Cambridge, Mass., 1971).

market capitalism in the Jacksonian era has enjoyed considerable success among labor historians in particular.[9]

More recent evaluations of the Second Great Awakening have stressed its liberating effect on a people long accustomed to thinking and acting in deferential terms toward established elites (whether in the religious or political realm). For scholars such as Gordon Wood and Nathan Hatch, the relevant context for understanding the origins of antebellum revivals is not the market revolution but the political revolution of 1776, in which a deferential political culture was replaced by a voluntaristic, participatory one. However encrusted with older notions of republican virtue, the ideal of democratic citizenship that took shape in the partisan squabbles of the early nineteenth century can be seen as emblematic of a new cultural "type" that emerged full-blown in Jacksonian America: the self-made, self-directed man. Recognizing no allegiance to a higher authority beyond that which was voluntarily given and contractually secured, the self-made man of the 1830s insisted on the right to think and act for himself in matters of the spirit as well. The anticlerical rhetoric of the revivals and their extravagant celebration of the vernacular are taken to be evidence of the populist spirit that animated figures as diverse as Lorenzo Dow and Richard Allen. In this reading, the revivals of the Second Great Awakening embodied the democratic pulse of America itself.[10] It was thus not the labor demands of the market economy that formed the seedbed of evangelical Protestantism but rather the political transformations associated with the fashioning of a liberal democratic order.

These two readings of the Second Great Awakening—one emphasizing the conservative function of revivalism, the other its liberating potential—are not as far apart as they might at first glance appear. Both lead ultimately back to the individual, arguing (as evangelicals themselves did) that the experience of conversion created a new set of attitudinal and behavioral imperatives that imbued each individual convert with a new spiritual character. Whether the "new birth" fitted one to labor diligently in the factories of rural New England or to found a sect in defiance of established ecclesiastical elites, the social effects of revivalism (industrial discipline or democratic populism) are understood as the residual consequences of a renewed sense of self. This emphasis on the self lies at the heart of the disparate interpretations of evangelical Protestantism's rise to cultural dominance in the early nineteenth century. Questions of alienation or empowerment

9. See, for example, Paul Johnson, *A Shopkeeper's Millennium: Society and Revivals in Rochester, New York, 1815–1837* (New York, 1978); and Paul Faler, *Mechanics and Manufacturers in the Early Industrial Revolution: Lynn, Massachusetts, 1780–1860* (Albany, 1981).

10. Gorden Wood, "Evangelical America and Early Mormonism," *New York History* 61 (October 1980): 359–86; Gordon Wood, *The Radicalism of the American Revolution* (New York, 1992); Hatch, *Democratization of American Christianity.*

follow from the larger question of how evangelical religion transformed the hearts and souls of Americans searching for new social identities.

For evangelicals themselves, the biblical injunction that in Christ "there is neither Jew nor Greek, slave nor free, male nor female" was no mere spiritual bromide but an urgent moral imperative. Their task was both facilitated and complicated in the early republican period by the wholesale assault on all conventional—i.e., man-made—social distinctions mounted by the American Revolution and its embrace of the "natural" rights of mankind. Eschewing the artificial divisions upon which an aristocratic society thrived and insisting that all human beings were endowed by their Creator with inalienable rights and liberties, the revolutionary generation embarked on an ambitious program of social deracination. From outlawing aristocratic titles to abolishing laws of primogeniture and entail, the new constitutions sought to ensure that the ancient prejudices and privileges that had nourished a corrupt political regime would be rooted out and destroyed. In its place would arise a society in which merit and virtue were the only marks of distinction, in which individuals would come together to form new social and political associations on the basis of their voluntary commitment to the public good.[11]

This commitment to equality and natural rights was, however, only one face of the republican experiment, its public face. The hidden, private face of American republicanism was the hardening of the "natural" hierarchies of race and gender.[12] The political liberation of white male Americans was secured by the continued enslavement of blacks and the domestication of white women, who together provided the necessary class of "dependents" whose labor sustained the independence of a virtuous citizenry. Yoked together as negative referents of republican virtue, women and blacks suffered a debilitating ideological loss in the decades following the Revolution, a period that both created new political and legal disabilities for them and reinforced existing ones. This is not to say that the material conditions of life were substantially different for women and slaves after the Revolution, since both remained essentially tied to the domestic cycle of production and reproduction that had governed their lives throughout the colonial period. Rather, white men experienced a striking reappraisal of their own position, which threw into bold relief the continued subjection of women and slaves. For white women in particular, old disabilities became newly gendered as the burden of economic and political dependency shifted entirely onto their shoulders.[13] For African Americans, especially those

11. Wood, *Radicalism of the American Revolution.*

12. Stephanie McCurry, "The Two Faces of Republicanism: Gender and Proslavery Politics in Antebellum South Carolina," *Journal of American History* (March 1992): 1245–64.

13. Joan R. Gundersen, "Independence, Citizenship, and the American Revolution," *Signs* 13 (1987): 59–77.

enslaved, race became as never before the distinguishing mark of servitude and the degradation that followed. Whatever remnants of social and political disadvantage whites had shared with blacks under colonial rule were forever destroyed by the Revolution and by the electoral reforms of the early nineteenth century that established universal white male suffrage.

So the "two faces of republicanism"—the public face of civic equality and the private face of domestic inequality—converged in the common designation of women and blacks as permanent dependents in a society that valued independence above all. But of what consequence was this ideological reformulation of the barriers of race and gender for evangelical Americans, who presumably rejected such secular barriers altogether? Does it make sense to speak of the "two faces" of evangelical Protestantism, one that accepted women and blacks as equal in the eyes of the Lord and another that designated them as inferiors in the secular affairs of the church? There is a problem of translation here. For "equality" has never meant the same thing in spiritual terms as it has in the political realm. Indeed, as Donald Matthews has argued for the South, "fellowship" is a more appropriate term than "equality" to denote the sense of collective bonding that evangelicals forged in their congregations, since these bonds leave secular distinctions intact. A southern planter could experience "fellowship" with his slave during worship without accepting him as an equal, socially or morally.[14] Without overstating the degree of equality implicit in the evangelical notion of fellowship, one can discern a new disjuncture in postrevolutionary evangelical Protestantism between the rhetoric of spiritual equality and the reification of social differences within the community.

In the late eighteenth century the language of dependency and debility came to define the position of women in evangelical churches in ways that mirrored their exclusion from the public life of the new republic. Again, problems of translation intrude. For evangelical Christians, dependence (upon God, upon the church, upon the community of saints) was the goal of spiritual endeavor, not the measure of inability as it was in the political realm. Yet evangelical women experienced their own kind of declension in the decades following the Revolution, when they found themselves excluded from positions of authority and modes of public expression that had previously been open to both sexes.[15] It is no accident that most seekers and prophets who came of age during the spiritual chaos of the early republican era were men, in sharp contrast to earlier periods of political and social

14. Donald Mathews, "Christianizing the South" (Paper presented at the 1993 Wingspread Conference, "New Directions in American Religious History: The Protestant Experience," Racine, Wis.).

15. For a discussion of how women were disenfranchised within the Baptist churches of New England after the Revolution, see Susan Juster, *Disorderly Women: Sexual Politics and Evangelicalism in Revolutionary New England* (Ithaca, 1994).

disruption. Access to divine authority was constrained by the same set of conditions that governed access to secular authority in the new republic: the privileging of masculine reason over feminine passion.

The severing of spiritual authority from "embodied" religious experiences such as ecstatic prophecy was an unintended consequence of the Enlightenment's celebration of human reason over the passions. Previous generations of mystics and spiritualists (largely female) had used their bodies as direct conduits between the natural and supernatural worlds. As the more "carnal" sex, women were considered ideally suited to be the vessels of divine revelation because they were more easily penetrated by external forces. The permeability of the female self to outside influences, whether of a divine or demonic nature, gave women a distinct advantage over men in the art of prophecy (as well as a tragic vulnerability to accusations of witchcraft).[16] This advantage was eclipsed during the nineteenth century by the medical and pedagogical reformulation of women as "passionless" creatures, distinguished by their moral purity rather than their carnal excess.[17] By the early nineteenth century the ideological vindication of "passionless" womanhood, combined with the suppression of erotic piety in evangelical Protestantism, had rendered the female mystic a spiritual anachronism. The trope of erotic piety, which as Amanda Porterfield has shown was intimately related to the trope of female sanctity in Puritan ecclesiology, was gradually supplanted during the eighteenth and nineteenth centuries by a model of spiritual union that accented the emotional side of the relationship between saints and God. The idealized vision of spiritual communion among Victorian Protestants was a desexualized version of the "bed of loves" so celebrated by earlier divines like John Cotton and Edward Taylor.[18] Women were certainly not excluded from this vision—indeed, their emotional nature made them particularly susceptible

16. For the connection between women's carnality and their mysticism, see Caroline Walker Bynum, "Bodily Miracles and the Resurrection of the Body in the High Middle Ages," in *Belief in History: Innovative Approaches to European and American Religion,* ed. Thomas Kselman (South Bend, Ind., 1991), and her *Holy Feast and Holy Fast: The Religious Significance of Food to Medieval Women* (Berkeley, 1987), which argues that medieval writers treated the body less as a trap or hindrance than as a means of access to the divine. On the association of women with mystical experiences in Anglo-American Puritanism, see Marilyn Westerkamp, "Puritan Patriarchy and the Problem of Revelation," *Journal of Interdisciplinary History* 23 (1993): 571–95.

17. Nancy F. Cott, "Passionlessness: An Interpretation of Victorian Sexual Ideology, 1790–1850," *Signs* 4 (1978–1979): 219–36.

18. On the trope of female piety, see Amanda Porterfield, *Female Piety in Puritan New England: The Emergence of Religious Humanism* (New York, 1992); Ivy Schweitzer, *The Work of Self-Representation: Lyric Poetry in Colonial New England* (Chapel Hill, N.C., 1991); Philip Greven, *The Protestant Temperament: Patterns of Child-Rearing, Religious Experience, and the Self in Early America* (New York, 1977); and Margaret Masson, "The Typology of the Female as a Model for the Regenerate: Puritan Preaching, 1690–1730," *Signs* 2 (1976): 304–315. The phrase "bed of loves" is taken from a sermon by John Cotton, quoted in David

to the revivalists' call—but they were no longer able to use their closeness to God as a vehicle for temporal empowerment.

Evangelical women, in other words, could attain spiritual union, but not spiritual authority, for only those in a position to transcend the confining bonds of emotion were able to speak for others. The blessings and dangers of emotional union were well known to republican citizens. Love was necessary for the republic to reproduce itself, but passionate affection could also undercut the disinterested virtue that was equally necessary for a republic to succeed.[19] Those who would govern must be able to transcend their particular attachments to people and place and act for the good of the whole. Women, whose very beings were rooted in the domestic world of marriage and motherhood, were constitutionally incapable of governing under these precepts.[20] As Linda Kerber has argued, republican theorists considered female patriotism a contradiction in terms, because the disinterested stance of the patriot was fundamentally incompatible with the particularistic affections and loyalties of a wife or mother.[21]

Where does this leave women who aspired to a larger role in the political or religious life of the new republic? What options were open to female seekers who, in the spirit of Anne Hutchinson or Anne Eaton, sought to speak the word of God outside the confines of the domestic parlor? We can glimpse some of the possibilities and constraints faced by female visionaries in postrevolutionary America by examining the life and career of one particularly intriguing figure, Jemima Wilkinson of Rhode Island. Her ministry and its appeal to a people frightened by war are revealing of the gender paradoxes implicit in the "democratic" revolution of the late eighteenth century. She was, to be sure, an atypical figure, both as a woman and as a preacher. But as Gordon Wood has observed, radical enthusiasts and visionaries warrant the attention they receive, since they represented "the advanced guard" of a popular evangelical movement that changed the face of American Protestantism.[22]

Leverenz, *The Language of Puritan Feeling: An Exploration in Literature, Psychology, and Social History* (New Brunswick, N.J., 1980).

19. The republican theory of gender, as described by Hanna Pitkin in her analysis of Machiavelli, identifies women as objects of male sexual desire who thereby corrupt civic virtue by their appeal to the passions. See Hanna Pitkin, *Fortune is a Woman: Gender and Politics in the Thought of Niccolo Machiavelli* (Berkeley, 1984). As Mary Ryan argues, "by equating women with sexuality, American republicans justified their exclusion from the political citadel of rationality and virtue." See Mary Ryan, *Women in Public: Between Banners and Ballots, 1825–1880* (Baltimore, 1990), pp. 27–28.

20. On the importance of women as "republican wives," see Jan Lewis, "The Republican Wife: Virtue and Seduction in the Early Republic," *William and Mary Quarterly* 44 (1987): 689–721.

21. Linda K. Kerber, *The Republic of Women: Intellect and Ideology in Revolutionary America* (New York, 1980).

22. Wood, "Evangelical America," p. 373.

Jemima Wilkinson, the Publick Universal Friend

The Society of the Publick Universal Friend was founded when a young ex-Quaker from Rhode Island, Jemima Wilkinson, proclaimed to a skeptical world that she had died and been reborn as the second coming of Christ. Her story is quickly told: in 1776, after undergoing a lengthy illness of an undetermined nature, Jemima (then aged 24) arose from her sickbed and announced to her family that she had died and would henceforth no longer answer to the name "Jemima Wilkinson." As the spirit of Jesus Christ had taken possession of her body, she assumed the title of the "Publick Universal Friend" and began a lifelong ministry. She left the following account of her transfiguration:

> The heavens were open'd and she saw too Archangels descending from the east bringing a Sealed Pardon from the living God; and putting their trumpets to their mouth, proclaimed saying . . . The time is at hand when God will lift up his hand a second time to recover the remnant of his People, whose day is not yet over; and the Angels said, the Spirit of Life from God had descended to earth, to warn a lost and guilty, perishing, dying World, to flee from the wrath which is to come . . . and was waiting to assume the Body which God had prepared for the Spirit to dwell in . . . And then taking her leave of the family between the hour of nine and ten in the morning, dropped the dying flesh & yielded up the Ghost. And according to the declaration of the Angels, the Spirit took full possession of the Body it now Animates.[23]

Enjoining celibacy on her followers and preaching the imminent and violent end of the world, the Friend (as she was now called) traveled from town to town in war-torn Rhode Island. Hounded out of New England and later Philadelphia by angry crowds who accused her of everything from whoremongering to blasphemy, she and a small band of devoted followers eventually settled in western New York in a community she named "Jerusalem." By 1800, the settlement had some 260 inhabitants, and the Friend had become deeply involved in secular affairs, from mediating disputes between white settlers and the local natives (who called her Squaw Shinnewanagistawge, or "Great Woman Preacher") to attacking slavery. This utopian experiment did not long survive her death in 1819 at the age of 67; within two decades the sect had entirely disappeared, leaving behind a complicated legal tangle over property claims and a dim regional reputation.

This is not exactly the stuff of historical epics. But it is a cautionary tale of sorts for those who would read into the religious climate of the early republican period a commitment to sexual equality. For the most salient

23. "A Memorandum of the Introduction of the Fatal Fever," undated, Jemima Wilkinson Papers, 1771–1849, Department of Manuscripts and University Archives, Cornell University Library (hereafter cited as JW Papers).

feature of Jemima Wilkinson's inauspicious career as a minister of God is that she deliberately remade herself into a masculine figure in order to legitimate her spiritual authority. Draping herself in severe clerical garb (long black robes unadorned with any accessories save a plain black hat), refusing to answer to any name but the "Publick Universal Friend" (even forbidding her followers to address her in gendered pronouns), and insisting that she was Christ incarnate, Wilkinson's masculine persona was complete.[24] Her only published work, an address entitled *Some Considerations by a Universal Friend of Mankind,* appeared anonymously under the signature "your friend and *brother* in the communion and fellowship of the gospel."[25] She was, in truth, "more like a man than a woman," as one fascinated observer noted.[26]

We can glimpse the dramatic effect of Wilkinson's persona on those who flocked to see her performances in the account left by Abner Brownell, a former disciple who later left the Society and wrote a searing indictment of his former mentor. "In the year 1778," Brownell records, "I heard of a remarkable Person of a Female Preacher from a back Town of Providence, call'd Cumberland, about which there was a Report of something very remarkable and extraordinary, that she was a Person that was said had been dead for the Space of an Hour, and by the mighty Power of God had been rais'd immediately to a State of Health, and had an immediate call to appear in public Testimony to preach to the People." His first glimpse of the Friend was a startling one. Her "outward Appearance seem'd to be something singular and extraordinary, appearing in a different Habit from what is common amongst Women, wearing her Hair curl'd in her Neck, without any other Covering on her Head, except it was when she travel'd out, she put on a Hat much like a Man's, only the Brim flap'd down." With a "Voice very grum and shrill for a Woman," Wilkinson made quite an impression on Brownell, who immediately left his home and family and began to itinerate with the Friend.[27] Her closest female followers imitated her masculine dress and mannerisms—one, Sarah Richards, was described in 1787 as a woman who "would be a comely person were she to dress as becomes her sex. But, as she imitates the person they call the friend in her external appearance and particularly in wearing her hair down like a man, she is by that means disfigured."[28]

---

24. Abner Brownell claimed that some of Wilkinson's followers "call her *him.*" See Abner Brownell, *Enthusiastical Errors Transpired and Detected* (New London, Conn., 1783), p. 18.

25. [Jemima Wilkinson], *Some Considerations Propounded to the Several Sorts and Sects of Professors of this Age . . . by a Universal Friend of Mankind* (Providence, 1779), p. 94. Emphasis added.

26. Jacob Cox Parsons, ed., *Extracts from the Diary of Jacob Hiltzheimer of Philadelphia,* (Philadelphia, 1893), p. 85.

27. Brownell, *Enthusiastical Errors,* pp. 4–5.

28. *American Museum* I (Feb. 1787), p. 153.

Whether "disfigured" or transfigured, Wilkinson and her female follow-ers repudiated their gender identity in order to assume the prophetic mantle. In other eras, there would have been alternative paths open to them: the history of dissenting religion in England and America is full of figures of women prophets who appear in politically turbulent times (the English Civil War, to cite the obvious example) and preach repentance *as women*. Claiming to be passive vessels of the divine spirit, such women lay claim to spiritual authority through, not in spite of, their feminine nature.[29] Jemima Wilkinson was no female prophet—she was Jesus Christ himself, the Son of God. The very title she chose for herself—Publick Universal Friend—suggests how consciously she positioned herself within a mascu-line universe of symbols. While the phrase has its roots in Wilkinson's Quaker past (Quaker traveling ministers were called "public friends"), the three terms had come to represent the masculine half of a series of indelibly gendered oppositions by the late eighteenth century: public/private, univer-sal/particular, and fraternal/hierarchical. In revolutionary discourse the notion of the public sphere carried connotations of transparency and universality, traits that were distinctly associated with the fraternal world of men.[30]

Wilkinson not only repudiated the female side of her own nature, she also embraced the misogynistic tradition of western Christianity that associated women with the fallen Eve. Her sermons invoked all the standard images of female monstrosity current in eighteenth-century religious and political discourse—witches, whores, fornicators, "painted Jezebels." She reserved special scorn for her religious rivals, those "false teachers" who inundated the American countryside during the war years and immediately afterwards preaching repentance and redemption. The many religious impostors of the revolutionary age were whores who flatter and seduce their followers into error:

> The strumpet, or false church, is forced, as God discovers her nakedness and lewdness, to change her dresses and appearances, to new trick and adorn her bed; and then, as if she also were changed, and were now no longer the same, she comes forth again with boldness, and tempteth the young man again to come in to her. And thus she casteth down many wounded; yea, many strong men have been slain by her, who otherwise would have pondered the path of life, had they not been ensnared by her flatteries.[31]

29. See, for example, Esther Copes' biography of perhaps the most famous of these Civil War prophets, Dame Eleanor Davies. Davies, Copes claims, refused to relinquish her identity or responsibilities as a woman when acting the prophet. Esther Copes, *Handmaid of the Holy Spirit: Dame Eleanor Davies, Never Soe Mad a Ladie* (Ann Arbor, 1992).

30. For a discussion of how the concept of the public sphere was gendered male in the discourse of the French Revolution, see Joan Landes, *Women and the Public Sphere in the Age of the French Revolution* (Ithaca, N.Y., 1991).

31. [Wilkinson], *Some Considerations*, p. 82.

Imposture itself was "the great witch of the age," who ensnares the weak and unprincipled, consigning all who stray from the path of righteousness to "her burning bed of torment."[32] Many conservative clergymen would have agreed wholeheartedly with these jeremiads against the allures of false prophets, for the early republican era was "the golden age" of impostors, the "most centrifugal epoch in American church history" according to Hatch.[33] Religious innovation was rampant, new sects were springing up like weeds in the fertile soil of American democracy, and orthodoxy was everywhere on the defensive. Wilkinson was not alone in her denunciations of such spiritual promiscuity, nor was she the only one to single out the corruptions of women as the source of this disorder. "Everything that has the smell of woman must be destroyed," warned another charismatic preacher, the Prophet Matthias, in the 1820s. "Woman is the capsheaf of the abomination of desolation—full of all deviltry."[34]

Historians searching for benign images of republican mothers or wives in the public discourse of religion after the Revolution would be disappointed. Rather than those benevolent figures of domestic nurture so cherished by later Victorian reformers, populist religion offered its audience powerful images of women of monstrous appetite who devoured their lovers and destroyed the fragile spiritual health of the new republic. In the Society of the Universal Friend, it was men who assumed the kind of nurturing roles women were supposed to perform for their communities. The masculine appearance of Wilkinson and her female disciples is dramatically highlighted by the effeminacy of her male followers. "Those male members who by long submission have become accustomed and reconciled to this petticoat discipline," one critic wrote, "discover its effects in their looks and actions so plainly, that they are apparent even to a stranger."[35] These "looks and actions" were readily apparent to another observer, who believed her male followers to have made themselves literal as well as figurative "eunuchs for Christ." Sporting "large round flipped hats, and long flowing straight locks," Wilkinson's male entourage exhibited "a sort of melancholy wildness in their countenances, and an effeminate dejected air."[36]

Where the Friend is stern and uncompromising, her male followers are

---

32. Ibid., pp. 79–80.

33. Hatch, *Democratization of American Christianity*, pp. 36, 15.

34. Quoted in Paul Johnson, "Democracy, Patriarchy, and American Revivals, 1780–1830," *Journal of Social History* 24 (Summer 1991): 846.

35. David Hudson, *History of Jemima Wilkinson, A Preacheress of the Eighteenth Century; Containing an Authentic Narrative of Her Life and Character, and of the Rise, Progress, and Conclusion of Her Ministry* (Geneva, N.Y., 1821), p. 134.

36. Marquis de Chastellux, *Travels in North America in the Years 1780, 1781, and 1782,* trans. Howard C. Rice, Jr. (Chapel Hill, N.C., 1963), 1:322.

thus described as sentimental and effete. The romantic air they projected in person was echoed in their sentimentalized sermons. While the Friend preached vengeance and death, her male followers preached love and compassion. The diary of one devotee, Abner Brownell, provides a direct comparison between the sermons delivered by Jemima and her male disciples. In the span of one month, Brownell recorded a sermon by the Universal Friend in which she warned of the imminent destruction of the world: "Therefore will I number you to the Sword and you shall all bow down to the Slaughter, because when I called you did not Answer and when I Spake you did not hear but did evil before mine eyes." Several days later Brownell himself preached on a very different scriptural text. "My beloved Spake and Said unto me Rise up my Love, my fair one and come away, for lo, the winter is past, the rain is over and gone, the flowers appear on the Earth . . . Arise my love my fair one and come away." Render not evil for evil, he pleaded, but rather "have compassion of one another."[37] In the Society of the Universal Friend, women appeared like men and men spoke like women. The semiotics of gender were truly in disarray in the evangelical universe in the postrevolutionary years.

Wilkinson's assumption of a masculine persona was not accidental or inconsequential. Only men could participate in political discourse of any kind in the early republican period, whether pertaining to the secular nation or the spiritual kingdom. And only men (or women who had become men) could speak the language of divine revelation. It is abundantly clear from Wilkinson's sermons that she aimed at a higher level of meaning than that circumscribed by spiritual allegory. Her constant and pointed calls for reformation were directed to a people distressed at their own inability to sustain the virtue required of republican citizens, and her apocalyptic message clearly resonated with more secularized versions circulating in political pamphlets and broadsides. The "visionary republic" was one beset with danger from all corners, from women unable to restrain their consumption habits to men unwilling to act the role of disinterested patriot to religious apostates of all stripes. "Although the Seas Roar yet the Lord on high is mightyer than the Noise of many waters . . . The fearfull and unbelieving and abominable & Dogs & Socrcers & Whoremongers and all Lyers shall have their part in the Lake that Burns with Fire & Brimstone," she warned in 1787.[38] Far from being unconcerned with the revolutionary

---

37. Diary of Abner Brownell, 1779–1787, vol. 2, pp. 73, 83, American Antiquarian Society, Worcester, Mass.

38. The Publick Universal Friend to Sarah Richards, 11 March 1787, JW Papers. On revolutionary millennialism, see Bloch, *Visionary Republic*; Melvin B. Endy, Jr., "Just War, Holy War, and Millennialism in Revolutionary America," *William and Mary Quarterly* 42 (1985): 3–25.

struggle and its discursive battles, as Wilkinson's most recent biographer claims, her ministry followed both literally and figuratively on the heels of the military campaigns that tore through her native Rhode Island.[39]

The apocalyptic dimension of Wilkinson's preaching, with its bloody imagery and martial cadences, suggests the depth of the Friend's ambivalence to the revolutionary war. Her illness and subsequent reincarnation as the Son of God was attributed to the "fatal fever" introduced into America by a "Ship of War" in 1776. This "awfull and allarming disease" caused numerous deaths in the port cities of Rhode Island before "Spreading more universally across the Country."[40] Torn between the urge to confront the beast in his own lair, or to flee into the sanctuary of the frontier, Wilkinson counseled her followers in both violent retribution and redemptive suffering. The ambivalence of her counsel, however, is less significant than the form in which it was expressed: she spoke not in the language of female prophecy or republican motherhood but in the uncompromising voice of God himself. To offer herself up as a public figure, a participant in the political discourse on republican virtue, was in effect to deny her feminine self altogether.

The masculine bias of Wilkinson's ministry is important precisely because her message was militantly *democratic* in its overturning of conventional religious hierarchies. In her sermons and religious allegories, the chief instruments of evil in the world are the established clergy and their elevation of book-learning over revealed truth. In one vision recorded in the Wilkinson papers, the Friend does battle with Satan disguised as a rich and powerful Emperor. Riding at the head of "a great Company of Friends ranged along as it were in martial order in Twelve Columns," the Universal Friend confronts her enemy across a desolate wasteland. The Emperor's attendants consisted primarily of "priests and Deacons," all of whom carried "Books looking like bibles under their right arms and under their Left a dagger which they Endeavoured to Conceal." In the ensuing battle the company of Friends triumphs by issuing a collective blast of heavenly sound that makes the walls of the Emperor's city crumble before their very eyes, crushing underneath all his men. The vision concludes with the image of "the Friends in great numbers walking on the men, Stamping them small with their feet, small as the dust of the earth."[41] Bible-wielding priests fall again and again to the apocalyptic sword in Wilkinson's allegories, vivid testimony to the virulent anticlericalism that Nathan Hatch claims was the heartbeat of democratic religion. Such democratic visions, however, were

39. Herbert Wisbey, *Pioneer Prophetess: Jemima Wilkinson, the Publick Universal Friend* (Ithaca, N.Y., 1964).
40. "Memorandum of the Fever."
41. "Religious Allegory," undated, JW Papers.

inescapably masculinist as well as populist—and this is the point. Insisting, as she always did in her sermons, that wealth, status, and above all learning were no bars to spiritual truth, the Friend betrayed in her own person an acute awareness that the division separating men from women was one barrier that could not be breached. Like those Mormons who believed that the individual self is gendered for all eternity, "a male/female division [was] lodged at the heart of ultimate reality" in the Society of the Publick Friend.[42]

Wilkinson's assumption of a masculine persona represents an extreme response to the suppression of the female religious expression in postrevolutionary America. Like the female spiritualists studied by Ann Braude, Wilkinson disclaimed any personal authorship for her spiritual message.[43] If, by positioning the self as a passive vessel, spiritual mediumship represented a compromise between the need for self-expression and the devaluation of the female voice, then Wilkinson represents the final denial of female spiritual authority. The empty shell of the female medium was now filled by a male presence, Christ himself. Significantly, the right to speak—authorized in the figure of Jemima herself by sexual transfiguration—was a jealously guarded one in her Society, exercised only by those whom she personally anointed as disciples. Among the six "apostles" who accompanied her to Philadelphia in 1782, the Marquis de Barbe-Marbois reported, were "three men whose duty is to speak, and three women who keep silent."[44] Detractors mocked the "silent fasts" she imposed on her followers, in which all speech was forbidden for a period of time. Those who "broke the fast" found their mouths "sealed up with wafers and slips

42. Caroline Walker Bynum, "Introduction: The Complexity of Symbols," in *Gender and Religion: On the Complexity of Symbols*, ed. Caroline Bynum, Stevan Harrell, and Paula Richman (Boston, 1986), p. 3.

43. Ann Braude, *Radical Spirits: Spiritualism and Women's Rights in Nineteenth-Century America* (Boston, 1989). Wilkinson's exact contemporary, the famed British evangelist Joanna Southcott, similarly attributed her prophetic utterances to the "Spirit" of God who spoke through her. Unlike Wilkinson, however, Southcott never abandoned her identity as a woman in the pursuit of religious authority; indeed, she proudly proclaimed herself the "Woman" of Revelation come to redeem the world of the corruptions introduced by her biblical forebear, Eve. See Anna Clark, "The Sexual Crisis and Popular Religion in London, 1770–1820," *International Labor and Working Class History* 34 (1988): 56–69; and James Hopkins, *A Woman to Deliver Her People: Joanna Southcott and English Millenarianism in an Era of Revolution* (Austin, Tex., 1982). Women novelists, too, often presented themselves as the "vessels" of an external authority in penning their stories. Such metaphorical representations of authorship, Margaret Homans has argued, reflect an essentially passive relation to language among nineteenth-century women. Homans, *Bearing the Word: Language and Female Experience in Nineteenth-Century Women's Writings* (Chicago, 1986).

44. *Our Revolutionary Forefathers: The Letters of Francois, Marquis de Barbe-Marbois*, trans. and edited by Eugene parker Chase (New York, 1929), p. 164.

of paper, or linen rags."[45] Far from representing the ultimate liberation of women's voices in postrevolutionary America, as some scholars have suggested, Wilkinson's Society reinstated a kind of patriarchal authority over language.[46]

Moreover, in her denial of sexuality, Wilkinson prefigured the Victorian preoccupation with virtuous womanhood as the cornerstone of respectable religion. Like the famed English founder of the Shakers, Mother Ann Lee, Wilkinson advocated celibacy for herself and those closest to her. The similarities between the Society of the Universal Friend and the Shakers—both were formed in America in the 1770s in the heat of revolutionary battle—have long intrigued scholars looking for evidence of a significant public female presence in postrevolutionary society. Despite their obvious similarities (both, for instance, used dreams and visions as vehicles of prophetic expression, and both incorporated millennial themes in their soteriology), the Shakers and the Universal Friends offered dramatically different models of spiritual authority in the figures of their respective leaders. Lee, it is true, also laid claim to divine powers; but in her reading of the Second Coming male and female elements of the Godhead were joined into a single persona. Representing the female half of this dual Godhead, Lee affirmed rather than repudiated her feminine nature, especially its maternal aspect. As "Mother" of the Shaker movement, Lee drew on the long tradition of Quaker female ministers who styled themselves "Mothers in Israel." This celebration of the maternal role of women among eighteenth-century Quakers and Shakers was, Phyllis Mack has suggested, a retreat from earlier models of female leadership that stressed the transcendent power of ecstatic experience. In contrast to seventeenth-century religious visionaries, "Mothers in Israel" remained circumscribed within the patriarchal model of familial relationships, however much they stretched the bounds of female behavior.[47] Motherhood is a powerful role, to be sure, but mothers answer to a higher earthly authority, whereas visionaries answer to God alone.

While the ecstatic model of spiritual authority may have remained a potent vehicle for African American women (who were entirely excluded

45. Hudson, *History of Jemima Wilkinson*, pp. 55–56. Whether or not such reports were true, it is interesting that so much of the public commentary about Wilkinson centered on questions of verbal power. Her own voice was a powerful instrument, according to most observers, who uniformly described it as both "masculine" and "authoritative"; see the accounts in *American Museum* 1 (1787), pp. 152–53, and in John F. Watson, *Annals of Philadelphia and Pennsylvania in the Olden Time, Being a Collection of Memoirs, Anecdote, and Incidents of the City and its Inhabitants* (Philadelphia, 1870), p. 554.

46. Those who see Wilkinson as an exemplar of the expanded opportunities for public expression offered women by the Revolution include Stephen Marini (*Radical Sects in Revolutionary New England* [Cambridge, Mass., 1982]) and Ruth Bloch (*Visionary Republic*).

47. Mack, *Visionary Women*, chap. 9.

from the republican formulation of virtuous womanhood), white women had little choice but to cloak their femininity behind the veil of linguistic and sexual chastity or abandon it altogether.[48] Wilkinson chose the latter route. Her cross-dressing and relentless barrage of martial and apocalyptic imagery may have confused the scoffers and seekers who flocked to her performances (they rarely persuaded), but they are poignant evidence of the aversion to femininity that so deeply marked the age of democratic revolution.

Early Methodist Visionaries

It is difficult to assess the importance we should attach to the admittedly peculiar ministry of the Publick Universal Friend. In order to place her career in perspective, it may be helpful to look at another religious society spawned by the revolutionary era, one far more successful in terms of numbers and longevity: the Methodists. There are important points of comparison between the two sects. Both emphasized dreams and visions as vehicles of spiritual awakening; both emphasized (at least initially) celibacy for the society's leaders if not for followers; both spoke the language of republicanism while distancing themselves from the political and military entanglements of the war effort. And, most importantly, both exhibited an intensely masculine religious culture, which calls into question the overly simplistic notion that evangelical Protestantism was "feminized" in the early nineteenth century.[49]

In the early years, American Methodist itinerants resembled to a striking degree the monastic brotherhoods of medieval Catholicism, as Jon Butler has noted. Drawn together by a commitment to poverty and spiritual asceticism, isolated from family and friends by the rigors of circuit riding, and celebrating their intense sense of fellowship with each other through rituals of brotherhood, the Methodist clergy of the late eighteenth century created an all-male religious culture that was phenomenally successful. Their spartan way of life was more than offset by the emotional richness of their communion with their "yokefellows" in Christ. In the all-male gather-

48. On African American female visionaries, see Jean M. Humez, "'My Spirit Eye': Some Functions of Spiritual and Visionary Experience in the Lives of Five Black Women Preachers, 1810–1880," in *Women and the Structure of Society*, ed. Barbara Harris and JoAnn McNamara (Durham, N.C., 1984), pp. 129–43.

49. For discussions of the "feminization" of American Protestantism in the late eighteenth and early nineteenth centuries, see Ann Douglas, *The Feminization of American Culture* (New York, 1977); Richard Shiels, "The Feminization of American Congregationalism 1730–1835," *American Quarterly* 33 (1981): 46–62; Barbara Welter, "The Feminization of American Religion 1800–1860," in her *Dimity Convictions: The American Woman in the Nineteenth Century* (Athens, Ga., 1976); David Schuyler, "Inventing a Feminine Past," *New England Quarterly* 51 (1978): 291–308; David Reynolds, "The Feminization Controversy: Sexual Stereotypes and the Paradoxes of Piety in Nineteenth-Century America," *New England Quarterly* 53 (1980): 96–106.

ings of the quarter session and yearly conference, Methodist preachers were "melted" together by the Holy Spirit. An abundance of tears, hugs, and heartfelt groans (presumably the preserve of the weaker sex and their literary representatives in sentimental fiction) were sanctioned by the very absence of women. Whereas Jemima Wilkinson cultivated an austere and dispassioned demeanor in her travels, Methodist preachers allowed themselves to display the emotional excesses commonly attributed to women at the preachers' "love feasts," secure in their masculine enclave. Where women were absent, feminine behaviors could be indulged.

This perhaps explains the popularity of dreams and visions as means of spiritual empowerment among the early Methodists.[50] Like many other religious pioneers in the early republican era, the Methodists exhibited a fascination for supernatural portents of any kind. "Early Methodist itinerants invoked the dream-world images already endemic in postrevolutionary society," Jon Butler notes.[51] Methodist preachers not only placed great weight on the ability of dreams to predict the future, they also regaled their audiences with vivid descriptions of these visions. As a form of sacred theater, dream telling was a particularly effective revivalist tool. The overtly public nature of Methodist visions places them squarely in the apocalyptic tradition of Jemima Wilkinson, who never missed an opportunity to warn her audiences of the gruesome future in store for unrepentant sinners. But there is a crucial difference in the eschatology of early American Methodists, who—in sharp contrast to the Universal Friend—tended to emphasis millennial rather than apocalyptic themes in their public addresses. The dark visions of death and destruction that filled the dreams of Jemima Wilkinson played but a minor role in Methodist literature, which tended instead to offer optimistic visions of the heavenly future that would follow the destruction of the world. Indeed, Jon Butler has argued that apocalyptic thinking in general declined after the Revolution, to be replaced by a kind of popular secular optimism that "millennialist propagandists" of all stripes offered the new nation.[52] If optimism about the future is a mark of security about one's position in the world, then it is surely significant that the most vivid images of apocalyptic destruction are to be found in the writings of Jemima Wilkinson, a woman masquerading as a man, a seeker without the social authority to seek.

The Methodists also offered America a more palatable version of the American Revolution than the Universal Friend. Like Wilkinson, early American Methodists were noted for their apolitical stance, even to the

---

50. On the Methodist fascination with dreams and visions, see John H. Wigger, "Taking Heaven by Storm: Enthusiasm and Early American Methodism, 1770–1820," *Journal of the Early Republic* 14 (Summer 1994): 167–94.

51. Butler, *Awash in a Sea of Faith*, p. 238.

52. Ibid., p. 217.

point of being unjustly accused of harboring Loyalist sentiments. Because they disavowed any direct connection to the war effort, their patriotism was as suspect as their piety. Yet, like Wilkinson, they spoke in an idiom that was implicitly political. The Methodist celebration of the ideal of fraternity—articulated in both the vernacular and institutional languages of the movement—recast in spiritual terms the political ideal of republican brotherhood that so animated the first generation of revolutionary leaders.[53] Both the Methodists and the Friend attached the political discourse of the Revolution to their respective religious agendas in ways that sought to deny rather than affirm a connection between them.

Here again, the Methodists were far more successful than their charismatic rival. In reaching for a new mode of spiritual communion, Jemima Wilkinson succeeded only in creating a shadowy version of an ancient and discredited form of religious authority, the Old Testament patriarch. Both sects recognized that public authority was a masculine prerogative after the Revolution, but the Methodists invested that authority in the republican notion of fraternity, while the Friend tried to resurrect the patriarchal ideal that the revolution had apparently dismantled.[54] The charge of political sabotage that accompanied the Friend as she traveled throughout southern New England was no mere chimera; it was an accurate, if misplaced, characterization of Wilkinson's archaic brand of Old Testament prophecy. When she thundered against those who "have persisted in rebellion against the King of heaven," when she invoked the power of "thou righteous, pure, eternal King, eternal Father" and spoke of the triumph of the heavenly "Emperor," it was difficult for critics not to hear the voice of treason.[55] Yet women who would be prophets in republican America had few options. Utterly excluded from the fraternity (political and religious) that governed the new republic, women had no choice but to reach backwards to an earlier age for models of spiritual authority. In this sense, Wilkinson's ministry was destined from the beginning to be the quaint anachronism it has become in historical annals.

53. Russell Richey, *Early American Methodism* (Bloomington, Ind., 1991).
54. On the Revolution as a struggle against patriarchy, see Jay Fliegelman, *Prodigals and Pilgrims: The Revolution Against Patriarchal Authority 1750–1800* (New York, 1982).
55. [Wilkinson], *Some Considerations*, pp. 90, 92.

CHAPTER 2

"Ethiopia Shall Stretch Forth Her Hands Unto God": Laura Kofey and the Gendered Vision of Redemption in the Garvey Movement

BARBARA BAIR

In an evening meeting in March 1928, Laura Adorker Kofey stood before her congregation in a storefront church in Miami and began exhorting her audience from scripture. Kofey was a charismatic evangelist and preacher. She had been a highly successful organizer for Marcus Garvey's Universal Negro Improvement Association in Alabama and Florida, and she was the founder of her own independent religious organization, the African Universal Church. Her powerful voice filled the meeting place as she stood with her Bible in her hands. As the worship began to build with enthusiasm, just as it had at many meetings before under Kofey's ministration, gunshots rang out from the back of the church. The bullets struck Mother Kofey in the head. Stopped short in mid-sentence, she slumped to the floor. She had stood at her place at the pulpit tall with dignity, vital and articulate with the word. Moments later she lay deprived of agency, her voice silenced by death.

The story of the violent martyrdom of Laura Kofey can serve as a metaphor in examining the gender politics and ideas of power and authority that imbued the Garvey movement. Her fate at the hands of an assassin in her storefront church was not the work of a moment. Rather it was the culmination of a series of events that elucidate debates within Garveyism over the place of women and their rightful access to leadership and public voice. Her experience speaks, in both its opportunities and its limitations, to other women's experiences in the movement. The varied responses to her success highlight the fact that among Garveyites, discourse—about whether women should preach or lead, about the gendered nature of spirituality and its link to political forms of redemption, and about the directions of the movement vis-à-vis the teachings of the church—was lively and multidimensional, a polyphony of multiple voices that defies a singular focus on Garvey himself or on a neat dualism of women and men.[1]

1. I am indebted, in this consideration of gender and religion in the Garvey movement, to

Garveyism is often seen as a grassroots nationalist phenomenon springing from the heightened political consciousness that imbued the Black community in the years surrounding World War I. Founded as a benevolent association by Marcus Garvey and Amy Ashwood in Jamaica in 1914, the Universal Negro Improvement Association (UNIA) was reformulated as a Black separatist and Pan-Africanist organization in Harlem in 1917 and 1918. The organization took root in the post-war environment of intellectual reconstruction and defiance, but it was equally produced by the nationalist aspects of the social movements of the past, and thus was part of an ongoing infrastructure of communal resistance and redefinition created by African Americans since emancipation. That infrastructure, including spiritual and social dimensions of religious practice, was itself built on foundations laid by African Americans and African West Indians during the period of slavery. Garveyism had its roots in the colonization movements of the nineteenth century and in the structures of Black self-help that belied the negating aims of Jim Crow: business enterprises, financial institutions, schools, masonic orders, benevolent associations, and community organizations organized by women such as mother's clubs, Bible bands, and neighborhood unions. Most pointedly, the Garvey movement was built on the social foundation of the Black church, particularly the church as it existed and evolved in the last decades of the nineteenth century and the first decades of the twentieth. It was on the foundation of the church that Garvey built a mass movement, and it was from the same population of the working poor and the petit bourgeoisie that both the Black church and the UNIA drew their memberships.[2]

Church men and women recognized in the UNIA familiar gender roles and patterns. Like the Black church, the UNIA developed a very strong women's auxiliary, in which women formed their own leadership and carried on their own functions. At the same time women participated in the gender-integrated hierarchy of the organization and strongly supported the concept of manhood rights upon which the organization was founded. Like

---

the important prior work of Richard Newman, who has written the definitive biographical profile of Laura Kofey, and Randall Burkett, who has documented the history of Garveyism as a religious phenomenon, as well as to current feminist scholars studying various aspects of women's roles in African American denominations, many of whom who have identified patterns and issues similar to those I have found in the Garvey movement. See Richard Newman, "Warrior Mother of Africa's Warriors of the Most High God: Laura Adorkor Kofey and the African Universal Church," in *Black Power and Black Religion*, ed. Richard Newman (West Cornwall, Conn., 1987), pp. 131–45; Randall K. Burkett, *Garveyism as a Religious Movement: The Institutionalization of a Black Civil Religion* (Metuchen, N.J., 1978); Burkett, *Black Redemption: Churchmen Speak for the Garvey Movement* (Philadelphia, 1978); Burkett, "The Religious Ethos of the Universal Negro Improvement Association," in *African American Religious Studies*, ed. Gayraud S. Wilmore (Durham, N.C., 1989), pp. 60–81.

2. Among the black denominations, the National Baptist Convention of America held the largest membership.

women active in the church, UNIA women sometimes challenged the secondary and separate roles assigned to them within the organization as a whole. They offered both a feminist theology and a call for expanded opportunity for women to speak and interpret. The UNIA, like the Black church, was an oasis of racial dignity, affirmation, and self-determination within a dominant society of oppression. Within the UNIA, as within the church, African American gender relations and understandings were continually being challenged and defended, reevaluated and redefined through discourse and action. Much of this debate centered on religious conceptions of political and moral duty and on women's and men's relations to the power of the word.

The UNIA encouraged the writing and performance of plays, recitations, pageants, historical dramas, essays, and poetry, and women were among its most prominent dramatists, poets, elocutionists, and performers. They also dominated musical performances as soloists and as singers in choirs. Speeches, sermons, and songs were central to UNIA meetings and conventions. Many were paraphrased or reprinted in the *Negro World*, which also carried reports of local division meetings and auxiliary functions, published letters to the editor, and printed essays by readers. Women as well as men participated in these forms of expression. Laura Kofey gained prominence in a world where Black women were writers and editors, speakers at local and national meetings, delegates to international conventions, and division organizers.

Different visions of liberty and redemption were encoded in male and female form in the UNIA auxiliaries, based on the models of Black soldiers in battle and the nurses who ministered to them. Military drills of the male African Legion auxiliary displayed the organization's commitment to assertiveness and self-defense, while plays and demonstrations of the nursing arts presented by the Black Cross Nurses, a female UNIA auxiliary, proclaimed a similar commitment to the safety and protection of people of color in a more nurturing manner. The military uniforms of male UNIA leaders and of the paramilitary auxiliaries—imperial in design—conveyed an image of manhood that belied the dominant white construction of Black male subordination and substituted determination, dominance, and nationhood.[3] The African Legion motto, "For God, For Africa, For Justice," encapsulated the sense of the auxiliary as Christian soldiers marching unto war, spiritual and political. The Black Cross Nurses presented a different iconography of African liberation and resistance. The white habits worn by

3. Wilson Moses is quite correct in observing that much of Garvey's vision of government, power, diplomacy, and policy was "based on the imperial model of Victorian England" (Wilson Moses, "Marcus Garvey: The Resurrection of the Negro and the Redemption of Africa," in *Black Messiahs and Uncle Toms: Social and Literary Manipulations of a Religious Myth* [University Park, Mcl., 1982], pp. 124–41).

the Black Cross Nurses signified a revised image of Black womanhood, also imbued with Christian meanings. Not the wanton Jezebels of white imagination, the nurses were instead angels of charity and mercy, holy sisters united in purity and devotion to their own community and its redemption. The popular conception of the nurses as a religious sisterhood, with a calling to serve their people, was underscored by descriptions of the auxiliary in the *Negro World* as "Ministering Angels of Humanity" and "noble, self-sacrificing" women "following in the footsteps of Our Savior."[4]

The religious connotations of gender in the male and female auxiliaries were also extended to the UNIA vision of Africa and its redemption from colonial rule. In the discourse of the Garvey movement Africa was metaphorically conceived as a woman. The scripture repeated most often in the Garvey movement spoke directly to the Garveyite longing for redemption, personifying Africa (often the ancient Africa of Egypt and Ethiopia) as a woman and promising her succor. This was the prophecy of Psalms 68:31—"Princes shall come out of Egypt; Ethiopia shall stretch forth her hands unto God." It was precisely this vision of African redemption that Mother Laura Kofey used to urge her followers on to a Pan-African consciousness—an image underscored by her own self-definition as an African and as a representative, in female form, of West Africa in America.

Gender, Authority, and the UNIA

The central force of religion, the missionary attitude of many Garveyites toward Africa, the call for collective Pan-African identification, and the prevailing unity of authority in the Garvey movement were all reflected in the various meanings of the official motto of the organization: "One God, One Aim, One Destiny" (a motto that Laura Kofey also adopted for her African Universal Church). The philosophy of the Garvey movement was framed by both religious ritual and a revised, neopolitical theology that stressed the importance of Africa and was often expressed in male and female terms.

The UNIA had official religious leaders who helped standardize the movement's religious practices. The national Parent Body, a council of officers, included a chaplain general who served as spiritual adviser to the movement's leaders, conferred ceremonial titles upon honored members, and offered prayers to open UNIA meetings and conventions. Each local division also had its own chaplain, required by an amendment to the 1918 UNIA Constitution to be an ordained minister or one with his first license.[5]

4. *Negro World*, 31 January 1925.

5. See the UNIA Constitution (1918), article 5, section 15, and amendments to the UNIA Constitution (1920), article 3, section 63, in Robert A. Hill et al., eds., *The Marcus Garvey and Universal Negro Improvement Association Papers*, 7 vols. (Berkeley, 1983–1990), 1:263, 2:681.

Reverend George Alexander McGuire, a Protestant Episcopal priest, emerged as the UNIA's principal chaplain general. He was the author of two key texts from 1921, the *Universal Negro Ritual* and *Universal Negro Catechism*, which were used as the foundations for the movement's official religious teachings and ceremonies.[6] McGuire's neo-Anglican liturgy and his ecclesiasticism, combined with Marcus Garvey's Roman Catholicism, gave the religious ritual of the UNIA a hierarchical, High Church tone (despite the fact that a majority of Garveyites were affiliated with Baptist, African Methodist Episcopal, or Holiness/Pentecostal denominations, with a strong minority interested in Islam).[7] Garvey turned to Papal decrees for precedents for some of his positions on UNIA policies. Also, in a pattern consistent with his criticism of Black folk and street culture and of the primitivism he saw manifested in much contemporary Black literature, Garvey scorned enthusiasm in worship and found the singing of spirituals denigrating to the race.

Although the preamble Garvey wrote for the UNIA Constitution spoke of the Fatherhood of God, the movement had an attraction to Marianism that was in accord with Garvey's Catholicism. The UNIA's veneration for Black womanhood, the strong spiritual and political meanings attached to mothering and motherhood, and the frequent rhetorical association of both Mary, the Mother of God, and the crucified Jesus with suffering and self-sacrifice were all manifested in the 1924 UNIA convention in New York. During the convention proceedings, religious ceremonies took place deifying the Lord Jesus Christ as the "Black Man of Sorrows." And, in a motion from the floor, the delegates Hannah Nichols and Carrie Minus moved that "the canonization of the Virgin Mary as a black woman be adopted as the ideal of the Negro race."[8] This willingness to conceive of God's will and goodness as manifested in female as well as male form may have contributed to converts' acceptance of "Mother" Laura Kofey as a female spiritual and political guide. The Garvey movement went one step further in this theological revisionism by presenting Marcus Garvey himself as a Christ figure. In her Liberty Hall speech Mme. M. L. T. De Mena applied the connection between the Black Madonna, the importance of UNIA women

6. The *Ritual* and *Catechism* were based on the *Book of Common Prayer*. McGuire (1866–1934) became chaplain general of the UNIA in 1920. He and Garvey had a falling out in 1921 over McGuire's founding of the African Orthodox Church. He returned to the UNIA in 1923.

7. The Major denominations were the African Methodist Episcopal Church; the African Methodist Episcopal Zion Church; the Colored African Methodist Episcopal Church; the National Baptist Convention, USA, Inc.; the National Baptist Convention of America (unincorporated); and the Pentecostal Church of God in Christ. Catholicism and, in the 1930s, Father Divine's Peace Mission movement also had significant influences on Garveyism.

8. *Negro World*, 16 August and 6 September 1924.

as mothers of sons, and the religious interpretation of Garvey's stature when she proclaimed that "even as from the womb of a good woman came the Son of Man who came to save the world, so from the womb of a good and lovable woman had Marcus Garvey come to save the Negro race."[9]

While religion permeated the UNIA and the constructions of gender and authority it created, reaction to the Garvey movement from the Black religious community at large was mixed. Church historians continue to debate the relative conservatism and progressivism of the Black church, which could in different communities and under different leadership be either a force for accommodation or a center for social activism. Just as some preachers in Miami resented Laura Kofey and her Sunday gatherings, so Black ministers in some locales disparaged the UNIA and aided white authorities in their repression of the movement. Meanwhile other pastors supported Garveyism and were among the strongest UNIA leaders in their towns and cities. In his extensive research on the UNIA as a religious movement, Randall Burkett has documented over 250 Black clergy active in the UNIA, most of them from Baptist and African Methodist Episcopal denominations.[10] In the opposite vein, Nellie G. Whiting, a UNIA delegate from Newport News, Va., stood up at the August 1920 UNIA convention in New York to talk about the negative impact of "troublesome preachers" on the movement in her neighborhood. She told the story of how the UNIA had held a meeting in a church to celebrate the launching of a Black Star Line ship, only to be told they could not meet there again. Trips to the pastors of other Black churches yielded the same results. Whiting said that one minister had asked a deacon to go to the town's mayor "for assistance in suppressing us" and that the mayor had reportedly told him that it seemed the "thing for you to do is to go and join them too." At issue were the Black pastors' worries over the pool of funds available within the Black community. The pastors feared that congregants' investment in international UNIA business enterprises would siphon off those funds from local use.[11] Despite such opposition, local and mass meetings were often scheduled in churches and drew on church networks. Regular weekly meetings were held Sunday evenings to accommodate attendance at both UNIA affairs and Sunday morning church services.

Despite Marcus Garvey's claim that "Liberty Halls [UNIA meeting places] were not to be used as churches, and we did not organize as any church," creating new UNIA divisions was not unlike "digging out" new churches, with organizers in the role of evangelists.[12] Amy Jacques Garvey

9. *Negro World*, 19 May 1928.
10. Burkett, *Black Redemption*, p. 9.
11. *Negro World*, 14 August 1920.
12. Garvey's speech of 18 December 1921 is printed in *Negro World*, 24 December 1921. Garvey had an announcement inserted in the *Negro World* (8 October 1921) that "We are in sympathy with all Negro Churches, but we have no particular Church to support."

has recalled that as a youth, Marcus Garvey listened carefully to different local sermonizers, modeling his own oratorical style on that of pastors he had heard in Jamaica.[13] (Later Garvey was phenomenally successful in winning followers during organizational tours of the United States.) Jacques Garvey herself defied standard gender boundaries when she described her own role in visiting grassroots divisions as that of a preacher. On one organizational tour of the South she recalled that at a meeting in Baton Rouge "after the prayers and the singing of hymns, I preached the sermon. My text was from Isaiah 40, verses 1–6, 'Comfort ye my people.' By the moans from the 'Amen corner', and expressions such as 'Tell it Sister, tell it! Hallelujah!' I felt that they were indeed comforted."[14] Successful founding of new divisions often meant that an organizer demonstrated an intimacy with the rich oral tradition of which the Black church played a part—the norms of which were well understood among those converted to the movement, and the good practitioning of which won respect. It was just such a command of discourse, honed in her experience as a preacher in churches in West Africa, that brought Laura Kofey so many converts. For many new listeners drawn to the UNIA, political dedication to freedom was an extension of their deep-seated religious faith. Religious metaphors, cadences of worship, and celebratory and participatory rituals infused the ceremonies and gatherings of the UNIA. Local UNIA meetings closely followed the format of a church service. Small rural divisions often began as gatherings in private homes, similar in form to prayer meetings. As they garnered membership, they moved into church buildings.

The Structure of the UNIA and the Roles of Women

The sociological structure of the UNIA mirrored in many ways that of the Black church—both the dominant Baptist and Methodist Episcopal denominations and such Sanctified churches as the Church of God in Christ. Church scholars studying the role of women in Black denominations have discussed how men recognized women as the "backbone" of the church. They have also pointed out that a practice lies behind this recognition: women worked hard in supportive positions, creating their own realms of collective activism and enabling the work of key men, who occupied most of the official leadership roles and positions of control within the denominations.[15] Garvey similarly acknowledged that over the years male leadership had proven transitory and opportunistic while women, working mostly

13. Amy Jacques Garvey, *Garvey and Garveyism* (reprint, New York, 1978), p. 5.
14. Ibid., p. 166.
15. See, for example, Jualynne Dodson and Cheryl Townsend Gilkes, "Something Within: Social Change and Collective Endurance in the Sacred World of Black Christian Women," in *Women and Religion in America*, vol. 3: 1700–1968, ed. Rosemary Reuther and Rosemary Keller (San Francisco, 1987), pp. 80–130; Cheryl Townsend Gilkes, "Together and in Harness: Women's Traditions in the Sanctified Church," *Signs* 10 (1985): 678–99;

out of the limelight, were the most steadfast and faithful supporters. Many women in the movement had been making this claim all along.

Like the Black church, the structure of the UNIA was bifurcated by gender and hierarchical in authority. Each local UNIA division had a male president and slate of main (male) officers, who had authority over the division as a whole (male and female). Each division also had a "lady president" and a female slate of officers who oversaw the work of the women's division, the female auxiliaries, and the juvenile division. The lady president was answerable to the president in the affairs of the women's division, and he had censorship rights over her reports to the division at large. Similarly, women in the female paramilitary auxiliary, the Motor Corps, were under the jurisdiction of the male officers of the African Legions. Male presidents of divisions were in turn guided and regulated by the Parent Body leadership. Over it all reigned Garvey as president general. Women could be delegates to international conventions, but they had difficulty being recognized from the floor by the men, who presided over the sessions. Women were also in the minority in the committee assignments and the diplomatic positions that shaped the policy of the UNIA and represented it in the world at large.[16]

In this environment, women UNIA activists, like women in the Black church, "created for themselves a variety of roles, careers, and organizations with great influence but with variable access to structural authority."[17] Black Cross Nurses in some divisions were highly organized, with networks throughout the community and a high profile in weekly programs and meetings. The foundation of the Nurses in the healing arts also had its religious meanings and bore a direct relation to historical avenues of Black women's power. As healers, the Nurses were part of a long African-American tradition of respected community midwives and herbalists—a tradition that reached back to African religions in which women held ceremonial roles as healers and prophetesses.[18]

Jacquelyn Grant, "Black Women and the Church," in *All American Women: Lines That Divide, Ties That Bind*, ed. Johnetta Cole (New York, 1986), pp. 359–69; C. Eric Lincoln and Lawrence H. Mamiya, "The Pulpit and the Pew: The Black Church and Women," in their *The Black Church in the African American Experience* (Durham, N.C., 1990), pp. 274–308. Grant uses the "backbone" metaphor to begin her discussion of the African Methodist Episcopal Church, p. 359.

16. On the structure of the UNIA and women's roles in it, see Barbara Bair, "True Women, Real Men: Gender, Ideology, and Social Roles in the Garvey Movement," in *Gendered Domains: Rethinking Public and Private in Women's History*, ed. Dorothy O. Helly and Susan M. Reverby (Ithaca, N.Y., 1992), pp. 154–66.

17. This quotation is in reference to women in the Sanctified Church, from Gilkes, "Together and in Harness," p. 680.

18. See Bennetta Jules-Rosette, "Privilege without Power: Women in African Cults and Churches," in *Women in Africa and the African Diaspora*, ed. Rosalyn Terborg-Penn, Sharon Harley, and Andrea Benton Rushing (Washington, D.C., 1987), pp. 99–119.

As in the church, the UNIA gave respect to women who may not have received it in the labor force. As in the Sanctified church, many Garveyite women chose to be identified by their first initials rather than by their first names, and the term "ladies" was applied to all women of any class or occupation (as in the official titles of "lady president" and "ladies' division"). "Lady" was also a title bequeathed to the two outstanding women organizers on the national and international level—Lady Henrietta Vinton Davis and Lady M. L. T. De Mena—a trend that reflects both Garvey's affinity with British traditions and masonic orders (there were titles of nobility bestowed on men as well as women, such as "knight commander of the Nile") and the honor given these women leaders by the mass membership (much as in the church women leaders are given the respectful title of "mother").[19] Like women in the Church of God in Christ, who wore uniformlike dresses, the Black Cross Nurses had a dress code and a daily uniform (green with white cuffs) as well as their white parade habits.[20]

UNIA women were teachers. Just as women in the church taught Sunday school and led prayer bands, so Garveyite women ran women's meetings and taught courses preparing young people to join the adult auxiliaries and to work in the divisions. Women had an important economic function within the UNIA, just as they did as tithers and fundraisers in the church. They raised funds and supplied unpaid labor for the administration of the divisions. They bought stock in UNIA enterprises (like the Black Star Line) and contributed to the divisions from their pocketbooks. Women were also important as managers and workers in UNIA enterprises—the restaurants, millinery shops, and other small businesses begun in Harlem—and as stenographers or secretaries in offices at the Black Star Line, the *Negro World*, and the UNIA headquarters. As in many churches, they ran supper kitchens, grew community gardens, and distributed food and help in times of sickness or death to the poor and shut-in.[21] Professional women— educators, social workers, musicians, nurses, businesswomen, editors, elocutionists—brought their skills into the movement just as they did into the church.

19. On the honorific use of the title "mother" for respected, usually older, church women, see Lincoln and Mamiya, "Pulpit and the Pew," p. 275.

20. On titles as a strategy of resistance and on the wearing of standardized dress, see Gilkes, "Together and in Harness," pp. 683, 685. The white habits of the Black Cross Nurses were also similar to garments later worn by women in the Nation of Islam. On the larger issue of the Black church (like the UNIA) as an institution through which Black women struggled toward greater dignity and respect, see Katie G. Cannon, "The Emergence of a Black Feminist Consciousness," and Letty M. Russell, "Authority and the Challenge of Feminist Interpretation," in *Feminist Interpretations of the Bible*, ed. Letty M. Russell (Philadelphia, 1985), pp. 30–40, 137–46.

21. Cheryl Greenberg has described the nature of these tasks during the Depression. See "Black Religious Sisterhood: Harlem Political Action in the Great Depression" (working paper, Trinity College, Hartford, Conn., 1986).

Like church conventions, UNIA conventions featured "women's days," when clothes, food, and other products produced by women members were displayed (exhibiting women's skills and artistry, as well as their economic importance to the movement). During the business sessions of women's days women were given unusual opportunities to speak from the floor and debate the policy issues at hand, but these sessions were still presided over by men; women had to be called on or recognized before they could speak.[22] Thus while many outstanding women succeeded in fulfilling roles on the local, regional, or national level based on an individualistic, hierarchical model (like male leaders), the majority of women exercised their skills and alternative modes of authority locally and in collective ways.

Cheryl Townsend Gilkes has argued that in the Church of God in Christ different styles of leadership developed between women and men: Women were oriented toward consensus and the group, and were inclusive and egalitarian, while men were "hierarchical, individualistic, and dominating."[23] The idea of the existence of "multiple authorities" in the church, and the embracing of women as inclusive and consensus building, is at the heart of modern Black womanist or feminist theology.[24] In some ways the split in styles of leadership that Gilkes observed in the church is true of the Garvey movement as well; in other ways it is not. The dominant models of leadership were those of male agency and authority versus female support and collectivity. The Black Cross Nurses offered a perfect model for feminine separatism and group action mixed with assertive female leadership and wider female networking through community interaction and service. Women attending the UNIA conventions definitely made efforts to build consensus among women delegates. However, many individual women acted in autonomous "male" ways, and there is little evidence of many close ties of affection or camaraderie among leading women in the movement. Also, while Garvey represents a clear case of autocratic leadership, the male African Legions were based on principles of domination and authoritarian values, but were collective, not individualistic, in nature. A small coup staged by women at the 1922 UNIA convention, when a core group of women delegates conspired to seize temporary control of the proceedings in

---

22. See, for example, *Negro World*, 2 September 1922. On women's days in the Sanctified Church, the economic clout of women members, and the formation of a separate convention for women, see Gilkes, "Together and in Harness," pp. 690, 691. On the formation in 1900 of the Women's Convention Auxiliary to the National Baptist Convention, USA, Inc. see Evelyn Brooks, "The Feminist Theology of the Black Baptist Church, 1880–1900," in *Class, Race, and Sex: The Dynamics of Control*, ed. Amy Swerdlow and Hanna Lessinger (Boston, 1983), p. 31, and Evelyn Brooks Higginbotham, *Righteous Discontent: The Women's Movement in the Black Baptist Church, 1880–1920* (Cambridge, Mass., 1993).

23. Gilkes, "Together and in Harness," p. 695.

24. See Russell, "Authority and the Challenge," pp. 143, 144–46; see also Patricia Hill Collins, "The Social Construction of Black Feminist Thought," *Signs* 14 (Summer 1989): 745–73.

order to voice their concerns, offers one of the rare documented accounts of representative women discussing their own status and the principles of leadership within the organization. While calling for women's access to leadership positions that had up to that time been reserved for men, and for women's greater control over the affairs of women in the organization, the debate led to no consensus. The discussants presented a plethora of viewpoints that ranged from "sameness" to "difference" in the essential nature of women, and from free agency to complementarity or subordination in their relation to men.[25] Women's desire for greater access to top leadership positions and for an unfettered voice can be seen as an inclusive impulse. It was a desire to serve, not for individualistic ends but in loyalty to the group endeavor, without squandering the abilities of any who could contribute—as in the biblical injunction, neither slave nor free, neither male nor female in Christ Jesus.

Despite their lack of access to higher office and their usually secondary status on convention floors and speaking platforms, a small number of individual exemplary women emerged among the movement's most important orators. The "teacher" (female) versus "preacher" (male) division of the Black church and its "double pulpit" practices (woman not supplanting the male pastor but complementing his function) had their parallels in the place of the exceptional women on the national UNIA platforms.[26] Like female evangelists in the church, women such as Henrietta Vinton Davis, M. L. T. De Mena, Amy Jacques Garvey, and Laura Kofey spoke and traveled independently as regional organizers, encouraging the formation of new divisions and reforming old ones. Sometimes they were spectacularly in the spotlight: Davis was revered by the local divisions where she had traveled over the years, and she chaired a historic mass meeting of the UNIA at Carnegie Hall in 1919; De Mena epitomized the movement in female form when she led one of the UNIA convention parades through the streets of Kingston, on horseback like a Black Joan of Arc.[27] But their primary role in programs where Garvey was present was to give the preliminary address before his keynote speech, warming the audience for his approach to the podium. The relative importance given their words was reflected in the coverage given such meetings in the *Negro World*. Women's speeches were often briefly paraphrased, while Garvey's were usually

25. See *Negro World*, 9 September 1922.

26. On "teaching" versus "preaching" as a gender distinction, see Gilkes, "Together and in Harness," pp. 682, 688; Higginbotham, *Righteous Discontent*; and Lincoln and Mamiya, "Pulpit and the Pew," p. 279.

27. On the woman warrior as a female image within the Garvey movement, see Barbara Bair, "Gendered Pan-Africanism: The Male and Female Auxiliaries of the UNIA and the African-American Vision of Africa" (paper delivered at the annual conference of the American Studies Association, Costa Mesa, Calif., November 1992).

printed word for word. As in the church, where the pastor's wife was often the most powerful woman in the congregation, UNIA women often derived power from their relation to a prominent male—lady presidents were frequently married to (male) presidents or other officers, and Amy Jacques Garvey wielded great influence as Garvey's wife. Just the wives of deceased or debilitated church founders would sometimes succeed their husbands in an unofficial capacity as pastors, so Amy Jacques Garvey, who had never held official office in the movement, acted in her husband's stead during his incarceration in the federal penitentiary.[28]

Women, Christianity, and the Pulpit in the *Negro World*

UNIA women had the power of the word in many ways in addition to oratory.[29] They became distributors of the *Negro World*. Like women who worked on church publications like *Tidings* or *Home Mission Echo*, UNIA women contributed articles, poems, and essays to the paper; they served as reporters on the affairs of local divisions; and over the years they had some presence on the editorial staff.[30] Amy Jacques Garvey played a crucial role as the major propagandist of the movement. She edited the *Philosophy and Opinions of Marcus Garvey* during the period of her husband's trial and imprisonment, and during his incarceration she edited a new page for the *Negro World*. Called "Our Women and What They Think," the page served for three years (1924–1927) as a unique forum for women's views and for the debate over masculinity, femininity, and women's proper roles.

28. Garvey benefitted a great deal in his career from the intelligence, extreme competence, and determination of his two wives. His first wife, Amy Ashwood Garvey, helped him found the UNIA in Jamaica; his second wife, Amy Jacques Garvey, emerged as the primary propagandist of the movement during Garvey's imprisonment. In both cases, the labor of the women was subsumed by the larger reputation of the man, but in reality theirs was dual-career leadership, with the woman/wife's role crucial to the man/husband's success. On the hidden place of women in the structural power of the Black church, see Jualynne Dodson, "Power and Surrogate Leadership: Black Women and Organized Religion," *Sage* 5 (Fall 1988): 37–42; see also James H. Cone, "Black Theology, Black Churches, and Black Women," chap. 6 in *For My People, Black Theology and the Black Church* (Maryknoll, N.Y., 1990), pp. 122–39.

29. UNIA women teachers, writers, editors, and poets counteracted a history in which literacy and the empowerment inherent in written expression had been denied to Black people. Access to the scriptures, opportunities for interpretating Biblical texts, and freedom of worship all formed part of the issue of literacy and its uses. On the issue of Black women's intellectualism and literacy in relation to political oppression and leadership, see Patricia Hill Collins, *Black Feminist Thought* (New York, 1991), pp. 3–18, 147–48.

30. There were no female members of the *Negro World* staff until 1924, when Amy Jacques Garvey joined the paper as associate editor. Four women and twenty-two men were listed on the masthead of the paper during its fifteen years of publication. Ethel Trew Dunlap was one of the most important women poets published in the *Negro World*; her poetry about the Middle East and the Muslim faith counteracted the UNIA's dominant focus on Christianity and gave voice to those in the movement who were attracted to the connections between nationalism and Islam.

Under Amy Jacques Garvey's direction, the page featured a range of Black feminist, womanist, and feminine perspectives. She encouraged women to extend their "holy influence outside the realms of the home, softening the ills of the world."[31] Motherhood and parenting were highly valued, as was the vision of the wife as valued helpmate to her husband, a good comrade in the home and in the arena of racial politics. Motherhood was particularly discussed in relation to the Madonna-like role of a woman, to be as the mothers of future leaders who would work for the cause of racial redemption. Maternity was also valued as a matter of group survival, a contribution to racial continuity and resistance. The home as much as the world represented a sphere of spiritual and racial calling.[32]

Comparisons with Joan of Arc, who was called by God to go forth as a leader of men in battle, was a major theme in women's page debates about the status of women in the movement. Women often expressed disappointment over the failure of UNIA men to take action, and they frequently threatened to go forth instead of men. In androgynous imagery that combined the religious aspects of the Black Cross Nurses with the militarism of the African Legions (and of Garvey's vision of God), and in violation of the supposedly clear gender boundaries that dominated the movement, UNIA women spoke of themselves as self-sufficient women warriors. "If our men hesitate," wrote Henrietta Vinton Davis in an article for the women's page, "then the women of the race must come forward, they must join the great army of Amazons and follow a Joan of Arc who is willing to be burned at the stake to save her country. Africa must be saved!"[33] Amy Jacques Garvey echoed this militancy in her editorials, stating that UNIA women were notifying the men that they demanded "equal opportunity to fill any position in the Universal Negro Improvement Association or anywhere else without discrimination because of sex." She apologized if this hurt men's "old-fashioned tyrannical feelings," but the women not only made the demand, they intended to enforce it.[34] They were tired of hearing from Black men that there is a better day coming "while they do nothing to usher in the day." Women were impatient and getting into the front ranks themselves, brushing aside cowards, and "with prayer on our lips and arms prepared for any fray, we will press on and on until victory is ours. . . . Ethiopia's queens will reign again, and her Amazons protect her

31. *Negro World*, 24 October 1925.
32. In many ways the vision of womanhood that the UNIA women upheld was very Victorian, linked to ideas very similar to those that Evelyn Brooks Higginbotham has identified as prevalent among Black Baptist women and feminist theological scholars in the 1890s. See Brooks, "Feminist Theology" and Higginbotham, *Righteous Discontent*, pp. 185–229.
33. *Negro World*, 17 October 1925.
34. *Negro World*, 9 January 1926.

shores and people."[35] It was the success of just such compensatory displacement that made male leadership view Laura Kofey as such a threat, although her earlier role as a prophet of Garveyism—leading in Garvey's name—had been acceptable.

The women's page of the *Negro World* also debated religious issues and questions regarding the place of the Black church in the community and the roles of women in the church. A scriptural citation was part of every page in its first several months of publication. Women were disturbed by the connections they saw between Christianity and world aggression, citing occurrences in the world where forces from Christian nations were acting in barbaric fashion toward Third-World peoples. They discussed the intellectual deterioration of the church and its failure to uplift the people. The page featured articles about the economic position of the Black church and its centrality to the social organization of African Americans, arguing that the investment that went into churches might best be broadened into establishing Black industries and economic enterprises. There were also debates over whether or not churches should be politically active.[36] Evangelical issues were discussed in regard to African Americans' relationship to Africa, including arguments that Black churches should do all they can to support the spread of Christianity and the suppression of Islam in Africa, so no "further breach will be created between Africans at home and Africans abroad."[37] The women's page also announced women's affairs and talks

35. *Negro World*, 24 October 1925. The rhetoric of war and religious battle also emerged in earlier Black Baptist women's writings, indeed Evelyn Brooks Higginbotham has observed that "this aggressive, warlike attitude commonly identified with male self-perception underlay the female insistence upon women as leaders, not merely helpmates" (Brooks, "Feminist Theology," p. 48; Higginbotham, *Righteous Discontent*, pp. 146–47). The militant stance taken by UNIA women who were deeply dedicated to the cause resembles what Higginbotham terms "loyal dissent," "radical obedience," or "righteous discontent." Like UNIA women, the Baptist women thinkers that Brooks profiles "claimed their right to intellectual, theological, and ethical discourse," and did so out of their dedication to their church/organization, not in defiance of it (Brooks, "Feminist Theology," pp. 31, 32; Higginbotham, *Righteous Discontent*, p. 122). See also Rosemary Radford Reuther and Eleanor McLaughlin, *Women of Spirit* (New York, 1979), p. 19.

36. On Third-World peoples, see "When Christians are Silent" and "The Christian Barbarians," *Negro World*, 5 September and 10 October 1925. For a domestic application of this critique, see "Mob of 2,000 Christian Whites Lynch One Negro," *Negro World*, 12 June 1926. For the deterioration of the church, see "Preach the Gospel or Plough, Which?" and "Thin Congregations," *Negro World*, 31 October 1925. On economic investment, see Amelia Sayers, "Half Million Dollar Churches and No Jobs," *Negro World*, 29 November 1924. On political activism, see "Opposition to the Church in Politics" and "Methodist Defends Church Political Aims," *Negro World*, 12 December 1925 and 4 December 1926.

37. Editorial, "Christian or Moslem Africa?" *Negro World*, 15 November 1924. In addition to this kind of Christian chauvinism, the UNIA was frequently guilty of an African-American imperialist view of Africa. On the issue of African American women's views of African women, see Sylvia M. Jacobs, "Afro-American Women Missionaries Confront the African Way of Life," in *Women in Africa and the African Diaspora*, ed. Rosalyn Terborg-Penn, Sharon Harley, and Andrea Benton Rushing (Washington, D.C., 1987), pp. 121–32.

and discussed the place of personal faith in community life and in organized worship.[38]

Just as the women's page presented news of women in secular professions and occupations usually filled by men, so it debated women's access to authority and leadership positions in the church. Amy Jacques Garvey printed news of successful women preachers—sisters to Laura Kofey in the outer world.[39] Efforts by male church leaders to bring greater equality to women were also reported, such as Rev. Dr. John Howard Melish's criticism of the Episcopal church as "too undemocratic and asked that women have an equal voice with men in the affairs of the church." During a diocese convention in Long Island Melish entered a resolution that the "womanhood of the church should be represented in the councils of the church equally with the manhood of the church," arguing that "educated young women" were being pulled away into settlement work because no opportunities for self-expression existed for them in their church homes. The measure failed by a vote of 191 to 49.[40] The *Negro World* addressed this argument, that church positions on the status of women were driving female members elsewhere, in a women's page article titled "Women Should Be Working Inside Church, Not in Vestibule: Empty Pews Caused Through Discontent."[41] This article spoke to women's reaction to the General Council of the Presbyterian Church's denial "to grant women equality in the government of the church." A woman member interviewed on the subject spoke of how the churches had for decades profited from women's free labor. Women defrayed church expenses by cooking church suppers, organizing fundraisers and festivals, "blinding herself" sewing for bazaars, and packing missionary barrels when they really wanted to do more: change child labor laws, reform schools, encourage the use of diplomacy not war to solve world problems, and have a voice in questions of spirituality and the work of the church. Not using women in these capacities was like letting a limb of the body atrophy—it would in time affect the body as a whole and bring about its annihilation.[42]

The women's page also kept abreast of various denomination's policies on the ordination of women.[43] Arguments in favor of women pastors ranged from references to the roles women had played in biblical history to the

38. See *Negro World*, 2 August 1924; 26 December 1925; 9 January, 6 March, and 12 June 1926.

39. See *Negro World*, 31 May and 5 July 1924; 22 May and 26 June 1926.

40. *Negro World*, 7 June 1924.

41. *Negro World*, 1 November 1924.

42. A similar argument about the need for the church to recognize the growing equality of women in the public sphere was made in "English House of Clergy," *Negro World*, 6 December 1924.

43. "Women Allowed to Join Ministry" and "More Women Preachers," *Negro World*, 2 October and 4 December 1926.

need for compensatory action due to the failures of men—"Women want to enter the ministry, and they have the right to do so, mainly because men ministers have nearly let the copyright of Christianity run out."[44] One article reported on a 1926 speech by Dr. Anna Lee-Starr before the International Association of Women Pastors claiming sexism in the translation of the Bible. She argued that male translators, personally "unable to grant equality to women," had reworded original meanings that had since been taken as gospel and used to silence women in the church. Dr. Lee-Starr went so far as to suggest that the names of "accomplished women" had been altered in translation "to read masculine," so that some of the apostles and ministers of Biblical times that Biblical scholars chose to describe as men had actually been women.[45]

"Should Women Preach?" was the title of a key article reprinted in the 24 May 1924 women's page. It covered the furor created during a Baptist Minister's Alliance meeting when Rev. George E. Stevens, pastor of the Central Baptist Church of St. Louis, was called to task for "allowing a woman to occupy his pulpit in the capacity of a preacher." Instead of humbly recanting, Reverend Stevens told his tribunal that not only did he not regret his action, "he would ordain a woman to preach if he thought she was called by God," citing the examples of Deborah acting as a judge for the Israelites and Huldah declaring God's law in the time of King Josiah. He went on to say that God "in the face of this age-long contempt for women, signally honored" these. He also pointed out that the resurrected Jesus had first appeared to women, who were his witnesses to men, and that women present at the Pentecost "had that same tongue of flame as the men"—a fulfillment of Joel and Peter's prophetic claim that God had said, "I will pour out my Spirit upon all flesh, and your sons and your daughters shall prophesy." Reverend Stevens felt that these ancient events pointed "to this day when women as the result of gospel emancipation are coming gloriously into their own" and should be used by God "not in any limited, circumscribed capacity, but on a par with men." He went one step further, arguing that God's will should be done through women not only as pastors in churches but in the public arena. "What a glorious galaxy of women we could name whom the gospel has emancipated, that are leaders on the mission fields, in the Salvation Army work, in the temperance cause, in the Sunday School work and in all forms of social uplift, which work requires that they stand out on the lecture platform as well as in the pulpit to direct and inspire the people in all this work. Truly this is woman's day of opportunity in Jesus Christ."[46] It was in this spirit, and within the context

44. "Women of Britain Urged as Minister," *Negro World*, 20 November 1926.
45. "Women Were Apostles," *Negro World*, 20 November 1926.
46. *Negro World*, 24 May 1924.

of such ongoing debates over women's rights as orators and preachers, that Laura Kofey emerged on the scene as a prophet of Garveyism.

Laura Kofey and the UNIA

Laura Kofey emerged on the horizon of Garveyism during a time of crisis in the movement's history, and she came, to use one of her own favorite metaphors, like a meteor brightening the sky. Marcus Garvey had been imprisoned in the Atlanta federal penitentiary in February 1925, and the controversies surrounding him had dimmed enthusiasm for the UNIA in many circles. Kofey, along with Amy Jacques Garvey and De Mena, emerged as major organizers in the movement during this period of doubt and crisis. Kofey began her career in the UNIA through invitations from women in Central America and the United States to appear as a guest speaker at division meetings. Everywhere she appeared her presence was described in the language of conversion and revival.

In the summer of 1926 she was the guest speaker at a series of UNIA meetings in Panama, introduced as a "distinguished traveler and missionary from Acra Gold Coast, West Africa." She addressed the meetings on the subject of Africa and African culture and showed the UNIA members African arts and wares. New members gathered at the altar of Garveyism after each of her appearances, pledging loyalty to the imprisoned Garvey and expressing their commitment and devotion. As one Panama City member put it, they showed adherence to the "doctrine of 'stick-to-itiveness.'" In the next year Kofey moved from involvement in the UNIA division in Detroit to guest speaking at the often-troubled division in New Orleans, not far from Garvey's location in Atlanta. She "spoke for several weeks at meetings sponsored by the Garvey organization" in New Orleans in the fall of 1926, then moved from city to city through Alabama and on to Florida. "Through her," as a Garvey representative later acknowledged, "thousands joined in Mobile, Ala., Jacksonville, Tampa, West Palm Beach, St. Petersburg and Miami, Fla." She established a number of new divisions in small Black communities in Alabama. Jacksonville UNIA leaders proclaimed that Kofey came to them "as a real conscientious race-lover, and a real product and representative of Garveyism."[47]

By the spring of 1927 her influence as a highly charismatic apostle of Garveyism had gained her wide recognition. She was now a stellar phenomenon on the UNIA scene. She held camp-style revival meetings that drew thousands of new members into the movement, with parts of Alabama and Florida as the "burned over" district that responded to her electrifying call. She came to the Jacksonville UNIA division in early April 1927 and held the capacity audience in the regular Sunday meeting at the local Liberty Hall

47. *Negro World*, 7 August 1926, 17 July 1926, 7 April 1928, 14 May 1927.

spellbound for well over two hours. Her success was such that additional meetings were scheduled at the nearby First Baptist Church on Monday and Tuesday nights. After 257 new members joined at her meetings, Kofey announced she would stay "until the enrollment reaches 500." This turned out to be a modest goal. For the next three weeks Kofey spoke every night of the week and twice on Sunday, and at each meeting "from four to fifty-two persons [were] added to the UNIA." By the end of the month almost a thousand new members had joined the ranks of Garveyism, with larger crowds arriving each night as her reputation spread. "Billy Sunday can congregate no more people than the princess is now carrying in Jacksonville," a division member reported to the *Negro World*, adding that the new goal for converts had been upped to 1,500.[48]

Kofey's ascendency as a UNIA organizer, seemed so quick and dazzling because she appeared out of almost complete obscurity. Her origins were mysterious to those who followed her rise, and they remain so. Although J. A. Craigen, one of Garvey's representatives, later claimed that she was an African American from Georgia with a husband and sisters in Detroit and a brother in Cincinnati, it is likely that she was, as she claimed, from the Gold Coast. There is no question that she lived part of her life in West Africa. She claimed to be the daughter of a paramount chief (thus the title "princess" used by her admirers) and was part of African religious networks in the Gold Coast and Sierra Leone. She also had prior experience in the UNIA before emerging as a major regional organizer during Garvey's imprisonment. She had "always aspired to be a preacher and was a member of the Garvey movement in Detroit" in 1924, when she made a visit to West Africa.[49] While in the Gold Coast she became the pastor of a church in Asofa and a missionary in Kumasi.[50] Upon her return to the United Sates in 1926, she preached the combination of nationalist religion, Pan-Africanism, education, and enterprise that formed the core ideology of the Garvey movement, reinforcing it with her direct personal knowledge of Africa.

The murkiness of her personal history did nothing to dispel the impact of her public voice. By May 1927, the Jacksonville UNIA division was petitioning President Calvin Coolidge to pardon Garvey on the strength of signatures from fifteen hundred members—that membership goal having been reached through Kofey's electrifying organizing.[51] On Sunday, 29 May 1927, Kofey enrolled eight hundred new members in Miami and some three thousand persons "gathered on the grounds, in the hall and in the street,

48. *Negro World*, 7 May 1927, 14 May 1927.
49. *Negro World*, 7 April 1928.
50. Newman, "Warrior Mother," p. 142.
51. G. W. Parker and C. H. Frazier to Calvin Coolidge, printed in the *Negro World*, 4 June 1927.

hungry for the truth." The local secretary reported that "Mrs. Coffey is marvelous. Garveyism is spreading like wild fire down here in Miami. Mrs. Coffey has done untold good and is still doing it." By mid-June she was beginning a series of ten meetings for the UNIA division in Tampa, presiding over mass meetings held at St. Matthew's Baptist Church and at Lafayette Hall. Three hundred twenty-two men and women joined the movement at her call, and at the end of her stay the division sponsored a banquet in her honor to thank her for having captured the "hearts of the people."[52] Her success was capped by a personal audience with Marcus Garvey at the Atlanta penitentiary in August 1927.

The meeting with Garvey was a turning point in the reception given Kofey by the male leadership of the movement. At first praised as a witness to Garvey's greatness and as a female John the Baptist for his cause, she began instead to be resented as a rival to Garvey's autocratic control over the organization. Her phenomenal ability to draw people and win their adoration threatened to dilute the hero worship that sustained Garvey's power, and the threat she posed was all the greater because of his own removal from the public arena due to his imprisonment. In September, of the same year, Claude Green, the president of the UNIA division in Miami and a longtime UNIA activist in Florida, visited Garvey at the prison. In October, J. A. Craigen, an attorney and a respected leader in the Detroit UNIA who acted as a Garvey lieutenant, was sent down to Miami to investigate Kofey's influence. The campaign to discredit Kofey and cool the fervor she had awakened had been set into motion. Craigen pointedly warned UNIA members in Tampa not to confuse the UNIA with a church.[53] Soon after, Garvey began to malign Kofey and encourage local harassment of her through public notices he had printed in the *Negro World*.

Directives to UNIA members appeared in October and November 1927 ordering local UNIA divisions not to entertain Kofey and, if they heard that she was appealing for funds, to seek her arrest.[54] In December 1927 Garvey's personal representative announced that the UNIA charter of the Jacksonville division—the division that had so thrilled to Kofey's presence—was revoked, and in early 1928 Miami division members who had supported Kofey were expelled from the movement (including, significantly, the division's religious leaders, the chaplain and assistant chaplain).[55] By February 1928, Garvey felt it necessary to mention Kofey in a postscript to his weekly front-page editorial. "This woman is a fake and has no authority from me to speak to the Universal Negro Improvement

52. *Negro World*, 11 June 1927, 23 July 1927.
53. *Negro World*, 17 September and 22 October 1927.
54. *Negro World*, 22 October and 22 November 1927.
55. *Negro World*, 3 December 1927; see also 11 February and 18 February 1928.

Association," he told *Negro World* readers, "Should she attempt to raise funds from any member or division in the name of the organization or with the pretence of my authority, have her arrested."[56] Kofey had been officially declared a false prophet. She was arrested by local authorities in Florida on two occasions, held briefly (in one case subjected to a demeaning strip search) and released for lack of cause. Meanwhile, male leaders of the Garvey movement were not the only ones enlisting the help of the police in repressing Kofey's influence. Local Black ministers were none too happy with Kofey's presence in their communities. "Her program," as one UNIA member who witnessed her rise put it, "gave the churches a shake-up, so she then had two sets of enemies. So it was the old organization and the preachers that formed the mob" that opposed her and her meetings.[57]

In response to this organized opposition, Kofey founded her own organization and gave it a name similar to the UNIA—the African Universal Church and Commercial League.[58] She first held meetings in the Miami Liberty Hall (a UNIA division's meeting place was called the Liberty Hall in any given city or location). Most members of the local UNIA male paramilitary auxiliary, the Universal African Legions, remained loyal to Garvey in the factionalism. They appeared at Kofey's meetings in UNIA uniform, heckled her during her sermons, and disrupted the meetings by using such methods as shooting out the lights. She responded to these confrontative demonstrations by moving her congregation to a storefront church made available through one of the expelled Miami division members, but her opposition followed her. She continued to give her inspired sermons based on biblical texts, and she encouraged African Universal Church members to embrace the Pan-African and Afrocentric matters that had long been central to her Garveyite message—to look to Africa, to give funds for African development, to educate children in the love of blackness and a knowledge of African history, to treat one another as brothers and sisters, and to trust in God.

The murder of Laura Kofey took place on 8 March 1928. As Kofey lay dead at the front of the church, felled by her assassin's gunshots, her followers, witnesses to her martyrdom, erupted in shock and rage. They turned in pandemonium on a man they knew opposed Kofey's leadership, and in the anger of the moment they beat him to death there in the

56. Editorial by Marcus Garvey, *Negro World*, 18 February 1928.

57. Charles L. Harrison, Pittsburg Landing, Tenn., to Senator Theodore Bilbo of Mississippi, 2 May 1938, Manuscript Collections, McCain Graduate Library, University of Southern Mississippi.

58. The full name of the UNIA was the Universal Negro Improvement Association and African Communities League. The ACL was the business wing of the UNIA. Kofey also borrowed the UNIA motto for use in her new organization.

meetinghouse. The police were called to quell the riot, which had spread outside. The murdered man was Maxwell Cook. He was well known to Kofey and to her followers. He had been a bodyguard for Kofey when she was with the UNIA, and after the split between Garvey and Kofey he remained an officer in the Miami African Legion. Two other UNIA leaders—Claude Green, the Miami UNIA division president who had visited Garvey in prison and was a close ally to J. A. Craigen (Garvey's representative), and James Nimmo, Cook's commander in the division's African Legion—were arrested for the murder and held for four months without bail. Craigen handled their defense, with extended appeals for funds for legal expenses published regularly in the *Negro World*, along with castigations of Kofey and her ministrations. Though both Green and Nimmo were, like Cook, well known for their opposition to Kofey and readily admitted their loyalty to Garvey, no evidence linked them directly with the assassination, and both had alibis showing that they were elsewhere at the time of the shooting. Their case was finally heard and they were released from custody in the summer of 1928. Garvey at the time of the murder had been released from federal detention in Atlanta and deported from the United States. He was reestablishing his political life in Jamaica and directing UNIA affairs from a new headquarters there.[59] The case of Laura Kofey's murder was never solved. It was widely believed in the street and among UNIA members that Garvey had ordered the assassination, or had indicated to those loyal to him that he would not mind should Kofey in some way be removed from the scene.[60]

Though the execution was planned to silence Kofey, she lived on in her martyrdom. In the spring of 1928 her body lay in state in Miami, Palm Beach, and Jacksonville. At some points so many hundreds of people from the Black community crowded the sidewalks waiting to pay their respects to the slain leader that street traffic had to be rerouted. Kofey's African Universal Church continued in Florida. It sent missionaries to Africa, and it established prayer bands, industrial clubs, and classes in Black history. It had churches and church representatives in Florida and Alabama and in the Gold Coast, and in the early 1940s it established a utopian Christian community, called Adorkaville, on the outskirts of Jacksonville. Mother Kofey's image continued to permeate the church's memory. It was featured

59. For more detailed information about the case see Hill et al., *Marcus Garvey and UNIA Papers* 7:141–42, 166–71. Appeals for funds appeared in the 21 April and 28 July 1928 *Negro World* and other issues.

60. Garvey, released from prison and deported in 1927, was in Jamaica at the time of Kofey's murder and departed for a tour of Europe soon after her death. Some Florida newspapers claimed that Garvey had instigated the attack on Kofey (*Miami Daily News*, 20 March and 22 March 1928; see also *New York Times*, 21 March 1928). It is worth noting the similarities between the experiences of Kofey and the UNIA and Malcolm X and the Nation of Islam.

in church literature and on banners, and the day of her death was ritually commemorated.[61]

Kofey even achieved something of a victory in regard to having the last word in the *Negro World*, the paper that had been used to suppress her. In 1930 the paper announced that the Native African Union of America, Inc., was celebrating their first Ladies' Day by commemorating two great women from the UNIA—Mary Sharperson Young, the founder of the UNIA women's elite Royal Court of Ethiopia auxiliary in New York, and the "Martyred African Princess [Laura] Adorka Koffey." A representative of the Harlem Housewives League was the principal speaker.[62]

"This Woman . . . Has No Authority from Me to Speak"

Death is the most effective means of censorship, of quieting a voice you do not want heard. Laura Adorker Kofey's life is a metaphor for the dialectics of gender and religion that existed within the Garvey movement—both in the opportunities afforded her and in the limitations placed upon her when she overstepped the unspoken boundaries of what a woman in the movement should do and be.

Kofey, a riveting speaker whose interpretations of scripture stirred her hearers to action, is emblematic of the women orators and organizers who worked at every level of the Garvey movement. She was mirrored in the hundreds of other women who gave addresses in their local division meetings, who organized auxiliary work, who voiced their concerns from the floor of conventions, or who were in the forefront of public discourse, appearing at podiums and representing the UNIA on an international scale. But all these women operated within restrictions of deference that granted ultimate authority within divisions and within the Parent Body leadership to men.[63] Kofey the female apostle presenting Garvey as a savior figure and stirring audiences in his name was considered laudable; Kofey displacing Garvey as an authoritative voice and winning her own messianic following was not.[64] In crossing the lines from pew to pulpit—from the accepted rules of female self-actualization within the bounds of service and support to self-proclaimed autonomy and authority—she became a threat to the fundamental structure of the UNIA and to the constructions of gender with which its dominant male leaders were comfortable. Ceasing to be a servant,

61. See Ian Duffield, "Pan-Africanism, Rational and Irrational," *Journal of African History* 18 (1977): 597–620; and Newman, "Warrior Mother," pp. 140–41.

62. *Negro World*, 19 April 1930.

63. On male dominance of top leadership positions in Black organizations and the issue of Black male identity and the church, see Collins, *Black Feminist Thought*, p. 8; and Lincoln and Mamiya, "The Pulpit and the Pew," pp. 275, 278.

64. This is similar to the theological questions regarding the manifestation of Marianism in some congregations in the Catholic church and the mixed reception of it by male priests and bishops.

except to her God, and claiming to be a leader in her own right, she was silenced. Hers was the abbreviated voice.

There is a tendency to interpret the Garvey movement as a new phenomenon springing from the New Negro era, but the circumstances of Kofey's life and death connect her to a much larger tradition. Just as women's activism in the movement had its ties to the church and to Black women's neighborhood organizations, mother's clubs, and uplift work of the preceding generations, so Kofey's dedication to a life as a preacher and prophet is tied to the experiences of nineteenth-century Black women who felt similar callings (and to contemporary women who left established denominations and started storefront churches in order that they might speak).[65] Just as importantly, Kofey's career as an orator was part of Black women's ongoing roles in preserving and conveying oral tradition and in honoring literacy (including the reading of scripture and the knowledge of God's Word) as a medium of empowerment.

In emerging with such force and controversy upon the scene of Garveyism, Kofey made explicit some of the internal contradictions of the movement and laid bare its system of authority. Her success as a woman challenged the pyramidal hierarchy of control and gender dichotomy that prevailed in the UNIA. Kofey's career as a Black woman preacher and interpreter of scripture also looked to the future of contemporary Black womanist theology and thought. Her function as an organizer and pastor raised continuing debates about the ordination of women as pastors, their position in church power structures, and the respect due women as biblical and spiritual authorities.[66] Her success as an evangelist built on everyday ways of knowing rather than on formal intellectual conventions. Her power of voice and the loyalty shown her were testaments to a strong oral tradition and a consensual sense of ethics.[67] And her belief in her right to the pulpit demonstrated claims for equity and inclusion. Her experience added to the tales of female heroism already attached to other women in church history. The example of her martyrdom and her message of redemption weakened narrow Christological concepts and opened doors to less gender-based understandings of the person and work of the Savior. These principles of equality, transformative self-actualization, inclusiveness, and mutuality are at the heart of new feminist visions of the church and of Black feminism in

65. See, for example, the nineteenth-century narratives of ministers of the gospel Jarena Lee and Amanda Smith and the speeches of Maria Stewart.

66. Grant, "Black Women and the Church"; Lincoln and Mamiya, "The Pulpit and the Pew"; Cheryl J. Sanders, "The Woman as Preacher," in *African American Religious Studies*, ed. Gayraud S. Wilmore (Durham, N.C., 1989), pp. 372–91.

67. On the issue of women's ways of knowing, see Bettina Aptheker, *Tapestries of Life: Women's Work, Women's Consciousness, and the Meaning of Daily Experience* (Amherst, Mass., 1989); Collins, "Social Construction"; and Collins, *Black Feminist Thought*, pp. 15, 16, 17.

general.[68] Despite its censorship, Laura Kofey's life laid claim to female participation in the arena of secular and spiritual discourse. It signified women's right to speak, to interpret, and to lead with the same tongue of flame as the men.

68. See, for example, Cannon, "Emergence"; Katie G. Cannon, *Black Womanist Ethics* (Atlanta, 1988); Margaret A. Farley, "Feminist Consciousness and the Interpretation of Scripture," in *Feminist Interpretations of the Bible*, pp. 41–51; Jacquelyn Grant, "Womanist Theology: Black Women's Experience as a Source for Doing Theology, with Special Reference to Christology," in *African American Religious Studies*, ed. Gayraud S. Wilmore (Durham, N.C., 1989), pp. 208–27; and Russell, "Authority and the Challenge."

PART II
Ministers and Laity:
Sexual Politics
in the Protestant Church

CHAPTER 3

Resurrecting Man:
Desire and *The Damnation*
of Theron Ware

LISA MACFARLANE

She unlocked still another door as she spoke—a door which was also concealed behind a curtain.

"Now," she said, holding up the candle so that its reddish flare rounded with warmth the creamy fulness of her chin and throat, and glowed upon her hair in a flame of orange light—"Now . . . now I will show you what is my very own."[1]

With this invitation, the "New Woman" Celia Madden begins her seduction of Harold Frederic's young minister Theron Ware. Theron struggles barely a moment with his Methodist training before the scene climaxes with his confused arousal: "I want to get as close to you—to your ideal, that is, as I can" (p. 202). Frederic, of course, who once called sex "the mainspring of all activity," knows what Theron wants to get close to.[2] But critics often suppress a full treatment of the sexual politics in the novel as successfully as Theron does; indeed, except when dealing with some notable exceptions—the erotics of Puritan poetry, for example, or *The Scarlet Letter*—scholars have tended to repress much of the erotic dimension, even the blatant sexuality, represented in many American works that focus on religion. Yet the conflation between sexuality and religious belief and practice is surely commonplace; from the seventeenth-century confrontation between Anne Hutchinson and her ministerial brethren to the contemporary scandals of Jim Bakker and Jimmy Swaggert, religious fervor, sexual potency, and political power have coexisted in an explosive symbiosis.

In *The Damnation of Theron Ware* (1896), the convergence of gender and religion illuminates three related topics. First, focusing on gender resurrects a too often forgotten but stunning novel that confronts regional and cosmopolitan cultures and bridges realist and modernist aesthetics. Second, *The Damnation* illustrates how flexible a convention the minister as a feminized

Reprinted, with changes, from *Studies in American Fiction* (Autumn 1992). Copyright 1992 by Northeastern University.

1. Harold Frederic, *The Damnation of Theron Ware* (New York, 1986), p. 190. All further citations will be in the text.

2. George E. Fortenberry, Stanton Garner, and Robert H. Woodward, eds., *The Correspondence of Harold Frederic* (Fort Worth, 1977), p. 290.

man can be; the novel highlights his centrality to questions of cultural authority in nineteenth-century America by revealing the ambiguity and discomfort with which American writers and readers have viewed men of the cloth. Finally, Frederic's handling of Theron Ware as a feminized man implicitly deconstructs the idea of a monolithic masculinity, especially in its binary opposition to an equally uncomplicated femaleness; rather, the ministerial convention reveals the constructedness, malleability, and plurality of gender, even as the character himself may struggle to retain a rigid and socially orthodox masculinity throughout the novel. For all this discomfort, however, the feminized hero himself hardly challenges traditional notions of masculinity; indeed, in this and similar novels, established gender and power relations are reinforced, as women become either traditional tokens of exchange among men or repulsed threats to an allied patriarchal establishment that includes both clerical and secular men. In short, the feminized minister in American letters focuses attention upon a network of homosocial bonds that reinforces patriarchy even as it apparently challenges patriarchal power.[3]

The Damnation fits nicely into a group of novels from this period that focus on the place of denominational or sectarian faith in a larger social context, either by examining the religious practices of a particular community, as in William Dean Howells' *The Leatherwood God* (1916), or by following an individual whose religious values are challenged by the secular pressures of married life, politics, or capitalism, as in Margaret Deland's *John Ward, Preacher* (1886), Elizabeth Stuart Phelps' *The Gates Ajar* (1868), or Henry Adams' *Esther* (1884). Even a historical religious novel like Lew Wallace's *Ben-Hur: A Tale of the Christ* (1880) provides an implicit commentary on how the late nineteenth century confronted the related crises of spiritual life and gender identity.[4] In works by both canonical and lesser-known authors, in recognized classics and in examples of popular culture, in works that are explicitly meant to foster certain religious values as well as in works that use religious situations as occasions for other projects, the

3. In many instances "feminization" implies that men have becomes less aggressive and more family-oriented than their peers; if to some this is utopian, feminist critics have good reason to be skeptical of male feminization's leading to a political or social alliance with women. In this essay, the term acknowledges the concerns of late nineteenth-century ministers that Christianity was becoming irrelevant to men's lives; one case study of the efforts to promote a male-oriented "muscular Christianity" is Gail Bederman's "'The Women Have Had Charge of the Church Work Long Enough': The Men and Religion Forward Movement of 1911–1912 and the Masculinization of Middle-Class Protestantism," Chapter 5, in this volume.

4. See Paul A. Carter, *The Spiritual Crisis of the Gilded Age* (Dekalb, Ill., 1971). William Dean Howells, *The Leatherwood God* (Bloomington, Ind., 1976); Margaret Deland, *John Ward, Preacher* (Ridgewood, N.J., 1967); Elizabeth Stuart Phelps, *The Gates Ajar* (Cambridge, Mass., 1964); Henry Adams, *Esther* (New York, 1983); Lewis Wallace, *Ben-Hur: A Tale of The Christ* (New York, 1880).

minister provides a particularly fertile trope for examining masculinity and power.

Both in fiction and in the larger social and cultural world the minister bridges the worlds of men and women by his professional position. He figures as the most visible representative of church hierarchies controlled almost exclusively by men, hierarchies that oversee largely female congregations. The institution itself, of course, is responsible for policing not only the behavior but also the very thoughts and values of both the congregation and more broadly of society as a whole.[5] Yet the mechanism by which this policing is to be done is based on influence—that female means of control which depends upon the willing cooperation of those whose behavior is to be affected. The minister's position is therefore an equivocal one. On the one hand, he represents legitimate and substantive authority: he represents the patriarchal authority of God the Father. On the other, he appears as impotent and irrelevant: charged with influencing values and morals, he functions as female in the gendered disposition of cultural work in the nineteenth century.[6] The minister's characterization sometimes as feminized, sometimes as neutered, or even sometimes as a hybrid or androgynous figure (sometimes as all three, even within the same text), thematizes the challenge he poses to normative social constructions of gender.

The link between disordering sexuality and questioning faith is explicit, and not surprising, since part of the character's understanding of his faith is how it constructs or leads him to understand both male and female sexuality. But this feminizing, neutering, or androgyny do not necessarily lead to any genuine transformation of values. If Theron and other male ministers were truly "feminized," they might have adopted what Adrienne Rich calls a woman-based "transforming power" to foster a potential radicalism. But in works by both male and female authors, ministers return to traditionally patriarchal and authoritarian ways of dealing with others; they exercise what is for Rich a male-identified "power-over" others.[7] The feminized hero still asserts male privilege; as Christopher Newfield argues in his discussion of *The Scarlet Letter*, "Dimmesdale recovers his social power as a man by showing the variable feelings of a 'woman' . . . men do

5. The minister has no overt power; rather, he relies upon his congregation's belief that their lives are constantly monitored and judged, both by an all-powerful male God and by the minister who is his representative. Religion's power is based upon its capacity to transform inner lives rather than simply affect external behaviors; its exercise of power converges with that of the panoptic and patriarchal world of emergent consumer capitalism. See "Panopticism," in Michel Foucault, *Discipline and Punish: The Birth of the Prison*, trans. Alan Sheridan (New York, 1979), pp. 195–228.

6. The phrase "cultural work" is of course Jane Tompkins'; on the role of religion and cultural authority see her "Sentimental Power," in *Sensational Designs: The Cultural Work of American Fiction 1790–1860* (New York, 1985).

7. Adrienne Rich, *Of Woman Born: Motherhood as Experience and Institution* (New York, 1981), p. 86.

not only escape but dominate women by feminizing themselves—by affirming their marginality in a way that aligns them socially with women."[8] The powerful socializing forces of masculinity allow even feminized men to dominate woman; they appropriate the peculiar power of her "sphere," thus disturbing the balance of power between the sexes. They assert—by force, if necessary—their authority as ministers and as men over the destabilizing theological and social (and sexual) rebellions of women, even when it is the very quality of independence that they admire in the women they love.

Like many feminized men in nineteenth-century novels, Theron clings to rigid constructions of gendered identity over the fluidity of human experience; he accepts culturally ordained constructions of the self over individual needs; and he embraces hierarchy and legalism at the expense of a more experientially-based and peer-oriented ministry that might subvert gender ideology.[9] Theron's unstable gender identity becomes, moreover, a factor in his relationships to other men as he negotiates the paradoxes of his simultaneous authority over them and dependence upon them. The disordering of gender identity is therefore part of how the male minister negotiates his own political and economic positions within patriarchy, not evidence of how he is aligned with women to challenge it.

Until recently, most scholars have seen gender in nineteenth-century America as divided by the ideology of separate spheres, and much of this work has focused on women. Ann Douglas' pathbreaking *The Feminization of American Culture* (1975), for example, drew attention to the transforming power relations of the disestablished Protestant clergy and their subsequent gender dislocation; but in doing so, it stressed women's domestic writing, revealing the alliance formed by ministers and their largely female congregations. Recent work on gender in the nineteenth century recognizes competing notions of womanhood, and also therefore of manhood.[10] It therefore provides useful models for probing the relationships between masculinity, spirituality, and power, and thus for understanding both the figure of the feminized male minister and the larger relationships between religious and moral authority and patriarchy, both in *The Damnation of Theron Ware* and in America more generally.

8. Christopher Newfield, "The Politics of Male Suffering: Masochism and Hegemony in the American Renaissance," *Differences* 1 (1989): 58.

9. Joan Hedrick has characterized this as the difference between a ministry involved with patriarchal values, which privileges hierarchy and legalism, and a ministry that has a potentially radically transforming value because of its immersion in a more experientially-based and female-oriented "woman's culture." See " 'Peaceable Fruits': The Ministry of Harriet Beecher Stowe," *AQ* 40 (1988): 307–32.

10. Ann Douglas, *The Feminization of American Culture* (New York, 1975). See also Ruth Cogan, *The All-American Girl: The Ideal of Real Womanhood in Mid-Nineteenth-Century America* (Athens, Ga., 1989). On nineteenth-century American masculinity, see David Leverenz, *Manhood and the American Renaissance* (Ithaca, N.Y., 1989).

Men's relationships with one another, as well as with women, shape the historical contours of masculinity. Eve Kosofsky Sedgwick has recently argued that, as Carroll Smith-Rosenberg saw with women, relationships among men exist along a continuum of homosocial bonds.[11] Smith-Rosenberg finds that the varieties of women's relationships—from lesbianism to mothering—need not be sharply dichotomized into the sexual and the non-sexual in the nineteenth century; Sedgwick, however, sees a radical discontinuity among male relationships between the homosocial and the homosexual. This discontinuity is of course shaped differently at specific historical moments; as Sedgwick says, "the shapes of sexuality, and what *counts* as sexuality both depend on and affect historical power relationships."[12] Although Sedgwick and others have followed Foucault's lead in demystifying the systems of classification that cluster around the "homosexual" in the nineteenth century, she invites a look at "the treacherous middle stretch of the modern homosocial continuum."[13] It is in this treacherous landscape that Theron Ware is lost, caught from beginning to end between his professional "feminized" self and the self socialized as a man, able to negotiate neither the ideological contradictions of gender construction nor the ambiguous position of the minister in a heterogeneous and increasingly secularized dominant culture.

Sedgwick explores how the exchange of women defines the boundaries of masculinity, mediates male bonding, and reveals the repressed bond between male rivals in erotic triangles. This exchange, she argues, is necessitated by a culturally endorsed homophobia, which conditions even heterosexual relationships among men. Put another way, for Christopher Craft, "desire between anatomical males requires the interposition of an invisible femininity"; moreover, "this insistent ideology of heterosexual mediation [involves a] corollary anxiety about independent feminine sexuality."[14] In *The Damnation* and similar works, invisible femininity is embodied not only in women, but also in the feminized minister himself, whose relationships to other men are, as they are for women, economically and politically dependent. Independent female sexuality is then doubly threatening: if a woman is no longer dependent upon men, then the feminized minister too might lose his claim to protection from other men, even as he loses the last constituency over whom he has control.

11. Carroll Smith-Rosenberg, "The Female World of Love and Ritual," *Disorderly Conduct: Visions of Gender in Victorian America* (New York, 1985), pp. 53–76; Eve Kosofsky Sedgwick, "The Beast in the Closet: James and the Writing of Homosexual Panic," in *Speaking of Gender*, ed. Elaine Showalter (New York, 1989), pp. 243–68.

12. Eve Kosofsky Sedgwick, *Between Men: English Literature and Male Homosocial Desire* (New York, 1985), p. 2.

13. Sedgwick, "Beast in the Closet," p. 247.

14. Christopher Craft, " 'Kiss Me with Those Red Lips': Gender and Inversion in Bram Stoker's *Dracula*," in Showalter, *Speaking of Gender*, p. 224.

Peter Schwenger argues that "a nineteenth-century man could assume his patriarchy with the ease of one settling into a comfortable armchair."[15] But the clubby familiarity of this image masks the tension with which nineteenth-century men maintained and negotiated their position; indeed, the vigor with which they defended patriarchy is itself indicative of their anxiety. Looking at the dynamics of desire reveals how this anxiety represses and misdirects men's relationships, whether they are construed as "normal" or as "aberrant." Desire can refer to something other than sex; it can be an affective and social force—sometimes love, sometimes hostility, sometimes something less emotionally charged—that shapes relationships. In other words, desire provides a structure for—rather than being itself an— emotion. Moreover, desire allows for the meanings implicit in different positions of the triangle to circulate. As Peter Brooks says, "narratives both tell of desire—typically present some story of desire—and arouse and make use of desire as dynamic of signification"; desire is, in fiction if not in society, both "narrative thematic" and "narrative motor."[16] In *The Damnation of Theron Ware*, as with all the novels cited, desire is indeed in part erotic; sexual desire forms both the motivation for the plot and the symbolic framework by which other themes—money, political power, knowledge— are inscribed. But as his clumsy response to Celia's seduction shows, Theron's desires are themselves confused. In *The Damnation of Theron Ware*, Frederic not only, as his previous critics have acutely observed, provides us with a parable of the American innocent's confrontation with the modern world; he also, and more subtly, deconstructs the basis for the innocent's own identity, by showing American masculinity to be a fluid, negotiable, and, for Theron at least, dangerously unstable fiction.[17]

These themes are played out in Octavius, a small town in the burned-over district of upstate New York, to which Theron, a young Methodist minister, and his wife Alice have been called. Theron's new flock proves to be conservative (theologically, intellectually, and economically), and the

15. Peter Schwenger, *Phallic Critiques: Masculinity and Twentieth-Century Literature* (London, 1984), p. 9.

16. Peter Brooks, *Reading for the Plot: Design and Intention in Narrative* (New York, 1985), pp. 37, 54.

17. Edmund Wilson, in *The Devils and Canon Barham: Ten Essays on Poets, Novelists and Monsters* (New York, 1973), sees Theron as an allegory of American innocence beset by foreign influences; following him, among others, are Everett Carter, Introduction to *The Damnation of Theron Ware* (Cambridge, Mass., 1960); George Spangler, "Theron Ware and the Perils of Relativism," *CRevAS* (1974): 36–46; and Elmer Suderman, "Modernization as Damnation in *The Damnation of Theron Ware*," *Ball State University Forum* 27 (1986): 12–19. Many studies have helpfully scrutinized the treatment of women in the novel: see John Crowley, "The Nude and the Madonna in *The Damnation of Theron Ware*," *AL* 45 (1973): 379–89; Scott Donaldson, "The Seduction of Theron Ware," *NCF* 29 (1974–1975): 441–52; Robin Lent, "The Infantilization of Theron Ware," unpublished essay, 1988; and Fritz Oeschlaeger, "Passion, Authority, and Faith in *The Damnation of Theron Ware*," *AL* 58 (1986): 238–55.

Wares, who dream of moving socially into a more genteel middle class, are quickly demoralized. The town also has a large Irish Catholic population, and Theron becomes fascinated by some of its citizens: the cosmopolitan Celia Madden, the daughter of Octavius' wealthiest man; the broadminded priest, Father Forbes; and Dr. Ledsmere, a Rappaccini figure who performs particularly sadistic experiments with opium on his very own Chinaman. Among Theron's own flock, his only sympathizers are Levi Gorringe, a non-professing trustee, and the Soulsbys, professional fundraisers. Theron's infatuation with Celia, nourished by a particularly suggestive encounter in her room and encouraged by a kiss in the forest, leads him to follow her and Father Forbes to New York City, where he is roundly rebuffed: "we find," she tells him, "that you are a bore" (p. 321). In New York's seediest places, he miserably drinks himself into delirium, only to find himself finally banging on the Soulsbys' door; he is rescued and started in a new life with Alice in Seattle real estate—all the while fantasizing about a bullier pulpit, the U. S. Senate.

The main characters circulate in a series of gender-confusing triangles, each governed by female intervention. But since gender is of course not exclusively equated with biology, the female can shift precipitously within culturally conditioned relationships. The role of the female in Frederic's triangles wavers disturbingly as the novel progresses. When the triangle involves only men, Theron himself takes on the role of the female, as, for example, when he facilitates the revenge of church trustees Pierce and Winch on Levi Gorringe. Theron's feminized self is so dominant that he plays the role of the female in his relationships with other women, especially with Celia. Moreover, in triangles involving both men and women—most dramatically with Father Forbes and Celia—Theron occupies different positions at different moments in the text, as he sees Forbes and Celia each as both a possible mentor and a rival for the affection of the other. Theron's shifting role in these triangles reveals something of the contours of Sedgwick's "homosocial continuum." A triangle consisting of Theron, Alice, and Levi delineates what might be called a normative functioning of an intermediary female presence; another triangle comprised of Theron, Celia, and Father Forbes reveals the degree to which the normative conceals and adjudicates the repressed homoerotic dimensions of male bonding. Theron's unstable roles in these triangles unravel the fiction of a stable gender identity, even as he continually reconstructs events around him so as to preserve an uncritical belief in his own, male, importance. At the novel's end, after a literally life-threatening dissolution of his self-image, Theron reinvents himself as the hero in another drama of conventional male privilege, politics. Yet even there, Theron shivers with pleasure as he fantasizes about being the object of an adoring male gaze.

As a minister, Theron's relationship with his congregation is negotiated through Alice, whose social skills assured the Wares' popularity in their former community; in Octavius, her retreat from the social life of the parish reinforces Theron's disaffection from his church. Even the flowers she wears in her Sunday bonnet, for example, signal to the Octavius Methodists that both Theron's theology and his taste might be a little extravagant for them. Moreover, Alice's refusal to shop at the more expensive Methodist stores underscores the connections between economic, domestic, and church politics. Alice's behavior is a symptom of Theron's alienation; it provides the occasion for demonstrating Theron's impotence with the trustees, who deflower not only Alice but Theron as well. Only Levi Gorringe, the nonprofessing church trustee, sympathizes with the Wares; and again, it is through Alice, and the literal replanting of her garden, that this sympathy is built, and later destroyed.

If Theron's relationship with Alice is the most normative of his relationships with women, then Theron's relationship with Levi Gorringe involves Alice in a conventional way. Alice prepares Theron for Levi's wink of comradeship following the trustees' meeting. "He's got a soft side somewhere," she tells Theron (p. 23). The wink signals Levi's extending moral support and friendship to Theron. The men's exchanges depend upon Alice; as Theron's interpretations of her sexual identity shift, their relationship deteriorates from potential friendship to disguised rivalry to outright hostility. The central scene provides an overt demonstration of how women become the objects transferred among men as they negotiate money, power, and allegiance.

Levi confesses how his own religious sensibilities were awakened by an unrequited love interest: "there hasn't been another minister here since that I should have felt like telling this story to. They wouldn't have understood it at all . . . But you are different." Theron is flattered: "'It pleases me beyond measure that you should like me, then,' returned the young minister, with frank gratification shining on his face. 'The World is made all the sweeter by these—these elements of romance.'" Theron returns Levi's confidences with one of his own—the surprising one that the Methodist Discipline should not be taken literally: "'I declare! . . . I never talked like this to a living soul before . . . Your confidences were contagious.'" The conversation ends merrily, but significantly; Levi Gorringe reminds Theron that "'I reckon that the church still owes me a girl. I'll have one yet'" (pp. 122–23). Levi's and Theron's relationship is clearly defined by the woman Theron's church owes Levi: in this subplot, Alice. And yet the relationship is clearly between them: their confidences, their "romance," in Theron's word, but also their rivalry.

Theron's declaration of independence from his Church fathers underscores the complicated interconnectedness of religious and gender politics, particularly as they involve Theron's own self-interested state. In one sense, his statement severs the filial bonds that have marked his spiritual and intellectual connection to the significantly named "Elders" and the Methodist Discipline, even if out of economic need his actions necessarily conform. With that statement, he writes himself into the master narrative of the American (male) mythic hero: shedding the trappings of past tradition, striking out for, in his case, theological "territories" previously uncharted, at least by the Methodists he has known. But this act of ostensible liberation is highly qualified. Theron is moved to commit it only after the "contagion" of Levi's own confidences, almost as if he needs to reciprocate Levi's confidences with one of his own. The statement is itself confidential: a mildly stated, covertly made secret, clearly intended to establish a private relationship rather than strike a public stance that might risk a real disruption of his place within the Methodist community. Moreover, the only precedent for Theron's confession is his limited understanding of the ideas that Father Forbes and Dr. Ledsmere have introduced about the historical and literary exegesis of the Bible. Theron's infatuation with these two men, which is distinctly gendered and specifically tied to the power and class status he feels instinctively that their learning gives them, is deflected into an infatuation with what are for him revolutionary ideas about the symbolic nature of Biblical language. His declaration of independence thus reflects his seduction by men other than the Elders; it is more an act of adultery than one of liberation.

But if Alice's interpolation between Theron and Levi nurtures their friendship, the relationship is inherently unstable, since it depends upon the presence of a female other who ultimately stresses it. When Theron's fantasies about Celia transform his relationship with Alice, his relationship with Levi also inevitably changes. Levi's friendly jest about the church owing him a girl echoes in Theron's head when Theron discovers that Levi has been giving her expensive flowers for the parish garden, which for Theron also operates as a symbol for Alice, and the labor and status she has provided for him.

At the simplest level, Theron is made to feel guilty by the implication that he is neglecting Alice; his response is to jettison what he sees as the source of his guilt, Levi. More important, the scene reveals the indirect nature of Theron's desire: its object is as much Levi as Alice. When Levi is revealed to have an independent relationship with Alice, Theron feels jealous; he feels that the normal privileging of male priorities has been breached, since the men's relationship is disrupted when Alice takes on an independent role. Theron's semiconscious preoccupation with his own sexual desire for Celia, moreover, leads him not only to assume a similar desire between Alice and Levi, which may indeed at some level be true for Levi, but also to fantasize that their desire has been consummated—an illicit consummation which, as he converts fantasy into fact, he also envies. Theron's final confrontation with Levi translates all this into an accusation of Alice's infidelity, an accusation that prompts Levi's contempt. Theron thus reestablishes his position over Alice in their relationships with Levi, and returns her to a traditional role as a passive medium for male interaction. Theron avoids acknowledging the insecurities about his masculinity that his relationship with Levi uncovers by more rigorously policing Alice's (in this case imagined) sexual activities.

In Alice, Frederic provides us with a benchmark against which to compare Theron's later versions of the female, and therefore his normative model of relationships between men and women. Theron's ability to define himself as a man in opposition to the female becomes increasingly problematic, however, when he encounters women who do not fit his preestablished conceptions about gender, Celia and Sister Soulsby. If Theron's relationship with Alice reveals that his desire for women is related to the vicarious status that their class, education, beauty, and money reflect on him, then his meeting Celia transforms his views of Alice. With her higher social standing, her greater education, her better clothes, and, not incidentally, her father's larger and obviously more liberal checkbook, Celia appears both as far more desirable and as a more ideal woman. But Theron also sees Celia as virile; she thus challenges his construction of himself as male, casting him in the role of the female, the role that he has assigned to Alice. Theron resists this implicit identification; when Celia's conversation reveals to him the limits of his own knowledge, he protects himself by seeing those limits as Alice's. As Theron's attraction to Celia intensifies, his construction of Alice's femaleness as inferior becomes more complete, and his need to assert his own dominance as a man increases. One index of his developing anxiety about Alice's and his own gender identities is his growing rigidity about gender roles; whereas in the early days of their marriage the two shared household tasks with little self-consciousness, in Octavius Theron is dimly aware of the danger such domestic crossdressing poses to his fragile sense of self, and he resists any impulse to help Alice with the chores. The more dominant Celia becomes over him, the more Theron finds himself in the female position; the more inferior the female, the more Theron needs to displace and control it; hence his need to control absolutely Alice's behavior, particularly what he imagines as her sexual activity. In a sense, then, Theron's monitoring of Alice's gender identity and her behavior is a way of monitoring and protecting himself.

The triangle involving Theron with Alice and Levi is therefore conditioned by Theron's fantastic relationship with Celia; not surprisingly, she emerges as the focus of desire in another triangle which shadows the one with Alice. If the triangle with Alice and Levi delineates what might be considered normative homosocial relationships, then a second triangle involving Celia and Father Forbes exposes both the latent homosexuality and the homophobia that remain unarticulated by the first. In Christopher Craft's terms, the second triangle reveals the corollary heterosexual anxiety, or as Sedgwick would put it, the homosexual panic, behind homosocial bonds. While here too a woman, in this case Celia, mediates between two men, this triangle shows Theron's masculinity at its most fluid and, for him, strained. Theron clearly is attracted to Celia; he fantasizes about her, revels in the memory of her kiss, imagines a future in which they sail away together on a yacht, even wonders if she has invited him to convert to Catholicism. But he also, if less obviously, desires Father Forbes. Consider Theron's first encounter with Father Forbes: Theron sees "the flash of a silk hat" and "felt his blood tingle in an unaccustomed way" (p. 40). So intriguing is this sight that Theron temporarily loses interest in Celia. Instead, he is fascinated by the priest in his surplice, his "white fingers," and "his pale face [on which] shone a tranquil and tender light" (pp. 42–43). Later, Theron watches Father Forbes move across a room: Forbes "wore a long house-gown of black silk, skillfully molded to his erect, shapely, and rounded form. Though he carried this with the natural grace of a proud and beautiful belle, there was no hint of the feminine in his bearing" (p. 67). Theron sees the Catholic priest as the feminine other, but he also savors "a pleasurable thrill" as he tries out the phrase Dr. Ledsmere gives him—"we priests"— and "[pauses] again to enjoy the words" (pp. 218–19). Theron's confused feelings for Father Forbes deepen when he learns from Celia that Catholic priests are celibate: "the greatest sacrifice of all—to never know what love means, to forswear his manhood, to live a forlorn, celibate life—you have no idea how sadly that appeals to a woman" (p. 251). It appeals to Theron, too, while it connects the priest overtly for the first time in his mind with sexual desire—repressed, to be sure, but desire nonetheless. Theron equates celibacy with effeminacy, and he is frankly baffled that what he considers to be the unmanly form of Father Forbes could inspire such an aura of virility: "the enigma fascinated him" (p. 281).

The confusion and instability that arise from these conflicting feelings further undermine Theron's sense of himself as a man; if he is a priest, like Father Forbes, and Forbes is a belle with no hint of the feminine, it is not clear who or what is Theron. Theron in a sense feminizes himself through his identification with Forbes; he, not Celia, becomes the female other posing as the intermediary between the more dominant Celia and Forbes. Theron may see Forbes as a "hybrid female" (p. 111), but he himself occupies the (missionary) position of the woman in this exchange.

Theron's desire for both Celia and Father Forbes becomes fused and confused when he listens to Forbes talk about Celia:

"She always impresses me as a sort of atavistic idealization of the old Kelt at his finest and best. . . . When I look at Celia, I seem to see in my mind's eye the fair young ancestral mother of them all." Theron gazed at the speaker with open admiration. "I love to hear you talk." [Theron remembers that these are] . . . the very words that Alice had so often on her lips in their old courtship days. How curious it was! He looked at the priest, and had a quaint sensation of feeling as a romantic woman must feel in the presence of a specially impressive masculine personality. (pp. 280–81)

His confusion of Celia and Forbes leads him to project onto Forbes his own desire for Celia, just as he has projected his desire for Celia onto Alice and Levi. But he also reverses his own gender identity and projects onto Celia his desire for Father Forbes, wondering explicitly about the nature of the priest's relationship with Celia. Just as Theron's suspicions about Levi and Alice have begun to grow, so too have his suspicions about Father Forbes and Celia, and again he is jealous *of* each of them and jealous of being left out by both of them. But where Alice and Levi and Forbes and Celia must have their imagined affairs constructed as what is for Theron a titillating and vaguely pornographic narrative, Theron characteristically elevates his own desire for Celia into a more acceptable male fiction of romantic passion.

Theron sees himself as having outgrown Alice, and therefore as justified in pursuing a fuller, deeper understanding of himself with a woman whom he assumes to be more capable of appreciating him (financially as well as emotionally, since he assumes Celia will support them both). His idealized vision of himself as the victim of heroic, ungovernable passion is threatened by its gendered instabilities, however: Theron has begun to figure himself as female, to see himself as the female to both Celia and Forbes. When he and Celia buy the Ware piano, she negotiates with the salesman, while he stands "nursing her parasol in his arms" (p. 210). At the Catholic picnic, he hopes that "someone would bring him out a glass [of beer], as if he were a pretty girl" (p. 236). And when his fantasy about running away with Celia becomes stalled at the thought of his inadequate finances, he suddenly remembers Celia's equally desirable checkbook: "would she not with lightning swiftness draw forth that checkbook, like the flashing sword of a champion from its scabbard, and run to his relief?" (p. 266).

But Theron is also disconcerted by how virile his constructed image of Celia is. If his simplistic vision of masculinity renders his own gender identity blurred and muted, then his equally naïve vision of femaleness leads to his confusion about Celia: "there was a deliciously feminine and sisterly intuition in her speech, and in the helpful, nurselike way in which she drew his arm through hers" (p. 186). Theron oscillates between constraining his fantasies, constructing Celia as the passionless, empathic nurturer who complements his own maleness, and reveling in them, his "visions full of barbaric color and romantic forms" (p. 199). Celia's room seems deliberately to foster this confusion: it is decorated with billowing curtains, delicate white canopies, and "pyramidal rows of tall candles . . . each masked with a little silken hood" (p. 192). And even Theron cannot miss the contradictions solidified by Celia's art work. A statue of a female nude, naked and pliant from the waist up, stiff and "decently robed" from the waist down, confronts a portrait of a fully-clothed, full-length Virgin with a "radiant, aureoled head": "the incongruity between the unashamed statues and this serene incarnation of holy womanhood jarred upon him for an instant" (p. 195).[18] Theron connects Celia with the Virgin, but as he looks at the coils of red hair wound around her head, "like a nimbus, . . . there was no mistaking the sudden fascination its disorder had for his eye" (p. 193).

Celia's sexuality—sisterly, sensual, virginal, passionate—disconcerts and disorients Theron, partly because Celia brings together traits he has sharply dichotomized as "good" or "bad," partly because he is excited to find himself attracted to both, and also because it is clearly a sexuality beyond his control, beyond even his capacity to move it, except in his fantasies. Certainly it is a sexuality that has no place in the Methodist world; far from tolerating Celia's disordered hair, the Methodist brethren do not even allow Alice's flowered bonnet. Theron's lack of control over a sexuality his church means rigorously to police arouses him, but it also threatens both his institutional and his gendered identities.

As Theron's desires and his behavior become more unstable over the course of the novel, the feelings that Celia and Forbes have toward him change, like Levi Gorringe's, from friendly mentoring to outright dislike. By the time Theron intrudes on them in a New York hotel, where Celia and Forbes are attempting to extricate her brother from trouble, Theron himself has become a token of exchange in the relationship between Celia and Father Forbes, a token of no further value, since his worth has been simply his passive and inadvertent ability to bring together the other participants. He can be discarded by them because he has been spent, in both the economic and phallic senses of the word. If this triangle demonstrates Theron's occupation of the female role pushed to its logical extension, his disintegrating conceptions of himself push his behavior beyond the parameters of social acceptability. Theron is spent in a third sense as well, then; the disruption of the fictional constructions upon which he has depended undoes both narrative logic and discursive consistency. In his odyssey among New York's rougher citizens, he simultaneously tries to commit suicide, but is afraid to die; he drinks excessively, but is unable to get drunk. He is rejected even by the strangers he meets on streets, by other derelicts,

18. For a thorough and incisive analysis of Celia's artwork, see Oeschlaeger, "Passion, Authority and Faith."

as Frederic has him revel in melodrama: "they saw that I was a fool whom God had taken hold of, to break his heart first, and then to craze his brain, and to fling him on a dunghill to die like a dog" (p. 335).

Recovery for Theron does not imply that he will achieve even a semiconscious recognition of the ways in which gender construction has trapped him. Instead, Theron's metaphorical rebirth at the hands of Sister Soulsby signals a reconstruction of the masculine for Theron. Like the professional actress that she is, Sister Soulsby plays for Theron a most traditional female role of midwife and mother through the long gestation of his winter illness. She and Brother Soulsby find the Wares a new home in Seattle, secure for Theron a job in real estate, and reunite Theron with Alice. Sister Soulsby restores Theron's faith in an essential female nature that he can uncomplicatedly contrast to his original conceptions of masculinity. Frederic stresses the fictional qualities of this reconstruction: his descriptions of Sister Soulsby emphasize her muscular neck, her Amazonian power and her masculine mind. She is not as solidly feminine as Theron would like to believe. But she represents for him a necessary social fiction, which Theron, who doesn't read fiction, misreads as a natural imperative.

In the novel's best-known speech, Sister Soulsby borrows a theatrical analogy to explain to Theron how cultural values are socially constructed:

> You'll understand when I say that the performance looks one way from where the audience sit, and quite a different way when you are behind the scenes. *There* you see that the trees and the houses are cloth, and the moon is tissue paper, and the flying fairy is a middle-aged woman strung up on a rope. That doesn't prove that the play, out in front, isn't beautiful and affecting, and all that. It only shows that everything in this world is produced by machinery—by organization. The trouble is that you've been let in on the stage, behind the scenes, so to speak, and you're so green—if you'll pardon me—that you want to sit down and cry because the trees *are* cloth, and the moon *is* a lantern. And *I* say, don't be such a countrified goose!" (p. 171)

She is referring to the fundraising techniques she and Brother Soulsby use to stir Theron's penurious flock into paying off the church debt and raising Theron's salary; and the speech has long been regarded as Frederic's commentary on Jamesian pragmatism.[19] But it also, and importantly, is Frederic's acknowledgment of the inherent constructedness of all social experience, including gender roles, and as such, the speech suggests that infinite production of roles to suit individual scenes. "The real wisdom is to

19. For a variety of assessments of Frederic's views on pragmatism, see Stanton Garner, *Harold Frederic* (Minneapolis, 1969); Austin Briggs, *The Novels of Harold Frederic* (Ithaca, N.Y., 1969); Luther S. Leudke, "Harold Frederic's Satanic Soulsby: Interpretation and Sources," *NCF* 30 (1975): 82–104; Patrick K. Dooley, "Fakes and Good Frauds: Pragmatic Religion in *The Damnation of Theron Ware*," *ALR* 15 (1982): 74–85; David Heddendorf, "Pragmatists and Plots: *Pierre* and *The Damnation of Theron Ware*," unpublished paper, 1990.

school yourself to move along smoothly, and not fret, and get the best of what's going," Sister Soulsby argues (p. 172). But this advice implies that "the best of what's going" is continually in flux; that gender, and cultural authority, and religious practice, all are shifting and contingent; and that to fix oneself in relation to these is not only to misunderstand one's own interests but also to risk moral and social stasis. It is precisely this wide-ranging indeterminacy to which Theron cannot temperamentally or intellectually adjust. Sister Soulsby understands the practicality of social fictions; Theron, who significantly has never seen a play, cannot conceptualize how the social is fictional. Thus his physical recovery recovers also the binary conceptual framework that caused his trouble to begin with; that framework remains both as self-serving and as incapacitating as it was at the beginning of the novel. The final scenes of the novel echo the opening where Theron preaches before his fellow clergymen; here, in his fantasy, he delivers a political speech, imagining "some faces of men, then more behind them, then a great concourse of uplifted countenances, crowded close together as far as the eye could reach. They were attentive faces all—rapt, eager, credulous to a degree. Their eyes were admiringly bent upon a common object of excited interest. They were looking at him . . . He smiled, shook himself with a little delighted tremor" (p. 344).

The other characters are disillusioned as they come to believe that the innocence they see as so inviting in Theron is apparently false. But Theron's innocence is not entirely false; rather, it is his innocence that invites him to create himself anew in every situation, even as it remains fundamentally unchallenged by what he has been through. Both the American and the English titles (*The Damnation of Theron Ware* in America, *Illumination* in England) can be read ironically and straight.[20] If Theron is damned, it is because he cannot reconceive the social constructions of gender that got him in trouble in the first place. But Theron has indeed been illuminated as well, for he now knows far better how to manipulate those codes for his own advancement. Politics are indeed a much better realm for him than the ministry: Theron doesn't have to disguise his desire for power; his rhetorical skills will command a higher price; and in politics, the homosocial bonds among men are orchestrated within institutions that seem at least to be more protected from the disruptive presence of the female. Even Alice has learned better what it means to be a man in America. When Sister Soulsby mentions visits east, Alice responds, "Oh, it isn't likely *I* would ever come East . . . Most probably I'd be left to amuse myself in

20. *The Damnation of Theron Ware* was published simultaneously in England under the title *Illumination*. In his examination of the confusing history of the title, Stanton Garner argues that *Illumination* was likely the intended title, and that its choice "testifies to Frederic's growing skill as an ironist"; see "*The Damnation* or *The Illumination*: The Title of Harold Frederic's Novel," *Proof* 5 (1977): 64.

Seattle" (p. 344). If Theron has become resettled in the landscape of masculinity, then Alice has by default been relegated to the separate sphere of femaleness. If this is Theron's "illumination," it is central to his ability to manipulate the "damnation" that attends Frederic's vision of American manhood. Theron's difficult, static relationship to the complicated cultural constructions of gender in America makes the damnation to which the title refers not a process but an inevitable condition with which Theron unwittingly struggles from beginning to end.

Frederic's novel has long been considered, quite rightly, as an allegory about isolationism, as a critique of American chauvinism, and as a commentary (more or less favorable) on pragmatism as the quintessential American philosophy. But just as the "others" represented in the text—Catholicism, scientific humanism, the New Woman—are themselves gendered, the novel is also an allegory about the social constructions of gender. If the novel confronts America's interaction with the world, then America's interactions with the world must be read as a series of gendered relationships.[21] Moreover, reading desire in *The Damnation* highlights how religion is gendered as an institution, in its language, and as it is experienced. The figure of the feminized minister, which Frederic uses so enticingly, shows that gendering to be continually in flux, contingent upon the changing positions of the participants, and thus a potent vehicle for understanding the dynamic between gender formation and cultural power. The feminized minister is not an androgynous creature, selecting judiciously from an orderly list of binarily gendered characteristics. Rather, he is an unstable, fractured being whose multiply gendered identity shifts as he negotiates his professional and personal positions. He is a particularly suggestive trope for examining how limber nineteenth-century constructions of gender were, and how those constructions framed religious expression both in and out of the church.

When Sister Soulsby attempts to instruct Theron in the virtues of acting—how in effect to exploit his multiple selves—Theron characteristically responds that "the point is that I'm to be a good fraud." Sister Soulsby replies, "I'm afraid you'll never make a really *good* fraud . . . you haven't got it in you. Your intentions are all right, but your execution is hopelessly clumsy" (p. 179). It is this very clumsiness in Frederic's beleaguered minister that makes him so revealing, and makes the novel so perversely appealing. Theron's clumsiness, so familiar and therefore endearing, opens up some of the spaces needed to read gender in American culture.

21. See Amy Kaplan, "Romancing the Empire: The Embodiment of American Masculinity in the Popular Historical Novel of the 1890s," *ALH* 2 (1990): 659–90.

CHAPTER 4

Ministerial Misdeeds:
The Onderdonk Trial and
Sexual Harassment in the 1840s

PATRICIA CLINE COHEN

In late 1844, the Right Reverend Benjamin T. Onderdonk, Episcopal Bishop of New York, was brought to trial before an ecclesiastical court of his peers on nine counts of "immoralities and impurities" committed against Episcopal women. Followed with intense interest by the public and covered with rapt attention in the secular and religious press, the Onderdonk case generated a best-selling trial book and a heated pamphlet war, focusing sharply on questions of correct gender deportment between ministers and female parishioners. To his supporters, Onderdonk was a man wrongfully accused by enemies within his church who in reality opposed his theological politics. To his antagonists, the bishop was a powerful man who abused his position to prey on women within his circle. The Onderdonk controversy has all the hallmarks of what today would be called a case of sexual harassment. But, lacking a concept of sexual harassment to frame the issues, commentators on both sides of the case remained perplexed and at odds about how to interpret Onderdonk's intimate touches.

The story unfolded in a place and time already alert to serious charges of misconduct by the clergy. News of an apparent epidemic of clerical vice oozed from the presses in antebellum America, from the urban penny newspapers to the respectable secular and religious papers. The New York Observer, a Presbyterian weekly, ran a series of articles in the summer of 1844, assuring readers that no minister trained properly in a theological seminary had ever fallen into "gross sins"—which implied a warning about irregularly trained ministers.[1]

Attentive antebellum newspaper readers could probably easily recall a dozen errant ministers who ran afoul of the law. Most of the clerics landed in court on charges of seduction and generally lost reputation and job in short order. There was the Rev. Barnabus Phinney, a Congregational

Reprinted, with changes, from the *Journal of Women's History*, volume 7 (Fall, 1995). Copyright 1995 by Indiana University.
1. New York *Observer*, 22 June, 6 July, 13 July, 1844.

minister in Westborough, Massachusetts, who seduced and impregnated his servant girl and whisked her off to a house of refuge in Boston; he disappeared on the eve of his ecclesiastical trial.[2] A Catholic priest from Lowell, the Reverend Peter Connelly, met by arrangement a young lady in a hotel room in Nashua, New Hampshire, only to be shamefully exposed by a curious stagecoach driver who, after conveying him there, had surprised the lovers in bed.[3] The *New York Herald* covered the 1836 trial of Rev. Joseph Carter, charged with attempted rape of a widow. Carter was an English-born Episcopalian who had applied to Bishop Onderdonk for a license but was turned down—for his Methodist leanings, not for his long history of trouble with women, which emerged at the trial. In the wake of the Carter case, the *Herald* reported (probably jokingly) that a Catholic priest was promising five hundred dollars "to any handsome woman, widow or maid, who will set a trap for a Presbyterian Parson, and catch one of them *flagrante delicto*," in retaliation for the then-raging news interest in the anti-Catholic tract *The Awful Disclosures of Maria Monk*, an exposé detailing sexual sins alleged to be rampant among priests and nuns.[4] The Rev. John N. Maffitt, a popular itinerant Methodist minister, surfaced repeatedly in the penny press as a outrageous womanizer, but nevertheless won appointment as chaplain of the House of Representatives in 1841. In 1848 the Baptist minister Issachar Grosscup endured both civil and ecclesiastical trials in Canadaigua, New York, for impregnating a local girl.[5] And surely the most serious and well known of antebellum clerical crimes was the murder trial of Rev. Ephraim Avery, of Fall River, Massachusetts, who was charged with seducing and then strangling a girl in his congregation in 1833. Avery was acquitted, but, not surprisingly, he never held forth in another pulpit.[6]

The fixation on clerical sexual sin soon spilled over into fiction, and "reverend rakes" crowded the landscape of popular romances and racy novels in the 1840s. The guilty adultery of the Reverend Arthur Dimmesdale, the fictional Puritan minister created by Nathaniel Hawthorne in his 1850 novel, *The Scarlet Letter*, seems tame by comparison to the brothel-haunting ministers in George Lippard's *The Quaker City*.[7]

---

2. Phinney's story can be tracked in the *Boston Recorder* 21 (14 Oct. 1836): 1–2; *Advocate of Moral Reform*, 1 Nov. 1836, p. 158; *Illuminator*, 4 Oct. 1836, p. 170, and 26 Oct. 1838, p. 164.

3. *Advocate of Moral Reform*, 1 Oct. 1836.

4. *New York Herald*, 1, 4, 7, and 8 Mar.; 9 Apr. 1836.

5. *The Trial of Rev. Issachar Grosscup, for the Seduction of Roxana L. Wheeler* (Canandaigua, New York, 1848). His trial was noted in the Rochester newspapers as well as the nationwide publication, the *National Police Gazette*.

6. David R. Kasserman, *Fall River Outrage: Life, Murder, and Justice in Early Industrial New England* (Philadelphia, 1986).

7. George Lippard, *The Quaker City* (Philadelphia, 1845). Two other well-known

To some extent, the attention to sordid sex crimes and fictionalized hypocrites of the 1830s and 1840s was partly a product of new forms of print culture that leaped on sensational stories and played them up. But features of the sociology of antebellum religion promoted a climate of fear about increased sexual temptation and awakened its logical consequence, a measure of public caution and distrust of some of the clergy. The rapid growth of denominations in the wake of the Second Great Awakening created space for irregularly trained ministers to make their way in the world; lax educational and licensing requirements inevitably allowed an occasional charlatan to move into a position of trust. An adversarial denominational press eagerly publicized questionable behavior as a way of discrediting the competition. Any amount of sexual sin stood a good chance of being widely broadcast by rivals whose righteous denunciations perhaps contained a certain element of unseemly satisfaction.

The emotional religious style of the evangelical movement helped to encourage an atmosphere conducive to sexual disorder as well. Evangelism brought passion and sensuality to the fore and privileged the immediate experience of piety over more traditional, ritual-bound forms. A spirituality that manifested itself in ecstatic moments, altered states of being, uncontrolled weeping, or speaking in tongues clearly drew on sources of psychic energy that modern-day skeptics might identify as subconsciously sexual. But the link could well have been a great deal more direct. Camp meetings and all-night revivals provided a new kind of mixed-sex social space where older rules of gender deportment might be observed less rigidly. Emotional religion allowed for more unrestrained touching, embracing, and general physical intimacy among adherents than did orthodox Congregationalism or High Church Episcopalianism.

Even among the staid unemotional denominations of the period, the renewal of religious fervor and the necessity to compete with charismatic clerics inevitably led to a greater cultivation of ministerial showmanship. Some men might ease into the presumption that their spiritual magnetism, displayed so dramatically in the pulpit, betokened sexual magnetism as well. And finally, in an age where religious styles were increasingly emotional and thus feminized, some clerics might have felt the need to compensate by overemphasizing traditional masculine prerogatives in their repertoire of gendered behaviors. Ministers battling to secure their masculinity could find quick reassurance of maleness by exercising dominance gestures over women, which, for the daring

---

examples are *The Awful Disclosures of Maria Monk* (New York, 1836) and George Thompson, *Venus in Boston* (New York, 1849). David Reynolds analyzes the genre and its relation to Hawthorne in *Beneath the American Renaissance: The Subversive Imagination in the Age of Emerson and Melville* (Cambridge, Mass., 1988), pp. 260–62.

or foolish, might extend to subtle or open flirtation or to other sexual initiatives.[8]

Whatever the causes, antebellum religious leaders were coming to realize that sexual temptation posed an important occupational hazard for members of the clergy, exacerbated by their unparalleled and intimate proximity to women. No other male occupation offered such easy access. Protected by a traditional assumption of unimpeachable morality, ministers could approach strange women in public and open conversations without benefit of introduction; for other men, this was rude or risky forwardness. ("Ah, your parsons know the way to the women! Would that I did!" wrote an envious young man in his diary on an Erie Canal boat trip in 1833, upon observing a minister approach some likely young women and propose a checkers game.[9]) Ministers were expected to nurture a tender solicitude for the emotional and spiritual states of their devoted followers. They were entitled to converse about deeply felt personal matters. Meetings with female parishioners might take place in rather private spaces—the parlor, the sickbed room, the minister's study. Intimacy and trust characterized a good pastoral relationship, and usually awe as well, based on ministers' religious learning and their stature and authority in the community. Such men were supposed to be above the ordinary temptations of life, so that women could assume their motives were pure. Usually, ministers took their responsibilities as honorable guardians of the hearts and souls of their followers as a sacred trust, but a few succumbed to temptation. The resulting cases of seduction testified to the nearly imperceptible threshold a man might cross, corrupting a proper love for a member of his flock with selfish needs for sex and power.

The Onderdonk case, however, was sharply different from the several dozens of tales of ministerial misconduct retailed in the press. No actual sex crime—seduction, rape, attempted rape—had been alleged. The behavior that the women complained of was universally regarded as inappropriate; there was no possible innocent interpretation for a man's burrowing his hand into a woman's neckline and fondling her naked breast. But in context, the behavior made no sense to the 1840s commentators, because Onderdonk seemed to engage in his frontal assaults in quite public places, when male protectors of the women were nearby. His defenders were thus sure that some less intimate act of tenderness—an arm around a shoulder

8. Two excellent studies of how gender is enacted and accomplished through body language are Nancy M. Henley, *Body Politics: Power, Sex, and Nonverbal Communication* (Englewood Cliffs, N.J., 1977); Candace West and Don Zimmerman, "Doing Gender," *Gender and Society* 1 (1987): 125–51.

9. Julia Hull Winner, ed., "A Journey Across New York State in 1833," *New York History* 46 (Jan. 1965): 60–78. The diarist was a 32-year-old New Hampshire bachelor.

that happened to brush the breast—was somehow misconstrued. They acknowledged that he was a man of free, affectionate manners to whom the caressing touch came naturally. But then how much affection and body contact could be permitted between ministers and women parishioners?

Rarely, before the twentieth century, have such minute, gendered interchanges of body language been the subject of so much discussion in print. Not surprisingly, the trial report created a sensation. The entire transcript was published in a 330-page softcover book within three weeks of the verdict. D. Appleton's, a leading New York publisher, paid eight hundred dollars to secure the copyright, and there were jibes in the press about how the church leaders should have waited a day or two more, to send the bidding war higher still.[10] The trial report was followed by at least a dozen pamphlets and circulars rehashing the case, as well as by innumerable commentaries in newspapers and national publications stretching over several months. The fullness of the testimony and its wide distribution allowed a throng of people to participate in defining, interpreting, rationalizing, or condemning sexual harassment.

Two themes dominated the public discussion. One focused on the women's testimonies and the inappropriate familiarities. Why did the women not complain at the time? Why did their male relatives fail to defend them? What could the bishop have possibly had in mind? Under what circumstances *could* a man presume a woman's willingness to engage in intimate touching? As so often happens in modern sexual harassment cases, questions were raised about the encouragement some of these women might have given the bishop.

The other significant and weighty subject of discussion was the issue of warring factions within the Protestant Episcopal church. Many were convinced that the entire prosecution—or persecution, his supporters said—of the bishop was the product of hidden motives. The presentment for trial came in November of 1844, just one month after the most searing General Convention the Episcopal Church had ever witnessed in America, where the controversy over the English "Oxford Movement" erupted. The struggle pitted High Church adherents against Low Church defenders, the former group advocating a Romanizing move in the direction of Catholic doctrine and especially liturgy.[11] The debate turned on symbolic ritual acts:

10. *The Proceedings of the Court Convened Under the Third Canon of 1844, on Tuesday, December 10, 1844, for the Trial of the Right Rev. Benjamin T. Onderdonk, D. D. Bishop of New York, on a presentment made by the Bishops of Virginia, Tennessee, and Georgia* (New York, 1845). On the bidding war, see the *New York Herald*, 9 Jan. 1845. The *New York Herald* of 19 Dec. 1844 predicted the book would draw sales on a par with the salacious novels of Eugene Sue and Paul de Kock.

11. William Stevens Perry, *The History of the American Episcopal Church, 1587–1883*, 2 vols. (Boston, 1885), pp. 269–82.

the lighting of candles, kneeling at the mention of Jesus's name, the color of the surplice worn, facing the congregation or not. Bishop Onderdonk was on record as a strong supporter of the High Church (or Puseyite) position, a minority view in American Anglicanism. The bishop's supporters claimed that the morality charges were a smokescreen for a sinister ulterior plot to oust the bishop and thereby divest the church of Catholic leanings.

The modern experience of adjudicating sexual harassment grievances suggests that the two motives to unseat Onderdonk were not mutually exclusive, as commentators in the 1840s thought. Women who suffer sexual harassment often get heard more quickly and clearly when the alleged harasser already has acquired powerful enemies on other grounds. The theological dispute, then, could well have been an important precondition that enabled the charge of immorality to be taken seriously. And of course the two objections were not completely unrelated to each other: ornate High Church ritual and aberrant sexuality could be seen as dual manifestations of an aristocratic posture now under attack by an increasingly bourgeois American Episcopalianism.

Onderdonk's defenders would naturally never agree that elaborate liturgy had anything to do with sexual irregularities. They insisted that a theological attack was being mounted under the guise of spurious and scandalous charges. And there was some foundation for this view. In the complicated religious and political terrain of antebellum America, gendered ideas were often invoked as a strategy to distill debates and simplify disagreements. Stereotypes of masculinity and femininity tend to be widely shared in a culture and can thus be used as a kind of shorthand to make accessible other, more complicated ideas. For example, depicting the concept of Liberty as a white woman in revolutionary-era political cartoons conveyed in a glance the idea that liberty was vulnerable to attack and in need of constant male protection. Fundamental ideological tensions between the emerging political parties of Andrew Jackson and John Quincy Adams in the 1828 election became readily accessible to voters in the famous campaign fight over Jackson's alleged adulterous marriage, as historian Norma Basch has recently shown.[12] And impugning the masculine honor and sexual purity of a clergyman was a quick way to bring him down.

The difficulty in the Onderdonk case was that using stereotypes of masculine and feminine behavior did not simplify things. Gendered behaviors lay at the heart of the case; they were not metaphors for larger questions of character. But they eluded quick comprehension. Onderdonk did not fit the mold of a lecherous man out to seduce a woman; the women also

---

12. On the use of gender as a trope for early Jacksonian political parties, see Norma Basch, "Marriage, Morals, and Politics in the Election of 1828," *Journal of American History* 80 (Dec. 1993): 890–918.

behaved unintelligibly according to 1840s notions of female delicacy, by keeping quiet for years. Without a vocabulary of sexual harassment, of the intricate interrelations of sex and power, commentators of the 1840s were at a loss to make sense out of the case. Ultimately, only one interpretative strategy succeeded: a translation of the Onderdonk phenomenon into blackface, where racist stereotypes distilled and simplified the complex issues the Episcopalians struggled with. Where gender metaphors no longer sufficed, racial metaphors worked.

In order to capture the perplexing nature of the incident with its gendered and racial configurations, we must first reconstruct the players and the stage and hear the testimony of the women themselves. Then we will turn to the contested explanations and interpretations, nearly all offered by men, from lawyers and clergy to acknowledged libertines and the jokester-creators of "Black Under-Donk-En Doughlips; or, De Feelin Deacon." The celebrity of the Onderdonk case derived from its famed centerpiece personality—the Bishop of New York; but this was far more than a seamy tabloid story of an individual public figure's fall from grace. Its richness, then and now, derives from its resonance with complex public attitudes about sexuality, gender, and race that preoccupied antebellum America.

Benjamin T. Onderdonk (fig. 4.1) was 53 years old when the charges against him were announced. He was born in New York City in 1791, of an old Long Island Dutch family. Both he and his brother Henry attended Columbia University and became ordained ministers in the Protestant Episcopal Church. He married at 22, fathered seven children, and spent his whole career in New York City, with successive posts at St. Paul's Chapel and Trinity Church. Onderdonk was an energetic and ambitious church leader; in addition to his priest's duties, he was for 15 years the secretary of the New York diocesan convention and professor at the General Theological Seminary in New York. In 1830, at the relatively young age of 39, Onderdonk was consecrated Bishop of New York. By that time, his brother Henry was already Assistant Bishop of Pennsylvania, and would rise to Bishop in 1836.[13] As bishops, both brothers were articulate and powerful proponents of the High Church party; both made enemies.[14]

In the fall of 1844, tantalizing gossip about Onderdonk's alleged immo-

13. There have been no biographies of the either of the Onderdonk brothers. See entries for each in the *Dictionary of American Biography*. See also Elmer Onderdonk, *Genealogy of the Onderdonk Family in America* (New York, 1910), 104–5.

14. The two examples most commonly cited at the time to explain the ire against the New York bishop were, first, a controversial ordination he performed, against others' advice, of a very Catholic-leaning seminary student; and second, a moment when he was chairing the 1843 General Convention and he imperiously refused a powerful opponent the right to speak. Matthew Hale Smith, *Sunshine and Shadow in New York* (Hartford, Conn., 1869), pp. 581–85.

Figure 4.1. Bishop Benjamin T. Onderdonk, by William S. Mount, 1830. Collection of The New-York Historical Society.

ralities was whispered about at the October Episcopalian convention in Philadelphia. On the surface, the rupture over the Oxford Movement was the main fireworks attraction. Press coverage of the convention also noted that a set of new procedures governing resignations—forced and voluntary—of American bishops got hammered out in tense sessions. Henry Onderdonk had just been forced to resign his Pennsylvania bishopric on grounds of habitual intemperance, and in early October he was showing signs of remorse for his hasty capitulation to the morals charge.[15] The new procedures sealed the door against his change of heart and set up the mechanism soon to be used against Benjamin Onderdonk. Obviously, insiders anticipated further bishop toppling. In November, the women

15. Henry Onderdonk's defensive account of his drinking problem appears in the *New World* 9 (14 Sept. 1844): 344–46.

complainants and their husbands submitted affidavits (held secret) to a team of three other bishops, as per the new procedures, and a presentment against Bishop Onderdonk was issued.

At the trial, held in mid-December at St. John's Chapel on Hudson Square in New York, the seventeen bishops sitting in judgment heard for the first time the women narrate their stories and elaborate on them under cross-examination by professional lawyers. A news blackout meant that the press coverage in December was limited to poking at the embers remaining from the October General Convention and speculating about why so few women were appearing at the trial, when the earlier rumors hinted of vast numbers of insulted females. In other words, for a few weeks the reigning published theory was that the bishop was being railroaded by his enemies on charges that seemed suddenly very slender and perhaps in danger of evaporating. James Gordon Bennett, the crusty editor of the *New York Herald*, advanced the theory that the massive Manhattan real estate hold-ings of the Trinity Parish were the real reason someone wanted to unseat of the bishop.[16] At the close of the trial, the testimony of the four women was released, printed piecemeal in New York newspapers day by day, and then issued unabridged in the hefty trial report. It was at this point, with explicit accounts of hands fondling breasts, that public opinion turned against the bishop: either the women were lying, or he had actually done such things— there seemed to be no way to reconcile those points of view.

The first woman to testify, Mrs. Frances L. Butler, described an encoun-ter with the bishop in June 1837. Then twenty and a newlywed living in Syracuse, New York, Mrs. Butler was the daughter of an Episcopal minister and knew the bishop in her maiden days. Onderdonk had come to Syracuse to ordain her husband, Clement Moore Butler. The couple met him in Ithaca and drove all night with him in a two-seat wagon, Mrs. Butler in the back seat with the bishop, and her husband and the driver in front. Accord-ing to Mrs. Butler, Onderdonk had had too much to drink, and as the sun set, he became unusually voluble and attentive, which alarmed her.

> He first put his arm around my waist and drew me towards him; this he repeated once, perhaps twice. He had often done this when I was unmarried, and I had permitted it, although always disagreeable to me; because I believed him incapable of wrong. At this time, however, I removed his hand each time, because I saw that he was not himself. I was exceedingly fearful lest our driver should discover it. . . . The bishop persisted in putting his arm about me, and raised his hand so as to press my bosom. I then rose and withdrew the arm from behind me, and laid the hand upon his knee, and said to him in a raised tone of voice . . . that a Bishop's hands were sacred in my eyes, and that his were particularly so, because they had been laid upon the heads of many I loved in

16. *New York Herald*, 22 and 29 Dec. 1844.

confirmation, and were about to be laid upon my husband's head in ordination. He made but little answer, but for some little time let me alone.

Mrs. Butler hoped it was just the alcohol and that the bishop meant no intentional insult. But

> while sitting in thought, I found he was again moving: I waited to see whether he might not be merely steadying himself in his seat, as the roads were rough, when he suddenly and violently again brought his hand upon my bosom, pressed and clasped it. In some horror I struck the hand with all my force, and he withdrew it; but immediately grasped my leg in the most indelicate manner.[17]

This was too much for Mrs. Butler, and she clambered into the front seat onto her husband's lap and whispered her fears to him. Both Butlers felt obliged to keep their concerns from the driver. Mr. Butler got the impression the bishop had actually lifted her skirt and touched her naked leg. At a rest stop he and his wife debated what to do. Mr. Butler, very agitated, wanted to confront the man, but Mrs. Butler, mindful of the ordination ceremony just hours away, counseled silence. "My whole efforts were needed by my husband, to soothe him, he being violently incensed, and declaring that Bishop Onderdonk should not ordain him." Mrs. Butler finished the ride on her husband's lap, or at times on the floor of the wagon at his feet.

Under oath, Mr. Butler confirmed his wife's story. He went through with the ordination the next day but afterward coldly avoided the bishop. He divulged his painful story—only to other ministers—when he began to hear rumors of similar incidents. His wife broke her silence by confiding in her sister-in-law, a close female friend, and later her father, who did not believe her. The Butlers' complaint constituted two counts: undue familiarities and improper inebriation.

The third formal charge against Onderdonk involved an unknown woman who shared a stagecoach with him in upstate New York in 1838. Also on board was another minister, the principle and reluctant witness who now clearly wished to minimize the incident. The young country woman, about 25, got on at LeRoy and sat on the back seat of the coach behind the bishop, who was sitting on the middle seat. Onderdonk reversed his direction (the middle seat not having a back) to converse with her. The woman put her hand down on the leather strap between the seats, and he leaned forward and put his hand on top of hers and held it. She blushed, withdrew her hand, said the witness, but the bishop took it a second time. Soon after the woman got out and ordered her trunk down, before reaching her stated destination. The inference drawn by the witness was that the

17. *Proceedings*, p. 15.

young lady was leaving the stage on account of the bishop's untoward familiarity. But he was careful to state that he did not think the bishop acted out of impure motives; "in a notoriously bad man such conduct would have been indicative of a bad design; but it did not occur to me, nor do I think, that the Bishop had any impure or lustful desires towards this woman." Nevertheless, the clergyman was sufficiently uneasy about the event that he mentioned it soon after to another Episcopal minister, whence the story spread.[18]

The next witness presented a much more damning picture of what the bishop's hands were capable of in a carriage. In 1841, Miss Helen Rudderow of New York City, then 29, shared an eight-block ride from church to her home with the bishop next to her and the Reverend James Richmond driving the horses in the front seat.

> We had not proceeded very far from the church, when Bishop Onderdonk put his arm around my neck, and thrust his hand into my bosom: this he continued to do. I was very much surprised and agitated, and would have jumped from the carriage, had it not been for exposing him to the Rev. Mr. Richmond. He kept repeating the offense until we reached home, where he was to dine with us.[19]

Careful questioning elicited the information that his hand was well below her neckline on her naked breast, under her shawl. Remarkably, the bishop continued to converse with Mr. Richmond all the while. Helen tried to squirm away from him and contemplated leaping out of the carriage but concluded it was too dangerous. Upon arrival at the 61st Street house, "I immediately went to the room occupied by my sister and myself, and told her what had happened. I entreated her to go down and entertain him, as the family were not yet prepared to do so; she consented, upon condition that I should follow as soon as I could sufficiently compose myself." Jane Rudderow, the next witness, bravely went to the drawing room and greeted the bishop, who led her to the sofa where he immediately "thrust his hand in my bosom." Jane retreated to the end of the sofa, but the bishop followed and repeated his attack, wordlessly, stopping only when a sister-in-law entered the room moments later. Jane said she did not cry out because her brothers were close by in the hall: "I was fearful for his personal safety, and did not expose him for the sake of the Church." Significantly, both Helen and Jane thought first of protecting him.

Jane's ordeal was not over. Despite great "fright and astonishment," she and Helen sat through a midday meal with Onderdonk and the family, remaining mostly silent while their mother chattered on with the distinguished guest. After dinner the bishop twice more maneuvered to be alone

18. *Proceedings*, pp. 30–39.
19. *Proceedings*, p. 40.

with her for just a few seconds, once out on the piazza where he put an arm around her, and a short time later by a parlor window, where he again put his hand inside her neckline, she testified.

The sisters commiserated with each other that day, and told a sister-in-law a few weeks later. But they waited until the next fall—some six months later—to tell their mother, and did not tell their brothers at all until they were called to produce affidavits in late 1844.[20] They feared "lest an ignominious if not bloody vengeance should speedily visit the anointed offender," delivered by their brothers' hands.[21]

The next charge against Onderdonk had to be dropped because the complainant suddenly refused to cooperate. Five years before, when the woman was a governess in Westchester, the bishop came to call. He steered her aside in the garden and quickly put his hand into her bosom, according to her affidavit. She now lived in New York City about a block from the unfolding trial at St. John's; servants at her door deflected all inquiries from the trial prosecutors.[22] Her refusal to testify underscores the difficulty these young women had withstanding close questioning by sharp trial lawyers about deeply embarrassing incidents before a roomful of Episcopal bishops, including of course Onderdonk. (One newspaper reported that one witness had received anonymous threats in the days before the trial. Another asserted that the women had agreed to testify only with "solemn assurance that their evidence would never be divulged."[23] They, as much as the bishop, must have been chagrined at the decision to publish the entire proceedings.)

The last witness was Charlotte Beare, wife of the Rev. Henry Beare of Bayside, Long Island. Like Mrs. Butler, Mrs. Beare was a bride of just a few months in 1842 when the bishop accosted her. Again, a carriage was the scene: Mrs. Beare sat with him in back, with her mother-in-law and nephew in the front. The bishop put his arm around her and pressed her bosom, and she shrank away from him, she testified. She told her husband soon after that the bishop was "too familiar in his manners," and Mr. Beare advised her to keep distant but remain civil.[24]

After the service, the Beares returned home for dinner with their important guest. The bishop came up to Mrs. Beare in a doorway, she testified, addressed her as "my daughter," lifted her chin and kissed her, all while her mother-in-law looked on. When asked on cross-examination if she interpreted this as an insult, she replied "I should have done so from any one else

20. *Proceedings*, pp. 39–62.

21. James Richmond, *The Conspiracy Against the Late Bishop of New-York, Unravelled by one of the Conspirators* (New York, 1845), p. 10.

22. *Proceedings*, pp. 7, 139–40.

23. *Morning Sun*, as quoted in the *New York Herald*, 17 Dec. 1844; *New York Herald*, 10 Jan. 1845.

24. *Proceedings*, p. 63.

but the Bishop . . . I had too much confidence in him to suppose that he
would offer me an insult in my own house."[25] But in the context of his
unexpected squeeze in the carriage earlier, she was now unsettled and wary.

Her caution was thoroughly shaken by a third incident later that day,
during another carriage ride. While her husband and nephew sat in the
front seat, Mrs. Beare took her proper place with the bishop in the back.

> The Bishop put his arm around my waist; then raised it, and put it across the
> back of my neck; he thrust his hand into the neck of my dress, down in my
> bosom. I threw his hand from there; he immediately put it upon the lower part
> of my person. I pushed it aside from there, and he then with the other hand
> repeated the same upon the other side of my person; but removed it towards
> the centre of my person. I threw it aside.[26]

The carriage was in the lane at the Beare's house at this point, and Mrs.
Beare quickly alighted and went to her room. Her husband followed, to see
why she was so agitated. His reaction was to "say no more now; let us join
the family, and have our evening devotions." The bishop stayed the night,
but Mrs. Beare swore that she spoke not at all to him during the rest of his
stay. She avoided his move forward to bid her goodbye the next morning,
worried about another unwelcome kiss. Except for her husband, she told no
one of her concerns until eighteen months later, when she confided in three
aunts.[27]

Mr. Beare, when more fully informed, was not inclined to let the matter
pass, and he consulted with some other Episcopal clergymen who joined
him on a visit to the bishop in New York to demand an apology. In Beare's
version of that meeting, the bishop acceded to the truth of Mrs. Beare's
accusation; he apologized but added that she had "misconstrued my motives." The bishop's version of that same meeting contended that Mrs.
Beare's accusations as conveyed to him by Mr. Beare were muddled and
indistinct, and when he said he "did not mean to impeach her veracity" he
had only meant to comfort his distraught young friend, Mr. Beare, by not
accusing his wife of lying.[28]

These, then, formed the substance of the first eight charges against
Bishop Onderdonk. The ninth and last was a dark hint of a continuing
pattern of immorality: "that at sundry times . . . [he] has impurely
and unchastely laid his hands upon the bodies of other virtuous and
respectable ladies, whose names have come to the knowledge of the
said Bishops, so that he is of evil report within the limits of the said

25. *Proceedings*, pp. 64, 73.
26. *Proceedings*, p. 64.
27. *Proceedings*, pp. 65, 66.
28. *Proceedings*, pp. 77–79; Benjamin T. Onderdonk, *A Statement of Facts and Circumstances Connected with the Recent Trial of the Bishop of New York* (New York, 1845), pp. 20–21.

Diocese."[29] With this charge, the church made it clear that its concern lay in the "evil report" and scandal to the church caused by an immoral bishop. The four women who came forward were merely witnesses, not parties to the action. The sense of a larger field of victims was aptly conveyed in a pamphlet by Rev. James Richmond, who drove with Helen Rudderow and the bishop, and who, it develops, played a key role in marshaling all of the witnesses' affidavits and orchestrating their testimonies.

> Where is the presbyter who walked on the banks of the Hudson, and related to a fellow clergyman that gross insult to his family, (worse than any on the trial,) which will yet be dragged to the light, unless all parties make up their minds to abandon so forlorn a hope as this man's *restoration*? Where is the lady in Bond-street who related to me her daughter's refusal to be confirmed these four years? Where the bevy of young ladies on Long Island who declared, if the spiritual father was coming, they could escape by wearing dresses high in the neck? . . . Where is the other young lady on York Island, who long refused to be confirmed, and at last actually tittered, as she went up, at the sad and yet ludicrous idea, that he might make a mistake, through old habit?[30]

If it was true that a bevy of young women on Long Island shared lore about the bishop's unusual interest in necklines, we are here tapping into a collective female response to sexual harassment in the 1840s: the girls practiced avoidance, deterrent dress, and sororal humor, assuaging individual embarrassment by a shared knowledge of the bishop's habitual behavior. Evidently such girls were unwilling to be witnesses, however; they did not appear at the trial.

The four women witnesses together constituted the first interpretative gloss on Onderdonk's strange behavior. Singly, each woman reported confusion and disbelief; each kept quiet for fear of bringing dishonor on their bishop and their church. The married women put their husbands' careers first. The Rudderow sisters feared their brothers would seek vengeance; Mrs. Beare's husband was at first unreceptive to her concern, and Mrs. Butler's father, himself a minister, flat-out refused to believe her. So the women confided in trusted females and abandoned the idea of correcting the bishop. Together, at the trial, their individual experiences still perplexed them, but their conviction of Onderdonk's immorality was validated by knowing that three other women had been through same experience. They bravely told their stories, facing an intimidating array of lawyers and the entire top administration of their church, and then retired to the shadows while their testimony was blasted to the world in newsprint.

Lawyers were the next in line to attempt a coherent account of the puzzling actions. Onderdonk opted to hire top professional lawyers, not

---

29. *Proceedings*, p. 8.
30. James Richmond, *Mr. Richmond's Reply to the "Statement" of the Late Bishop of New York* (New York, 1845), pp. 9–10.

customary in church trials, and the presenting bishops were forced to follow suit. Lawyers brought their sense of constitutional rights and legal wrongs to the case; evidence was held to a strict standard. Undermining the women's credibility became the prime defense strategy. The result was "a very rigid examination of witnesses," according to the *Morning Sun*. "We will suppose that a most virtuous, honorable and excellent female is called upon the stand; she testifies to a certain gross, immodest act on the part of a prelate, she does it with reluctance and with tears. Is it fair, is it just, in order to destroy the testimony thus briefly, thus modestly given that most indelicate and disgusting questions should be asked on the cross examination . . . ?"[31]

Lawyers reduced the case from the lofty realm of cultural politics to a legalistic examination of the individual complaints. The charge involving the unknown woman on a stage near LeRoy was immediately dispensed with, since no one could name the woman. The ninth charge, of a broad pattern of immoralities and general "evil report," was similarly dismissed, because no evidence had been presented to support it. What was left were four women, testifying to events many years in the past. The defense argued that the four incidents—three of which lay beyond the customary statute of limitations for many crimes in regular law—were hardly enough to prove that the man was at present immoral. They stressed the error of arguing from accumulation: a parade of weak evidence was not made stronger by the length of it.

Their main defense strategy invoked gender stereotypes: none of the women had responded as an insulted woman of true virtue. None summoned help, even though help was nearby. Mrs. Butler's concern to keep quiet for the sake of the driver was dismissed as ludicrous beyond belief. Much was made of the Butlers' confusion as to whether the bishops' hand was on top of or under her skirt, suggesting they had not gotten their concocted story straight. It seemed preposterous that the Butlers themselves had hardly spoken of the details of the incident after the day of the event, such that Mr. Butler persisted in his apprehension of the hand-on-naked-thigh scenario for several years. Maybe the simple explanation was that the jolting of the carriage on the bad roads out of Ithaca fully accounted for Mrs. Butler's complaint.

Doubt was cast on the Rudderow sisters and Mrs. Beare, because of their unwomanly silence. Mrs. Beare had only to lean forward and tug on her husband's sleeve when she apprehended the bishop's hand moving up her leg; Jane Rudderow could have leaped from the couch and run to her brothers in the hall.

> The feelings of a virtuous woman would in such circumstances have broken forth irresistibly—the feelings of the family would have been excited and aroused—and the aggressor, be he Bishop or any thing else, would have been

31. *Morning Sun*, quoted in the *New York Herald*, 17 Dec. 1844.

expelled the house, whose inmates he had insulted, and whose hospitality he had so grossly outraged. I say this, because it is not in human nature that any man could so grossly insult two virtuous females—again and again insult them—and yet not only have escaped summary vengeance, but not even the slightest intimation have been conveyed to him from any quarter that he had been guilty of the least misconduct. But yet such is the story these young ladies would have us believe.[32]

What is more surprising, the lawyers said, was that the women continued to be civil to him. Why would Helen Rudderow send Jane down to be alone with him, and why would Jane go? How could they possibly have shared a meal with him, as did Mrs. Beare? Helen Rudderow even visited him months later in a delegation of young women pleading support for a charitable activity and was polite with him then, a point established at great length in the trial. And why had all of these victims failed to complain in a timely fashion; why were they only now coming forth with such stories?

The defense lawyers' attempt to discredit the women in the end did not persuade. The presiding bishops finally found Onderdonk guilty on a vote of 11 to 6, based on the accumulated weight of evidence. Those who voted against him found it hard to imagine a conspiracy of perjury large enough to encompass all the ministers, wives, and parishioners who had testified. On the question of punishment, the vote was also 11 to 6, 11 voting for indefinite suspension of the bishop from his duties, while six voted for the harsher sentence of complete deposing from office. (The six who had voted for acquittal and lost now shifted their votes to the lesser penalty of suspension.) The Diocese of New York was put into ecclesiastical limbo, its leader suspended from all priestly functions but still technically occupying the office.

The verdict in, the pamphlet war began, each writer vying with the last to impose a credible account on the evidence. The pamphleteers were mostly clerical leaders well accustomed to putting their words in print. But instead of sermons and closely reasoned religious treatises, now they were writing blistering personal attacks. While the trial had limited itself to the women's allegations of immoralities, the pamphlets opened up the ulterior theological motives. In their rush to publish, the writers adopted a style more closely resembling the barbed and chatty penny press. This was white-heat writing by angry writers, all men; no women fought the pamphlet war.

Bishop Onderdonk, silent at the trial, now produced his own carefully crafted *Statement of Facts*. He avoided any comment on the women's particular charges, except to say that it was his impression that Mrs. Butler was unwell and had gratefully leaned on him in the carriage out of Ithaca. The changes were all very old, and he was given no chance to respond to

32. *Proceedings*, p. 173.

them before the trial. In short, the case amounted to a conspiracy against him, he felt, instigated chiefly by Rev. James Richmond, who was motivated because of a bad letter of recommendation Onderdonk had written for him four years before.[33]

Quickly more pamphlets entered the fray, some claiming party spirit while others emphasized a keen concern about immorality staining the church.[34] The *Churchman*, the official national publication of the Episcopal Church, stood by the bishop.[35] And James Richmond, accused by Onderdonk of nursing the grudge that cause him to spearhead the plot, gave his version of events that led to the trial.

Richmond of course denied any personal grudge over a negative letter of recommendation, just as he denied that animosity over High Church/Low

33. Onderdonk, *Statement*, p. 7. An oddly disproportionate amount of space in the pamphlet was filled by a long affidavit from Onderdonk's 26-year-old son, Henry M., a religious bookseller and printer in New York City. The son told of frequent bookshop visits by Rev. Beare, who always spoke in a friendly manner about the bishop. Since Henry M. was also the printer of his father's "Statement," that might well explain the attention he lavished on his own grand act of witnessing. He was not called at the trial; if he had appeared, he risked revisiting his own painful moment of public disgrace. Back in 1835, at age 17, he had sat in his father's study at Trinity and counterfeited two fifty-dollar bank notes. He was arrested, tried, and convicted, and in an extraordinary move, all twelve jurors who found him guilty simultaneously signed a petition asking the governor of New York for clemency. Young Onderdonk's brush with the law and his obliging pardon by the governor packed a wallop in the penny press in 1835; it suggested a bias in the legal system toward coddling the sons of influential fathers and gave new meaning to the old phrase "benefit of clergy." (District Attorney's Indictment Files, 14 July and 10 August 1835, Municipal Archives, New York.) At the time of his pardon, the *Sun* complained that "because he is a bishop's son, he is let loose upon the community to defraud others as he may see fit." If he had gone to prison, the *Sun* editorialized, he would probably have worked "white marble, at Sing Sing, in white kid gloves—such are the blessings of a virtual union of church and state" ("Young Onderdonk, the Forger," *New York Sun*, 10, 14, and 16 Nov. 1835).

34. Pamphlets include: Paul Trapier, *A Narrative of Facts which led to the Presentment of the Rt. Rev. Benjamin T. Onderdonk, Bishop of New York* (New York, 1845); Laicus, *The Trial Tried: or, the Bishop and the Court at the Bar of Public Opinion* (New York, 1845); *Statement of Bishop Meade, in reply to some parts of Bishop Onderdonk's Statement of Facts and Circumstances Connected with his Trial* (New York, 1845); John Jay, *Facts connected with the Presentment of Bishop Onderdonk* (New York, 1845); Charles King, *Review of the Trial of the Rt. Rev. B. T. Onderdonk* (New York, 1845); William Barlow, *A Letter by the Rev. William Barlow to a Committee of New-York Clergymen* (New York, 1845); James C. Richmond, *Mr. Richmond's Reply to the "Statement" of the Late Bishop of New York* (New York, 1845); James Richmond, *The Conspiracy Against the Late Bishop of New-York, Unravelled by one of the Conspirators* (New York, 1845); *An Appeal from the Sentence of the Bishop of New York; In behalf of his Diocese; Founded on the Facts and Improbabilities Appearing on Both Sides in the Late Trial* (New York, 1845); Spectator, *The Verdict Sustained at the Bar of Public Opinion* (New York, 1845); *The Laugh of a Layman, At a Pamphlet entitled The Conspiracy Unravelled* (New York, 1845); *Richmond's Pamphlets Reviewed; Or, the Priest of Cedar Grove Called to Order by a South Carolinian* (New York, 1845); *Is the Diocese of New York Vacant?* (1845).

35. The *Churchman* printed blandly reassuring letters from Onderdonk in November and early December. In January, after the verdict, the editor urged readers to pray for the bishop; his sins were "comparatively light" and people should be steadfast to him as a penitent bishop. Letters: 2 and 16 Nov. 1844; editorials: 21 and 28 Dec. 1844, 11 Jan. 1845.

Church differences formed his motive. But bitter remarks linking the High Church position with personal self-indulgence betrayed Richmond's view that the religious controversy cut deep into the sexual one. (He accused the Puseyites of enjoying "fat dinners and good wines" during Lent.) Still, he insisted that sexual sin was the chief concern, not ritual: "Did the Bishop really think that by raising such a hue and cry about his Puseyism and Popery he could throw dust in all our eyes, and that nobody would dream of looking under that cloud into his irregular life?"[36] Richmond, 36, was something of a maverick cleric. Harvard- and Gottingen-trained, and with several years of missionary service in Turkey under his belt, he now had a tame job as rector of St. James in upper New York City.[37] It was he who had driven the carriage with Helen Rudderow in 1841, uneasy about what was going on behind him—but too timid to turn and look. After hearing rumors of the bishop's unchaste attentions to other women, he returned to the Rudderow family in 1843 and boldly asked the women exactly what had happened, and with evident relief they unburdened themselves. Richmond quoted a letter he wrote to his brother that year, warning that Onderdonk's indecencies were "now a matter of notoriety in the female portion of the Diocese, here, there, and everywhere. I know no man whom I would watch *so closely, every minute* in my house. No lady is safe from the grossest, most palpable, and almost open insult. If he is not admonished, he *must* blow up."[38]

Soon thereafter, at a dinner party of ministers and deacons, Richmond turned the conversation to "Pope Benjamin I," hinting at his intemperate, licentious ways. The other diners became instantly tense; some cautiously asked him what he meant, while others called "order! order!" to shut him up. "I looked through my fingers, and said to one and another, 'you know'; '*you know*,' and some of them did know." A nearby cleric said darkly to another: " 'Don't ask him . . . for he will tell you.' "[39]

To challenge that obstinate denial at the highest levels of church hierarchy, Richmond commenced gathering women's stories and securing agreements to testify. Most turned him down, he reported; this countered the complaint of Onderdonk supporters that the women witnesses were insufficiently modest. Mrs. Beare only finally agreed when it appeared the October Convention was considering adding a statute of limitations of three years on any evidence in a bishop's trial. Richmond described a dramatic late-night visit to the Beares, in the midst of a furious storm. At first Mrs. Beare stayed out of the room altogether while the men talked, only slowly

36. Richmond, *Conspiracy Unravelled*, pp. 8–9.
37. See "James Cook Richmond," in *Appleton's Cyclopedia of American Biography* (New York, 1888).
38. Richmond, *Conspiracy Unravelled*, pp. 5, 6.
39. Ibid., p. 7.

consenting to sit in a corner of the room behind Richmond, such was her modesty. From her position on the margin, she finally was emboldened to intimate to Richmond worse deeds yet than any could imagine: "Mr. Richmond ... *I am afraid he takes advantage of the deacons!*"[40] Here was an explosive assertion of wrongdoing, hinting that the bishop had an eye for young men as well. Richmond did not follow it up.

With good reason, women were reluctant to go public. Most of the pamphlet writers were polite enough to try to demolish their stories without impugning their virtue, but it proved to be a tricky task. For example, one writer took pains to claim that Mrs. Butler and Mrs. Beare, "ardent and impulsive" brides presumably in the fresh bloom of sexual awakening, might well have misinterpreted affectionate gestures that they would have gladly and innocently accepted when unmarried. Recall, this was intended to be a defense of the bishop—that his accusers confused his pure caresses with the preliminaries of lovemaking, simply because they were delicately ripe for sex.[41]

Much harsher treatment of the women came from a New York literary writer editorializing in the *New York Evening Mirror*. Nathaniel P. Willis set out "A Man of the World's View of the Onderdonk Case." Willis was a noted man of the world himself; in his 15-year literary career in New York he chronicled the city's foppish dandies.

> In our opinion, no modest woman has ever been outraged by such liberties as are charged upon the Bishop. . . . Every man knows—and the most vicious man knows it best—that no woman is ever invaded till the enemy has given a signal from within! . . . We declare our belief that no woman whose virtue is above suspicion, was ever insultingly spoken to—far less, insulting touched—by a man in his senses. . . . The look of surprise only, with which the first shade of a questionable sentiment is met by a completely pure woman, is enough to arrest, and awe from his purpose, the boldest seducer. . . . We are recording what we have heard confessed by libertines in their cups—defining what we know to be an impassable gulf between female purity and its destroyer.[42]

Profligate men all over New York City, Willis knowingly reported, were laughing to think that a woman could be surprised when a man put a hand on her breast. Worse still, Willis declared that clergymen everywhere would of course sympathize with Onderdonk, because of "the caressing character of the intercourse between the clergy and the women in their parishes whose affections are otherwise unemployed." Worldly men all knew that ministers took advantage of affection-starved women.

40. Ibid., p. 15.
41. *Appeal from the Sentence*, pp. 7, 14.
42. Quoted in full in both the *New York Herald*, 11 Jan. 1845, and the *Advocate of Moral Reform*, 1 Feb. 1845, p. 20.

Indignation greeted Willis's article. The secular press castigated him as a vulgar libertine who had libeled all of American womanhood.[43] Willis's essay provoked a sharp reply from female pens as well. The women editors of the bimonthly *Advocate of Moral Reform* had up until now steered clear of the Onderdonk case. But Willis's indictment of womanhood prompted a response. To think that a look of surprise alone was sufficient to deter harassment was ridiculous, the editors said. Thousands of women knew the contrary; what the *Mirror* was in effect saying was that women, not men, are to blame for sexual sin.[44] Another woman moral reformer elaborated the idea that "certain familiarities . . . [are] always indicative of a wrong state of feeling on the part of those who use, or permit them"; there simply was no possible pure construction of Onderdonk's touches. But she also criticized the women victims and their husbands for continuing to pay respect to the bishop. Here was the moral reformers' favorite, robust theme: virtuous women have a duty to expose licentious men to public shame.[45]

The inexplicable failure of the victims to raise an outcry seems to have been the sticking point for many commentators. A pamphlet by "Spectator" produced the most closely reasoned analysis of the complex power dynamics at work. As individuals, he pointed out, the women must have feared their accusations would not be believed; even four together testifying under oath were still met with skepticism. With no possibility of official redress, they took the only other path: avoidance and aloofness, but with enough civility to avoid raising questions that simply could not be raised without risk to themselves.

"Spectator" had a grasp of what prevents harassed women from complaining. But he could not explain the bishop's conduct; no one could, because of a persistent resort to the models of courtship or sex crimes as the context for interpreting his actions. One Onderdonk supporter, the Bishop of New Jersey, dismissed the alleged acts of immorality by simply asking, "What was to come of it?" With people all around, the bishop could not have intended to carry his misdeeds any further, so even if he touched a breast, there was no true evil intent. "Spectator" pounced on the absurdity of this idea, but his objection was still grounded in the assumption that sexual intercourse was the ultimate goal of a man with roving hands. "Every body, including Bishop Doane, knows that seduction is insidious in its beginning, gradual in its progress, and because insidious . . . and gradual, the more sure in its end. It always begins in 'passages that lead to nothing' in the eyes of its victims."[46]

---

43. The *Herald* of 11 Jan. 1845 reprinted condemnations of Willis from the *Courier and Enquirer*, the *Express*, and the *New York American*, along with its own.

44. *Advocate of Moral Reform*, 1 Feb. 1845, pp. 20–21.

45. S. T. Martyn, "The Case of Bishop Onderdonk," *Advocate of Moral Reform*, 15 Feb. 1845, pp. 30–31.

46. Spectator, *Verdict Sustained*, p. 10; *Proceedings*, p. 291.

Feelings ran high on the Onderdonk case precisely because it was difficult, in the 1840s, to create a narrative that accounted for the bishop's conduct and the women's silence. To the bishop's High Church supporters, the only narrative that made sense was a conspiracy by theological opponents. His normally affectionate manner toward women had been misinterpreted; whatever he had done, he had no ultimate evil intent to seduce or rape. From the victims' point of view, the story was equally puzzling. How could such a touch be anything but immoral? Why would he touch them without trying to do more? Why would he take such a risk with people nearby? The ambivalent outcome—removing Onderdonk from duty without removing him from his bishop's office—perfectly reflected the bafflement religious leaders felt.

Framing the events through the lens of modern sexual harassment concepts helps bring several features of the case into focus. The four women, widely separated in location, each reported a very similar experience, suggesting a pattern of behavior indulged in by the bishop. He had enormous institutional power over his victims and, as importantly, over their male relatives. He picked virtuous churchwomen—wives of ministers, single women active in church circles—to make sure of their allegiance to the larger entity of the church. He picked wives of young clergymen at precisely the point of their husband's greatest vulnerability to pressure, the moment of ordination or of grand visitation. If Richmond's allegations about the female lore on Onderdonk were true, the bishop even engaged in his compulsion during holy services, when young women knelt at the communion rail before him. Onderdonk's preference for apparently risky situations, with male protectors close by, actually ensured silent acquiescence from his victims. If no one had been within earshot, the women would have been freer to complain to him, to push him away, to make a scene. But these women well understood the cultural pressure for male protectors to respond with violent anger, and they thus feared for their bishop's safety and by extension the reputation of the church.

Onderdonk had no intention to seduce or rape; the quick, unauthorized plunge into forbidden territory carried a sexual charge and enhanced his sense of power over women. His thrill was to touch naked bosoms in crowds and get away with it. Over many years, he had gotten away with it, by picking his moments and victims carefully. During the years of rumors, his fellow clerics deliberately looked the other way; they really hoped James Richmond would not tell them anything unpleasant at that rancorous dinner party. Women told their war stories chiefly only to other women, rarely to men, and never to authorities, knowing that the outcome of telling would be bad for them and bad for the church they respected.

But not everyone was baffled. Cynics and libertines in New York's night spots had a laugh over Onderdonk's scandalous plight. The *Herald* reported that during an intermission at Niblo's, a popular New York City music garden on Broadway, four or five copies of the Onderdonk trial were seen circulating through the audience and made the basis of choice humor.[47] One mild joke that did make it into print told of a fancy evening party where the gas lights went out all of a sudden. "Ladies, don't be afraid, the Bishop is not here!" called out a man's voice in the darkness, "followed by an ungenerous burst of laughter."[48]

Nathaniel Willis, the self-appointed spokesman for libertine men, found the bishop's actions completely comprehensible: affection-starved women subtly but surely invited his caresses. A somewhat different humorous take on the libertine worldview was offered by George Thompson, a fiction writer and sometime radical social critic, who devoted a chapter to licentious clergymen in his 1848 book, *New-York Life*. He characterized Onderdonk as "a man so full of wine and lust—a high liver, a full eater of flesh, and a man of fleshly lusts, which war against the soul."[49] Women were innocent victims of such men, Thompson claimed. Evil ministers easily seduced young women into believing that pleasing God and pleasing the minister were closely related undertakings. They knew how to excite tender feelings, both religious and sexual, in young women: "So far from a sin, it seems to be an act of duty and of piety to submit to his desires, and when the object is once accomplished, the reward is a devout blessing and thanksgiving, that removes every scruple of conscience and the pleasing duty of comforting a beloved pastor is performed as an act of religious merit." In Thompson's view, unscrupulous men under the camouflage of clerical robes took advantage of incredibly naive girls, who remained naive even after sexual favors were cleverly coaxed out of them. As absurd as that seems, Thompson's fantasy spoke to a deep and abiding male desire, even among libertine men, to maintain an illusion of female sexual innocence.[50]

Thompson's cynical view of ministers' sexual powers over women apparently had widespread currency, judging from this glimpse of male adolescent banter from the 1820s, contained in a letter from a young man clerking in New York City to his chum in rural Connecticut. In the midst of a passage on big-city brothel frolics he advised his country friend:

> I think if I were in your skin, I would turn minister—assume the garb of priesthood, and under the ministerial cloak gain conquest which it is impossible to do in a citizens dress; monopolize the whole, turn hypocrite, d——d rascal, seducer; still be on the same footing with the ministers who are now working wonders in that part of the globe; only work your own card and I'll assure the

47. *New York Herald*, 31 Jan. 1845.
48. Spectator, *Verdict Sustained*, p. 9.
49. George Thompson [Paul de Kock, pseud.], *New-York Life; or, The Mysteries of Upper-Tendom Revealed* (New York, n.d.), p. 54. Internal evidence in the book points to an 1848 publication date.
50. Thompson, *New-York Life*, p. 54.

office of minister plenipotentiary from the devil's dominions, invested with full power to work wonders and take maiden heads when you choose.[51]

The most interesting and pertinent social commentary interpreting the Onderdonk case took the form of a blackface parody of the bishop's carriage rides (see fig. 4.2). It appeared in a scurrilous Philadelphia almanac for 1846, titled "De Darkie's Comic All-Me-Nig." The illustrated story, "Black Under-Donk-En Doughlips; or, De Feelin Deacon," recounted in exaggerated Negro dialect the tale of a buggy driver who drove Deacon Doughlips to a purity meeting along with another clergyman and his wife. First the driver hears sounds "berry much like niggar lips comin in contract." He turns and sees the Deacon kissing the clergyman's wife. Next he hears the sound of a dress coming undone, and beholds "a sample ob dark underdonkation to parfection: dar was Mrs. Frogpaw's bare black beautiful bosom fast in de Deacon's boff hands, an his black fist war worken its way along like a black snake under de loose bark ob a gum tree." The text and accompanying illustration make clear that the black clergyman in the front seat looks on the whole scene of his wife and the bishop with full approval. The woman, in contrast, looks utterly astonished.[52]

The almanac, of course, was the production of whites, for a white audience, just as blackface minstrelsy in theaters of the 1840s involved whites speaking to other whites using the semantics of race.[53] The mediation of race transposed the bishop's behavior from the realm of privileged, religious whites—where it seemed to make no sense—to the realm of black burlesque and broad comedy, where infantile jokes and wishes could be given full expression. Rendering the Onderdonk story in blackface allowed white men to indulge in the forbidden fantasy of touching a woman's breasts at will and without punishment. The female victim as black woman is understood to be open game for sexual attack; no system of patriarchy protects her, as it would white women. This black woman victim has a husband, to be sure, but he looks on with approval and enjoyment, since the conventions of blackface exaggerate his prurient sexuality, along with his dialect and facial features.

In the world of privileged whites, men could not touch women disrespectfully as a social rule, and if they did, male relatives were supposed to spring to the women's defense. Even harboring the thought of such an

51. T. D. Stewart to John A. Taintor, 24 Jan. 1825, in the Taintor–Davis Papers, American Antiquarian Society, Worcester, Mass. I thank James O. and Janet C. Robertson for bringing these letters to my attention. The Robertsons' book, *All Our Yesterdays: A Century of Family Life in an American Small Town* (New York, 1993), pp. 115–25, discusses this set of sexually frank letters exchanged between young men.

52. *De Darkies Comic All-Me-Nig for 1846* (Philadelphia, 1845). My thanks to Joanne Chaison of the American Antiquarian Society for locating this document for me.

53. My reading of the "All-Me-Nig" owes a debt to Eric Lott, *Love and Theft: Blackface Minstrelsy and the American Working Class* (New York, 1993).

BLACK UNDER-DONK-EN DOUGHLIPS;
OR, DE FEELIN DEACON.

Yu, yu, ya! by smash, I blebe dar's no more human natur any more, when a bit o' women natur am about, for all our Deacon's am getting so fat d..t de spiritual feelin am all smashed out ob 'em like de yolk out ob geese egg, an dar all flesh like ebery oder boddy else. Fader Miller am been about, all de preachers am takin toll ob de fair black sheep ob dar flock. Dar's only last October I went to drive de Rev. Doctor Frogpaw down to de purity night meetin house, when dey took a notion to stop for Deacon Dough-lips on de way, an earry him down to de meetin at de same time. Well, de Deacon got in de bugbee, an Doctor Frogpaw gib him his seat along side of Mrs. Julep Frogpaw ob course, and took a seat next behind me, so as he could look me face to face in de back, an tell me which way to drive. Now somehow or todder how, as soon as de Deacon got to de bugbee, I tought dat he smelt berry loud ob dat little house below de cider press, an his two eyes walked out like de risen moons; so tinks I, I'll jist keep one eye behind my back, for I'se berry lately had a berry loud suspicion ob dese he black sheep Well, as we war gwan along de road, I seed sebral wery queer sounds dat look berry much like niggar lips comin in contract; I turned boff eyes around, an smash me up into corn cakes, if de ole Deacon wasn't biting de tallest kind ob a buss from de innocence an dullifferous forbidden lips ob Mrs. Julep Frogpaw. Well, I drove on a little furder, an I soon heered furder sights; I tought dat I seed de bosom ob de dress crack an come apart, an look around some more, an oh, bullglory an seductionation, if I didn't dar behold a sample ob dark underdonkation to parfection: dar was Mrs. Frog-paw's bare black beautiful bosom fast in de Deacon's boff hands, an his black fist war worken its way along like a black snake under de loose bark ob a gum tree. I gib Dr. Frogpaw a wink wid de corner ob my elbow, and he turned right around backwards, an dar he seed de hull sight for nothin,—a Deacon's hand on a new edition ob de bible,—a she nigga's bosom; de hosses laughed, I fainted in exprise, as de Doctor called de Deacon a most feel-in fader; an de next ting I he red ob, was dar making up a purse ob money as a reward for his feeling so fur into de bosoms an hearts ob de black flock.

Figure 4.2. A scurrilous blackface parody of the Onderdonk scandal. Courtesy, American Antiquarian Society.

invasive action was so foreign—forbidden—to white commentators in the Onderdonk case that they could not imagine why the bishop might do it in actuality. In the negative figuration of blackface, immature and inappropriate fondling could be seen to be an end in itself, an infantile compulsion and not a preliminary to serious seduction or courtship as might be expected from a grown man. The childlike and stupid black caricatures served to mark Onderdonk's behavior as childlike, a giving way to an impulsive urge that most men in real life would quickly censor were they even to allow the thought to creep into their heads. "Deacon Under-Donk-En" revealed the sexual fantasy for the forbidden thrill that it was. The racial inversion played off of an ambivalent identification some whites felt for blacks and black culture in the 1840s, a potent mixture of fear, ridicule, and desire. The caricature also expressed a sense of cross-race male solidarity at the expense of women: the almanac story invited masked men, white or black, to take delight in a sexual insult to women. This is why the black woman in the illustration had to look surprised and scared—a reversal of the prevailing stereotype of black women's freer and easier sexuality, of welcoming sexual advances. The thrill of the Onderdonk grab relied precisely on the fact that the victim did not welcome it and felt great consternation and distress.

Bishop Onderdonk was suspended from office, but his friends in the New York diocese refused to turn him out completely. He continued to occupy the bishop's house near Trinity Church and to draw his full bishop's salary. He attended church daily and led the procession to communion. He ceased all social life, rarely left his house, and retired from church politics. The confusion occasioned by having a suspended bishop finally led to the appointment of an interim bishop, and the death of this substitute in the late 1850s prompted Onderdonk's supporters to try, yet again, to have the suspension lifted. But the Convention of Bishops refused, and in 1859 the cleric died, unrepentant and officially unforgiven. His supporters installed an elaborate marble memorial in the All Saints' Chapel in Trinity Church. Chiseled on it was an unintentionally multivalent symbol depicting a "serpent darting his venomous fangs at the bishop."[54] Onlookers and mourners could wonder whether the serpent represented the external enemies (the snakes) who drove the man from power or the internal temptations of serpentine sexuality that bedeviled him.

The power of the Onderdonk case to amaze, in 1845 as surely now, is that it emerged in the midst of one of the most traditional, hierarchical, and ritual-bound religious institutions in America. Theological controversy for the Episcopalians involved struggles over minute details of ritual; the new

54. Smith, *Sunshine and Shadow*, pp. 584–85. The memorial cenotaph still occupies its niche at Trinity, but the head of the snake has been broken off.

and "radical" opinion lay with the High Church proponents, who wanted more symbolic punch in their liturgical arrangements.

Americans in the 1840s were more prepared to find altered gender relations and aberrant sexuality among the liminal, anti-ritual, democratic religious groups pioneering on the margins of the major denominations. The religious upheavals of the antebellum period opened the doors to divergent styles of gendered interactions between a largely male clergy and an increasingly feminized congregation. Some of these new movements forged deliberately new styles of sexuality—the Oneida Community, the Shakers, and the Mormons, to name three very distinct examples. Fragmentation lessened the possibility for institutional oversight and control. Irregular ministers had the irregular lives, insisted the religious press; it was most comfortable to isolate unbridled sexuality on the margins of society.

But when the figure of the clerical seducer emerged in the highest pillar of respectable society, different explanations had to be invoked. For his Low Church opponents, Bishop Onderdonk's sponsorship of neo-Catholic symbolism was congruent with his sexual lust in that both were expressions of an indulgent sensuality—the man who ate rich foods during Lent and argued for opulent surplices also had fleshly desires he could not control. They framed their explanation in terms of undisciplined desire; but they could not fully comprehend the peculiar form his desire took, the quick and compulsive grab, that seemingly accomplished so little and yet incurred such risk.

But in the frame of modern understandings of sexual harassment, a pattern takes shape. The bishop preferred a church that maximized hierarchy and consolidated lines of authority to the top, one that contained women and men congregants within ritual forms. Elaborate liturgy distanced the minister from the congregation and operated as a symbolic language to express social arrangements honoring status and privilege. Individual congregants did not have individual voices within his institution, and so they found it hard to speak back to authority figures. Onderdonk's compulsion to grab breasts was at heart idiosyncratic and unrelated to any aspect of religion, but his insistence on a vast privilege and power inherent in a clerical elite gave him scope and cover to indulge with a remarkable degree of security his intimate frontal attacks. His authority and eminence became his safety net, giving him a sense of entitlement to do as he did and assuring him that no one would ever believe him capable of it. And it very nearly worked.

CHAPTER 5

"The Women Have Had Charge of the Church Work Long Enough": The Men and Religion Forward Movement of 1911–1912 and the Masculinization of Middle-Class Protestantism

GAIL BEDERMAN

In 1911 and 1912, an interdenominational religious revival, the Men and Religion Forward Movement (M&RFM) caused a stir across the United States. Over a million people attended M&RFM events; organizers spent hundreds of thousands of dollars; seventy-six major cities and 1,083 small towns participated. But the most unusual aspect of the revival was not its scope but its sex. The Movement's purpose was not to Christianize America, but to masculinize the Protestant churches by getting as many men as possible active in religion. According to *Collier's*, the common sentiment was unmistakably, "The women have had charge of the church work long enough."[1]

The declared purpose of the M&RFM was to "vitalize" the churches by bringing in more male church members: "To help find the 3,000,000 men missing from participation in church life. There are 3,000,000 more girls and women in the churches of America than men and boys."[2] Addressing primarily a white, native-born, middle-class audience, the Movement was sponsored by nearly every national Protestant men's organization: ten denominational brotherhoods,[3] the International Sunday School Committee, the Gideons, and most actively, the YMCA. The organizers played

Reprinted, with changes, from *American Quarterly* 41 (September 1989): 432–65. Copyright 1989 by Johns Hopkins University Press. Reprinted by permission of the Johns Hopkins University Press. For helpful criticisms of earlier drafts, many thanks to Sherri Broder, Mari Jo Buhle, Gary Kulik, Louise Newman, William McLoughlin, Don Scott, Joan Scott, and Julie Weiss.

1. Arthur H. Gleason, "Going After Souls on a Business Basis," *Collier's* 23 Dec, 1911, p. 14.
2. "For Men," *Christian Advocate* (Boston) 36 (Aug. 1911): 1026.
3. The Baptist Brotherhood, the Brotherhood of Andrew and Philip (Presbyterian), the Brotherhood of Disciples of Christ, the Brotherhood of Saint Andrew (Episcopalian), the Congregational Brotherhood of America, the Lutheran Brotherhood, the Methodist Brotherhood, the Otterbein Brotherhood (United Brethren), the Presbyterian Brotherhood of America, and the United Presbyterian Brotherhood.

Figure 5.1. The crowning event of the Forward Movement was to be the six-day Christian Conservation Congress. Here, William Jennings Bryan addresses a crowd of men in Union Square. *Current Literature* 52 (June 1912): 674.

down all denominational differences in order to concentrate on their main goal: recruiting male church members, or, as their slogan put it, providing "More Men for Religion, More Religion for Men."[4] Because of this focus, it was able to attract the active support of an unusually wide spectrum of prominent Protestant churchmen: businessmen like John D. Rockefeller and J. Pierpont Morgan; social activists like Charles Stelzle and Raymond Robins; theologians like Washington Gladden and Walter Rauschenbusch; and politicians like William Jennings Bryan and Governor W. J. Northen of Georgia.

The campaign opened September 18, 1911, with meetings in Protestant churches all over the country, and closed, as planned, with a widely heralded "Christian Conservation Congress" in New York City the next April. (See figs 5.1 and 5.2.) According to historian of religion Charles Howard Hopkins, it was "the most comprehensive Evangelistic effort ever undertaken in the United States."[5] And except for one mother's meeting per campaign and an occasional city which allowed women to attend one or two meetings "in the gallery," the Men and Religion Forward Movement was

4. For slogan, see William T. Ellis, "A Movement: A Message: A Method," *Independent* 72 (May 1912): 985.

5. Charles H. Hopkins, *The Rise of the Social Gospel in American Protestantism* (New Haven, 1940), p. 296.

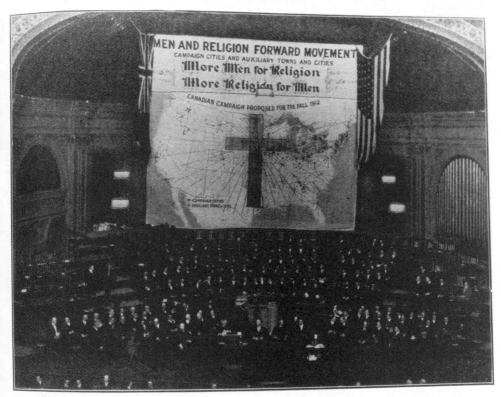

Figure 5.2. Meetings were held in large theaters like the Hippodrome or, here, Carnegie Hall. *Independent* 72 (May 1912): 985.

explicitly and exclusively for men and boys only—the only widespread religious revival in American history that explicitly excluded women.[6]

While cultural historians recently have paid a great deal of attention to widespread cries for a muscular Christianity as an aspect of a larger cultural transformation during the years 1880–1920, they have been surprisingly insistent that the movement for manly Christianity had very little to do with issues of gender. The call for a virile Protestantism, they claim, addressed gender-neutral cultural issues such as the loss of middle-class hegemony and the breakdown of the Victorian worldview far more than it addressed

6. In other campaigns, individual revival meetings might target working girls, mothers, laboring men, or businessmen. See W. G. McLoughlin, "Billy Sunday and the Working Girl of 1915," *Presbyterian Church History* 54 (1976): 376–84. However, there is a clear difference between organizing one meeting for a special interest group and organizing an eight month campaign designed to appeal to all members of only one sex.

"women's" issues like feminism or suffrage.[7] Yet it cannot be ignored that these men addressed issues of power and cultural dominance in emphatically gendered terms—celebrating the virility of Protestantism and condemning "effeminate religion."

The advocates of the Men and Religion Forward Movement, like other muscular Christianity advocates, used this sexualized language because they understood power and religion in terms of gender.[8] Between 1880 and 1920, many middle-class men experienced the social and cultural changes tied to the development of a corporate, consumer-oriented society as dangerous challenges to their manhood.[9] Since they did not compartmentalize "gender" and "cultural" issues, as today's historians sometimes do, these men addressed their cultural crisis in gendered terms, and their masculinity crisis in cultural terms. Worried that middle-class men were becoming "effeminate," they moved to reclaim their threatened cultural dominance by redefining gender. By focusing on the Men and Religion movement as one representative example of a much wider struggle, we can see some of the ways gender shaped the social and cultural tensions of the period and, perhaps, how men's moves to reformulate male identity limited women's options.

7. See David I. Macleod, *Building Character in the American Boy: The Boy Scouts, YMCA, and Their Forerunners* (Madison, 1983), esp. xv–xvi; and T. J. Jackson Lears, *No Place of Grace: Anti-Modernism and the Transformation of American Culture 1880–1920* (New York, 1981), pp. 97–139, esp. 104. Inadequate attention to gender remains a weak spot in Lears's otherwise excellent discussion. While Lears does consider what he calls the "masculine" and "feminine" poles of anti-modernism, he tends to use these terms in a static fashion, as synonyms for "active" and "passive." He ignores the way masculinity and femininity articulated actual social power, as opposed to mere metaphoric categories. Similarly, he neglects to consider how constructions of masculinity and femininity were themselves issues of contention and being actively transformed over the period as an integral part of the very processes he discusses. See pages 217–60.

8. I am influenced here by historians who, following Michel Foucault and other postmodernist critics, see language and power as mutually constitutive. Since language—defined as not merely words, but as systems of meaning—is based on differentiation, sexual difference has often been crucial in establishing those systems of meaning. For a theoretical discussion of language, gender, and power, see Joan W. Scott, "Gender, A Useful Category of Historical Analysis," *American Historical Review* 91 (1987): 1053–75; and Joan W. Scott, "On Language, Gender, and Working Class History," *International Labor and Working Class History* 31 (1987): 1–13. For historical examples of ways gender and power have been mutually encoded through language, see Ruth H. Bloch, "The Gendered Meanings of Virtue in Revolutionary America," *Signs* 13 (1987): 37–58; Denise Riley, " 'The Free Mothers': pronatalism and working women in industry at the end of the last war in Britain," *History Workshop* 11 (1981): 59–118; Joan W. Scott, "Work Identities of Men and Women: The Politics of Work and Family in the Parisian Garment Trades in 1848," in *Gender and the Politics of History* (New York, 1988), pp. 93–112; and Carroll Smith-Rosenberg, *Disorderly Conduct: Visions of Gender in Victorian America* (New York, 1985), pp. 11–52, 245–96.

9. On cultural reorientation, see Lears, *No Place of Grace*, and John Higham, "The Reorientation of American Culture in the 1890s," in *Writing American History: Essays on Modern Scholarship* (Bloomington, Ind., 1978), pp. 73–102. On the "masculininty crisis," see Peter G. Filene, *Him/Her/Self: Sex Roles in Modern America* (Baltimore, 1974 & 1986), pp.

Historical Roots: How Did Feminized Protestantism, Once a Blessing, Become a Problem?

In their celebrations of red-blooded revivalists and virile, masculine Bibles, the Men and Religion activists were actually attempting to transform the Victorian gender system. During the late eighteenth and early nineteenth centuries, religion and morality had been coded female, while politics and business had been coded male; and the "male" sphere of business and politics had been set in opposition to the "female" sphere of religion and morality. The point of the Men and Religion Forward Movement was to collapse these oppositions. Thus, the gender specificity of its message stemmed directly from the gendered coding of contemporary languages of religion and of power. A quick review of the history of gendered Protestantism in America can give some idea of what was at stake in the move to masculinize the churches.

Although Men and Religion organizers saw the preponderance of women in the churches as evidence of a new and modern crisis, in actuality the American Protestant churches had been two-thirds female ever since the 1660s. Yet despite this sexual imbalance, seventeenth- and eighteenth-century Protestants saw religion as gender-neutral—neither feminine nor masculine. The disproportionate numbers of women might occasionally be a matter for comment, but rarely concern.[10] Even during the early nineteenth century, when religion was first coded feminine, few Protestants were alarmed.[11] The actual number of men and women in the churches

---

69–93; Elliot J. Gorn, *The Manly Art: Bare Knuckle Prizefighting in America* (Ithaca, N.Y., 1986), 179–206; Michael S. Kimmel, "The Contemporary 'Crisis' of Masculinity in Historical Perspective," in *The Making of Masculinities*, ed. Harry Brod (Boston, 1987), pp. 121–54; and Joe L. Dubbert, "Progressivism and the Masculinity Crisis," in *The American Man*, ed. Elizabeth H. Pleck and Joseph H. Pleck (Englewood Cliffs, N.J., 1980), pp. 303–20. See also Margaret Marsh, "Suburban Men and Masculine Domesticity," *American Quarterly* 40 (1988): 165–86. Marsh's fine article provides a needed corrective to the simpleminded view that the "masculinity crisis" was reflected in a male flight from home life. Although Marsh questions the existence of a "masculinity crisis," I believe her findings support my contention that it is primarily on the level of cultural, and not social, history that we should understand the Progressive Era's "cult of masculinity." The masculinity crisis was a crisis of cultural meaning, and not a growth of male aggressiveness spawned by urbanization or office work.

10. Nancy F. Cott, *The Bonds of Womanhood* (New Haven, 1977), pp. 126, 128; Mary Maples Dunn, "Saints and Sisters: Congregational and Quaker Women in the Early Colonial Period," in *Women in American Religion*, ed. Janet Wilson James (Philadelphia, 1980), pp. 27–46; Gerald F. Moran, "Sisters in Christ: Women and the Church in Seventeenth-Century New England," in ibid., pp. 47–66; and Laurel Thatcher Ulrich, *Good Wives: Image and Reality in the Lives of Women in Northern New England 1650–1750* (New York, 1980 & 1982), pp. 215–36.

11. Ann Douglas, *The Feminization of American Culture* (New York, 1977), pp. 1–143; and Barbara Welter, "The Feminization of American Religion, 1800–1860," in *Clio's Consciousness Raised: New Perspectives on the History of Women*, ed. Mary S. Hartman and Lois Banner (New York, 1974), pp. 137–57.

cannot explain why feminization was suddenly discovered as a danger in the late nineteenth century.

The feminine church only became a problem after 1880, when the Victorian gender system had begun to lose coherence in the face of a cultural reorientation connected to the growth of a consumer-oriented, corporate order.[12] In the early decades of the nineteenth century, American Protestants had adopted a feminized religion because feminization provided a means of combining the benevolence of a Christian moral order with the untrammelled self-interest of laissez-faire capitalism. After the American Revolution, the potential rewards of the growing free market attracted the new middle classes; yet they feared the moral results of unrestrained individualistic competition. If every man pursued his own self-interest, they worried, perhaps nothing would hold society together; American society might degenerate into a mob of rapacious self-seekers greedily pursuing their own private interests.[13]

In order to minimize the moral dangers of the open market while maximizing its potential rewards, middle-class Americans used gender to marry morality to productivity—literally. During the early Republic, for the first time, they defined women as the naturally religious sex, and men, the naturally productive sex. By joining the two, they constructed the middle-class family as the basis of the moral commercial society. Pious women would keep their husbands and sons moral; productive men would work to become successful entrepreneurs in order to provide for their wives and children; and together they would form godly homes, the epitome of Christian progress.[14] Of course, women did not stop engaging in productive labor, any more than men stopped going to church.[15] What changed was the *cultural significance* assigned to these activities.[16] By using gender to marry market relations to religion, in the form of coupling productive men to

12. On gender and the cultural crisis 1880–1920, see Lewis A. Erenberg, *Steppin' Out: New York Nightlife and the Transformation of American Culture 1890–1930* (Chicago, 1981); Elaine Tyler May, *Great Expectations: Marriage and Divorce in Post-Victorian America* (Chicago, 1980); and Lary May, *Screening Out the Past: The Birth of Mass Culture and the Motion Picture Industry* (Chicago, 1980 & 1983).

13. Cott, *Bonds of Womanhood*, pp. 97–98; Mary P. Ryan, *Cradle of the Middle Class: The family in Oneida County, New York, 1790–1865* (Cambridge, 1981), pp. 1–17, 60–144; Bloch, "Gendered Meanings," pp. 54–58.

14. Cott, *Bonds of Womanhood*, pp. 70–71; Ryan, *Cradle of the Middle Class*, pp. 83–105, 145–85; Katharine Kish Sklar, *Catharine Beecher: A Study in American Domesticity* (New York, 1973), pp. 135–37, 155–75.

15. For a good discussion of the strong nineteenth-century prescriptive norms for male piety, see E. Anthony Rotundo, "Learning about Manhood: Gender Ideals and the Middle Class Family in Nineteenth-Century America," in *Manliness and Morality: Middle-Class Masculinity in Britain and America, 1800–1940*, ed. J. A. Mangan and James Walvin (New York, 1987), pp. 35–51, esp. 36–40. See also Rotundo, "Manhood in America: The Northern Middle Class 1770–1920" (Ph.D. diss., Brandeis University, 1982), pp. 213–35.

16. Although historians say that Protestantism was "feminized," this doesn't necessarily mean that women actually gained power. Male dominance remained a central tenet of the

pious women, the middle classes were able to construct a moral capitalist order and to engage—with all their hearts and souls—in the free market.[17] Thus, the Victorian gender system linked feminized Protestantism and entrepreneurial capitalism from the very beginning.

The feminization of piety then, was not caused by dissatisfaction with the relations between men and women; but by dissatisfaction with the relation of religion and business within the world, as signified through gender.[18] Similarly, the masculinization of religion would be catalyzed, in part, by dissatisfaction with the relation of religion and business, as signified through gender. As entrepreneurial capitalism gave way to an increasingly corporate order, the voice of feminine restraint embodied in Victorian Protestantism began to seem sissified and effeminate. And when, at the same time, woman's movement activists translated woman's moral mission to restrain male rapaciousness into a mission to expand woman's sphere, the value of a feminized Protestantism came to appear increasingly dubious.

On the one hand, the feminization of piety had allowed the development of a massive Gilded Age woman's movement. Many women, taking their cultural constructions literally, believed that women's superior sense of morality made it their duty to be "social housekeepers" and by becoming active in politics and the professions, to clean up the mess that men, because of their competitive, materialistic natures, had made of society.[19] Yet by extending women's sphere, based on their moral mission to restrain male selfishness, women ultimately threatened another linchpin of the Victorian gender system—male dominance. By the 1890s, genteel maga-

---

gender system as well as a fact of life in the Protestant churches. While a handful of women did manage to be ordained, mainly in small liberal denominations, the theologians, ministers, governing bodies, and entire power structure remained almost exclusively male.

17. It would be misleading to assert, as historians like Ann Douglas and Barbara Welter have done, that morality was assigned to women because religion was dwindling in importance to the middle class. The antebellum middle class cared deeply about Christian values. Many people even hoped to perfect society on Christian principles. See John L. Thomas, "Romantic Reform in America," *American Quarterly* 17 (1965): 656–81. It was because they cared so deeply about Christian values that they organized much of their gender system around delegating this part of society to women.

18. Although I am arguing that most of feminizers' main object was never to give women major social or political power, this doesn't negate the by-now well-established point that many antebellum women actively worked to feminize morality and to carve out a new, more powerful role for middle-class women. The point is that they could not have been successful—and perhaps would not even have proposed the solutions that they did—if the middle classes were not already wrestling with the problem of morality under competitive individualist capitalism. In other words, we do have to focus on women's agency in forming their lives in history; but they form their lives within cultural limits.

19. Ruth Bordin, *Woman and Temperance: The Quest for Power and Liberty 1873–1900* (Philadelphia, 1980); and Barbara Epstein, *The Politics of Domesticity: Women, Evangelism and Temperance in Nineteenth-Century America* (Middletown, Conn., 1981), pp. 125–27.

zines were publishing dozens of anxious articles wondering how woman's advancement might affect American men. As Charles Dudley Warner editorialized in *Harper's*, "[I]f the young men of our Republic do not bestir themselves mentally and physically, they are apt . . . 'to be left'."[20]

But at the same time that feminine morality and manly dominance were seeming increasingly antagonistic, other social forces were undermining the conditions that had fostered the feminization of religion in the first place. The old constructions, in which female piety facilitated male economic competition, had been tailored for a small-scale, competitive capitalism—a capitalism which had all but disappeared by the 1890s. In the context of a bureaucratic interdependent society, the old imperatives lost meaning, leading to a pervasive sense of unreality. Bourgeois domestic moralism— the fiefdom of the Victorian moral mother—began to appear stifling and hypocritical.[21] Now, consumer pleasures and commercial leisure promised men more palpable rewards than Christian self-denial and hard work.[22] In short, the feminized Protestantism that informed an individualistic, producer-oriented middle class had been rendered obsolete by the development of a corporate, consumer-oriented order.

The crisis of cultural "effeminacy" developed in part because feminized religion, tailored for laissez-faire capitalism, no longer answered the needs of the new modern society. "Feminine" religion no longer balanced "male" self-interest in American society. Now, "she" threatened to overwhelm "him." The "ladylike" voice of higher morality remained embedded in men's overworked superegos, urging thrift, hard work, and self denial— increasingly irrelevant values in a corporate, consumer society. And, as archaic "feminine" morality grew increasingly oppressive, American culture seemed increasingly effeminate.

Protestant men mourned the loss of a morality that let them feel manly, and of a gender/cultural system that had seemed—so deceptively—to provide a firm foundation for cultural and personal identity. As one writer put it in 1896, "We are drinking the dregs of the immaterial and have touched the dingiest bottoms of purity. . . . Nature and commonsense crumble, and sincerity has long since withered away. Complexions are of wax when feminine; when male of pale peach-blossom!"[23] With purity (defined as

20. Charles Dudley Warner, "Editor's Easy Chair," *Harper's New Monthly Magazine* 78 (1889): 324. See also William S. Walsh, "The Conceited Sex," *North American Review* 159 (1894): 372; Charles Dudley Warner, "The Subjection of Man," *Harpers New Monthly Magazine* 80 (1890): 972–73; and William Ward Russ, "Our Boys," *Outlook* 54 (1896): 1138– 39 for representative examples. On men's reaction to the woman's movement, see Filene, *Him/Her/Self*, pp. 69–93 and Kimmel, "Contemporary 'Crisis'," pp. 121–54.

21. Lears, *No Place of Grace*, p. 6.

22. John F. Kasson, *Amusing the Million* (New York, 1978), p. 107. See also Filene *Him/ Her/Self*, pp. 71–74.

23. Laurence Jerrold, "The Uses of Perversity," *Chapbook* 5 (July 1896): 194–98, cited in Lears, *No Place of Grace*, p. 48.

feminine in Victorian parlance) looking "dingy" and men reminiscent of "pale peach blossoms," Victorian gender definitions had lost coherence. They neither provided a satisfying model of relations between the sexes, nor constructed a convincing model of an acceptable capitalism. In short, cultural changes, as signified through gender, had made feminized religion a problem.

Yet many believed this problem could be solved. The "effeminacy" of American culture could be cured with a healthy dose of masculinity, augmented and redefined for changed circumstances.[24] Masculinizers who were committed Protestants concentrated on reversing the feminization of religion. By the early 1880s, American Protestants had begun to work to align Christianity with manliness, focusing initially on boy's work. Dozens of organizations like the Boys' Brigades and the Knights of King Arthur formed to attract boys to religious activity, using athletics and a quasi-militaristic organization as bait.[25] When progressive reformist fervor replaced popular enthusiasm for armed force, the more militaristic of these faded, but the perceived dangers of feminized religion continued. Increasingly, Protestants from Billy Sunday to local YMCA organizers linked religion to sports, business, or whatever seemed most manly at the moment.[26]

Around the turn of the century, churchmen escalated their tactics. Now, ignoring the fact that the churches had been two-thirds female for over two hundred years, they discovered—or, more accurately, constructed—a "crisis," pointing to the "excess of women over men in church life" as a new and dangerous threat, requiring immediate attention.[27] In 1905, influenced by reports of this so-called "crisis," the U.S. Census of Religion compiled its first report on the statistical proportion of men and women in the denominations, and confirmed it officially—the mainline American Protestant churches were two-thirds female.[28] Churchmen treated this news as

24. See note 9 for citations of efforts to redefine masculinity.

25. Macleod, *Building Character*, pp. 44–50, 72–94; Joseph F. Kett, *Rites of Passage: Adolescence in America 1790 to the Present* (New York, 1977), pp. 189–210. On American muscular Christianity see also Gerald F. Roberts, "The Strenuous Life: The Cult of Manliness in the Era of Theodore Roosevelt" (Ph.D. diss, Michigan State University, 1970), pp. 52–77. For a good account of muscular Christianity in Britain, see Norman Vance, *The Sinews of the Spirit: The Ideal of Christian Manliness in Victorian Literature and Religious Thought* (Cambridge, 1985), pp. 1–29.

26. For examples of Billy Sunday's linking religion to sports, business, and show-business stars, see William G. McLoughlin, *Billy Sunday Was His Real Name* (Chicago, 1955), pp. 154–88, esp. 179–80.

27. George Coe, *The Spiritual Life: Studies in the Science of Religion* (New York, 1900), pp. 6–7, cited in Kett, *Rites of Passage*, p. 210. See also Josiah Strong, *The Times and Young Men* (New York, 1901), pp. 179–80; and "Religion for Men," *Century Magazine* 58 (1910): 153–54.

28. For the official Census results, see Bureau of the Census, *Religious Bodies: 1906, 2 vols.* (Washington, D.C., 1906); and H. K. Carroll, *The Religious Forces of the United States* (New York, 1912), lvii–lix.

confirmation of their worst fears and made strenuous efforts to meet the "crisis." To attract men back to the churches, they published books calling for a manly Christianity, such as Carl Case's *The Masculine in Religion* (1906), Alfred Thayer Mahan's *The Harvest Within* (1909), Harry Emerson Fosdick's *The Manhood of the Master* (1911), and Jason Pierce's *The Masculine Power of Christ* (1912).[29] They formed new denominational men's clubs.[30] And some of them organized the Men and Religion Forward Movement.

Thus, the Men and Religion Forward Movement itself should be seen as merely one manifestation of a much broader cultural trend. When the consolidation of a consumer-oriented, corporate capitalism made Protestant men feel that their identity as men was uncertain and their religion was effeminate, many middle-class men moved to recodify religion as especially manly. Even the origins of the Men and Religion Movement show how widespread this desire had become by 1910: According to M&RFM literature, several churchmen got the idea for the Men and Religion campaign simultaneously. When Fred B. Smith, head of the Religious Work Department of the YMCA, approached other Protestant men's groups to propose a massive, continent-wide religious revival aimed at men alone, he found that several groups including the International Sunday School Association were already considering such a plan. After hearing Smith's presentation, Hubert Carleton, secretary of the (Episcopal) Brotherhood of Saint Andrew, "took from his suitcase a typewritten document in essential points similar to the one [Smith had] just described."[31] Although Movement literature repeatedly referred to the three leaders' simultaneous inspirations as proof of the movement's "providential origins,"[32] where they saw the hand of God, we might see further evidence that in the face of a gender-based cultural crisis, a broad spectrum of American churchmen had conceived a burning desire to masculinize the churches.

This spectrum was broad, but not unlimited, however. Most Men and Religion Forward Movement organizers, assuming that "religion" meant only the practices of white, native-born Protestants like themselves, ignored immigrant and nonwhite Protestants. The black Protestant churches had an even larger proportion of female church members than the white Protestant

29. Joe L. Dubbert, *A Man's Place: Masculinity in Transition* (Englewood Cliffs, 1979), pp. 136–37.

30. See Daniel W. Martin, "The United Presbyterian Church Policy on the Men's Movement—An Historical Overview," *Journal of Presbyterian History* 59 (1981): 441–42.

31. Henry Rood, "On the March with the New Crusaders," *Everybody's Magazine* 26 (1912): 638. Rood was Publicity Chairman of the Men and Religion Forward Movement Committee of 97.

32. "For Men," *Christian Advocate* 86 (1911): 1026. See also Rood, "On the March," p. 638; and "The Buffalo Resolutions," the founding document of the Movement, reprinted in Men and Religion Forward Movement, *The Program of Work* (New York, 1911), p. 63.

churches, yet M&RFM organizers seem to have ignored black Protestant organizations altogether.[33] Although the "Negro Problem" was discussed at the M&RFM Christian Conservation Congress, the "problem" under review was not the feminization of the black churches, but simply the "Negro."[34] And when one congregation of Italian Presbyterians requested a Movement speaker during the New York City campaign, the situation was evidently unusual enough to warrant the attendance of a *New York Times* reporter. The M&RFM speaker addressed the Italian men in the most patronizing tones, enjoining them to "stop the bad moving picture shows, cooperate with the officers of the law, and never fail to vote."[35]

Although Movement literature occasionally expressed pious hopes that Catholics and Jews would participate, real outreach to those communities was practically nonexistent, too. For example, although one *New York Times* advertisement urged Jewish men, as well as Protestant and Catholic men, to find out more about the Men and Religion Forward Movement, the

33. Bureau of the Census, *Religious Bodies: 1906* 1:29, 136. The Protestant churches (black and white) were 60.7 percent women; the black Protestant churches, 62.5 percent women.

Since this article was published, Evelyn Brooks Higginbotham's excellent *Righteous Discontent: The Women's Movement in the Black Baptist Church, 1880–1920* (Cambridge, Mass., 1993) has cast new light on this issue. *Righteous Discontent* provides a rich and persuasive analysis of gender issues at stake in some of the black Protestant churches and suggests that black Protestants might have had important reasons not to care about the whites' masculinization movement.

Higginbotham demonstrates that, unlike mainline white Protestants, who moved either to masculinize religion or to defend its femininity, black Baptist men and women deployed religion in a far more complex and less dualistic fashion. For them, the gendered aspects of racism complicated the question of gender and religion. Romantic racialism had long associated masculine characteristics with the white race and feminine characteristics with the black race. Higginbotham shows that turn-of-the-century black Baptists "destabilized and blurred" these codings of race and gender in order to synthesize an anti-racist theology. On the one hand, black Baptists, both men and women, represented their church as incorporating valuable feminine characteristics: Black Protestants' highly Christian spirit of meekness and forgiveness was depicted as challenging notions of white spiritual superiority. But on the other hand, both men and women frequently used masculine imagery to describe black churchwomen and their valiant efforts to combat racism (Higginbotham, *Righteous Discontent*, pp. 142–48). Thus, blurring masculinity and femininity as a tool to erase racism, black Protestants might well have found little meaning in white Protestants' efforts to masculinize their churches.

34. W. J. Northen "Constructive Christianity and the Negro Problem," *Messages of the Men and Religion Forward Movement*, 7 vols. (New York, 1912), 1:127 42; Booker T. Washington, "The Church in Relation to the Negro Problem," in ibid., 1:143–51; "Revivalists Reach 100,000 Men," *New York Times*, 22 Apr. 1912, p. 13.

Booker T. Washington, the only African-American I found who participated in the movement, shrewdly gauged the limits and possibilities of his racist white audience, as always. His speech consisted of a warning that unless northern white Protestants donated large amounts of money to the southern black churches, the needy blacks would migrate to the northern cities where most of his audience lived. This threat to "move next door" was probably the most effective fundraising argument he could have made.

35. "Real Fishers of Men," *New York Times*, 27 Mar. 1912, p. 22.

ad's tasteful border of sixty-eight little crosses was unlikely to attract many Jewish participants. Catholics, as well, found the Men and Religion Movement's Protestant imagery and assumptions unappealing.[36]

Yet there is some evidence that middle-class Catholics, too, had been trying to masculinize their churches. Despite the fact that, according to the 1906 census, the Catholic church was almost evenly split between men and women, by the late 1890s even middle-class Catholics were worrying about a lack of active male participation in their church and defining it as—if not a crisis—at least a matter needing attention.[37] In 1911, for example, one publication argued that it was a mistaken idea to think that "to receive often the Holy Eucharist one must be a woman." Some parishes designated special hours for men to take communion and make confession, and in New York some parishes instituted "a type of 'express lane' service for male-only confession" on busy Friday and Saturday nights.[38] If, in spite of the equal numbers of men and women in the Catholic Churches, middle-class Catholics worried about the feminization of religion and tried to masculinize their churches, just as middle-class Protestants did, this provides additional evidence that the masculinity crisis stemmed from conditions that both Catholic and Protestant middle-class men shared—from the gender coding inherent in Victorian culture, and its irrelevance for a corporate, consumer-oriented capitalism.

The Men and Religion Forward Movement

The Men and Religion Forward Movement is historically important because it provides a window into the motives and logic behind the widespread cultural impulse to masculinize middle-class religion. The M&RFM organized yearnings common among middle-class men into a national campaign. Its copious publications and press reports gave voice to those yearnings and explained what was at stake in the move to masculinize. The

36. The ad was located on the sports page of the *New York Times*, 11 Mar. 1912, p. 12. For Catholic reaction, see "Farley Reproves Secular Education," *New York Times*, 13 May 1912, p. 5.

37. Sex ratio statistics from Bureau of the Census, *Religious Bodies: 1906* 1:29.

The statistically high proportion of men stemmed in part from the different ways in which Protestants and Catholics defined church membership. Unlike Protestants, who needed to join their churches formally in order to be counted as church members, all Catholics were automatically born into the Church, where they remained until they either overtly left the Church, or died.

38. Colleen McDannell, "'True Men as We Need Them' Catholicism and the Irish-American Male," *American Studies* 27 (1986): 22–23. McDannell, who is concerned primarily with documenting ideas about masculinity within the Catholic church, argues that issues of gender and religion for Catholic men differed substantially from those for Protestant men. She defines those Protestant issues quite differently from the way I am defining them here, however. In addition, because she assumes that the years 1870–1900 formed one relatively homogeneous block, she never considers whether masculinity issues might have changed during those years, as her own evidence suggests they may have.

basic purpose of the Men and Religion Movement was to make Protestantism manly by collapsing the polar opposition between (feminine) religion
and (masculine) business, which had worked well for entrepreneurial capitalism but had become obsolete in the new corporate order. With religion
part of the manly world of commerce and social affairs, activists felt, it
would loss the taint of association with stifling Victorian sentimentalism.

Movement literature repeatedly emphasized the earthshaking importance
of getting the "3,000,000 missing men" into the churches. "If all the men of
any city upon any given Sunday morning should say to their families, 'We
will go to church with you today,' the churches would overflow and pack
the streets with the crowds which could not be accommodated, and shouts
of happiness would fill the air. This is not an overestimate of the effect,"
wrote the Movement's most visible leader, Fred B. Smith.[39] According to
another leader, "The well recognized facts regarding the inadequate
proportion of adult males who are church members make emphatic the
demand for unusual effort."[40] To the men involved, the "need of new
masculine material in the church" was "constant and self evident."[41] A need
so "self-evident" rarely required explanation, but once, *Collier's* reported,
Fred B. Smith was "asked by a reporter why he didn't leave church work to
the women, who already had a monopoly of it. 'When a man is drowning,
you don't send a lady out to rescue him. You send a great, big, he-man,'
said Smith."[42] To become modern and powerful the church needed, not
"ladies," but "he-men."

To counteract the feminine taint and attract the missing men, movement
literature emphasized the masculine qualities of the church and churchmen,
continually referring to "virile hymns," "Christian manliness," and most
often, "strong men." Men who attended M&RFM activities were no
pantywaists, but were "ready for the strongest utterances of the strongest
men."[43] These strong men found the "exacting masculine pages of their
Bible" to be "worthy of the best time and mightiest effort of the manliest
man."[44] The "battalion of experts" who conducted the campaign, all
"hearty meat eaters," engaged in "strenuous physical exercise" regularly on
tour.[45]

Conversely, churchmen insisted upon real Christianity's lack of "feminine" traits. Nineteenth-century evangelical Protestantism had been emotional, emphasizing the heart over the head; and the Men and Religion

39. Fred B. Smith, *Men Wanted* (New York, 1911), p. 16.
40. Clarence A. Barbour, *Making Religion Efficient* (New York, 1912), p. 54.
41. Men and Religion Forward Movement, *Messages of the Men and Religion Forward Movement* 5:128.
42. Gleason, "Going After Souls," p. 13.
43. *Messages of the Men and Religion Forward Movement* 1:2.
44. *Messages of the Men and Religion Forward Movement* 3:45–46.
45. Rood, "On the March," p. 639; Gleason, "Going After Souls," p. 14.

activists identified this, rightly, with Protestantism's feminization. From now on, they maintained, their religion would be manly and businesslike— and thus, useful for the masculine world of daily affairs.

> There is one thing that should be clearly understood: there will not be a trace of emotionalism or sensationalism in this entire campaign. The gospel of Jesus of Nazareth—and its practical application to our practical daily life—is presented calmly, sanely, logically, so that it will convince the average man, who is a man of sane, logical, common sense. Women have no part in this movement, the reason being that Mr. Smith believes that the manly gospel of Christ should be presented to men by men.[46]

Above all, they maintained, "The spirit of religion is not dead . . . and not mere ineffective sentimentality."[47] Sentiment had no appeal to scientific, middle-class men, who feared that as men and as Protestants they were becoming "ineffective."

In order to construct a masculine religion, Men and Religion activists insisted that church work should be understood as part of the modern, twentieth-century world of corporate business. During the nineteenth century, feminized Protestantism had been a restraining foil to the male sphere of commerce. Now, Men and Religion activists aligned their religious movement with the masculine world of business by using new corporate techniques such as bureaucratic organization and aggressive advertising. Religion was not ladylike, they insisted. It was as manly as the biggest, strongest corporation president.

Although many Progressive Era revivalists, working to make religion manly and relevant, had attempted to conduct efficient, businesslike campaigns, the Men and Religion Movement took this businesslike ethos to hitherto unknown lengths, organizing the entire revival like an up-to-date, rationalized corporation.[48] The Movement's central headquarters in New York provided plans for a standardized bureaucratic structure, suitable for all cities organizing campaigns. This structure consisted of an executive committee of fifteen men, eleven subcommittees, and another committee "composed of the one hundred strongest men in the city."[49]

Men and Religion organizers also adopted the latest advertising techniques in order to depict their religion as an integral part of the masculine world of business and politics. The use of paid commercial advertising did

46. Henry Rood, "Men and Religion," *Independent* 71 (1911): 1364. M&RFM activists seemed to find this quote especially meaningful; portions were repeated elsewhere. See, for example, this letter to the editor: "Men and Religion Forward Movement Explained as of Experts Lecturing to Teachers," *New York Times*, 29 Dec. 1911, p. 10.

47. Rood, "On the March," p. 645.

48. For other revival campaigns organized in efficient, businesslike manners, see W. G. McLoughlin, *Modern Revivalism* (New York, 1959), pp. 378–83.

49. *Program of Work*, p. 6. See this source for the entire campaign blueprint.

not only publicize the Movement; more important, it was meant to align religion with the modern, corporate-consumer order, and disentangle religion from association with the old "feminine sphere." According to the *New York Times*, Eugene M. Camp, chairman of the M&RFM Publicity Committee, held a press conference and "urged that what is good for the merchant with ggods [*sic*] to sell ought to be good for the church with souls to save, and that the advertising of church services ought to be considered wholly ethical."[50]

The next week, the front page of the *Times* announced, "Salvation, preached with electric bulbs, that he who runs may read, appeared on Broadway last night in letters eighteen and a half feet high."[51] The actual messages on the billboards were bland: "Welcome for Everybody in the Churches of New York," read the first New York billboard. "The Church Wants Men in Her Work for Man," read another. (See figs. 5.3 and 5.4.) Yet the controversial medium of "electric signs" outshone the innocuous slogans. "The Church" might still be depicted as a "her," but "her" message stood proudly next to signs for "Dioxogen," the circus, and a poolroom—portraying it as an up-to-date part of a consumer-oriented world.

Similarly, the movement bought ads in newspapers across the country. Again, the messages were often traditional, but the method of presentation was highly unorthodox. As often as possible, organizers bought ads on the sports pages, where Men and Religion messages competed for consumers' attention with ads for automobiles, burlesque houses, and whiskey. (See figs. 5.5 and 5.6.) Putting ads on the sports pages suggested that religion was as enjoyable and as manly as football or baseball.[52] And the entire revival, from beginning to end, was occasionally depicted as one gigantic advertising campaign. For example, *Collier's* announced that the Movement's experts "have taken hold of religion, and are boosting it with the fervor and publicity skills which a gang of salesmen would apply to soap that floats or suits that wear."[53]

The Men and Religion Forward Movement not only advertised itself like Dioxogen and organized itself like Standard Oil, it also attempted to borrow the most scientific management techniques possible. (See fig. 5.7.) For one charismatic evangelist, the Men and Religion Forward Movement substituted teams of seven "experts," who were "specialists on conducting

50. "For Church Advertising," *New York Times*, 28 Feb. 1912, p. 10. See also "The Church and the Press," in *Messages of the Men and Religion Forward Movement* 7:99–106.

51. "Piety Sign in Broadway," *New York Times*, 6 Mar. 1912, p. 1.

52. At the same time Christian Manliness advocates moved to make religion manly by tying it to sports, sports themselves were taking on some of the transcendence and moral attributes previously associated with religion, according to Donald Mrozek. See Mrozek, *Sport and American Mentality 1880–1910* (Knoxville, 1983).

53. Gleason, "Going After Souls," p. 13.

Figure 5.3. Billboards along Broadway, New York City. *Literary Digest*, 20 Apr. 1912, p. 814.

religious revivals on scientific lines."[54] Each man on the team was responsible for one area of expertise: Bible Study, Boy's Work, Community Extension, Evangelism, Missions, or Social Service. During each campaign, the experts held nightly "institutes," envisioned as "teachers colleges" to transfer their expertise to local laymen. Men needed training to be lay evangelists, Bible teachers, and social service workers—to do work challenging enough to attract real men to the churches. Soul saving remained an

54. "Hasten Religious Campaign," *New York Times*, 8 Jan. 1912, p. 6. Men and Religion organizers found that this strategy, while it attracted laymen, backfired among the ministers, who resented the idea that they needed outside "experts" to show them how to do their jobs. See Ellis, "A Movement," p. 984; and "Men and Religion Movement," *Zion's Herald* (Boston) 90 (Jan. 1912): 119–20.

Figure 5.4. Although this "electric sign" advertises a welcome for "Everybody" in New York's churches, the full message is directed exclusively to men: the crosses on either end bear the ever-present messages (partially obscured here) "Men for Religion," and "Religion for Men." The very space the sign dominates—Madison Square after dark—itself comprises a "male" public space, where few middle-class women would venture unescorted. *Independent* 72 (May 1912): 987.

important component of the revival, as it had been for the old-fashioned evangelistic meetings: at the final meetings, men were encouraged, in a dignified fashion, to make a commitment to Jesus. Yet in the most visible Movement publications, old-fashioned conversion nearly disappeared behind the newer emphasis on the connection with corporate organizations, as publication after publication announced that the Men and Religion Forward Movement was *Making Religion Efficient* and "Going After Souls on a Business Basis."[55]

In short, the M&RFM's corporate organization, like its advertising and businesslike rhetoric, carried the message that manly Protestantism spoke the language of a new, consumerist world. As we have seen, the growth of a consumer-oriented society had made the old feminized evangelicalism of a producerist society obsolete. Now, these laymen believed they could revitalize the church by aligning their religion with "masculine" aspects of the new social and economic order. As *Collier's* put it. "Capitalized by the money and the brains of the biggest business men of the country, the

55. See notes 1 and 40 for citations.

Figure 5.5. This ad from the sports page was surrounded by ads hawking vaudeville performances, movie shows, tours to Florida, and Fatima Turkish Cigarettes. *Providence Journal,* 13 Jan. 1912, p. 5.

movement is going after souls in just the same way that the Standard Oil Company goes after business."[56]

Yet Men and Religion activists understood that Protestantism would never be truly masculinized unless men found modern, manly outlets in church work itself. It wasn't enough to simply advertise religion as a business and organize it as a corporation. Men and Religion organizers didn't want merely to *sell* their religion. They wanted to *vitalize* it—to make it as important to twentieth-century man as the stock exchange or the railroads. The old feminized Protestantism had been set in *opposition* to the market and other "manly" concerns. A truly masculinized religion would need to be put in *congruence* with the world of twentieth-century business and politics.

56. Gleason, "Going After Souls," p. 24.

†††††††††††††††††††

Men and Religion

To Readers of the Sporting Page

Sport is pleasure —
but it is not pleasure
enough for a well-
rounded man

"Man *has* a body; he *is*
a living spirit."

If you want to know more about the Men and Religion
Forward Movement, ask the editor or the nearest clergyman.

†††††††††††††††††††

Figure 5.6. The M&RFM's New York ads used modern advertising techniques, and featured catchy slogans and a characteristic graphic design. Their "product," manly religion, provided "pleasure," instead of restraint, and was a commodity which no "well-rounded man" could do without. Feminized religion, which repressed earthly enjoyment, was last year's model, and no longer for sale. *New York Times*, 2 Apr. 1912, p. 6.

In order to make the churches an integral part of the world of men, then, the churches had to provide a new sort of church work manly enough for men to do. Only by providing meaningful, masculine work more "important" than the work of women could the Protestant churches attract those "missing men." According to Ray B. Guild, the executive secretary of the Movement, "Men have hitherto felt that the task assigned to them in the Church was too petty to be of much importance. There was the position of Sunday school superintendent, and a few others which needed men, but for the mass of male membership, there was nothing to do."[57] Fred B. Smith, the Movement's most visible leader, agreed. *Collier's* reported that Smith "believes in giving men a man's job to do in church work. 'I found one church committee of twenty-three men—men capable of organizing a bank

57. "Men of Churches Begin a Campaign," *New York Times*, 10 June 1911, p. 27.

THE FIVE-FOLD MESSAGE.
Symbol used on the programs of the Men
and Religion meetings.

Figure 5.7. Some local campaigns used this logo, reminiscent of early corporations' first efforts to develop recognizable symbols for their products. Here again, religion was shown to use the most up-to-date business methods. *Survey*, 3 Feb. 1912, p. 1673.

or running a railroad—engaged in the work of buying a rug for the vestry floor,'" Smith complained.[58] The churches' very survival was at stake, for, as Charles C. Albertson warned during the Providence campaign, "unless men and boys were attracted to the church by some definite program of work for them to do, the church would die."[59]

It was this provision of a definite program of manly church work that turned the Men and Religion Forward Movement into what some historians have labelled a Social Gospel campaign.[60] But the real story is more complex. Advocates of the Social Gospel and proponents of masculinization had entirely different aims, but each group allied itself with the other in order to pursue its goal. On the one hand, Social Gospel ministers, anxious for wider acceptance of their controversial call for a religiously mandated social activism, were able to use the Men and Religion Forward Movement as a vehicle for propagating the Social Gospel. They accomplished this by showing that the Social Gospel and social service activity could provide the churches with that elusive but all-important element: masculine church work fit for manly men.

On the other hand, the more conservative M&RFM activists who adopted the Social Gospel appropriated its visionary message to the more

58. Gleason, "Going After Souls," p. 13.
59. "Gang Spirit Among Boys is Discussed," *Providence Journal*, 10 Jan. 1912.
60. See, for example, Hopkins, *Rise of Social Gospel*, p. 296.

crabbed purposes of masculinization. When these churchmen were finally convinced (partly by the popularity of manly social service work) that the Protestant church was not merely an arena for women, they began to take the masculine quality of the church for granted, and to lose interest in the reconstructive vision of the Social Gospel. In the short run the Social Gospelers appropriated the Men and Religion Forward Movement to spread their theological message; but in the long run the advocates of masculinization appropriated the Social Gospel to the services of defeminizing the church.

The earliest organizers of the Men and Religion Forward Movement, like Fred B. Smith, had expected the Social Gospel–based social service committees to be "a minor feature" of the campaigns.[61] Smith and his colleagues were hoping to unite the broadest possible coalition of Protestants behind the banner of manly Christianity, and the Social Gospel threatened to be too controversial for inclusion. "Is this to be radicalism?" Smith and his associates worried. "Will this mix us up in politics?"[62] According to Social Gospeler Charles Stelzle, it took a great deal of time and persuasion to convince the organizers to include the social service committees at all.[63]

Once included, however, the Social Gospelers lost no time in attempting to transform the Movement into a platform to convert laymen to Social Gospel activism. They believed—correctly, as it turned out—that men looking for manly church work would respond to their vision of establishing the Kingdom on earth by vigorously reforming the urban environment. As the Social Gospel contingent predicted before the Movement began, "The Social Service Committee of the Men and Religion Forward Movement has an unusual opportunity to demonstrate that Social Service is a vital part of Christianity. It has a chance to enlist in the social work of the church a group of men who have been looking for their kind of 'man's job'."[64] Enthusiastically, radical Social Gospelers like Stelzle and Raymond Robins—who each traveled as a social service "expert" in an M&RFM traveling "team of experts"—threw themselves into the task of directing laymen towards involvement in social service.[65] As Robins put it, "This is the platform I have been waiting for through ten years."[66]

61. Fred B. Smith, *I Remember* (New York, 1936), p. 97.

62. Smith, *I Remember*, p. 93.

63. Charles Stelzle, *A Son of the Bowery* (New York, 1926), p. 154.

64. *Program of Work*, p. 37.

65. On Robins's activities traveling with the M&RFM see Smith, *I Remember*, p. 94; Arthur P. Kellogg, "In Hartford as it is in Heaven," *Survey*, 3 Feb. 1912, pp. 1673–78; "Raymond Robins in Hippodrome," *Survey*, 30 Mar. 1912, pp. 1993–94; "The Forward Movement," *Survey*, 6 Apr. 1912, pp. 37–63. On Stelzle's activities traveling with the M&RFM see Stelzle, *Son of the Bowery*, pp. 111–16; "Campaigning with the Men and Religion Teams," *Survey*, 23 Dec. 1911, pp. 1393–96; Charles Stelzle, "Men and Religion in the South," *Survey*, 6 Apr. 1912, pp. 11–13.

66. Quoted in Gleason, "Going After Souls," p. 14.

Their success exceeded even their own expectations. The Social Gospel did, indeed, enlist churchmen looking for "their kind of 'man's job.'" In nearly every one of the seventy-six cities which held M&RFM campaigns, the activities organized by the Social Service committees far outdrew more traditional activities like evangelism or Bible study. From Los Angeles to Minneapolis, from Little Rock to Hartford, laymen flocked to hear the Social Gospelers' message.[67] By 1913, Social Gospel theologian Walter Rauschenbusch could write of the M&RFM, "The movement has probably done more than any other single agency to lodge the social gospel in the common mind of the Church. It has made social Christianity orthodox."[68]

One reason for this great success was that the Social Service Committees addressed many of the same concerns that had originally led to middle-class men's fears of social effeminacy: cultural upheaval, a consumer economy, threats to class dominance. Working on Social Service Committee projects allowed laymen to resist those threats both as Protestants and as men. For example, local M&RFM Social Service Committees were required to conduct extensive surveys of local conditions before the campaigns. In South Bend, Indiana, for instance, they spent three months compiling information on

> the number of saloons, dance-halls, theatres, burlesque shows, and their character; arrests and convictions of men, women, children, for what causes, under what conditions; detailed, definite statements as to water-supply, sewerage, taxation; condition of bakeries and meat markets; the sanitary condition of tenements, factories, restaurants, hotels; an exhaustive inquiry concerning public schools, playgrounds, libraries; the number of boys and girls at work in shops, stores, factories; wages paid them, and actual cost of living under decent surroundings.[69]

Armed with this new "scientific" knowledge, local Men and Religion Forward activists could move, as men, to take control over their communities by acting on a virile moralism which had nothing to do with the old feminized religion—by closing brothels, working to improve housing regulations, or addressing labor unrest.[70]

Here, finally, was masculine church work[71] more virile and important than "buying a rug for the vestry floor," and churchmen around the country

67. Ellis, "A Movement," p. 985; Rood, "On the March," pp. 646–49; Smith *I Remember*, pp. 97–98; Hopkins, *Rise of the Social Gospel*, pp. 296, 298.
68. Walter Rauschenbusch, *Christianizing the Social Order* (New York, 1913), p. 20.
69. Rood, "On the March," p. 642.
70. See Rood, "On the March," pp. 646–49; Gleason, *Going After Souls*, p. 14; and "Men and Religion: A Review," *Outlook* 100 (1912): 891–93.
71. Ironically, Progressive Era women were claiming precisely the opposite—that this sort of reform activity was especially suited for *women* to do. Frequently, women even addressed the same reforms as the M&RFM, arguing that as "social housekeepers" and as moral mothers, they were peculiarly fitted to close dance halls, protect working-class children, etc.

enthusiastically engaged in this manly work. After the M&RFM campaign in Des Moines, for example, men formed committees to establish a public shelter, to improve conditions in the local jail, and to erect a Labor Temple. In Dallas, they concentrated on reforming garbage collection, inspection of water and milk, and improving communication with labor unions.[72] In several cities, Men and Religion activists focussed their attention on prostitution, sometimes exposing "respectable" citizens who were profiting from "vice." In one midwestern city, M&RFM activists claimed the credit for removing a police chief who was preying on young girls.[73] Of course, all Men and Religion activists did not focus on Social Service work. The M&RFM also inspired committees to encourage prayer meetings, Bible study, and other traditional activities.[74] Nonetheless, as intrigued journalists pointed out, those men who were looking for a new and more "virile" church work could find it in the M&RFM's social service work and in the application of the Social Gospel.[75]

Fred B. Smith himself was converted to the Social Gospel through his work with the Men and Religion Forward Movement. Before participating in the Movement, his main field of work was a strenuous evangelism targeted toward men and conducted through the YMCA. Mildly hostile to the Social Gospel, Smith was at first "embarrassed" when Raymond Robins showed up at an early organizing conference of the Men and Religion Forward Movement, and he tried to think up ways to "dispose of him."[76] But when Smith discovered how effectively the Social Gospel message recruited "More Men for Religion," he began to reconsider his criticisms. By the end of the campaign, Smith was enthusiastically echoing themes raised by Robins and Stelzle. At one Boston M&RFM meeting, for example, Smith went so far as to suggest "many who were listening to him were guilty of 'white slavery'"—horrifying Boston's more conservative ministers, who accused the longtime YMCA worker of being as hotheaded and inappropriate as radical Social Gospelers Stelzle and Graham Taylor.[77] And

---

See Mary P. Ryan, *Womanhood in America* (New York, 1983), pp. 198–210. These women believed women were peculiarly suited to restrain vice in the public sphere, because of the feminine moral mission. Conversely, the M&RFM activists engaged in these same reforms in order to *refute* the notion that women had any such an exclusive moral mission. For a more detailed discussion of ways these opposing views of gender motivated male and female anti-porstitution reformers, see Ruth Rosen, *The Lost Sisterhood: Prostitution in American 1900–1910* (Baltimore, 1982), pp. 52–58.

72. Rood, "On the March," pp. 646–49.

73. Rood, "On the March," p. 648; "Men and Religion," pp. 891–92.

74. "Men and Religion," p. 893.

75. In addition to the above citations, see "Social Service as Vital Christianity," *Literary Digest* 44 (20 Apr. 1912): 814; and Gleason, "Going After Souls," pp. 13–14.

76. Smith, *I Remember*, pp. 93–94.

77. "Men and Religion Movement," *Zion's Herald* (Boston) 90 (Jan. 1912): 120.

in 1914, after the Men and Religion Forward Movement ended, Smith left the YMCA after twenty-five years of service, explaining that his new awareness of the Social Gospel, acquired through his travels with the Men and Religion teams, made it impossible for him to continue his old, individually oriented evangelistic work.[78]

On the one hand, then, the Social Gospelers succeeded in imbuing much of the Men and Religion Forward Movement with their own message of Social Christianity. Yet most of the new Social Gospelers were inspired less by an awakened social conscience than by a search for manly church work to counter the churches' "excessive feminization," It's not surprising, then, that many also opposed the movement for women's advancement. Official Men and Religion Forward publications ignored the woman's movement entirely, as a depressing example of unbridled feminine influence. Indeed, the Woman Question is almost the only major social issue of the day M&RFM literature did *not* mention. The daily newspapers which reported M&RFM activity were full of articles and letters to the editor denouncing the feminists and suffragists. Yet Movement literature is suspiciously, if not deafeningly, silent on those issues. To read only M&RFM publications, one might assume that all Progressive Era women were either Sunday School teachers, mothers, or prostitutes.

Yet in non-Movement publications some M&RFM activists, like Fred B. Smith, condemned the woman's movement in no uncertain terms. In tune with middle-class men's fears of masculine "weightlessness" and effeminacy, they rejected any strengthening of femininity in American society. Smith believed that while men should expand their influence in the churches, expanding women's sphere of influence led only to disaster:

> In greatest numbers the conspicuous poets, musicians, artists, politicians, merchants, generals, have been men. This seems to have been the wisdom of God, for about every departure from this rule has caused unhappy friction. I could write a volume upon the tragedies with which I am familiar concerning the homes of women who have felt it necessary to assume masculine functions. . . . Whatever may be true in exceptional cases, the general fact remains that in a very real sense this is a man's world. . . . [79]

Dr. Gaius Glenn Atkins, a prominent Congregational minister and the "Conservation Committee" chairman of the Providence Men and Religion Forward Movement agreed. In a 1914 sermon on "The Right and Wrong of Feminism," Atkins found more "Wrong" than "Right." Most women belonged in the home, not the workplace or the polling booth, Atkins insisted. Above all, he maintained, the biggest problem with feminists was their unnatural efforts to displace men and to take on masculine attributes. He

78. Smith, *I Remember*, pp. 85–87.
79. Fred B. Smith, *A Man's Religion* (New York, 1913), p. 71.

deplored "the discontent of women with the very facts of womanhood itself," and warned that "We shall gain nothing in the end by displacing manhood by womanhood or the other way around. . . ."[80]

Radical Social Gospel activists like Robins and Stelzle did not share the moderates' fear that women were displacing men, or distrust women's advancement. Robins was married to a national labor reformer and suffrage supporter, Margaret Dreier Robins; he actively supported her work. Stelzle, too, supported suffrage and wider opportunities for women.[81] More moderate Social Gospelers, however, were not as egalitarian as Stelzle or Robins. Washington Gladden, the best known and most popular of Social Gospel ministers, equated the M&RFM's popularization of the Social Gospel with its move to masculinize:

> The conception of the Church and of Religion which finds expression in this movement [which he later defines as the Social Gospel] comes nearer to being sane and adequate than any popular evangelism which I have ever had to do with. It was high time that something should be done to bring men and religion into closer relation. Men needed religion and religion needed men. It was getting to be quite too much the business of women. This movement has done much to redress the lost balance and to restore to the Church the element of masculinity which it sadly needed.[82]

In short, those churchmen who organized the Men and Religion Forward Movement in order to counter the perceived dangers of too much female influence appropriated the Social Gospel to the cause of masculinization, just as the Social Gospelers were able to use the Movement to popularize their own message. Indeed, Gladden's enthusiastic response to the Men and Religion Movement's masculinizing efforts suggests that moderate Social Gospelers suffered from their own masculinization anxieties, despite the more egalitarian stance of radicals like Robins and Stelzle. Thus, the Social Gospel's success in appealing to the mass of M&RFM participants was integrally tied to the Movement's goal of masculinization.

Women's reactions to the Men and Religion Forward Movement as a whole are difficult to assess, since all Movement literature was written by and for men, but scattered evidence suggests most women approved. After all, women's mission had long been to make men better Christians.

---

80. [Gaius Glenn Atkins], "The Right and Wrong of Feminism: A Sermon Preached at the Central Congregational Church, Providence, R.I." (Providence, 1914), pp. 12, 15. For Atkins's affiliation with the M&RFM, see "The Conservation of the Men and Religion Forward Movement," *The Church Messenger* (Providence, R.I.) 21 (1912): 41.

81. Stelzle, *Son of the Bowery*, p. 210.

82. Washington Gladden, "Men and Religion Forward Movement: A Personal Conviction," *Christian Advocate* (Boston) 87 (1912): 369. On masculinization and the Social Gospel, see also Janet Forsythe Fishburn, *The Fatherhood of God and the Victorian Family* (Philadelphia, 1981).

Women's secular and religious organizations had long criticized masculine culture as inimical to women's interest because of male immorality.[83] Not surprisingly, then, many women greeted with delight a movement to make men enthusiastic church members. Women as diverse as Jane Addams, author and social worker, and Evangeline Booth, national commander of the Salvation Army, vocally supported the Men and Religion Forward Movement. Addams, the only woman to publicly participate in the movement, addressed the Conservation Congress on the evils of prostitution.[84] Booth—an evangelical Christian who was rarely one to agree with Jane Addams on anything—also applauded the Men and Religion Forward Movement as evidence that "good by no means lies supine . . . this movement must inevitably work wonders in the way of good."[85]

Other women seemed to have had mixed feelings about the move to masculinize the churches. Perhaps they sensed the churchmen's dislike of woman's advancement without being able to object to the self-evident good of greater male piety. In Providence, for example, a few weeks after the M&RFM campaign, a group of churchwoman dredged up a three-year-old survey on women's church work, and improbably found in it a mandate for a "Church Woman's Forward Movement." The Church Woman's Forward Movement was clearly modeled on the Men and Religion Forward Movement. Like the Men and Religion Forward Movement, it pointed to statistical research as its inspiration. Its slogan, "A Work for Every Woman and Every Woman at Work" mimicked the M&RFM's slogan, "More Men For Religion, More Religion for Men." Yet it was pitifully tiny in comparison, and there is little evidence it garnered much enthusiasm.[86]

And some women objected to old-fashioned feminized piety and called for masculinization, just as the M&RFM did. One Social-Gospel-influenced writer who identified herself only as "A Minister's Wife" complained that feminized churches had degenerated into irrelevant domesticity. Women concentrated on "the domestic type" of church work, like church suppers or bake sales, whereas the real work of the world was "man-made." In order to do important church work, women must study "the

83. See, for example, Epstein, *Politics of Domesticity*, pp. 125–27.
84. Jane Addams, "Challenge to the Contemporary Church," *Survey*, 4 May 1912, pp. 185–90; "Closing Strides in Men and Religion Movement," *Survey*, 30 Mar. 1912, pp. 1992–93.
85. "Spiritual Influence of Women Decreasing—Eva Booth," *New York Times*, 8 Oct. 1911, p. 5. Though she began her career in England, Booth had become the commander of the American Salvation Army by this point.
86. Georgia M. Root, "The Church Woman's Forward Movement," *The Church Messenger* 21 (1912): 76. For a description of the Church Woman's Forward Movement's tepid reception, see "Women's Forward Movement Starts," *Providence Journal*, 12 Oct. 1912, p. 16; "Urge Religion in Social Work," *Providence Journal*, 16 Oct. 1912, p. 9; and "Missionary Conference Held," *Providence Journal*, 19 Oct. 1912, p. 12. The M&RFM's Providence press coverage was considerably more extensive.

business methods employed by their husbands, brothers and sons," and work for justice for the poor. Although the feminization "crisis" had more to do with cultural changes than the activities of actual women, "A Minister's Wife" blamed women personally, believing them "in great measure responsible for the failures of the past":

> While the church is officered and administered by men [she concedes], the pews are largely filled by women. It is the latter whose presence sustains the mid-week meeting, who teach in the Sunday School, and carry on the philanthropic activities. They, in fact, create the atmosphere of the church, and determine its relation to the community. There may be a wholesome though bitter truth in the sentiment of the four hundred young men who met recently to further the Men and Religion Forward Movement: "Women have had charge long enough."[87]

Results of the Move to Masculinize Protestantism

Americans in 1912 disagreed as to whether the Men and Religion movement had been a success or a failure. Boston's *Congregationalist and Christian World*, for example, believed that as a whole, the movement had succeeded: "It has sounded forth from sea to sea the message that religion is for men and men are for religion. It . . . is drafting the masculine strength of the nation for great tasks." But the journal conceded that "Neither before, during nor after the meetings has the main thought of the masculine portion of a community been directed to the things of religion."[88]

Others claimed failure when Census figures showed that the Movement had come nowhere near its goal of finding "3,000,000 missing men." In January 1913 a *New York Times* headline sneered, "Growth of Church Fails to Meet Hopes: Men and Religion Not the Success Expected. . . ." It turned out that in 1912, 15,000 *fewer* people had joined the church than had joined in 1911. In their defense, Movement leaders pointed out that they had always said the proposed increase would take about five years. Still, the drop in new converts during the M&RFM campaign year must have discouraged Movement organizers.[89]

And yet, although the Men and Religion Forward Movement of 1911–12 failed to achieve its organizers' most grandiose goals, it had an impact nonetheless. Within fifteen years, American Protestants had effectively masculinized their churches. By the mid-1920s, although the M&RFM itself had been forgotten, many of its aims had been met. Protestant churchmen had finally collapsed the old opposition between the "male"

---

87. A Minister's Wife, "Woman's Present Opportunity in the Church," *The Church Messenger* (Providence, RI) 22 (1912): 11; reprinted from the June 1912 issue of the *Gospel of the Kingdom*.

88. Quoted in "Net Results for Men and Religion," *Literary Digest* 44 (27 Apr. 1912): 886.

89. "Growth of Churches Fails to Meet Hopes," *New York Times*, 30 Jan. 1913, p. 22.

sphere of commerce and the "female" sphere of religion. Ministers and popular theologians were celebrating Protestantism's businesslike nature. More men were joining the mainline Protestant churches. And in several denominations, women were losing their influence on Protestant church life.

The M&RFM didn't cause this defeminization single-handedly, of course. As we saw earlier, churchmen had been calling for masculinization since the 1880s. In the late nineteenth century, as laissez-faire began to give way to corporate capitalism, and producerism to a culture based on leisure, middle-class Americans lost confidence in a gender system which made "feminine" piety counterbalance "masculine" self-interest. In order to revitalize their religion—which now seemed "effeminate" instead of "feminine"—Protestant churchmen had improvised new ways to align religion with things masculine. For example, they organized the M&RFM. And by the mid-1920s, their cumulative efforts had finally succeeded—the Protestant churches had been masculinized.

According to the 1926 census, the Protestant churches were finally attracting many of the M&RFM's "3,000,000 missing men." In the years following the Men and Religion Movement, the proportion of men in the Protestant churches had increased significantly. According to census figures, in 1906 the Protestant churches, combined, had been 39.3 percent male. By 1926, that proportion had grown 6.4 percent, to 41.8 percent male.[90] Some denominations—especially those with a large proportion of urban, middle-class adherents—had gained even more new men. For example, the proportion of men in Congregational churches grew by 10.9 percent. In the Northern Presbyterian (U.S.A.) churches, male membership was up by 11.2 percent. The proportion of Episcopalian men grew by a whopping 20.8 percent.[91]

In order to definitively explain these statistics, more research into the conditions of each denomination would be necessary. However, their class and cultural position made these churches the most likely candidates for a revolt against Victorian feminized religion. Their members were more likely to be the urban, educated, native-born middle class who, in gaining the benefits of the new corporate world, needed to recast Victorian gender definitions; these were the men who had "discovered" feminized religion as

90. Bureau of the Census, *Religious Bodies: 1906* 1:30–31; Bureau of the Census, *Religious Bodies: 1926*, 2 vols. (Washington, D.C., 1926), 1:82–91. To compute the 1926 figures, I applied the criteria the Census Bureau used in 1906 to define "Protestants," and subtracted Jews, Roman Catholics, Eastern Orthodox, Mormons, and Spiritualists from the aggregate data. Interpreting such aggregate data is difficult. However, since overall American Protestant church growth kept up with or slightly exceeded population, it seems likely that this growth is due to men actually joining the churches, not merely to women leaving them.

91. Computed using Bureau of the Census, *Religious Bodies: 1906* 1:30–31; Bureau of the Census, *Religious Bodies: 1926* 1:82–91.

a problem. Even with these increases, Protestant churches still had more women than men. Yet this significant change in middle-class denominations' sex ratio suggests that the churchmen who had felt the feminization "problem" most severely had, to some extent, succeeded in masculinizing their churches.

Contemporaries noticed these shifts, and some believed the intentional masculinization campaigns had caused this "defeminization." In 1925, Progressive home economist Martha Bruère reported in *Collier's* that for the six largest Protestant denominations, male converts had nearly equalled women converts during the past several years. Ministers all agreed—men were "flocking" to the churches, and due to this awakening male interest, the churches were "in process of becoming defeminized." Bruère believed this "defeminization" resulted from a conscious campaign which began "a dozen years ago" (i.e., 1913 or so). "At the time when there were twice— sometimes three times—as many women as men in the churches . . . the churches died like flies under woman's gentle hand! . . . In the face of this disaster the churches themselves tried to get the men back." And by 1925, church membership statistics showed they were succeeding.[92]

One way Protestants lured men into the churches was by associating religion with masculine leisure activities. "Virtually every denomination was organizing men's clubs, fostering boys' sports, installing bowling alleys and billiard tables when they could get some sort of a club house," Bruère continued. In Missouri, for example, she found "a new baseball league between the neighboring churches," while the constitution of a new Iowa church organization mandated "two baseball games, one field meet, three literary contests and a competitive hunt and clay-bird shoot every year."[93]

The men who came to church for baseball games and field meets were not attracted by manly social service work, as laymen had been during the M&RFM campaigns. Once the churches had been masculinized, popular interest in Social Gospel activism waned, suggesting that from the beginning, most laymen had cared more about masculinization than about social justice.[94] In Atlanta, for example, the social service arm of the Men and Religion Forward Movement remained active through 1916, but it grew increasingly conservative and gradually lost the spirit of the Social Gospel altogether. Between 1912 and 1914, the Atlanta M&RFM worked on prison reform, child labor laws, prohibition, and establishing a home for unwed

92. Martha Bansley Bruère, "Are Women Losing Their Religion?" *Collier's* 7 Feb. 1925, pp. 17, 42. During the 1920s, Bruère published a number of books and articles on a variety of reform and feminist topics, especially in *Survey* magazine.

93. Bruère, "Are Women Losing Their Religion?" p. 42.

94. On the decline of the Social Gospel in the 1920s, see Robert Moats Miller, *American Protestantism and Social Issues 1919–1939* (Chapel Hill, 1958), pp. 17–47; and Paul A. Carter, *The Decline and Revival of the Social Gospel 1920–1940* (Ithaca, N.Y., 1956).

mothers. In 1913 and 1914, they were particularly active in labor issues, vocally supporting unionized textile workers in a lengthy strike against the Fulton Bag and Cotton Mills. During 1915 and 1916, however, the Movement's interests narrowed, until they revolved primarily around the issue of alcohol and prohibition. In late 1916, the Atlanta Men and Religion Forward Movement dissolved itself, requesting the local Minister's Association to form a committee to take over the responsibility of addressing social concerns.[95]

As we saw earlier, many of the M&RFM's converts to the Social Gospel, like Fred B. Smith, had been motivated more by their distaste for feminization than by real enthusiasm for Christianizing the social order. Thus, when laymen became more confident about the church's masculinity, they mostly lost interest in the Social Gospel's reconstructive agenda. In 1912, the M&RFM's Social Gospelers had gained laymen's interest by convincing them that social service committees provided "manly church work," and thus that the churches were not merely arenas for women. Once Protestants succeeded in masculinizing their churches, widespread interest in the Social Gospel evaporated.

In short, despite Rauschenbusch's claim that the Men and Religion Forward Movement "had made social Christianity orthodox," it is more accurate to say that the Social Gospel had helped make middle-class Christianity masculine. Although the M&RFM's masculinizers and its Social Gospel proponents had each tried to appropriate the other's movement, the masculinizers were more successful. In the long run, from the perspective of the 1920s, the Men and Religion Forward Movement was more influential in defeminizing the Protestant churches than as a vehicle of the Social Gospel.

Although by the 1920s popular enthusiasm for the Social Gospel had dissipated, another of the M&RFM's masculinizing tactics had been widely adopted—the move to identify the churches with the manly sphere of commerce. During the 1920s, churchmen extolled Protestantism as the perfect religion for the masculine world of the stock exchange and the corporate boardroom. In *Babbitt*, published in 1922, Sinclair Lewis lampooned the results: the new stereotypical minister "wrote editorials on 'The Manly Man's Religion' and 'The Dollars and Sense Value of Christianity'." He "often said that he was 'proud to be known primarily as a business man' and that he certainly was not going to permit the old Satan to monopolize all the pep and punch."[96]

95. Harry G. Lefever, "The Involvement of the Men and Religion Forward Movement in the Cause of Labor Justice, Atlanta, Georgia, 1912–1916," *Labor History* 14 (1973): 524, 533–34.

96. Sinclair Lewis, *Babbitt* (New York, 1922, 1946), p. 208.

Two years later, Lewis's portrait was echoed—*not* satirically—by Bruce Barton's phenomenal 1924 best-seller, *The Man Nobody Knows*. Barton depicted Jesus Christ as the virile prototype of a prosperous, powerful business executive. In writing the book, Barton intended to refute the old-fashioned, feminized religion he had learned from the "kindly ladies" who had taught him Sunday school. Their Jesus was feminine: "a frail man, undermuscled, with a soft face—a woman's face covered with a beard."[97] The real Jesus, Barton maintained, was precisely the opposite—the epitome of modern masculinity. Barton's Savior was a brawny carpenter with arms muscular from hard physical labor. While the Sunday school's feminized Jesus was sad and meek, Barton's manly Jesus was hearty and popular. Women found him irresistible, and he was in great demand for Jerusalem's dinner parties. Jesus also had a head for business, and the organizational skills to whip his twelve Apostles into a fabulously successful advertising agency which promoted the product of "abundant life" throughout the world.[98] In short, Barton and his followers, like the M&RFM before them, made religion manly by making it an integral part of the business world rather than a restraint to business, as feminized religion had been in the nineteenth century. Yet the degree to which Barton's Jesus was part of the materialist, commercial world exceeded even the M&RFM's businesslike rhetoric, and demonstrates the popular success of the move to masculinize middle-class Protestantism.

Attention in the 1920s' masculinized Protestant churches, then, tended to revolve around men. Religious leaders rejoiced that men were joining the churches in record numbers. Churches incorporated billiards, baseball, and Boy Scout troops. Popular religion had finally collapsed the opposition between masculine business and feminine religion. Protestant men celebrated manly religion's businesslike ethos.

And Protestant women? According to Bruère, "Nobody was bothering about the women and girls. They were safely within the fold and there was no other place for them to go. Anyway, there was more joy over one man who joined the church than over a dozen women. That campaign is now bearing fruit."[99]

97. Bruce Barton, *The Man Nobody Knows: A Discovery of the Real Jesus* (Indianapolis, 1925), p. 43.

98. For an excellent discussion of Barton as an exponent of 1920s therapeutic consumerism, see T. J. Jackson Lears, "From Salvation to Self-Realization," in *Culture of Consumption*, ed. Richard Wrightman Fox and T. J. Jackson Lears (New York, 1983), pp. 29–37. Here too, however, Lears misses the strong gender component of Barton's message. According to Barton's introduction, he wrote primarily in order to set the record straight about Christ's masculinity. He was not merely providing a religious version of "abundant life" and revitalized selfhood; he was creating a *manly* version of God and religion. Barton concentrated on the therapeutic ethos and the consumer economy precisely in order to show Jesus's masculinity. Unlike the false feminized savior, the real Jesus was at home in the world.

99. Bruère, "Are Women Losing Their Religion?" p. 42.

The effect of masculinization on church women needs further study, but if the Presbyterian experience is at all typical, it was devastating. Churchmen disbanded women's organizations; women church leaders lost their authority. Presbyterian women had built up a flourishing and effective network of charitable and missionary groups, and had created effective national coordinating bodies. During the late nineteenth and early twentieth centuries, these bodies had wielded considerable influence.[100] In 1923, however, without consulting women's group leaders, the all male Presbyterian General Assembly disbanded the women's boards and merged them with several men's groups, in the name of "efficiency."[101]

Churchwomen's private responses show that they understood this move—correctly—as a power play designed to increase male control over local women's activities. Women complained of the men's utter failure to consult with them before making this move; of women's lack of equal representation on the new, mixed-sex boards (women were allotted only about one-third of the seats); and of male leaders' propensity to expropriate funds collected by women's groups for their own aims.[102] For the next ten years, women struggled unsuccessfully to regain some independent power in church organizations. Unnerved by the vehemence of women's opposition, male church leaders commissioned an analysis of "Causes of Unrest Among the Women of the Church," but took few effective steps to quiet that unrest.[103] In a masculinized church, women could no longer expect to carve out female organizations with any significant power. Church leaders could finally follow through on the M&RFM's judgment, "the women have had charge of the church work long enough."

In itself, the Men and Religion Forward Movement was a minor movement; it caused a stir for a time, and then was forgotten. But its history illuminates the complex interconnections between gender and culture during the Progressive Era and the way those gendered cultural meanings shaped peoples' actions.

The widespread movement to masculinize religion can only be understood in the context of the earlier move to feminize religion. Religion was

100. Lois Boyd and R. Douglas Brackenridge, *Presbyterian Women in America: Two Centuries of a Quest for Status* (Westport, 1983), p. 35. See also Elizabeth Howell Gripe, "Women, Restructuring and Unrest in the 1920's" in *Presbyterian Church History* 52 (1974). On other denominations' efforts to merge women's missionary societies into men's societies during these years, see R. Pierce Beaver, *American Protestant Women in World Mission* (Grand Rapids, 1980, 1968), 179–201.
101. Boyd and Brackenridge, *Presbyterian Women*, pp. 61–63.
102. Boyd and Brackenridge, *Presbyterian Women*, pp. 63–65.
103. Boyd and Brackenridge, *Presbyterian Women*, pp. 61–75.

originally coded feminine during the early Republic, in order to reconcile Christian morality with the new laissez-faire market economy. When laissez-faire capitalism gave way to a corporate, consumer-oriented economy, the "marriage" between feminine religion and masculine market no longer worked. Protestant religion, which had seemed appropriately feminine before, now appeared uncomfortably effeminate. Neither the theology nor the proportion of women in the churches had changed; nonetheless, Protestant churchmen proclaimed that they had discovered a masculinity crisis within the churches.

Protestants now moved to change the relation between religion and commerce by reshaping constructions of gender. In the new corporate order, feminized religion's restraint of masculine commerce felt stifling. Protestantism's vitality seemed awash in a sea of effeminacy. Therefore, Protestants like the organizers of the Men and Religion Forward Movement took steps to masculinize their religion. They advertised it as strong and virile. They organized it like a modern business. They urged Protestant laymen to assert manly civic authority over social unrest through social service work. They tried to find "3,000,000 missing men." Only by decoding the gendered nature of religion and its place in Victorian middle-class culture can the logic of the masculinizers' strategies and the meaning of their actions become clear.

Although motivated by culturally constructed metaphors, the masculinizers' actions affected men and women of the Protestant church in real and concrete ways. The masculinizers first popularized and then discarded the theology of the Social Gospel in their quest for masculine church work. Church leaders instituted new programs stressing sports and masculine leisure in order to attract men to the churches. Ministers preached "dollars and sense" sermons in order to attract men to the churches. By the 1920s, men were joining the Protestant churches in record numbers. But at the same time, churchwomen were being ignored, and opportunities were dwindling for churchwomen to exercise leadership or power in their denominations. Thus, while some have argued that deconstructing cultural codings of gender only distracts historians from the business of understanding "real women's and men's lives and experience," the history of the masculinization of religion suggests this is a false dichotomy.

The history of the M&RFM and the larger cultural move to masculinize religion suggests the importance of understanding the subtle interrelations between gender, culture, and social change. Cultural historians who ignore the ways definitions of gender underlay constructions of culture risk overlooking important factors that explain social change. Those who ignore the interrelation between moves to transform culture and moves to transform gender risk dire oversimplification. And women's historians who ignore the ways in which men themselves were working to redefine gender risk overlooking significant factors that may have limited women's capacity for self-definition.

CHAPTER 6

"Theirs the Sweetest Songs": Women Hymn Writers in the Nineteenth-Century United States

MARY DE JONG

While Asahel Nettleton, New England's premier revivalist in the 1820s and 1830s, was compiling poems for a new hymnbook, fellow clergyman Lavius Hyde sent four lyrics by his wife, offering, "You may make them better, or leave them out entirely, as you please." A subsequent letter to Nettleton began, "Mrs. H continues to scribble hymns, and that sets me scribbling to you." Enclosing two more poems, the deferential Mr. Hyde, aware that his wife took her writing seriously, requested the return of manuscripts that would not be published. Nine lyrics by Abigail Bradley Hyde were included in Nettleton's *Village Hymns* (1824), which had already been reprinted eight times by 1835, when she thanked him for telling her of the "usefulness" of her contributions. That information was "a cordial to [her] spirit." Often ill, this woman who had borne seven children and buried two sometimes felt like a "useless being," a "cumberer of the ground." It was gratifying to know that her poems furthered the Lord's work.[1] The interaction of this trio—an itinerant evangelist, a woman who had been writing poems and praying for revivals since girlhood, and a settled Congregational minister almost as modest about his wife's abilities as about his own—reflects attitudes that governed hymn writing, editing, and publication.

Many Americans believed in the importance of hymns. Throughout the nineteenth century, hymn singing was credited with soothing, animating, and inspiring powers. Clergymen attributed conversions to hymns; other religious writers attested to their immediate and lasting emotional effects; and literary people joined career and lay evangelists in relating stories of hearts touched, characters formed, and lives transformed by sacred songs. It was widely agreed that the hymnal was "next to the Bible among religious

This essay first took shape in an NEH Summer Seminar, "Women's Writing and Women's Culture," directed by Elaine Showalter. Much of the research was done during a fellowship year at the National Humanities Center.
  1. Letters of Lavius and Abigail Hyde, 13 Nov. [1822 or 1823], 2 Feb. 1824, and 14 Aug. 1835, Nettleton Papers, Hartford Seminary. Information on Abigail Hyde from the Bradley-Hyde Papers, Schlesinger Library, Radcliffe College.

books in its influence over mind and heart."[2] Hymnody—the writing and performance of hymns—informed speech, private writing, devotional and evangelistic publications, and literary art. Protestants read, sang, and recited hymns from memory at every social level and at all manner of public and private occasions. But hymn writing and publication were not equally the prerogatives of both sexes or of both whites and people of color.

This chapter examines the relationship between gender and the production and criticism of hymns. Familiarity with hymnody and hymnology offers scholars of nineteenth-century American Protestantism new perspectives on the interaction between clergymen and women writers, for hymnody manifested clerical power as it channelled and extended "feminine influence." The study of gender and hymnody also enables a better-informed critical approach to nineteenth-century poetry—particularly poems by women, whose culturally mandated investment in religion and morality encouraged hundreds of them to write pious lyrics, often in hymnic meters. For more than a century, hymnologists have remarked on the sweetness and plenitude of "songs from the hearts of women."

The Second Great Awakening of 1790–1835 generated a virtually insatiable demand for lyrics that articulated religious ideals and experience. Hymnody flourished with the antebellum evangelical movement, and popular hymnbooks proliferated rapidly from the late 1860s into the twentieth century. Women writers became increasingly active during the same period. While compiling an anthology of American women's poetry in the late 1840s, Thomas Buchanan Read remarked, "If our country has one great peculiarity, it is in its production of female poets, not in name only, but true children of Song."[3] Literary critics and women poets portrayed "ladies" as natural versifiers. Lyric poets, especially women, were called "singers" and compared with songbirds. Assessing women's writings as qualitatively different from men's, critics characterized the "poetess" as one who records the "graceful, unpremeditated effusions, that come from the heart."[4] This notion of artless expression derived from the cultural construction of feminine sensibility: (white) woman's "heart"—her susceptibility to love, beauty, joy, and sorrow—was considered the essence of her nature and source of her refining influence on man and child. Women's writing and publication of poems about religion, nature, and "the affections" were considered legitimate as long as authorship did not compromise womanly

---

2. Robert S. MacArthur, "Current Literature," *Baptist Quarterly Review* 11 (1889): 398. On hymns' influence see W. R. Goodwin, "Hymns—Their Writers and Their Influence," *Ladies' Repository* 22 (Sept. 1862): 531–34; Elizabeth Stuart Phelps, *The Gates Ajar* (1869; Boston, 1910), p. 34; C. L. Thompson, *Times of Refreshing, Being a History of American Revivals* (Rockford, Ill., 1878), pp. 327, 341–47; Lucy Larcom, *A New England Girlhood: Outlined from Memory* (Boston, 1889), pp. 58–73.

3. Letter of 9 Jan. 1848, Hoadly Collection, Connecticut Historical Society, Hartford.

4. Thomas Buchanan Read, *The Female Poets of America* (Philadelphia, 1849), p. 173.

modesty or interfere with domestic duties. For some middle-class women, versifying was a means of private self-expression or an accomplishment comparable to piano playing. Those who took their poetry more seriously were ambivalent about venturing into the "male" world of fame and literary distinction.[5] The experience of writing and conditions of authorship were somewhat different for women who wrote poems that were used as hymns.

There were two classes of women hymn writers. A few widely known professional authors wrote poems that appeared in formal hymnals—collections of dignified hymns for public congregational worship. Established poets were sometimes asked to contribute to new hymnals; often their poems were simply appropriated. For most literary women, hymn writing was not a vocation.

Poems by a larger, less famous group appeared infrequently in formal hymnals but often in "social hymnbooks"—ephemeral, relatively energetic collections for Sunday schools, revivals, prayer meetings, and family devotions. These poets thought of themselves as hymn writers and were utilized as such by hymn editors and composers. Hymnists of both sexes were not generally evaluated as creative intellectuals or literary artists, in part because of the common ascription of hymns to spiritual experience and divine inspiration. Hymn writing alone did not bring literary fame and rarely led to wide public recognition, for many antebellum hymnbooks did not identify poets; later books commonly named hymnists only in indexes. Poems written as hymns were not always published, but they were assessed with a measure of respect as offerings to God, forms of evangelistic "work," and evidence of the writers' piety.

Other sacred songs were composed orally by amateurs. Individually and communally, African Americans and "plain-folk" whites who attended frontier camp meetings improvised hymns and spiritual songs as they sang. Blacks created their own songs at work and at religious meetings separate from whites. Middle-class women wrote devotional lyrics in their letters and journals and composed them while doing housework or lying on sickbeds.[6] Poems by pious women appeared in literary magazines and newspapers as well as religious periodicals. Between 1800 and 1850, according to Emily Stipes Watts, over eighty American women poets published at least one

5. On women poets and "female poetry," see Cheryl Walker, *The Nightingale's Burden: Women Poets and American Culture before 1900* (Bloomington, 1982), and Emily Stipes Watts, *The Poetry of American Women from 1632 to 1945* (Austin, 1977). This essay also draws on my study of reviews in religious, popular, and literary periodicals.

6. Albert J. Raboteau, *Slave Religion: The "Invisible Institution" in the Antebellum South* (New York, 1978), pp. 67, 243–66; Dickson D. Bruce, Jr., *And They All Sang Hallelujah: Plain-Folk Camp-Meeting Religion, 1800–1845* (Knoxville, 1974), pp. 96, 122 n. 63; H. Wiley Hitchcock, *Music in the United States: A Historical Introduction* (Englewood Cliffs, N.J., 1969), p. 96. Religious lyrics, some of them original, appeared throughout the letters and autobio-

book or appeared frequently in anthologies, and "at least twice that number" published in magazines.[7] Three anthologies of American women's poetry appeared at mid-century: Read's *The Female Poets of America* (1849), Caroline May's *American Female Poets* (1848), and Rufus W. Griswold's *Female Poets of America* (1849). Many religious lyrics appeared in these books, which were repeatedly reprinted, and in other anthologies. I found hymns attributed to 530 women in social hymnbooks published in the U.S. in the nineteenth and early twentieth centuries.[8] But countless songs of prayer and praise were not anthologized or published at all. Most of the lyrics composed by African Americans, singers at camp meetings, and middle-class women were never authorized for congregational singing. Considered as texts alone, the poems in hymnbooks articulate experiences and perspectives approved by white male ministers.[9]

Men, many of them members of the clergy, wrote a large majority of published hymns. Nearly three-fourths (73.7%) of the male poets in *A Selection of Spiritual Songs* (1881), for instance, were identified as clergymen. In a representative sample of seventy hymnals for formal congregational worship published in the U.S. between 1849 and 1917, only 8.7% of the texts are attributed to women, 1.7% to women identifiable as Americans. In seventy social hymnbooks published between 1869 and 1909, 26.3% of the hymns are attributed to women, 13.7% to women known to be Americans. Women hymnists became more visible during the latter half of the century. Their contribution to the formal hymnals in the sample, just 5.9% in the 1850s, increased to 9% in the 1870s and 11.8% in the 1890s. American women's hymns, a mere 0.6% in the books published in the 1850s and 1860s, exceeded 2% during the 1880s. The proportion of women's hymns in social hymnbooks, more popular than formal collections but with less churchly and literary prestige, rose from 20.8% in the 1870s to 30.7% during the first decade of the twentieth century. The representation of women I have identified as Americans, just under 10% during the 1870s and 1880s, exceeded 16% in the 1890s and the first decade of this century. Still, only

---

graphical writings of Mary James; see [Joseph H. James], *The Life of Mary D. James* (New York, 1886), pp. 112, 121, 137, 151. On women who wrote while working or bedridden, see Charles H. Gabriel, *The Singers and Their Songs: Sketches of Living Gospel Hymn Writers* (Chicago, 1916), p. 28, and Samuel W. Duffield, *English Hymns: Their Authors and History*, 10th ed. (New York, 1886), p. 475.

7. Watts, *Poetry*, p. 65.

8. Since information on many of the writers named in social hymnbooks is not available, I cannot say how many of these 530 were Americans, how many were white, or whether there were actually 530 different writers. (Some hymnists used pseudonymns; surnames changed upon marriage.)

9. While accepting the Euro-American, androcentric perspective of the hymn as authoritative, singers could experience personal and communal resonances.

4.2% of the texts in the 140 hymnbooks in my combined samples were attributed to American women.[10]

In a century and a nation noted for female piety, why were so few women represented in hymnbooks? The factors of nationality and timing intersected with sex. Even white male American poets were at some disadvantage—first, because hymns by Britons Isaac Watts (1674–1748), Charles Wesley (1707–1788), and Anne Steele (1716–1778) were canonized in the U.S. by the early 1800s; second, because British literature was generally more prestigious; and third, because British texts, unprotected by international copyright laws, were available to U.S. publishers at no cost. If, as I suspect, there was an unacknowledged quota for hymns by "ladies," lyrics by contemporary Englishwomen Charlotte Elliott ("Just As I Am"), Sarah Flower Adams ("Nearer, My God, to Thee"), and Frances Havergal ("Take My Life, and Let It Be") were available to help fill it. Hymns by Watts and other English divines had special authority in most denominations. Methodists were attached to the texts of Charles and John Wesley (1703–1791), while Lutherans and Episcopalians favored their own church fathers. Many American collections also included hymns translated from the German by nineteenth-century Englishwomen. Examining eighteen major congregational hymnals published in the U.S. between 1826 and 1880, a knowledgeable hymnologist found "about one in seven" of the texts had originated in America.[11]

Collections for congregational use consisted largely of hymns already familiar or revered as classics. Clergymen knew that people in the pews resisted the introduction of new texts and tunes. More lyrics by contemporary women were included in social hymnbooks, whose compilers balanced novelty with familiarity and stood to profit by short-lived "hits." But the proportion of American women's lyrics in popular hymnbooks, especially gospel and Sunday school collections, is greatly inflated by the output of Frances J. Crosby (1820–1915). She wrote as many as nine thousand hymns, of which "at least three thousand

10. The precision of these figures is constrained by problems in attribution and identification. Many texts are unattributed in pre-1870 books, especially social hymnbooks. Authors of attributed texts are usually labeled "Rev." or "Mrs." When only first initials are given, however, it is not always possible to determine whether the poet was a woman; in such cases, I made no assumption about that person's sex. I did not count unattributed hymns as women's even when I recognized them as such, because I am assessing the conditions of authorship for women who wanted to write hymns. In short, I counted women's names. The only exception is the case of Frances J. Crosby, who used numerous pen names. When a hymnbook attributed texts both to Crosby and to her pseudonym "Grace J. Frances," for instance, I counted "Frances's" hymns as Crosby's in order to take her extraordinary productivity into account.

11. Frederick M. Bird, "American Hymnody," in *Dictionary of Hymnology*, ed. John Julian, 2d ed., 2 vols. (1907; New York, 1957), 1:59.

were published"[12]—some repeatedly ("Rescue the Perishing," "Blessed Assurance").

Women had little power in the hymn-publishing industry. American gospel hymns, routinely copyrighted by the late 1860s, were printed as the property of (male) publishers and (usually male) composers. Writers of both sexes received a fee for a religious poem deemed suitable as a hymn— typically a dollar or two, occasionally as much as $6.25.[13] There was no remuneration for donated poems or those used without the writers' consent. Copyright holders reaped the profits from hymns that appeared in many books. Whether or not women were deliberately held to a minority, the process whereby poems were published as hymns must have effectively silenced or muted some women while persuading others to put their poems at the disposal of clergymen and professional editors.

Ida L. Reed (1865–1951) of rural West Virginia believed that God called her to be a hymnist. Tied to the family farm, she struggled to earn a meagre living by mailing packets of hymns and other religious writings to urban publishers. Reed's correspondence reveals that some of her hymns were promptly accepted; others were rejected sooner or later without explanation or helpful suggestions. Editors' comments could be as frustrating as their silence. For a self-educated writer of experiential hymns (she called them "heart-cries to God") who had limited literary resources and professional contacts, it was not easy to learn or to do what editors wanted, given reports like these:

> Try to write more cheerful.
> Am sorry to say I do not find any of them that strike me just right.
> I am sorry that the mass of [your hymns] do not fit into our special needs, so that I find only two that seem to promise usefulness in our publications, for which you will find enclosed our check for $5.00.[14]

Reed's experience reflects women's historical vulnerability to professional men's judgments, a theme Mary Wilkins Freeman explored in her story "A Poetess" (1890). An amateur to whom writing seemed as necessary as breathing and natural as her canary's singing, Freeman's Betsey Dole served communal needs for expression by commemorating deaths in the village. She believed that she was a poet because she desired to write, because neighbors requested occasional poems, and because local papers

---

12. Donald P. Hustad, "Foreword," in *Fanny Crosby Speaks Again*, ed. Donald P. Hustad (Carol Stream, Ill., 1977), p. [2].

13. Hustad, *Fanny Crosby Speaks*, p. [3]; Sandra Sizer, *Gospel Hymns and Social Religion: The Rhetoric of Nineteenth-Century Revivalism* (Philadelphia, 1978), 186 n. 5.

14. Quotations from letters by publishers George F. Rosche (17 November 1893 and 17 March 1896) and the Rev. E. S. Lorenz (18 March 1931), Reed Papers, Barbour County Historical Society, Philippi, W. V. On hymn writing as her calling, see Reed, *My Life Story* (1912), p. 56; on "heart-cries," see p. 196.

printed them. Devastated upon learning that her minister (a "country college" graduate and a magazine poet) denigrated a verse obituary to which she had devoted a day and real tears, Dole lost the "innocent pride" that gave her life meaning. Some hymn editors' qualifications to pass aesthetic judgment on poetry were little more impressive than those of this self-appointed critic who did not realize what his remarks cost an ardent poet. Freeman's character raised a protest never recorded by pious writers like Reed: alone in her house, Dole inquired whether it was "fair" that she had been given the desire but not the talent to write good poetry. Reed, like many hymnists, indicated that some hymns were given to her, either directly, as if by divine inspiration, or through intense experiences beyond her control.[15]

Hymnbook making was subject to men's control. Almost 99% of nineteenth-century American hymnbooks were edited by men or by all-male committees that often consisted largely of ministers.[16] For generations, commentators have reiterated that women are uniquely qualified to write hymns for children.[17] Throughout the nineteenth century, it was British women who received Anglo-American Protestant recognition in that field. (The exceptions were Fanny Crosby and Anna B. Warner, author of "Jesus Loves Me.") Despite the ongoing discussion of women's rights, maternal "nature," and allegedly innate piety, and regardless of the mid-century literati's campaign to create a distinctive national literature, most hymnbook editors in the U.S. made no discernible effort to publish American women hymnists. "The sex" was urged to sing hymns and teach them to children—thus transmitting the Father's words and the fathers' perspectives to the next generation—but not to write them.[18] Men dominated the writing and compilation even of Sunday school hymnbooks. In sixty collec-

15. Mary Wilkins Freeman, "A Poetess," in *Short Fiction of Sarah Orne Jewett and Mary Wilkins Freeman*, ed. Barbara Solomon (New York, 1979), pp. 386, 382, 384. On the composition (or the allegedly instantaneous arrival) of hymns, see Reed, *My Life Story*, pp. 54, 72, 77, 83–87. Emily H. Miller recalled of her hymn "I Love to Tell the Story" that "the words were suggested rapidly and continuously as if I were writing from dictation" (quoted in Francis A. Jones, *Famous Hymns and Their Authors* [London, 1902], p. 278).

16. In a sample of 500 English-language hymnbooks published in the United States in the nineteenth century, six were compiled by women, two by the same individual (*Bibliography of American Hymnals*, ed. Leonard Ellinwood [New York, 1983]).

17. E[mma] R[aymond] Pitman, *Lady Hymn Writers* (New York, 1892), pp. 281–82; Nicholas Smith, *Songs from the Hearts of Women: One Hundred Famous Hymns and Their Writers* (Chicago, 1903), pp. 112–13; Eric Routley, *A Panorama of Christian Hymnody* (Collegeville, Minn., 1979), p. 116.

18. The literary nationalism of "Young America" is examined in Perry Miller, *The Raven and the Whale: The War of Words and Wit in the Era of Poe and Melville* (New York, 1956). For advice to women, see, for example, A. G. Stacy, *The Service of Song: A Treatise on Singing in Private Devotion, in the Family and in the School, and in the Worshiping Congregation*, 2d ed. (New York, 1874), pp. 69–70.

tions for Sunday schools published in the U.S. between 1865 and 1908, 24.2% of the hymns were by women, 12.3% by women identifiable as Americans. American women's contribution rose from 10.3% in the 1860s to 16.1% between 1900 and 1908. Among 301 pre-1900 American hymnbooks designated specifically for children and Sunday schools, twelve (just under 4%) were compiled by women, four by the same person.[19]

Why did clergymen exert themselves to control hymn publication, when they had the prerogatives to determine which hymns would be sung in the sanctuary and to influence hymn singing in other settings? An easy but legitimate answer is that a vast market for hymnbooks developed along with the expansion of evangelical Protestantism and the growth of a national publishing industry. The popular and financial success of Henry Ward Beecher's *Plymouth Collection* (1855) encouraged several commercial presses to publish hymnals.[20] The potential for a widely used book to earn a tidy profit was most significant to publishers, but some late-century composers and editors and a few poets earned livings from hymnody. An industrious clergyman could enhance his prestige and supplement his income by editing a hymnal. By amateurs' accounts, though, compilation was an arduous, time-consuming project, a labor of love and optimism. Many hymns already in print had been condensed, expanded, or otherwise altered by previous editors, so textual variants had to be compared, hundreds of choices made, a version of each hymn settled upon and copied by hand. To increase a congregational hymnal's usefulness and potential popularity, meticulous indexes had to be prepared. In the preface to her *Hymns of the Church Militant* (1858), an anthology for private reading, Anna Warner related, "many times [a] hymn had to be *collected* from various books,—I have had twelve open before me at one time, for one hymn."[21] Unlike most editors, Warner did not expend energy selecting or recommending appropriate tunes. Assisted by a sister and several clerical colleagues, Elias Nason spent more than a year working on his *Congregational Hymn Book* (1857).[22] Co-editing *Hymns for All Christians* (1869), the Rev. Charles F. Deems and his parishioner Phoebe Cary examined more than 20,000 poems "in several languages" in order to select one hundred lyrics for devotional reading.[23]

19. Figures derived from Samuel J. Rogal, comp., *The Children's Jubilee: A Bibliographic Survey of Hymnals for Infants, Youth, and Sunday Schools Published in Britain and America, 1655–1900* (Westport, Conn., 1983). The figure of just under 4 percent is based on my count of books published in English in the U.S. Among British collections, 10% were edited by women.

20. Louis F. Benson, *The English Hymn: Its Development and Use in Worship* (1915; reprint, Richmond, 1962), 474.

21. Anna Warner, *Hymns of the Church Militant* (New York, 1858), p. vi.

22. Elias Nason Papers, American Antiquarian Society, Worcester, Mass., box 3, folders 3, 4, 5; box 4, folder 1.

23. Joseph S. Taylor, ed., *A Romance of Providence: Being a History of the Church of the Strangers, in the City of New York* (New York, 1887), p. 165.

Only a hymnbook that sold exceptionally well paid painstaking editors generously for their time. It is unlikely that members of denominational hymnal committees received any monetary remuneration.

For evangelicals with faith in the edifying, refining, and redemptive powers of song, hymnbook making represented an opportunity to exert constructive influence. Writers who respected those powers and that motive often repeated an old saying: "Let me make the *songs* of a nation, and I care not who makes its *laws*."[24] I contend that the clergy dominated the publication of hymns because a significant number of its members considered hymn writing and hymnbook making too important to leave to laypeople. They regarded hymn singing as an invaluable medium for the expression, inculcation, and propagation of Protestant beliefs. Editorial alteration and restoration of religious poems indicate the desire to fix texts in print and in memory.

Editors were not mere collectors. They solicited new lyrics from established poets and culled uncopyrighted poems from other hymnbooks, poetry anthologies, periodicals, and manuscript portfolios. Most whites who engaged in this process ignored lyrics by nonwhites. Devotional poems passed through a rigorous editorial process before being authorized as hymns. Lyrics were edited to ensure doctrinal, grammatical, prosodic, and ideological correctness, to serve the editors' political interests, and to satisfy their tastes. Idiosyncratic expressions were routinely eliminated; uniquely personal content was obscured.[25]

In the names of propriety and universality, editors avoided content and attitudes not properly religious. They minimized sex-linked imagery and overt indications of the poet's sex—if the imagery or voice was marked as female. Editors' statements of policy and other hymnological documents reiterated that the hymn text must be both "singable" and true to universal Christian experience. The first criterion privileged regularity and conventionality.[26] Practical, moral, doctrinal, and aesthetic considerations (the

24. John Anketell, "A Brief History of Hymnology," *American Church Review* 31 (Nov.–Dec. 1879): 443.

25. By the 1870s, hymns by African Americans, mostly clergymen, appeared in hymnals for black churches (Jon Michael Spencer, "The Hymnody of the African Methodist Episcopal Church," *American Music* 8 [Fall 1990]: 280–86). On the erasure of "individualities" and "idiosyncrasies" see Austin Phelps, Edwards A. Park, and Daniel L. Furber, *Hymns and Choirs: Or, the Matter and the Manner of the Service of Song in the House of the Lord* (Andover, Mass., 1860), p. 247. The cited passage is in Park's chapter.

26. "Singable" occurs in James Warrington, "The Hymnal Revised and Enlarged," *Church Review* 54 (July 1889): 240, and "Church Poetry and Music," *Presbyterian Quarterly Review* 6 (Dec. 1857): 504–5. This ideal is constantly implied in hymn criticism. On the importance of formal regularity, see Lowell Mason (an influential musician and music educator) and David Greene, *Church Psalmody* (1831; Boston, 1866), p. vii; "The Revised Methodist Hymnal," *Methodist Quarterly Review* 61 (July 1879): 523; "Hymns and Hymn-Books," *Christian Examiner* 8 (Nov. 1832): 117.

latter typically class-related) were acknowledged; those implicated in sexual and racial politics usually were not. The criterion of universality actually admitted androcentric language and ethnocentric perspectives while excluding representation of experiences specific to women and people of color. Many texts equated whiteness with spiritual cleanliness. There were hymns for seamen but not seamstresses, for clergymen but not field- or factory-workers, hymns honoring "our [pilgrim] fathers" while proposing to illuminate "pagan darkness."[27] Unstated ideological concerns and psychosexual fantasies motivated editorial treatment of texts that characterized a performer as passively yielding to and resting on Jesus. Editors' attentiveness to sex and gender is revealed by their alteration of texts that explicitly or metaphorically portrayed the performer as female. Some fussed over lyrics that seemed amatory or inappropriately familiar; a few replaced the second word of "Jesus, Lover of My Soul."[28]

Editorial treatment of gender-marked and obviously personal content is illustrated in the initial alterations of poems that Phoebe Hinsdale Brown (1783–1861) and Washington Gladden (1836–1918) had not intended as hymns. Brown stated in her autobiography that her poem "My Apology for My Twilight Rambles," written in 1818, accounted for her habit of walking outdoors at dusk to pray: she had no place of her own in a small house with four young children, an ailing sister, and a husband. Preparing the poem for inclusion in *Village Hymns*, Asahel Nettleton toned down its Romantic appreciation of nature and willing anticipation of death; he excised the maternal reference from the second of these lines: "I love to steal awhile away / From little ones and care." Picked up by other compilers, the simplified version was widely published. Hymnologists approvingly related the story of the Rev. Nettleton's revision of Brown's poem. One remarked that a mother "might well sing" in private of her daily need for a few moments alone with God. In the sanctuary, however, she should "exalt" the lyric, as Nettleton had done, by eliminating the explicit reference to children.[29]

A poem that clergyman Washington Gladden wrote in 1879 became popular as the hymn "O Master, Let Me Walk with Thee" after an editor deleted a stanza that reflected contemporary disputes over theology and congregational polity in Gladden's church. Taking seriously the stated ideal of universality, one might infer that the stanza was cut because it reflected

27. Terms like "heathen," "pagan darkness," "fierce and naked savage," and "our fathers" recurred in missionary hymns. Quotations from *Plymouth Collection of Hymns and Tunes* (New York, 1860), nos. 943, 954, 958.

28. Mary G. De Jong, "'I Want to Be Like Jesus': The Self-Defining Power of Evangelical Hymnody," *Journal of the American Academy of Religion* 54 (1986): 464–69, 481.

29. Phelps, Park, and Furber, *Hymns and Choirs*, p. 213. Brown's original work and explication thereof are quoted in Duffield, 243–45; Nettleton's version is in *Village Hymns* (New York, 1828), no. 285.

public power struggles in which few women or people of color directly participated. It is more likely that the lines were removed because they were unworshipful. (They pointed to spiteful opponents who "taunt" and "hate" and whom "sincere" people cannot trust, and called the multitude "dull.") Whatever the clerical editor's rationale for the deletions, they modulated the remaining stanzas into a prayer with which most singers could identify.[30]

Sex and gender influenced the selection and editing of hymns. Among the few American women whose poems were included in hymnals for formal congregational worship, several had some connection to the editor or a clergyman of some standing or had already been approved by another clergyman-editor.[31] The less prestigious social hymnbooks printed established favorites but introduced more lyrics by contemporary Americans, including hymnists not known as authors. Social hymnbooks consisted largely of conventional, often formulaic gospel hymns by professional and self-defined hymnists. In addition to doctrinal and aesthetic standards, editors' selections were affected by financial and legal considerations: Was a particular lyric copyrighted? If so, who held the copyright—a fellow clergyman or evangelist, a powerful publisher, or a woman? Editors of social hymnbooks usually passed over copyrighted gospel hymns or copied them as they were. Lyrics that appeared in periodicals could be picked up at no cost and, if uncopyrighted, altered at will. On the whole, more extensive changes were made in women's lyrics than in men's.

Why would editors chose relatively few women's poems, only to change them? There were various considerations and several rationales, some of them probably rationalizations. To begin with the obvious, women were not clergymen. Ministers and other editors could readily assume that their brethren better understood congregational needs and the traditions of worship. But the predominance of male authors in hymnbooks was not simply a consequence of sex discrimination and clerical fraternalism.

Most nineteenth-century Americans, observing differences in the sexes' experiences and social prerogatives, assumed that women and men were different by nature. Clergymen were especially protective of women's subordinate status in the church. That (men's) poetry and "female poetry" would differ seemed obvious. Late nineteenth- and early twentieth-century hymnologists spoke of women's lyrics as "heart-songs" that expressed the poets' feelings and experience.[32] One listed "distinctively feminine qualities" in women's hymns: "intuitive spirituality, devout meditation, deep

30. For Gladden's poem and its textual history, see Jacob Henry Dorn, *Washington Gladden: Prophet of the Social Gospel* (Columbus, 1967), p. 155.

31. Examples include Harriet Beecher Stowe, Maria Frances Hill Anderson, Eliza Scudder, Phoebe Brown, and Abigail Hyde.

32. Quotation from Smith, *Songs from Hearts*, p. x. See also Pitman, *Lady Hymn Writers*, p. 162, and Lydia E. Sanderson, "The Contribution of Women to the Hymnody of This Century," *Hartford Seminary Record* 8 (May 1898): 232, 233.

and earnest piety, childlike simplicity, and general grace of form."[33] Like contemporary literary critics, hymn commentators reasoned that women could write for children because they cared for children and that their poems touched readers in general because women were emotionally sensitive. Women sympathized with sorrow and suffering because they had intimate knowledge of both. Accordingly, hymnologists discussed them in separate paragraphs, articles, and books with titles like *Woman in Sacred Song* (1885), *Lady Hymn Writers* (1892), and *Songs from the Hearts of Women* (1903).

The practice of segregation by sex persisted into the second half of the twentieth century. Women have been considered in separate paragraphs or sections and in chapters titled "Hymns Written by Ministers' Wives," "Women Hymn-Writers," "A Group of Gifted Women Hymnists," "The Contribution of Women," and "Women Writers before 1906."[34] Since the 1860s, popular hymnologists have related countless stories about hymns' autobiographical bases. Biographical sketches of women poets often stressed their personal piety, modesty, and pain; women were frequently called "great sufferers."[35] It was even suggested that they were providentially "appointed" to suffer as preparation for their work as hymnists.[36] Commenting specifically on nineteenth-century British women, hymn scholar Eric Routley suggested that some of them accepted the role of minister to domestic misery by compiling such collections as *Invalid's Hymn Book* (1834) and *The Name of Jesus, and Other Verses for the Sick and Lonely* (1861, 1878).[37] Gender may indeed have figured in projects of this

33. Sanderson, "Contribution of Women," p. 234.

34. These chapters appear, respectively, in Ivan H. Hagedorn, *Stories of Great Hymn Writers* (Grand Rapids, Mich., 1948); Eric Routley, *Hymns and Human Life* (London, 1952); E. E. Ryden, *The Story of Christian Hymnody* (Philadelphia, 1959); Hugh Martin, *They Wrote Our Hymns* (London, 1961); and Eric Routley, *A Panorama of Christian Hymnody* (Collegeville, Minn., 1979).

35. This phrase occurs in Pitman, *Lady Hymn Writers*, p. 147; Smith, *Songs from Hearts*, p. 235; and Charles S. Nutter and Wilbur F. Tillett, *The Hymns and Hymn Writers of the Church: An Annotated Edition of the Methodist Hymnal* (New York, 1911), pp. 402, 407, 437. On women hymnists' suffering and disabilities, see also Pitman, *Lady Hymn Writers*, pp. 120, 168, 253; Smith, *Songs from Hearts*, pp. 50, 91, 146; and Wilbur F. Tillett, *Our Hymns and Their Authors: An Annotated Edition of the Hymn Book of the Methodist Church, South* (Nashville, 1892). The tradition continued with Amos Russell Wells (1862–1933), whose hymnological articles were collected in Wells, *A Treasure of Hymns: Brief Biographies of One Hundred and Twenty Leading Hymn-Writers with Their Best Hymns*, (1945; reprint, Freeport, N.Y., 1971). Pitman, Sanderson, and Routley treated British and American women separately, but several nineteenth- and twentieth-century generalizations about women hymnists as a whole derived from Victorian hymnologists' selection of and commentary on British women. I do not doubt that women hymnists as individuals or as a group suffered or that certain illnesses and disabilities were compatible with, even conducive to, hymn writing. But I believe that post-Victorian hymnologists have modelled their sketches of women on the sentimental and evangelical pattern of the great (female) sufferer.

36. Quotation from Pitman, *Lady Hymn Writers*, p. 168; see also Wells, *Treasure of Hymns*, p. 59.

37. Routley, *Panorama*, p. 116.

kind. American gospel hymnist Eliza E. Hewitt (1851–1920), noted by popular hymnologists for writing hundreds of hymns and enduring a prolonged spinal disease, co-edited with a clergyman-publisher a book of religious lyrics called *Looking Sunward: Rays of Light for Darkened Rooms* (1895). To verify Routley's thesis, however, it would be necessary to determine how many men engaged in similar work and inquire whether there were significant correlations between invalidism, gender, and the writing and editing of hymns.

Two hypotheses emerge from a survey of hymnological discourse: first, hymnologists of the nineteenth and early twentieth centuries anticipated the current feminist position that women's writing reflects female experience and perspectives; and second, the individuals who edited and commented on hymns valued women's lyrics for their "female" characteristics. Close inspection of hymn criticism and edited hymns confirms that the first hypothesis is tenable, which is not to say that hymnologists advocated equal rights and privileges for both sexes. The second hypothesis is problematic.

Late-century champions of women hymnists, stressing women's emotionality and subjectivity, urged that their work was distinctive and worthy of recognition. Emma Pitman, author of *Lady Hymn Writers*, complimented them for not making "a trade" of hymn writing, as men had done. According to Pitman, most women's hymns were "composed under the pressure or stimulus of very special emotions"—which might explain why "so many are loved and remembered as household words," even though women wrote "comparatively few hymns."[38] Lydia E. Sanderson, contrasting general characteristics of men's and women's hymns, stated that women "dwelt more naturally" on the "gentler aspects" of Jesus, whereas men portrayed him as a powerful, relatively remote figure, a leader and hero.[39]

Yet in 1901 a male contributor to the *Methodist Review* exclaimed, "[H]ow few hymns have dealt adequately with [Christ's] humanity! We have had much about his meekness, patience, sufferings; how little about his manliness and strength!"[40] Such impressions of difference, sufficiency,

---

38. Pitman, *Lady Hymn Writers*, p. 140. More accurately, hymnals *published* comparatively few lyrics by women.

39. Sanderson, "Contribution of Women," pp. 233–34. Sanderson finally stated that the qualities she located in women's hymns "may be found among both men and women" (p. 234); in my judgment, she exaggerated general differences. Both sexes wrote hymns about the warrior Christ and the meek Jesus. Some commentators have perceived a tone of resignation in nineteenth-century women's hymns. (Surrender to God, it should be noted, was the orthodox expectation of both sexes.) But in her 1884 preface to *Woman in Sacred Song: A Library of Hymns, Religious Poems and Sacred Music* (Boston, 1885), editor Eva Munson Smith remarked that "recent hymns" by women portrayed "an aggressive warfare" on behalf of social reform (p. vii).

40. Frederic L. Knowles, "Hymns As Literature," *Methodist Review* 61 (Nov. 1901): 908. For comments on women hymnists' emphasis on Jesus, see also Eva Munson Smith's Preface to *Woman in Sacred Song*, [vi], and Nicholas Smith, *Hymns Historically Famous* (Chicago, 1901), p. 234. Whether such impressions would be confirmed by statistics remains to be determined. Nineteenth-century hymnody as a whole was Christ-centered.

and appropriateness are influenced by gender ideology and personal experience. Most published hymns were written and authorized by men; empirical research also reveals that many male hymnists depicted a gentle Jesus. Whether or not Sanderson's generalizations about female and male visions of Christ are accurate (which is possible, although her "dwelt more naturally" must be questioned), the *Review* contributor's discomfort with the feminization of Jesus illuminates gender's effect on the perception of hymns and, more generally, on the assessment of women's presence, success, and influence in enterprises in which both sexes participate. Gospel hymns starring the warrior Christ and male Old Testament heroes multiplied during the late nineteenth and early twentieth centuries; these interacted with the movement for a more "masculine" Christianity and with U.S. imperialism in America and abroad.[41]

Most hymnologists of the mid and late 1900s avoid sentimentality and pathos. While some react against the Victorian stereotypes of man and woman, others uncritically perpetuate the questionable notions that nineteenth-century women poets as a group were exceptionally frail and that their hymns (as published) were distinctive. In 1952, Routley explicitly justified his separate chapter about women hymnists on the ground that most of them "segregate[d] themselves by their subject-matter and style." "Theological, outward looking" (male) hymns were not their forte. They "specialized in hymns of personal devotion"; they wrote and compiled religious poetry for sick people because many were in poor health themselves.[42] Re-presenting Victorian commonplaces and commonplaces about Victorianism under a wrapping of historical knowledge, Routley stated in 1979 that, since most women hymnists in nineteenth-century England were members of the bourgeoisie, their lives were "totally different" from men's; spending most of their time in the domestic sphere, they did not address social issues. Though bourgeois women had "time to nourish" the imagination, most women's hymns "lack[ed]" that "faculty."[43]

Victorian, sexist, and feminist assumptions that women's religious poems as a group would be different from men's must be interrogated. In hymns, the issue of sex differences is triply complicated.

41. De Jong, "'I Want to Be Like Jesus,'" pp. 475–78.
42. Routley, *Hymns and Human Life*, p. 204.
43. Routley, *Panorama*, p. 116. Without defining "imagination," he says it is present in the hymns of Charlotte Elliott and Sarah Flower Adams. Middle-class women in Britain and the U.S. did not necessarily have "time," incentives, or preparation to produce the kinds of writing that were regarded as literature. As for Routley's remark about ladies' remoteness from social problems, British and American women writers campaigned against slavery, advocated women's rights, and published many temperance songs, some of which appeared in American social hymnbooks.

First, it was men who selected and edited texts, which goes far to account for the surface-level "sexlessness" apparent to some readers today.[44] Poems published in hymnbooks generally bore no obvious gender markers except, significantly, their authors' names. Women's religious activities were defined by gender. But as a recent researcher in nineteenth-century American gospel hymns points out, both sexes' evangelistic hymns reflected and helped to propagate "a more humanized, subjective view of God" than Calvinism had promulgated.[45] My conclusion, based largely on hymns published in the nineteenth-century U.S., is that commentators have overstated the dissimilarities between men's and women's hymns. A thorough comparison of nineteenth-century American women's and men's religious lyrics must draw on manuscript sources, which are not plentiful.[46] Such a study must recognize that the vast majority of texts in hymnbooks reflect the criteria of men, mostly clergymen. Like hymn writers and editors, most hymnologists—the critics of hymnic literature—have been men. They could emphasize, blur, or obliterate differences between male and female hymnists. Whereas textual editors have elected to minimize obvious or detectable differences, hymnologists have generally chosen to emphasize them.

Second, in prefaces, reviews, and essays, hymnologists specified their ideals of hymnic form, style, content, and "voice": metrical regularity, lyrical smoothness, sincerity, universality, humility, and a certain amount of subjectivity (though the proper extent and value of the last-named quality provoked debate). Aspiring hymnists of both sexes were capable of learning and, if they chose, observing those standards. Women's increasing representation in late-century social hymnbooks demonstrates their ability to satisfy editors.

Third, social constructionist theory would indicate that differences in men's and women's hymns as originally composed were not based in innate physiological or psychological traits but in culture. Editors' and critics' socially constructed preconceptions of "female poets" affected their treatment of women's manuscripts and texts. While selecting, editing, and evaluating religious lyrics, they considered who the poets were as well as what they wrote, interpreting the latter in light of their own concepts of gender.

To study hymn editing I assembled textual histories of twenty-one hymns by nine women and nine men with comparable credentials as

44. Samuel J. Rogal sees hymns as "sexless" (*Sisters of Sacred Song: A Selected Listing of Women Hymnodists in Great Britain and America* [New York, 1981], p. xi).

45. Esther Rothenbusch, "The Joyful Sound: Women in the Nineteenth-Century United States Hymnody Tradition," in *Women and Music in Cross-Cultural Perspective*, ed. Ellen Koskoff (New York, 1987), pp. 179–181.

46. The Nettleton Papers at Hartford Seminary include manuscripts of several poems edited for inclusion in *Village Hymns*.

poets.[47] Comparing at least ten hymnal appearances of each of these poems with the forms published by their authors, I found variants of seventeen of these hymns—changes ranging from the alteration of a single word to omission of one or more stanzas to substantial remodelling. To illustrate how gender figured in the reception and editing of women's hymns, I present textual histories of selected hymns, focusing on cases that yield suggestive and revealing comparisons.

Harriet Beecher Stowe's devotional poem "Still, Still with Thee" was published in six stanzas in *The Independent* in 1852 and in her *Religious Poems* (1867). Her brother Henry Ward Beecher reproduced it in his *Plymouth Collection* (1855). But five of the ten hymnbooks that picked up the lyric between 1857 and 1905 omitted two or three stanzas, and only two followed Stowe's text exactly.

"O Love Divine, That Stooped to Share" by Oliver Wendell Holmes was first published by the *Atlantic Monthly* in 1859 as part of "The Professor at the Breakfast-Table." The only male poet in my textual sample who was not a clergyman or licensed preacher, Holmes was an established author at the time his poem entered the hymnic domain. Nine of fourteen hymnals published his text intact; three altered a single word (it bothered them that Holmes's speaker "flings" burdens upon God); one editor omitted one of his four stanzas. A contemporary clergyman-hymnologist remarked of Holmes's religious lyrics that "what they may lack in fervor they make up in poetry—a feature in hymns which cannot be safely despised."[48] Literary critics who patronized women poets often remarked that they expressed appropriate emotions, but their poetic vehicles were flawed. The quoted comment about Holmes, read in the context of contemporary literary criticism, illustrates how an aesthetic consideration—a text's merit as

---

47. The poets and first lines of the hymns in my sample: Phoebe Hinsdale Brown, "I love to steal awhile away"; Phoebe Cary, "One sweetly solemn thought"; Frances J. Crosby, "Pass me not, O gentle savior"; Annie Sherwood Hawks, "I need Thee every hour"; Abigail Bradley Hyde, "Say, sinner, hath a voice within" and "Dear Saviour, if these lambs should stray"; Elizabeth Payson Prentiss, "More love to Thee, O Christ"; Harriet Beecher Stowe, "Still, still with Thee, when purple morning breaketh"; Anna B. Warner, "We would see Jesus"; George Washington Bethune, "There is no name so sweet on earth"; Arthur Cleveland Coxe, "How beauteous were the marks divine"; George Duffield, Jr., "Stand up, stand up for Jesus"; Joseph H. Gilmore, "He leadeth me! O blessed thought"; Washington Gladden, "O Master, let me walk with Thee"; Oliver Wendell Holmes, "O Love divine, that stooped to share"; Ray Palmer, "Jesu, Thou joy of loving hearts," "Jesus, these eyes have never seen," "My faith looks up to Thee," and "Take me, O my Father, take me"; Sylvanus Dryden Phelps, "Saviour! Thy dying love"; and William B. Tappan, "'Tis midnight, and on Olive's brow."

A tally of verbal changes in men's and women's poems does not reveal the nature and extent of editing. Some alterations changed sound, level of formality, or tone; some, meaning; some changed two or more of these features. The poems of Brown, Cary, and Coxe were subjected to various and substantial revisions; some editors of Cary and Coxe melded two originally separate stanzas.

48. Duffield, *English Hymns*, p. 426.

poetry—could be weighted differently depending on gender and genre. Fourth in a familial line of Presbyterian clergymen, this hymnologist evidently took into account that Holmes was a Unitarian and a poet. (To evangelical Protestants, denominations and sects that rejected revivalism were deficient in "fervor.")

Stowe was not known primarily as a poet, but her credentials as an evangelical writer had been established by the early 1850s. Morever, she had many connections in literary and churchly circles. "Still, Still with Thee" appeared in poetry anthologies and hymnals that maintained high literary standards—for instance, the Unitarian *Hymns of the Spirit* (1864). Yet her lyric was subjected to more extensive alteration than Holmes's. The reasons for different treatment cannot be known with certainty, but the operative factors seem to have been the poems' length and the poets' sex and occupation.

Anna Warner, recognized in her own time as a hymnist and compiler, was thoroughly familiar with the hymn as a genre.[49] She published "We Would See Jesus" in her novel *Dollars and Cents* (1852) and in *Hymns of the Church Militant* (1858). The lyric consisted of seven four-line stanzas. Each of the ten nineteenth-century hymnals in my textual sample deleted at least one stanza (all omitted the one that includes these words: "our souls have many a billow breasted"); seven editors cut three. In addition, nine editors changed between one and eight words; these alterations, apparently made to satisfy the editors' ears, did not substantively change the poem's meaning, but one sacrificed an exact rhyme for no gain in clarity or singability.

George Washington Bethune's "There Is No Name So Sweet on Earth," first published as a hymn in 1861, has a comparable textual history. Bethune's status as a clergyman and the author of *Lays of Love and Faith* (1847) did not protect his poem. Nine of ten hymnal editors omitted two of the six stanzas (always the two whose inverted word order compromised clarity); one deleted three stanzas. Seven editors also changed an adverb in order to portray God as ruling "ever" rather than "gladly." (They probably reproduced a common source.) Whether "There Is No Name" was originally composed as a hymn is unknown, but editors' alterations indicate that they found the whole somewhat long and certain passages awkward for group performance. Editorial considerations in the cases of the Warner and Bethune lyrics seem to have been identical (length, clarity, euphony, and propriety), but there was more, and more varied, small-scale tinkering with the woman's poem.

During the nineteenth century, congregations discontinued the practice of singing every stanza of long hymns. Social hymnbooks routinely omitted

49. Mary De Jong, "The Warner Sisters and Authorship: 'Special Work for Us to Do,'" in *Seventy-Fifth Annual Report*, Constitution Island Association (West Point, N.Y., 1991), 19–22.

stanzas even of classic texts. Editors reasoned that curtailing lengthy hymns made room for more numbers in each collection, potentially widening its appeal. For late-nineteenth-century editors, then, length was a legitimate practical concern.[50] As the foregoing hymn histories testify, however, editors also felt entitled to correct poets' vocabulary—especially, perhaps, when the poets were not clergymen.

Another likely influence on editorial choices was the widely shared perception that women were more loquacious than men and had less mental discipline. Literary critics reiterated that they tended to needless verbosity. Carefully distinguished from poets, poetesses were gallantly praised and patronized for artlessness. Critics who claimed to serve art withheld from most women "the sacred name of Poet," for the poetess of cultural myth did not stop to reflect or revise (some suggested that she was capable of neither), and she published too many unfinished effusions.[51] This early and mid-century paradigm of female poetic genius reflected the prevailing ideology of gender, which constructed women as essentially more subjective than men and weaker in intellect and concentration. Women were said to be naturally intuitive, sensitive, and religious; they learned quickly but were not analytical or deep. Satisfying as this formulation may have been for literary gatekeepers and compilers of sacred poetry, it left thoughtful observers with a question: Why were women, so vocal as "singers," so inconspicuous as hymnists? Another query promptly arose: What did women's poems lack?

In 1857 a contributor to the *Presbyterian Quarterly Review* bluntly stated that "very few good hymns have been written by women." One would have expected otherwise, considering their evident piety, emotional "warmth," and "delight" in congregational worship. The *Presbyterian* could explain. Great hymns are distinguished by "breadth or massiveness in handling," which enables them to "upbear the devotion of multitudes." Women did not write such lyrics.[52] The few women's hymns in common use were "plaintive and penitential." (Reviewers in mid-century literary magazines commented on the sadness, "misery and anguish" in contemporary women's poetry.)[53] It might be expected that the renowned British poets

50. Richard Storrs Willis, author of *Our Church Music: A Book for Pastors and People* (New York, 1856), justified the deletion of stanzas (see pp. 115–16). In *The Psalmody of the Church: Its Authors, Singers, and Uses* (Chicago, 1889), William H. Parker denied editors' right to make such choices for clergymen and congregations (p. 14).

51. Quotation from a review of *Passion-Flowers*, by Julia Ward Howe, *Knickerbocker Magazine* 43 (April 1854): 353. See also H[enry] T. T[uckerman], "Passion Flowers," *Southern Quarterly Review* 26 (July 1854): 180–91.

52. "Church Poetry and Music," pp. 510, 509. Sanderson expressed a similar view ("Contribution of Women," p. 233).

53. Quotation in parentheses from "Alice Cary," *Graham's Magazine* 48 (April 1856): 332. See also discussions of Cary's *Poems* (1855) in "Recent American Poetry," *Putnam's Magazine* 6 (July 1855): 48–51, and *North American Review* 80 (April 1855): 537–38.

Felicia Hemans (1793–1835) and Elizabeth Barrett Browning (1806–1861) would have written effective hymns. "But their poetry is too *recherché*; the imagination, or the fancy, is rather individual than general, and there is a want of that massiveness that fits a poem for popular use, just as a woman would be delightful in conversation but out of place as an orator."[54] Like many men who enforced literary standards, this commentator assumed that women's expression was not strong, their themes not universal. Hence their poems were found wanting.

Nineteenth-century literary, theological, and medical theorists took sex differences for granted or explained why they were inevitable. According to Charles D. Meigs, specialist in midwifery at the University of Pennsylvania, women lack the intellect and "poetic vision" to write with the "strength" of Milton and Shakespeare: "Such is not woman's province, nature, power, nor mission."[55] These remarks predated gospel hymnody, in which women more actively participated as poets and composers. Ida Reed and other late-century lay evangelicals could justify the writing of gospel hymns as their "mission." Meanwhile, clergymen who maintained hierarchical standards declared that gospel hymns "do not belong to legitimate hymnody at all, any more than the effusions of negro minstrelsy belong to poetry."[56]

A similar delimitation of female genius, with the trappings of logic and academic authority, was reinscribed in 1908 by a scholarly educator with three degrees. Analyzing the "psychology" of Protestantism as expressed in hymns, Charles W. Super noted that only 85 out of "about 750" texts in the Methodist hymnal of 1905 were attributed to women. (Had he examined *Gospel Hymns Nos. 1–6 Complete* [1894], he would have found over one-fourth of its 739 texts attributed to women.) "This proportion must be considered remarkable when we take into account that more than one-half of the verse in our current periodical publications is by women." He inquired, "How shall we account for the paucity of female contributors, seeing that women are more emotional than men and the great interest they take in the affairs of the churches?" Super had his answers ready. "Although more emotional by temperament and more demonstrative, their emotions are less profound" than men's, for they rarely commit suicide. Women's attachment to their children, which dissuades them from self-destruction, perhaps also "hinders the[ir] complete immergence into the religious feelings. It is also probable that the power of concentration is less in women than in men." Ignoring the probability that domestic responsibilities hinder

54. "Church Poetry and Music," p. 510. Lyrics by Hemans did appear in nineteenth-century American hymnals and social hymnbooks.

55. Meigs, *Woman: Her Diseases and Remedies* (1851), quoted in Paula Bennett, *Emily Dickinson: Woman Poet* (New York, 1990), pp. 150–51.

56. Rothenbusch, "Joyful Sound," pp. 182–91; quotation from Frederick M. Bird, "Sentimentalism in Hymns, New and Old," *American Church Review* 30 (1878): 217.

concentrated thought and composition, he concluded his paragraph on women and hymns with this assertion: "That [their] education has generally been inferior to that of men cannot have had much weight."[57]

Super's last word on women as "contributors" to hymnody needs qualification. It is true that an extensive formal, classical, or even bookish education was not a prerequisite for writing experiential or evangelistic lyrics. In my sample of 37 widely published women hymnists born in the U.S. between 1783 and 1865, one of the latest-born went to college; eleven attended a female seminary, normal school, or high school; the rest were educated at home. On the other hand, more women might have become authors and called themselves hymnists if both sexes had equal access to colleges, theological seminaries, and knowledgeable tutors who respected their abilities. Women who wanted to write hymns would have been likely to perceive hymn writing, like preaching, as normally a male prerogative. The fledgling nation's educational resources and derivative literary traditions were not conducive to American women's early emergence as hymnists. Privileged women in Britain had easier access than most of their American counterparts to instruction and practice in languages—notably German, with its wealth of hymns and Romantic lyrics. The Romantic movement and influence of German Romanticism reached the U.S. by way of Britain. Several British women secured places in American hymnals as translators of continental hymns.

For literary foremothers and sisters who wrote religious poetry, women in Britain could look to Elizabeth Singer Rowe (1674–1737), Felicia Hemans, Elizabeth Rundle Charles (1828–1896), and Adelaide Procter (1825–1864) and to poets known specifically as hymnists.[58] Anne Steele's hymns were canonized by British Nonconformists from the late 1700s and by American evangelicals throughout the 1800s. Steele was represented in 69 of 70 nineteenth-century American congregational hymnals I consulted, averaging over 18 texts to a collection. By mid-century, many Americans admired Connecticut's Lydia Sigourney (1791–1865) for her charitable and literary activities. Her poems appeared in religious and popular periodicals, literary annuals, poetry anthologies, collections of her own writings, and hymnals (including 37 of the same 69 books that included Steele, and averaging just over two texts per hymnal). But I have seen no evidence that American women who wanted to write hymns took Sigourney as a model. When Prof.

57. Charles W. Super, "The Psychology of Christian Hymns," *American Journal of Religious Psychology and Education* 3 (May 1908): 7–8. Biographical information from *Who Was Who in America*, vol. 1, 1897–1942 (Chicago, 1943), p. 1206.

58. On successful eighteenth- and nineteenth-century British women poets, see Marlon B. Ross, *The Contours of Masculine Desire: Romanticism and the Rise of Women's Poetry* (New York, 1989). See also Margaret Maison, "'Thine, Only Thine!' Women Hymn Writers in Britain, 1760–1835," in *Religion in the Lives of English Women, 1760–1930*, ed. Gail Malmgreen (Bloomington, Ind., 1986), pp. 11–40.

Super, president of Ohio University, dismissed education as a cause of women's underrepresentation in hymnbooks, he neglected to consider that privileged British women preceded—in effect, preempted—their American cousins as poets and specifically as hymnists. Nor did he recognize that the predominance of white male poets in American collections epitomized the hymnal-making process.

To put nineteenth-century generalizations on women's emotionality and intellectual resources in perspective, it is helpful to turn once more to the literary world's reception of women poets, for Presbyterian, Congregationalist, and Episcopalian ministers considered themselves literary men; and by the late 1800s so did Methodists and Baptists. Denominational journals and religious periodicals reviewed current literature; literary magazines, some edited by clergymen, reviewed religious books. The *Knickerbocker Magazine*'s 1854 review of a book of poems by New York native Julia Ward Howe includes some enlightening remarks. According to this Romantic critic, poetry is the "expression of the innermost of thought and feeling." The "inner-life" is "the source and scene of [a woman poet's] genius. Into her poems the personal element enters far more largely than into those of men. . . . [Women's] poetry is eminently subjective." Commenting on the celebrity of Elizabeth Barrett Browning's *Aurora Leigh* (1856), a verse novel with a poet-heroine, the editor of a Charleston literary magazine generalized, "No woman has yet created in literature a woman free from the alloy and restraints of her own individuality."[59] Again, the notion that women could only exude themselves. Browning and Howe were less reticent and "sweet" than most contemporary women poets. American reviewers who noted defects of art in Howe's poetry sometimes complimented her, rather gingerly, for passionate sincerity. But she was advised to overcome "the purely private cast of her song." *Putnam's Magazine* pontificated, "The poet is not a poet until he has mastered in his verse the emotion which mastered him in life."[60]

The expectation that women's poems world be wordy and highly subjective undoubtedly influenced hymn editors' selections. To complete this assessment of textual editing, it is necessary to inquire more closely whether two important—and, as we have seen, gender-related—criteria, length and subjectivity, were applied in specific cases. Phoebe Brown's poem "My Apology for My Twilight Rambles," mentioned earlier, was both lengthy and overly personal by hymnological standards. The defeminized lyric was widely approved for congregational performance. But even poems that satisfied hymnologists' stated criteria did not always escape alteration.

59. Review of *Passion-Flowers*, p. 357; "Editor's Table," *Russell's Magazine* 3 (Apr. 1858): 82.

60. Review of *Words for the Hour*, by Julia Ward Howe, *Putnam's Magazine* 9 (Feb. 1857): 220.

Professional hymnist Fanny Crosby's "Pass Me Not, O Gentle Savior," a prayer that might be uttered by any Christian or would-be Christian, consisted of just four four-line stanzas. It was copyrighted by her publisher. Nevertheless, four of ten nineteenth-century editors changed a line or omitted a stanza.

Men's poems were altered, too, even when professional courtesy might have arrested the editorial scalpel. The Rev. Sylvanus Phelps, who had published sonnets in *Graham's Magazine* and lyrics in religious periodicals, wrote "Savior, Thy Dying Love" as a hymn. A poem of four eight-line stanzas, it was copyrighted in 1871 by a New York publisher who specialized in Sunday school and gospel hymns. In seven out of 12 later collections, one ambiguous preposition in Phelps's lyric was replaced. By rewording a line that paraphrased the opening of the classic hymn "My Faith Looks Up to Thee," two late-century editors eliminated the allusion. The poet himself had authorized this unfortunate change in his revision of the text published in *Baptist Hymn Writers* (1888).[61] Clerical status and a hymnologist's cooperation enabled Phelps to fix his own text.

Phoebe Cary's experience in attempting to establish her preferred version of "One Sweetly Solemn Thought" was different. Not composed for congregational singing, the lyric prays for faith during the passage from mortality into eternity. In it, the speaker is chilled at the prospect of death, which may be "nearer than I think." The poem is metrically irregular, and it employs some unusual terms. Published in Cary's *Poems and Parodies* (1854), it was picked up—with numerous and various alterations—in nineteenth-century formal hymnals, social hymnbooks, magazines, poetry anthologies, and parlor songbooks. According to the authors of *Hymns and Choirs* (1860), an authoritative (and authoritarian) treatise, the poem was already extant "in at least four different forms." Though the lyric was "exquisite," the authors continued, it "must be either excluded from the songs of the sanctuary, or must be divested of its original rythmic [*sic*] inequalities." *Hymns and Choirs* presented in parallel columns Cary's "original form" and the tranquilized, regularized version that appeared in the *Sabbath Hymn Book* (1858), a collection edited by the same theologian-hymnologists who co-authored *Hymns and Choirs*. They remodelled Cary's heart-song of seven stanzas into a hymn with five stanzas. Besides standardizing the meter and removing unfamiliar expressions ("the dark abysm," "the awful chrysm"), these editors introduced two references to Jesus (Cary spoke only of and to "my Father"). They subdued the original poet-speaker's awe.[62] Emily Dickinson would not have been surprised to discover

61. Henry S. Burrage, *Baptist Hymn Writers and Their Hymns* (Portland, Me., 1888), pp. 387–88.
62. Phelps, Park, and Furber, *Hymns and Choirs*, p. 265. For further commentary on the alleged necessity of altering Cary's poem, see Edwin T. Hatfield, *The Poets of the Church*

that the version endorsed by *Hymns and Choirs* was singable and almost ordinary. Other hymnals published other versions departing in varying degrees from the original. Of the three books in my textual sample published in 1869 or earlier, none reproduced the text in Cary's *Poems and Parodies,* and each one was different.

Hymns for All Christians (1869), a collection without music edited by Cary and her pastor, included a six-stanza revision of the poem with a headnote announcing that "the author desires the following [text] to be considered hereafter her authorized version."[63] This text was not regular, either, though by 1869 Cary was aware of the expectations for congregational hymns. She stood by her poem intended for private devotional use. But only one of the seven post-1869 hymnals in my textual sample accepted her "authorized" text. Among the other six late-century versions in my sample, no two were alike, and one introduced a "chorus" (refrain).

Reduction of a hymn's length, copyright notwithstanding, was evidently a primary motive of editors who cut the lyrics of Crosby and Phelps. Cary's uncopyrighted poem raised, and therefore illustrates, more complex considerations. Editors who found the poem attractive proceeded to reduce its idiosyncrasies and temper the emotional intensity that had probably attracted them in the first place. As if aware that Cary had been a Universalist, some editors reworked this lyric into an appeal to Jesus as redeemer and intercessor. (Universalists rejected the concept of hell. For most orthodox Protestants, heaven was accessible only because Jesus had atoned for sin and would serve as Christians' advocate with the divine Judge.) In short, most editors thought they knew better than Phoebe Cary.

These textual histories yield several conclusions. The standard of appropriate length was applied more or less evenhandedly to the men's and women's poems in this sample. But editors' behavior bespeaks a stronger need to curtail and regularize the poetry of women. The dominant culture encouraged clergymen to perceive female poetry as "*recherché*" and lacking in "massiveness" and universality. Today's scholar must also consider that poets thought they were doing when they composed religious lyrics. Most of the women whose work was included in formal hymnals did not define themselves as hymnists. That their poems tended to be longer and less conventional than most hymns is evidence of neither lack nor failure. These women were occasional, unwitting, even unwilling "hymnists."

(1884; reprint, Boston, 1977), and Theron Brown and Hezekiah Butterworth, *The Story of the Hymns and Tunes* (1906; reprint, Grosse Point, Mich., 1968), p. 530. According to a popular story, Cary wrote the poem upon returning home from church—from which Hatfield concluded, "It was, doubtless, inspired by the morning sermon" (p. 135).

63. *Hymns for All Christians,* 6th ed. (New York, 1889), p. 223.

Though hymnologists idealized universality, editorial practice was actually ethnocentric and androcentric. I found hymns by only two nonwhites (a Native American and an Asian Indian) recurring in American hymnbooks. I have seen no instance of demasculinization of a man's poem parallel to the defeminization of Phoebe Brown's. Most editors approved the masculine pronouns that refer to the performer of George Duffield's "Stand Up, Stand Up for Jesus." Among fourteen nineteenth-century editors, just one dropped the stanza that contains this line: "'Ye that are men, now serve him'" (a quotation from Exodus 10:11). None touched Duffield's last four lines:

> To him that overcometh,
> A crown of life shall be;
> He with the King of glory
> Shall reign eternally.[64]

Hymn editors and critics rarely spelled out their views of women's poetry. But clergymen could hardly have been unaware that hymn writing would seem "natural" for women. It fitted perfectly within the sphere of Christian womanhood, for it offered small financial reward; it could be done at home, pseudonymously or anonymously; and it was a private activity with public benefits, justifiable as a useful endeavor and a legitimate avenue for "feminine influence." Hymns, like women's writing and behavior in general, supposedly originated in the heart, not in the intellect—not in men's domain, the realm of sermons and theological treatises. Hymns were experiential, not scholarly or theoretical. Female piety was everywhere evident: in church attendance, participation in religious and reformist societies, moral and financial support of missions. Furthermore, religious lyrics by women appeared in numerous publications. Compilers could collect potential hymns in the course of their daily reading. The public demand for evangelistic and experiential lyrics rose contemporaneously with the emergence of women poets who wanted to see their work in print. Gospel song composers (some of them clergymen and evangelists) and publishers approached women who had published hymns for new lyrics.[65]

Throughout the century, however, American women wrote a small minority of the poems published as hymns in the U.S. At least a partial awareness of this paradox—that women were not prominent in a form of expression and service apparently within their sphere—must have been one motive for clergymen's rationalizations of the hymnological status quo, effusive tributes to female devotion, and expressions of admiration for great sufferers who kept quiet or wrote usable poetry. The Rev. S. W.

---

64. Duffield, *English Hymns*, pp. 493–98.
65. Reed, *My Life Story*, pp. 54–55; *Fanny Crosby's Life-Story, By Herself* (New York, 1905), pp. 131, 147–48.

Christophers declared in 1867 that Steele and her sister poets had written hymns that spoke for "many other devout but suffering women." Echoing a point stated by countless clergymen and women, he noted that Jesus's closest followers included women. Furthermore, the earliest Christian hymns "were, doubtless, from the hearts and pens of sons of holy mothers." It was even possible that some "simple" and "rhythmical" anonymous verses addressed to the infant Jesus were composed by women. Throughout Christian history, "[t]heirs has been the deepest homage; theirs the warmest devotion; theirs the profoundest sympathy; theirs the sweetest songs."[66] The few hymnologists who openly acknowledged the relative dearth of women's hymns offered rationales compatible with contemporary views of gender and literary genius.

Christophers' attitude and rhetoric were typical. Nineteenth-century hymnologists and hymn editors who portrayed women as pious mothers (of sons) did not mean to offend them. Uncomplimentary or obviously patronizing remarks about their abilities—infrequent in hymnological discourse, which often ignored women completely—occurred mainly in statements intended primarily for clergymen. Perhaps some commentators did not consciously realize that hymnody and hymnology disadvantaged women poets. In many published compliments to women's piety and the "sweetness" of their songs, skillfully strategic flattery cannot be distinguished from sincere appreciation.

Some twentieth-century historians and hymnologists, overlooking or ignoring the obvious predominance of male poets and editors, have exaggerated nineteenth-century women's presence as hymnists.[67] Nineteenth-century editors' motives for praising, ignoring, excluding, and altering

66. S[amuel] W[oolcock] Christophers, *Hymn-Writers and Their Hymns* (New York, 1867), pp. 394, 49–50, 416. Parker remarked that women, "as would be expected, . . . wrote the sweetest hymns we have" (*Psalmody*, p. 143).

67. Among nineteenth-century writers, Pitman, author of *Lady Hymn Writers*, was unusual in openly admitting (but not before p. 140) that the proportion of women's lyrics in hymnals was small. Most commentators have ignored or glossed over the fact of women's underrepresentation unless they tried to explain how women's hymns differed from men's. Others have taken hymnologists at their word, or accepted their implication, that women published a great many hymns during the 1800s. The productivity of women hymnists in America is overstated in *The Woman Question: Society and Literature in Britain and America, 1837–1883*, ed. Elizabeth K. Helsinger, Robin Lauterbach Sheets, and William Veeder, 3 vols. (New York, 1986), 3:137, and in Ann Douglas, *The Feminization of American Culture* (New York, 1978). Douglas refers to the "largely non-evangelical and feminine authorship" of hymns sung in nineteenth-century churches and homes (p. 217; see also p. 218). The quoted generalization, based on Douglas's sampling of liberal Protestant hymnals, is not representative of American Protestantism. Analyzing the British and American women's hymns in fourteen nineteenth-century hymnbooks, Barbara Welter found "very physical imagery" used to depict the believer's relationship with Christ, and she noted an attitude of total submission to him ("The Feminization of American Religion," in *Clio's Consciousness Raised: New Perspectives on the History of Women*, ed. Mary S. Hartman and Lois Banner [New York, 1974], pp. 142–43). I would add that the same qualities are found in

women's lyrics were varied and complex. But finally, their reasons become clear enough, and —although paradoxical—not inconsistent. Clergymen wanted to channel hymns' evangelistic powers. They believed women's poetry was different but potentially useful. They *could* ignore, exclude, and alter women's devotional lyrics, all the while valorizing female sympathy and piety. They felt justified in appropriating women's poems or relegating them to oblivion. And they expected none of these attitudes and acts to entail unpleasant consequences.

In churches that did not follow a liturgical calendar, local ministers determined which texts would be sung. It was customary for the clergyman to announce a hymn and then read it aloud prior to group singing. Thus the text was delivered from a revered book in a sacred place, often from a raised platform, in an authoritative male voice. (Music, the "handmaiden of religion," was chosen by male song-leaders. When gendered language was used in hymnological discourse, music was feminine and subordinate to the word; texts could be ruined by "emasculation.")[68] Clergymen exhorted congregants to participate in singing and urged that they teach appropriate sacred songs in Sunday schools, in public schools, and at home.

Advocates of hymn singing reiterated that it unified worshipers in the pews and forged bonds within families and that it promoted "Christian unity" across denominational lines, "teaching us harmony despite diversity" and affirming the grand "legacy of the church catholic."[69] And, declared one clergyman, it should be used to bridge differences between Americans of different cultural backgrounds. Since the nation was "neither Anglo-Saxon nor Oriental nor Occidental exclusively," its church music ought to be eclectic.[70] As "Anglo-Saxons" were wont to do, this writer either omitted blacks from his census of Americans or lumped them with Jews and Asians as "Orientals."

Congregational singing guaranteed hymns' interaction with the social constructions of gender and race. The status of privileged or divinely chosen white males—implying the relative powerlessness of everybody else—was symbolized by role and position in all-white, biracial, and multi-

---

men's hymns. Commenting on late-century women's emergence as gospel hymnists, Sizer acknowledges that "men (primarily clergy) still dominated the field" (*Gospel Hymns*, p. 23; see also p. 87). She does not differentiate women's gospel hymns from men's. My view is that gender-based differences in religious expression did exist—but are best examined in genres other than published hymns.

68. Parker, *Psalmody*, p. 42. On religion itself as "muscular," "virile," or "effeminate," see "Church Poetry and Music," p. 496; De Jong, "'I Want to Be Like Jesus,'" pp. 475–78.

69. Quotations from Eliphalet Nott Potter, "Church Music and Its Future in America," *American Church Review*, no. 137 (April 1882): 110, 112, and Frederick Saunders, *Evenings with Sacred Poets*, rev. ed. (New York, 1885), p. 478. See also Lowell Mason, "Congregational Singing," *Musical Gazette* 3 (27 March 1848): 33.

70. Potter, "Church Music," p. 111.

racial sanctuaries. African-American formal worship, too, was led by men. Therefore, lessons about order and male authority were enacted at every service. Ministers did not dispute the claim of musicians, educators, and cultural critics that individuals who sang or played instruments in groups learned their places in the social hierarchy.[71]

Although most offices in the institutional church were held by men, piety was commonly associated with women and femininity; clergymen were not considered especially masculine. The performance, publication, and criticism of hymns expressed clerical power while it reinforced patriarchal norms, maintained distinctions between the sexes (especially those between churchly women and churchmen), and therefore participated in the re-creation of the sex/gender system. Clerical approbation of hymns' "universality" should not obscure the significant roles hymnody and hymnology have played in maintaining Protestants' consciousness of social differences.

71. On music and social order, see James H. Stone, "Mid-Nineteenth-Century American Beliefs in the Social Values of Music," *Music Quarterly* 43 (Jan. 1957): 38–49, and Joseph A. Mussulman, *Music in the Cultured Generation: A Social History of Music in America, 1870–1900* (Evanston, Ill., 1971).

PART III
Black and White in
the Spiritual Borderlands

CHAPTER 7

The Uses of the Supernatural: Toward a History of Black Women's Magical Practices

YVONNE CHIREAU

African American people are heirs to a religious diversity inspired by the meeting of old and the new worlds. African at its roots and American in its orientation, black sacred culture is a vibrant mélange of traditions, theologies, and styles. Part of the richness of African American spirituality derives from its complexity, the distinctive interplay of multiple meanings within unified conceptual frameworks and categories. An enduring element of the religious experience of black people in the United States is *supernaturalism*, a perspective that acknowledges the accessibility and efficacy of the spiritual realm in human life. This chapter is a preliminary exploration of the historical functions and meanings of supernaturalism, focusing on African American women and the significance of supernatural practices for women in black communities in nineteenth- and early twentieth-century America.

Historically, black American women's spirituality has extended well beyond the physical boundaries of church, mosque, and temple. However, in studying the spiritual experiences of black women many scholars have privileged institutionalized religious activities over those traditions that emerged external to ecclesial and parochial associations. Numerous studies have documented African American women's roles within the Christian denominations, independent networks, movements of organizational reform, and community-building efforts, but few have investigated the varied, elaborate meanings that emerge when women create alternative avenues for sacred self-expression *outside* of these established channels. Consequently, the history of African American women's spiritual lives consists of much uncharted territory.[1]

1. On black women and religion see Evelyn Brooks, "The Feminist Theology of the Black Baptist Church, 1880–1900," in *Class, Race, and Sex: The Dynamics of Control*, ed. Amy Swerdlow and Hanna Lessinger (Boston, 1983); Cheryl Townsend Gilkes, "'Together and in Harness': Women's Traditions in the Sanctified Church," *Signs* 10 (Summer 1985); Jualynne Dodson, "Nineteenth-Century A. M. E. Preaching Women," in Hilah Thomas and Rosemary Skinner Keller, *Women in New Worlds* (Nashville, 1981); Elsa Barkley Brown, "Womanist Consciousness: Maggie Lena Walker and the Independent Order of Saint Luke," *Signs* 14 (Spring 1989). An extensive (though uneven) bibliography is Marilyn Richardson's *Black Women and Religion: A Bibliography* (Boston, 1980).

Magic or Religion?

A perspective that emphasizes the supernatural elements in African American sacred culture can help to reorient historians' approaches to religion. We might start with the very terms we use to understand these practices. For example, when it is not part of the practitioners' conceptual framework, the word *magic* can be problematic. As used by historians, *magic* typically describes activities that are private, illicit, and coercive of spiritual powers, while *religion* primarily refers to those practices which are public, liturgical, and institutionalized.[2] As historian Natalie Zemon Davis has noted, these distinctions often have limited application to actual experience. She suggests that the magic/religion dichotomy carries unnecessary baggage and is therefore too narrow to be of practical use to the historian: "a premature evaluation of the functions of religion and magic, an insistence on sorting their function into those which are 'rational' and those which are not, may limit our historical insight unduly . . . We continue to examine distinctions between religion and magic, Christian and pagan, rational and primitive as they are made in varying ways . . . as evidence about the periods, not as categories which exhaust the possibilities for our analysis."[3] The typological distinction between magic and religion has not precluded the convergence of both categories within African American sacred traditions, where magical and religious elements are often combined. As I employ it, *supernaturalism* is a more appropriate term of description for this broad sphere of belief and practice, referring to a cluster of ideas concerning suprahuman agents and spiritual efficacy that includes traditional conceptions of divinity and other spiritual forces.

Among black Americans, ideas of the supernatural and the accessibility of supernatural powers have been passed down from early generations of slaves to their descendants in the present day. In particular, the practice of *conjure* has occupied a principal location in black folk tradition for at least two centuries. Conjure, or as it is known by its various appellations, *hoodoo*, *voodoo*, *rootworking*, *mojo*, or *goopher*, is the ritual harnessing of spiritual forces in order to heal, to harm, to predict the future, and to influence individuals or events.[4] As a magico-religious system, conjure was most

2. From the formulations derived from the sociologists of religion Emile Durkheim and Marcel Mauss. See Durkheim, *Elementary Forms of the Religious Life* (New York, 1915), and Mauss, *A General Theory of Magic* (Boston, 1972).

3. Natalie Z. Davis, "Some Tasks and Themes in the Study of Popular Religion," in *The Pursuit of Holiness in Late Medieval and Renaissance Religion*, ed. Charles Trinkhaus and Heiko Oberman (Leiden, 1974), p. 312.

4. *Conjure* is a term from the African American folk vernacular that refers to supernatural practices and powers. Prior to this time, the word *conjure* was used primarily by whites to refer to the sleight-of-hand tricks and performances of professional magicians. Other terms, as they are employed by blacks, vary by region. The sources of some words, like *goopher* or *voodoo*, are arguably African, but *conjure* is the appelation which comes into most common usage by the nineteenth century. See Newbell Niles Puckett, *Folk Beliefs of the Southern Negro* (Chapel Hill, 1926), pp. 15–20.

widespread among black slave populations in the United States during the early 1800s, but its roots predate this period by at least a hundred years. Accounts of conjure and conjuring among blacks were central to the cultural narratives perpetuated by African Americans in the oral tradition. As a supernatural system of belief and practice, conjure continues to draw freely from black religion and folklore.[5]

The Roots of Black Supernaturalism

To find the origins of conjure and supernaturalism one must go back to the initial encounters between Africans and Europeans in the American colonies. Cruelly enslaved, Africans were brought to the New World as laborers under brutal and inhumane conditions. Separated from their homelands, divorced from their native social and religious institutions, slaves forged relationships with white colonists that were defined by conflict and subjugation. In early America, black and white worldviews clashed and occasionally reinforced each other. The diverse impulses of post-Reformation Christianity in Europe informed popular notions of the invisible world, occultism, and the efficacy of holy objects. Many of these themes made their way to the colonies, redefining the barriers that church authorities had cast between supernaturalism and religion. Ultimately, the "worlds of wonder" that so captivated white colonists became a source of enrichment for African American sacred consciousness.[6] As historian Mechal Sobel has argued with respect to Africans and Anglican settlers in colonial Virginia, similarities in the two groups' perceptions of space, time, and the natural environment made for a "social-cultural" interplay of black and white perspectives:

> In the traditional cultures of both peoples the natural world was seen as a place of mystery and hidden powers that had to be taken into account. Africans

5. There are several published collections of African American magic and folk beliefs: Harry Middleton Hyatt, *Hoodoo-Conjuration-Witchcraft-Rootwork; Beliefs Accepted by Many Negroes and White Persons, these being orally recorded among Blacks and Whites,* 5 vols. (Hannibal, Mo., 1970–78); Wayland Hand, ed., *The Frank Brown Collection of North Carolina Folklore,* vol. 7 (Chapel Hill, 1964), and regional studies, such as Georgia Writers Project, *Drums and Shadows: Survival Studies among the Georgia Coastal Negroes* (Athens, Ga., 1940), Ray Browne, *Popular Beliefs and Practices from Alabama* (Berkeley, 1958), and Federal Writers Program, *South Carolina Folk Tales* (Columbia, S.C., 1941). There are no such collected works dating from the nineteenth century, but see the materials reprinted in Bruce Jackson, ed., *The Negro and his Folklore in Nineteenth-Century Periodicals* (Austin, 1967), and Donald Waters, ed., *Strange Ways and Sweet Dreams: Folklore from the Hampton Institute* (Boston, 1983).

6. Jon Butler, *Awash in a Sea of Faith: Christianizing the American People* (Cambridge, 1990), pp. 151–63. See also Albert Raboteau, *Slave Religion: The "Invisible Institution" in the Antebellum South* (New York, 1978); Lawrence Levine, *Black Culture and Black Consciousness: Afro-American Folk Thought from Slavery to Freedom* (New York, 1976). See also Mechal Sobel, *The World They Made Together: Black and White Values in Eighteenth-Century Virginia* (Princeton, 1987).

coming to America did not have a deviant rational tradition, but their view of the natural world was very close to the traditional view of most English people. Taboos were highly important; ritual acts were seen as having efficacy; holy places, holy times, and holy people could affect spirit or power. In this area of perceptions and values the possibility of confluence and melding was strong.[7]

Many beliefs were not completely unfamiliar. Europeans and Africans both tapped into a galaxy of otherworldly visions, including ideas concerning the mediation of the dead and the powers of unseen entities. As Africans were exposed to the spiritual imagination of whites, they absorbed many ideas that were compatible with their own. Practitioners of astrology, divination, and fortune-telling attracted both whites and blacks, and various occult activities thrived in the American colonies. Moreover, the cultural influences went both ways. Evidence indicates that whites borrowed heavily from African slave traditions, including folk beliefs in witches, ghosts, spirits, and other forces. Undeniably, early American folk tradition possessed black and white roots.[8]

Throughout the colonial period, traces of the supernatural pervaded the spiritual consciousness of blacks. But by the late 1700s dynamic new religious configurations stimulated the revivalism of the First Great Awakening and, later, the Second. African American culture blossomed in this lively environment of spiritual renewal. At the end of the eighteenth century the first independent African American churches were established, and slaves and free blacks converted to Christianity in increasing numbers. Many of these converts embellished their understandings of the Christian faith with visions that incorporated images and symbols from their African heritage. Nevertheless, the black embrace of evangelical Christianity represented only part of the religious picture. By the nineteenth century, slaves and freeborn blacks had developed a significant body of practices and beliefs, ones that were complementary rather than hostile to the interests and expressions of Christianity.[9]

A determination of the extent and significance of these complementary spiritual ideas among blacks has relied largely upon the remarks of

7. Sobel, *World They Made Together*, pp. 5, 78.

8. Beneath the mass of African American folk beliefs throughout the old South, for example, lies a storehouse of seventeenth- and eighteenth-century European legend and lore. See Sobel, *World They Made Together*, pp. 97–99. On the cross-fertilization of black and European supernatural beliefs, see Tom Peete Cross, "Witchcraft in North Carolina," *Studies in Philology* 16 (July 1919); Norman Whitten, "Contemporary Patterns of Malign Occultism among Negroes in North Carolina," *Journal of American Folklore* 75 (1962), pp. 311–25. Newbell Niles Puckett, "Religious Folk Beliefs of Whites and Negroes," *Journal of Negro History* 16 (1931), pp. 9–35.

9. Raboteau, *Slave Religion*, chap. 2; Levine, *Black Culture*, pp. 55–80.

nineteenth-century observers, who have often described African American religion with scorn or amusement. "In all instances which I remember to have noticed with reference to such fact," wrote one South Carolina plantation owner, "I have found among the religious slaves of the south traces . . . of a blending of superstition and fetichism, modifying their impressions of Christianity." Traveling in Virginia in the 1850s, the writer Frederick Law Olmsted observed that while a good portion of black folk were churchgoers, their religion was dominated by "a miserable system of superstition, the more painful that it employs some forms and words connected with true Christianity." Almost thirty years later, folklorist William Owens corroborated the presence of a strange admixture of Christianity and supernaturalism, remarking that black "American-born superstitions" were "interwoven with so-called religious beliefs," and represented "a horrible debasement of some of the highest and noblest doctrines of the Christian faith."[10] The frequent use of the term *superstition* by these commentators is a key indicator of the widespread perception that African American religion possessed supernatural elements. What were these elements, and what was their significance to the culture of the slaves?

Slavery and Supernaturalism

Religion was one of the foundations of black life in nineteenth-century America. Christian ideology informed the development of most of the primary institutions of African Americans, including their churches, voluntary associations, and schools. To the slaves, an oppressed and subjugated people, religious faith and community were significant sources of solace and comfort. The African worldview contributed a further, powerful dimension to the kind of Christianity that the slaves practiced. Belief in human access to an unseen world, a world that addressed specific concerns for power and control within the domain of the unpredictable, formed the bedrock of black folk religion. Anxieties involving the fear of punishment and abuse, possible sale and separation, and the unforeseeable risks of attempting to escape, were all part of the slaves' daily experience. Many of these concerns were addressed by a vast network of supernatural ideas. Slaves resorted to conjure, for example, when they confronted the physical threat of violence. Some slaves carried conjuring charms or amulets; some engaged in rituals that they believed would deter whippings and other forms of abuse; others wore protective "voodoo bags" on their persons or used powders, roots, and

10. Charles Raymond, "The Religious Life of the Negro Slave," *Harper's New Monthly Magazine*, August 1863, p. 816; Frederick Law Olmsted, *A Journey to the Seaboard Slave States in the Years 1853–1854, with Remarks on their Economy* (New York, 1856), p. 114; William Owens, "Folklore of the Southern Negroes," *Lippincott's Magazine* 20 (Dec. 1877), reprinted in Jackson, *The Negro and His Folklore*, p. 146.

potions that would shield them from unanticipated attacks by cruel slaveholders and slave drivers. Furthermore, conjure offered protection to the slave who dared to fight, rebel, or engage in destructive acts of sabotage. Supernatural beliefs thus had important functions for enslaved African Americans—they were a means of coping with and resisting slaveholder domination in situations of limited alternatives, and they were a culturally validated source of spiritual power.[11]

Written sources on African American conjure in the nineteenth century include narratives by former slaves, journals and diaries, and occasional firsthand accounts and commentaries. Abolitionists Frederick Douglass and William Wells Brown are two widely quoted authors who describe male plantation conjurers in their autobiographies.[12] Lesser-known portraits of female conjurers by antebellum writers allow for a more balanced picture of black women's roles as supernatural authorities in slave communities. The journal of British actress Frances Kemble, for example, provides a rare glimpse of an enslaved African American woman, Sinda, who possessed the gift of second sight. Sinda, according to Kemble's account, was so respected for her supernatural powers and predictions that when she prophesied that the end of the world was imminent, other slaves refused to work any longer, even upon pain of punishment. As a powerful prophetess acknowledged by other slaves, Sinda was not unique. A nineteenth-century journalist in North Carolina described a plantation slave woman who was believed to be "in communication with occult powers" and endowed with the gift of clairvoyance. "Her utterances were accepted as oracles, and piously heeded," remarked an observer, "for it was believed that "she could see through the mists that hide the future from others.""[13]

Other bondswomen used supernatural powers to participate in a clandestine system of occult subversion. Incidents recorded in the journal of James Henry Hammond, the proslavery ideologue of South Carolina, demonstrate the symbolic impact of supernaturalism in undermining the integrity of the slave system. Hammond, who was frustrated by the rampant destructiveness of conjurers on his estate, tried to root out and punish all blacks who were involved with occult activities, but he met with little success. In 1835 a female slave named Urana helped other slaves to steal wine from

---

11. Levine, *Black Culture*, pp. 70–75; Raboteau, *Slave Religion*, pp. 281–88; Elliot Gorn, "Black Magic: Folk Beliefs of the Slave Community," in *Science and Medicine in the Old South*, ed. Ronald Numbers and Todd Savitt (Baton Rouge, 1989), pp. 308–16.

12. Frederick Douglass, *Narrative of the Life of Frederick Douglass, an American Slave* (Boston, 1845), p. 81; William Wells Brown, *My Southern Home; or, The South and Its People* (New York, 1880), pp. 90–92.

13. Frances Ann Kemble, *Journal of a Residence on a Georgia Plantation in 1838–1839* (New York, 1863), p. 119; Elwyn Barron, "Shadowy Memories of Negro Lore," *The Folklorist* (Chicago, 1892): 50; see also Jacqueline Jones, *Labor of Love, Labor of Sorrow* (New York, 1985), p. 41.

Hammond's cellar. She apparently employed supernatural powers to "screen" those involved in the theft from his detection. As Hammond's biographer notes, this incident challenged his attempt at the total domination of his slaves, since what Urana had accomplished "lay entirely outside his system of control." The other slaves' belief that Urana was protecting them supernaturally allowed them to contest Hammond's ownership of property and his power over them—the foundations of his authority.[14]

These examples illustrate black women's supernatural empowerment, a fact that the historiographical focus on Christianity among slaves has obscured. It is likely that male preachers and female conjurers participated equally as spiritual leaders within African American slave communities. Such an equality would have been consistent with women's roles among enslaved blacks in the nineteenth century: bondswomen and bondsmen had complementary functions and participated in a nonhierarchical sexual division of labor within the private arena, even as their productive and reproductive capacities were ultimately subject to slaveholder demands. Similarly, enslaved female conjurers operated on a level of parity with male conjurers. Equal access to the supernatural world tended to level out gender-based hierarchies for African American males and females, particularly within the spiritual arena.

Conjure in the Black Community

While supernaturalism was a way of confronting the oppressiveness of slavery, the functions of conjure were primarily internal, and had little direct impact upon relations between blacks and whites. African Americans adopted supernatural beliefs to address their own specific concerns, such as healing and health. Among slaves and their descendants, for example, supernatural folk traditions were an important way of conceptualizing sickness; disease was often thought to have spiritual causes. One became unhealthy, it was commonly believed, because another person had "wished it," or because one was the object of someone's "bad feelings." Chronic sicknesses that did not respond to conventional treatment were considered to be the consequence of malign powers or forces. As historian Albert Raboteau has noted, this understanding of affliction placed random causes within an explanatory social context. "Slaves believed adversity was due not to fate or mere happenstance," he states, "but to the ill will of someone working through a conjurer."[15] For many blacks, supernaturalism revealed *why* suffering occurred and indicated *who* or *what* was responsible, thus explaining and locating the disease or misfortune within communally based

14. Drew Gilpin Faust, *James Henry Hammond and the Old South: A Design for Mastery* (Baton Rouge, 1982), p. 93.
15. Raboteau, *Slave Religion*, p. 276.

norms and idioms of the spiritual world. Furthermore, conjure and other beliefs offered numerous possibilities for remedying distressing situations, thereby facilitating individual agency and empowerment.

Such beliefs concerning the supernatural causes of disease and illness were salient among African Americans long after emancipation, especially among black women, who historically were entrusted with primary healing roles in slave and free communities. The recollections of educators and missionaries working among former slaves on the Sea Islands suggest that supernatural perspectives toward sickness were still viable early in the twentieth century. The following conversation between a New England schoolteacher, Grace Bigelow House, and an elderly black woman illuminates the manner in which some African Americans systematized their perspectives of physical ailments:

> One of the older women . . . had an affliction which she said no "medical doctor cayn' cure." "I had dis affliction before," she said, "and I been to Parris Island doctor and all de doctors, an' dey say it could do no good."
>
> "But you can tell me what the sickness is like?"
>
> . . . shaking her head, "dey is some illness come from God, and some come from man!"
>
> "Do you think this sickness came from God?" asked Miss House.
>
> ". . . No," she whispered, "No, no! Dishyuh sickness came from man."
>
> "Do you think some one wished some evil on you?"
>
> "Yes," came back the expected answer in a whisper.[16]

Similar notions of affliction circulated throughout the South and in other parts of the United States where blacks settled. The following testimony of an emancipated slave woman in Texas indicates that a variety of possibilities—sinful deeds, poor labor conditions, and supernaturalism—were all considered as explanations for the blindness that struck her unexpectedly. Ultimately she believed that the forces of "hoodoo," or malign conjure, were to blame:

> A man and he wife and I was workin' as woodchoppers on de Santa Fe route up Beaumont to Tyler County. After us git up and I starts "way, I . . . hear somethin" say, "Rose, you done somethin you ain't ought." I say, "No, Lawd, no." Den de voice say, "Somethin gwine happen to you," and de next mornin I's blind as de bat and I aint hever seed since . . . Some try tell me snow or sweat or smoke de reason. Dat aint de reason. Dey a old, old, slewfooted somethin' from Louisiana and dey say he de Conjure man, one dem old hoodoo niggers. He git mad at me de last plum-ripenin' time and he make up powdered rattlesnake dust and pass dat through my hair and I sho' ain't seed no more.[17]

16. Rossa Belle Cooley, *The Homes of the Freed* (New York, 1906), pp. 39–41, 55.
17. George Rawick, *The American Slave: A Composite Autobiography*, vol. 4, pt. 2 (Westport, Conn., 1972), p. 64.

Prominent as they were, supernatural interpretations of affliction did not apply only to illness and disease. Negative developments, unexpected losses, bad luck, adversity, and even death were also interpreted as having spiritual causes. Furthermore, underlying the spiritual causes of affliction were human intentions. Misfortune had meanings that emerged from the acts and thoughts of others. Conjure was a principal medium through which hostilities were articulated and characteristically "evil" emotions such as hatred, jealousy, fear, avarice, and lust were transformed into unseen spiritual agents—weapons—tangible, powerful forces that could be directed to attack others. Rather than openly displaying anger or bitterness one could assert one's hostility toward another by manipulating the spiritual realm.

Conjure and Interpersonal Relationships

Another face of the power of conjure was less negative: supernatural beliefs also functioned to arbitrate interpersonal and sexual relationships. In many cases of conjure, love was as powerful a force as hatred. Sometimes African American folk specialists were called upon to settle romantic disputes often conflicts or jealousies between wayward spouses or lovers. The Reverend Irving Lowery, a black Methodist minister born into slavery, described the ordeal of a female slave on a nineteenth-century South Carolina plantation, a victim in what he called a "love scrape." According to Lowery, after taking sick and suffering "a lingering illness of possibly four or six months' duration," the woman died. Her demise was attributed to malicious conjuring by a jealous rival.[18] Supernaturalism was also utilized within interpersonal relations as a means of enticement. Among slaves in the nineteenth century, folk recipes and spiritual prescriptions for matters of seduction were endless. In his narrative of southern plantation life in the 1800s, black abolitionist William Wells Brown observed that the conjurer Dinkie did a fair trade in providing consultations and charms for a clientele of lovelorn females.[19] Similarly, the fugitive slave Henry Bibb described a conjurer's talisman that promised to make any girl love him, "in spite of herself . . . no matter who she might be engaged to, nor whom she might be walking with." Though the charm ultimately failed to achieve the desired effect, Bibb was not deterred, for shortly thereafter he sought another specialist's assistance.[20] Many freed slaves recalled the power of the supernatural for attracting potential lovers. A report by Works Progress Administration interviewers in Oklahoma described a former slave from Tennessee who once bought a "sweetheart hand," or personal charm, from a "coal black" conjure man. In

18. Irving E. Lowery, *Life on the Old Plantation in Ante-bellum Days* (Columbia, S.C., 1911), pp. 84–85.
19. Brown, *My Southern Home*, p. 76.
20. Henry Bibb, *Narrative of the Life and Adventures of Henry Bibb, an American Slave, written by himself* (New York, 1850), p. 30.

his farcical account of failed courtship, the ambitious suitor narrowly escaped the wrath of the girl's parents, who had accidently discovered his amorous intentions.[21]

In the area of love relationships, conjure seems to have provided immediate and effective consolation for women. In northwestern Florida in the early part of the twentieth century, anthropologist Zora Neale Hurston described a female "hoodoo doctor," Eulalia, who dealt solely with sexual entanglements. Apprenticing with Eulalia, Hurston recounted one such incident: "I went to study with Eulalia, who specialized in Man-and-woman cases. Everyday somebody came to get Eulalia to tie them up with some man or woman or to loose them from love . . . So one day a woman came to get tied to a man." According to Hurston, the distraught woman declared that a man she wanted could not marry her because his current wife had "got roots buried" and kept him under her power. She believed that their relationship would be undone if she could "work roots" of her own. She sought Eulalia's supernatural assistance to resolve the situation. Hurston described the conjure woman's reaction: 'Eulalia sat still and thought awhile. Then she said: 'Course Ah'm uh Christian woman and don't believe in partin' no husband and wife but since she done worked roots on him, to hold him where he don't want to be, it t'aint no sin for me to loose him.'" Hurston and her teacher devised a ritual that effectively banished the man's spouse, and nuptials between Eulalia's client and her partner were secured.[22] The prominence of conjure in meaningful life events suggests that it functioned as a symbolic marker mediating the anxieties that accompany social and emotional distress.

As part of its function within interpersonal relationships, conjure also had important protective uses for black women. Supernatural beliefs provided women who were powerless in their domestic situations with spiritual resources to address their circumstances. Interviews by Works Progress Administration writers with former slaves throughout the South yielded narratives of crisis, loss, and reconciliation which resonate strongly with oral testimonies from the black Christian tradition. In one account an African American woman explains that she sought the counsel of a conjurer after suffering abuse, abandonment, and infidelity at the hands of her husband. She believed that her husband's mistress, Minnie, was responsible for her misfortune. After her first meeting with the conjurer she stated that he had diagnosed her situation with skill and accuracy: "He got some cards and started tellin' me about Minnie. And 'fore my Maker I wouldn't tell

21. B. A. Botkin, *Lay My Burden Down: A Folk History of Slavery* (Chicago, 1945), pp. 31–33; see also Puckett, *Folk Beliefs*, pp. 264–66, and Zora Neale Hurston, "Hoodoo in America," *Journal of American Folklore* 44 (Oct. 1931): 378.

22. Zora Neale Hurston, *Mules and Men* (1978; reprint, Bloomington, Ind., 1935), pp. 197–99.

you a word of a story, he told me everything dat happened. At first I didn't believe in fortunetellers and root-workers, but after he told me so much that I knowed was true, I couldn't help but believe him." The conjurer offered the woman a charm to wear on her person, and in a short time she was reunited with her spouse. "I knows it done me all the good in the world . . . and right now whenever I see anybody sick or anybody tells me anything 'bout somebody hurtin' 'em, I send 'em to this same man and all of 'em say he really does what he says. I knows he's good and I ain't afraid to tell nobody 'bout him."[23]

Protecting oneself from violence, coping with afflictions, and healing broken relationships—these are the primary themes of many women's personal stories. The conjure stories also show the anguished struggles of African American women to repair unfortunate relationships with men. In another narrative, a black woman explained how she went to a root worker about restoring order to her household, which she believed a second female had disrupted. For her, the supernatural power of conjure came not a moment too soon. "When us went to [the conjurer] he told me if I hadn't come to see 'bout it, my husband never would have come back . . . He said too dat my husband wuz thinkin' 'bout gettin' a divorce pretty soon . . . Sho' nuff dat Sunday my husband come back like de man said. He cried and said he didn't know how come he had left me . . . and wanted me to forgive him dat time and he was sho' it wouldn't happen again."[24]

As a kind of spiritual therapy, the relationship of trust forged between conjurers and their clients helped to solidify the inner resources of black women during periods of crisis. Conjure beliefs provided the women with supernatural assets for strength and survival. For women who were sexually and emotionally abused, supernaturalism was a means of recovery and of spiritual and physical empowerment.

Conjure practices illuminated disputes of a diverse nature within African American communities. Incidents of malign supernaturalism were most often intraracial, with blacks injuring other blacks. Even after emancipation, the majority of spiritual practices seem to have been of a negative nature. White observers were quick to characterize malign supernaturalism among African Americans as demonstrating black inferiority. "Negroes are not necessarily loyal as a race," remarked Myrta Avary, a white southerner and critic of postwar race relations. "They fear each other, dread covert acts of vengeance, and being conjured."[25] Philip Bruce, an early southern historian, asserted that Virginia blacks had "no compunction about inflicting

---

23. Undated interview in Richmond City, Ga., folklore folder, Manuscripts Division, Library of Congress, pp. 1–7.
24. Ibid., pp. 1–6.
25. Myrta Lockett Avary, *Dixie After the War* (New York, 1906), p. 234.

injury" upon each other. He noted that as a rule African Americans were "always suspicious that their enemies have turned the black art against them in the same spirit that they themselves have sought to turn that art against their enemies."[26] Of course, these remarks must be viewed in their context, as reflecting the general hostility of many southern whites toward blacks during Reconstruction. Nevertheless, the picture they present—a world of animosity and discord—raises questions concerning the meaning of conjure for blacks in post–Civil War America.

Meanings of Conjure

Negative conjure seems to have been relatively common among African Americans during the latter half of the nineteenth century and the early decades of the twentieth century. In many cases, resentment and revenge were the primary motives for supernatural affliction. Numerous accounts, both from the northern and southern states, attest to the various ways that conjure was used as tool for affliction, especially for women, who were often the most powerless within black communities. In rural Georgia after the turn of the century, ex-slave Mary Jackson told how one African American woman who "worked hard and got something for herself" became convinced that the entire community was resentful of her success and good fortune. When she was stricken with an illness, she believed that it had been put upon her by others who thought she was trying to be "more than anyone else."[27] Similar accounts are ubiquitous in black folk narrative. In one community, rivalry and avarice led one woman to conjure another so that she could corner a greater share of the neighborhood washing trade.[28] In another example of supernatural harming, a bitter woman was accused of supernaturally "fixing" her neighbor, her motive being that the other woman had been envious of the "nice clothes and dancing lessons" she had provided for her child.[29] Conjure-related conflicts could also reflect personal resentments involving the aesthetics of racial identity. An African American woman who disliked another individual's "light skin" and "straight hair" was held responsible for causing her affliction through conjure.[30] When a black woman living on the Georgia coast during the early decades of the twentieth century found herself sick, she explained to a white missionary that someone that she knew had "wished some evil" upon her because she was

26. Philip A. Bruce, *The Plantation Negro as a Freeman: Observations on His Character, Condition and Prospects in Virginia* (New York, 1889), pp. 120–22.

27. Mary Jackson, undated interview, Georgia, folklore folder, Manuscripts Division, Library of Congress.

28. Jeanette Robinson Murphy, "The Survival of African Music in America," in Jackson, *The Negro and His Folklore*, p. 335.

29. M. S. Lea, Two-Headed Doctors," *American Mercury*, Oct. 1927, p. 238.

30. Daniel Webster Davis, "Conjuration," *Southern Workman* 27 (1898): 251.

"so independent."[31] And in 1882, newspaper readers in the North learned of an unusual case that showed the extent to which faith in conjure could fuel an individual's drive for wealth and power: "The 'Philadelphia Press' . . . gives an account of the examination of a colored woman . . . [who] had rendered herself liable to indictment for fraud in professing to work charms by 'occult and crafty science'. The accusation was, that she had defrauded Charles Lecan, colored, out of one dollar, and had threatened to paralyze him if he did not give her more money in payment for services rendered in endeavoring to secure for him the presidency of the Reading Railroad by means of spells and incantations."[32]

It is clear from many accounts that suspicions of malign supernaturalism could fill members of black communities with distrust. Worry over malevolent conjure and people with hostile intentions was pervasive: one had to be constantly on the lookout for potentially dangerous enemies. Property and personal effects had to be guarded jealously; if they came into someone else's possession, one could fall under that person's control. Strange food could not be eaten for fear of ingesting dangerous objects. Dust from one's tracks, hair clippings, nail parings and objects of clothing could be used as ingredients in deadly charms. Katie Sutton, a former slave in Savannah, Georgia, took her suspicions to an extreme. "There are folks right here in this town that have the power to bewitch you," she claimed. Refusing to lend any of her personal goods to neighbors or friends, Sutton explained that some individuals were able to harm others supernaturally through borrowed items. "Evil spirits creeps around . . . and evil people's always able to hax [hex] you," she warned. Other black folk obsessively swept their tracks in order to cover their footprints, avoided having photographs taken, and pursued numerous countermeasures in order to divert the effects of malign supernaturalism.[33]

Each of these examples of conjuring involve women. They raise the question of how gender related to supernaturalism as a vehicle for harm. Were women more susceptible than men to the powers of conjure, either as clients or as victims?

Toward a History of Black Women and Supernaturalism

The religious world of African Americans during slavery and thereafter was a mosaic of conjuring and supernaturalism. It is a picture that enlarges our

31. Cooley, *Homes of The Freed*, pp. 40–41.
32. Stewart Culin, "Concerning Negro Sorcery in the United States," *Journal of American Folklore* 3 (1890): 284.
33. Rawick, *American Slave*, vol. 6, pt. 2, pp. 193–94; Georgia Writers Project, *Drums and Shadows: Survival Studies among the Coastal Georgia Negroes* (Garden City, 1972), p. 2; Sarah Handy, "Negro Superstitions," *Lippincott's Monthly Magazine* 48 (1891): 737.

understanding of the varieties and functions of spiritual power that were available to women and, to some extent, of gender relations and the formations of gender in black communities. As I view it, supernaturalism does not appear to be a predominant means of expressing gender controversies among slaves and their descendants; but gender did help to define the sorts of accusations that spiritual practices addressed—for example, spousal abandonment or marital infidelity. Like witchcraft allegations in many cultures, accusations of conjure followed the lines of fractured or damaged relationships, or emerged out of suspicions and rivalry due to economic, social, and sexual conflicts. For African Americans, conjure accusations emphasized "stress spots," where antagonisms over seemingly minor differences eventually erupted and bitterly divided members of a community.

Conjure complaints were leveled at co-workers, acquaintances, spouses, and family members. Community members were pitted against those who "stood out" in some way, either because they were successful or because they were disturbing or difficult. These supernatural beliefs had considerable utilitarian value for closely knit groups like plantation slaves or post–Civil War black communities, whose existence was constantly jeopardized by the threat of sale or separation and by racist intimidation. To take a functionalist perspective, then, conjure beliefs might have served to unite black communities against common enemies—anyone or anything that would threaten their insularity and cohesion.

The supernatural practices of African Americans also give us an alternative perspective on how women in particular used and experienced spiritual power for personal and pragmatic goals. Both men and women in African American communities were empowered by the supernatural, but it appears that black women's adoption of supernatural practices often had both a narrower emphasis and a wider implication. Like African American men, black women utilized spiritual resources for various ends, both private and public. Yet women had different needs from men, and supernaturalism served to address them. Women's concerns included protection, safety, and security within their interpersonal relationships. At times, their supernaturalism reflected their particular experiences as enslaved females within a rigidly oppressive social order or as women at risk in domestic situations. Yet it is unclear if black women were more attracted to supernaturalism by virtue of their dual subjugation or by the autonomy that conjure offered them. Although the activities of female conjurers are less conspicuous than those of males in the historical record, I suspect that women practitioners constituted a significant segment of those who were recognized within black communities as supernatural authorities.

Black folk traditions such as conjure have continued to hold a central location in African American life in the present day, and although class differences, education, and ambivalence toward "superstitions" have obscured them, supernatural beliefs and practices are to be found among blacks in all social strata. A subtle transformation occurred, however, when the significance of conjure shifted in black folk religious discourse. Gradually, many supernatural beliefs became folklorized, which means that they became part of an ongoing body of tales and traditions circulating within African American oral culture. One of the consequences of the new emphasis on folklore was the transformation of conjurers from flesh-and-blood individuals into mythic figures. In many folklore traditions, supernatural practitioners were identified with witches and hags.[34] "A witch is a *cunjuh man* dat somebody paid tuh tawment yuh," explained Christine Nelson, a descendent of slaves in Georgia.[35] "Dey's sho' hoodoos," remarked an unidentified informant in Mississippi, elaborating on the relationship of witches and conjurers. "Mos gen'ally dey rides you in de shape uv a black cat, an' rides you in de daytime too, well ez de night."[36] In the late nineteenth century, folklorist Mary Owen noted that the black folk practitioners she met living on Missouri's border regions "invariably speak of themselves as Witches, men or women, or conjurers."[37] Witch and hag stories became standard fare in African American narrative in the nineteenth century, and, true to the nature of verbal improvisation, these tales

34. An African American mythic figure, the hag seems to have been a particularly fearsome being in southern folklore. Witches and hags in southern folk narrative were often identified with the female, but ex-slave Jacob Stroyer, writing of his experience as a bondsman in Charleston, South Carolina, noted that there were certain persons, "both men and women, who when they had grown old, were supposed to be witches." See Stroyer, *My Life in the South* (Salem, Mass., 1898), p. 52; Puckett, *Folk Beliefs*, p. 147; also Cross, "Witchcraft in North Carolina," p. 226. For a reading of the purported practice of witch "riding" and its metaphorical sexual overtones, see William Grimes, *Narrative of the Life of William Grimes the Runaway Slave, written by himself* (New York, 1825), pp. 24–25; and Tom Peete Cross, "Folklore from the Southern States," *Journal of American Folklore* 22 (1909): 251.

35. Georgia Writer's Project, *Drums and Shadows*, p. 17.

36. Puckett, *Folk Beliefs*, p. 151. For other witch-riding traditions, see *Popular Beliefs and Superstitions from North Carolina*, Frank C. Brown Collection of North Carolina Folklore, vol. 7, Duke University (Chapel Hill, 1964), pp. 115–19.

37. Daniel Robinson Hundley, *Social Relations in Our Southern States* (New York, 1860), p. 330; Cross, "Witchcraft in North Carolina"; Mary Owen, *Among the Voodoos*, Proceedings of the International Folklore Congress (London, 1892), p. 241; Mary Owen, *Voodoo Tales, As Told Among the Negroes of the Southwest* (New York, 1893), pp. 10–11. The problem of the gender of witches in black American folk traditions is not easily resolved. Folklorist Fanny Bergen argues that most older black women were conceived of as witches, but Elsie Clews Parsons makes note of a "witch-man" who was a powerful specialist in one southern black community. See Fanny Bergen, *Current Superstitions Collected from the Oral Traditions of English-Speaking Folk* (New York, 1896), p. 128, and Elsie Clews Parsons, "Folklore of the Sea Islands," *Memoirs of the American Folk-lore Society* 16 (Cambridge, Mass., 1923), p. 61. Puckett describes some witches as evil succubi who steal wives, which suggests a masculine identity, as does Cross, who notes that "a male witch sometimes causes his neighbor to leave his bed, and then, entering the house, enjoys his wife." See Puckett, *Folk Beliefs*, p. 151; Cross, "Folklore," p. 251. While some accounts make reference to male witches, by far most witches in black folk narrative are female.

overlapped and merged with other folktales about spirits, ghosts, and other apparitions.[38]

The mythic transformation of the conjurer informed black perceptions of spiritual power as a gendered phenomenon. Supernatural tales made statements about women and the menace of potentially malign spirituality. Did the supernatural female figure signify danger, on some level, within African American culture and consciousness? More directly, did female conjurers, as actual persons, represent a threat to male spiritual authority? Evidence is sparse, but accounts indicate that some black women were chastised and punished by other members of the community for their use of the supernatural. In 1868, for example, a missionary on St. Helena Island described the battering of a black female by a family member in revenge for her "bewitching" a man.[39] In an earlier incident in South Carolina, a male slave was censured by the Welsh Neck Baptist Church for attacking an aged woman whom he was convinced had hexed him. In a separate case years later, former bondsman Jake McLeod recalled the hanging of an African American female slave who was accused of attempting to poison a white family. It was well known among other slaves, McLeod contended, that the woman practiced witchcraft.[40] Black women empowered by supernatural forces might have been seen as a threat to males' domination of sacred space, as well as an embodiment of the dangers of female spirituality, witchcraft, and maleficence within the larger society.

Unanswered questions remain in this exploration. In particular, the problem of the significance and tenacity of African American supernatural beliefs and traditions remains unexamined. What was the nature of relationship between supernaturalism and religion? Did conjure and Christianity overlap? Much of the evidence demonstrates that powerful, complex currents fed the spiritual beliefs of African Americans and that supernaturalism was indeed linked to religious belief. While there were strong objections to some of the ideas and assumptions of conjure, many blacks considered supernaturalism to be compatible with Christianity. A letter published in Hampton Institute's school newspaper in 1878 suggests that a relationship existed between Conjure and religious belief. A Hampton student had interviewed a local conjure woman, who declared that "she had a special revelation from God." The writer insisted that "all the conjure doctors [he] had ever heard of" had made similar claims.[41] Mary Owen

38. See, for example, Federal Writers Project, *South Carolina Folk Tales* (Columbia, S.C., 1941), and Charles Joyner, *Down by the Riverside: A South Carolina Slave Community* (Urbana, 1984), pp. 150–53.

39. *American Freedman* 3 (June 1868): 430, cited in Herbert Gutman, *The Black Family in Slavery and Freedom* (New York, 1977), p. 278.

40. Rawick, *American Slave*, vol. 3, pt. 3, p. 157.

41. *Southern Workman* 24 (July 1895): 117; see also Puckett, *Folk Beliefs*, p. 565 on the pious and reverential dispositions of Conjurers.

turned up similar evidence when she interviewed members of a "Voodoo" circle who met regularly at an African Methodist Episcopal church in northern Missouri. Among them was "Aunt Dorcas," who, like the other members, prepared charms, "jacks," and other objects that were endowed "with a familiar or attendant spirit in the name of the Lord."[42] For other blacks, Christianity and conjure combined as vital sources of healing power. Rossa Cooley, a white schoolteacher living in the South after the Civil War, explained how one local woman became desperately ill and, convinced she had been conjured, sought help from a "colored doctor" who prescribed medicine *and* prayer for relief from the affliction.[43] The overlap of Christianity and supernatural practices should not in itself be seen as unusual, given that throughout its history the church has manifested internal tensions between orthodoxy and popular notions of the efficacy of spiritual powers. The use of biblical sayings and prayers as ingredients in spells and charms, for example, is an occult tradition that dates far back to the origins of Christianity itself.[44]

While conventional religious accounts highlight the lives of African American male clergy or church elites, either they tend to overlook the roles of ordinary women or they obscure women's participation in noninstitutionalized spiritual traditions. At present we lack a paradigm that places black women's spirituality within an appropriate historical context. The personal stories and accounts of black women and their dealings with the supernatural highlight the intersection of race and gender within African American religious experience. Black women in the nineteenth and early twentieth centuries, like their present-day counterparts, utilized prac-

42. Owen, *Among the Voodoos*, p. 232.

43. Cooley, *Homes of the Freed*, p. 41; "Charles Chesnutt, Superstition and Folklore of the South," *Modern Culture* 13 (1901), reprinted in Alan Dundes, *Mother Wit from the Laughing Barrel* (New York, 1981), p. 374.

44. Supernaturalism also appears in the African American Protestant tradition. For example, the manipulation of the natural world was acknowledged by two black nineteenth-century female preachers, Rebecca Jackson and Amanda Smith. Although they did not perceive themselves as practitioners of conjure, both women adopted similar principles (the appropriation of spiritual power, control of forces) within their ministries. Both Jackson and Smith claimed that their abilities to control the weather, curtail threatening human behavior, and engage other skills was evidence of sacred power. See Jean Humez, "My Spirit Eye: Some Functions of Spiritual and Visionary Experience in the Lives of Five Black Women Preachers, 1810–1880," in *Women and the Structure of Society*, ed. Barbara Harris (Durham, 1984), pp. 136, 277; Jean Humez, ed., *Gifts of Power: The Writings of Rebecca Cox Jackson, Black Visionary, Shaker Eldress* (Amherst, Mass., 1981), pp. 22–23; Amanda Smith, *An Autobiography: The Story of the Lord's Dealings with Mrs. Amanda Smith, The Colored Evangelist* (1893; reprint, Chicago, 1988), p. 158. Eighteenth- and nineteenth-century white Methodist preachers were also among those who tapped into popular supernaturalist beliefs by claiming possession of spiritual gifts and attributes. See Butler, *Awash*, pp. 236–41, and Donald Byrne, *No Foot of Land: Folklore of American Methodist Itinerants* (Metuchen, N.J., 1975), pp. 155–70.

tices and beliefs that effectively accommodated eclectic understandings of spirituality and supernaturalism. Such beliefs were available to all persons. Conjure was an example of a fully democratic and egalitarian system of spiritual empowerment that provided explanation and control for men and women who experienced disempowerment, regardless of gender roles and expectations. Still, although both African American men and women utilized the supernatural to resist oppression, it appears that conjure had more significant implications for women. Conjure functioned as a cultural index of the vital issues that affected African American women's lives in slavery and in freedom: their health, safety, sexual competition, protection, status, and fulfillment.

The experiences of black women provide a window into the many levels at which African American life has been suffused with supernaturalism. For many black people, supernatural beliefs endure even today. African American religion provided black people with the basis for enduring, culturally specific visions of the world and the universe. Conjure and supernaturalism offered a worldview that promised limitless powers and possibilities. A full history of black women's appropriation of these spiritual alternatives waits to be written.

CHAPTER 8

"It's a Spirit in Me":
Spiritual Power and the Healing Work
of African American Women in Slavery

SHARLA FETT

African American communities have historically defined health as a
matter of the soul as well as the body. Spiritual power has therefore been
central to effective healing for a wide range of black practitioners from
conjure women to Holiness preachers.[1] Slave healers of the plantation
South, in particular, embedded their medicinal practices in a context of
sacred power. A formerly enslaved woman spoke to the spiritual significance of healing when she described how she had asked God to deliver her
from the misery of her swollen limbs. She testified that "the spirit directed
me to get some peach-tree leaves and beat them up and put them about my
limbs. I did this, and in a day or two that swelling left me, and I haven't
been bothered since. More than this, I don't remember ever paying out but
three dollars for doctor's bills in my life either for myself, my children, or
my grandchildren. Doctor Jesus tells me what to do."[2]

The appearance of this account within a longer conversion narrative
accentuates the connections between faith and healing. Deliverance from
illness through direct revelation from "the spirit" paralleled this woman's
deliverance from sin. Just as conversion propelled her to tell others of her
salvation, healing authorized her to cure others of their ailments. The
experience of healing by "Doctor Jesus" thus served as a point of transformation both in the woman's faith and in her labors to keep her family

I wish to thank Jerma Jackson, Charles Joyner, Suzanne Lebsock, John Rogers, and
Elizabeth Rose, who thoughtfully critiqued earlier versions of this chapter. A Dissertation
Grant from the National Endowment for the Humanities made much of the writing possible.

1. Albert J. Raboteau, "The Afro-American Traditions," in *Caring and Curing: Health and
Medicine in the Western Religious Traditions*, ed. Ronald L. Numbers and Darrel W.
Amundsen (New York, 1986), pp. 539–62. My title quotation comes from a conjure woman
named Seven Sisters who is quoted in Carl Carmer, *Stars Fell on Alabama* (New York, 1934),
p. 218. Oddly, the same quote is also attributed to a 1940 interview with a Virginia root
woman named Melviny Brown in the WPA Folklore Collection (box 2, folder 2, item 264),
Manuscripts Department, Alderman Library, University of Virginia, Charlottesville. The
dual attribution of this quote illustrates the challenges of working with folklore sources as
historical evidence.

2. Clifton H. Johnson, ed., *God Struck Me Dead: Religious Conversion Experiences and
Autobiographies of Ex-Slaves* (Philadelphia, 1969), p. 60.

healthy. Her experiences of affliction and restoration demonstrate the importance of healing, in scholar Beverly Robinson's words, as "a religious act, which places folk practitioners and their art in the world of the spiritual."[3]

This essay explores the collision of the "world of the spiritual" in black women's healing with the world of plantation labor. While healing work empowered enslaved women as spiritual leaders, it also put them in conflict with slaveholders who devalued both their faith and their skills. In the course of their labor, slave women healers had to contend with the conflicting notions of authority and subservience inherent in antebellum plantation healing. On the one hand, daily healing work was closely associated with related tasks of domestic servitude performed by slave women. On the other, many slave women invested their healing work with claims of spiritual empowerment. The work of slave healers was thus both a requirement of enslavement and a source of community autonomy. As such, it demonstrated a broader tension in slave women's labor between work as an outcome of exploitation and work as a source of pride and individual identity.

A broadly accepted paradigm for the tensions of opportunity and oppression in slave women's labor has been Jacqueline Jones' distinction between "labor of love" for kin and community and the "labor of sorrow" requisitioned by slaveholders.[4] However, slaveholders expected enslaved women to care for sick family and neighbors as well as resident whites. How, then, are we to understand forms of work that encompassed both "love" and "sorrow"? I will argue that the two sides of healing, as coerced labor and as spiritual expression, placed enslaved women in a position that was both vulnerable and transformative. The nature of nursing work made enslaved women vulnerable to the oversight of slaveholders and physicians who utilized their labor but denigrated their medical authority. Yet, the presence of women healers afforded enslaved communities a powerful resource for defining experiences of health and healing on their own terms. Furthermore, slave women transformed the meaning of their work through claims of spiritual authority that refuted planter notions of black female subservience.

Studies of spirituality in African American healing have not explored in depth the significance of women's herbalism and bedside care, the focus of this essay. Scholars of African American folkways have addressed questions of spiritual power in the practices of hoodoo, conjuration, and divination.[5]

3. Beverly J. Robinson, "Africanisms and the Study of Folklore," in *Africanisms in American Culture*, ed. Joseph E. Holloway (Bloomington, 1990), p. 219.
4. Jacqueline Jones, *Labor of Love, Labor of Sorrow: Black Women, Work, and the Family from Slavery to the Present* (New York, 1985), pp. 3, 29.
5. Eugene Genovese, *Roll, Jordan, Roll: The World the Slaves Made* (New York, 1976), pp. 215–29; Charles Joyner, *Down By the Riverside: A South Carolina Slave Community* (Chicago, 1984), pp. 142–50; Lawrence Levine, *Black Culture and Black Consciousness: Afro-American*

Yvonne Chireau's chapter in this book, a discussion of how African American women employed magic practices as alternative paths to spiritual expression, contributes a valuable gender analysis to this literature. Equally important to African American spiritual practice have been the mundane aspects of healing, such as the daily care slave women gave their families, the use of herbal medicines, and the labor of bedside nursing. Enslaved women, to a large extent, cared for the health needs of the slave quarters. They nursed the sick, birthed babies, treated injuries, and prepared the bodies of the dead for burial. Although the existing scholarship on slave women treats healing practices briefly in terms of female labor and slave community social structures, it does not examine them as expressions of religious belief.[6] As a result, the historiographical picture of slave community religion has been skewed in favor of male leadership (preachers and conjure men) and the institutional church, to the neglect of the spirituality of daily life.

An examination of bedside care and herbalism brings the neglected work of countless slave women into the history of African American spirituality during slavery. Historians of "slave religion" have examined how practices such as the ring shout and worship in secret brush arbors provided an autonomous space for spiritual renewal away from the demands of plantation labor.[7] However, unlike stealing away to the woods to worship, healing did not offer a reprieve from the demands of the plantation. It was instead another dimension of female slave labor. As such, healing practices stood at the intersection of plantation production, women's work in their communities, and African American spiritual expression. Examining notions of spiritual power in slave women's healing thus not only offers insight into antebellum black female spirituality but, more specifically, also highlights the ways in which African American women created and maintained forms of spiritual expression in the very midst of their lives as enslaved laborers.

Folk Thought from Slavery to Freedom (New York, 1977), pp. 55–80; Albert J. Raboteau, *Slave Religion: The "Invisible Institution" in the Antebellum South* (New York, 1978), pp. 80–86, 275–85. A gender analysis of the shifting character of voodoo practice and practitioners in New Orleans during the nineteenth century appears in Jessie Gaston Mulira, "The Case of Voodoo in New Orleans," *Africanisms in American Culture*, pp. 34–68.

6. Deborah Gray White, *Ar'n't I a Woman?: Female Slaves in the Plantation South* (New York, 1985), pp. 115–16, 124–26; Elizabeth Fox-Genovese, *Within the Plantation Household: Black and White Women of the Old South* (Chapel Hill, 1988), pp. 169–71; Jacqueline Jones, *Labor of Love*, p. 40. Martia Graham Goodson also discusses slave women's healing knowledge in "Medical-Botanical Contributions of African Slave Women to American Medicine," *The Western Journal of Black Studies* 11 (1987): 198–203. Todd Savitt discusses enslaved women nurses among other African-American practitioners in Virginia in Savitt, *Medicine and Slavery: The Diseases and Health Care of Blacks in Antebellum Virginia* (Urbana, 1978), pp. 179–81.

7. Raboteau, *Slave Religion*, pp. 212–19; Sterling Stuckey, *Slave Culture: Nationalist Theory and the Foundations of Black America* (New York, 1987), pp. 3–97.

"I Don't Do Nothing But Nurse, Nurse, Nurse": The Labor of Healing

The women designated in plantation slave rosters as "hospital nurse," "midwife," or "doctoress," contributed critical labor to southern plantation communities. One such healer was an elderly woman named Elsey, whose responsibilities suggest the potential for both autonomy and exploitation inherent in her work. In 1832, the Georgian planter Alexander Telfair left the following instructions for the Thorn Island Plantation: "Elsey is the Doctress of the Plantation. In case of extraordinary illness, when she thinks she can do no more for the sick you will employ a Physician." Though an overseer described Thorn Island as a place of sickness and death, the seventy-six year old Elsey assumed charge of all but the most severe illnesses in the slave quarters housing over thirty-five men, women, and children. She was also the midwife "to black and white in the neighborhood." In fact, Elsey was in such demand that the Telfair family became anxious about collecting the large outstanding debt owed by nearby free families in return for her midwifery services. When neither birth nor illness demanded her attention, Elsey served as the nurse for slave children and worked in the plantation yard.[8]

Elsey's position afforded her unusual mobility for an enslaved woman, but the labor she did was familiar to slaves and slaveholders alike as "women's work."[9] Nursing and midwifery involved a panoply of domestic skills, since slave healers did not merely keep watch over the sick and women in labor. They made medicines, prepared food, and washed the bodies and bedclothes of the sick. Healing work thus overlapped with domestic tasks of cooking, cleaning, and laundering. For example, in addition to nursing and midwifery, Elsey raised poultry and rendered tallow used to make soap, salve, and candles. What is more, women who understood the medicinal properties of plants often possessed similar expertise in the use of plants for food, dyes, cloth, and other household products. The close association between healing and female domestic labor imbued healing with elements of skill and servitude.

While all plantation residents seem to have agreed that nursing and midwifery were appropriately done by women, the gender division of healing work among enslaved African Americans differed from that of white, upper-class Southerners. White record keepers carefully distinguished between black male and female healers, calling them "negro doctors" and "doctoresses." Regardless of gender, however, African Americans referred

8. Thorn Island Rule and Direction Book, 11 June 1832, and 1837; "List of Negroes at Thorn Island," 1836; Stephen Newman to Miss Telfair, 28 February 1837, Telfair Family Papers, Georgia Historical Society Library, Savannah, Georgia.

9. Leslie Owens, *This Species of Property: Slave Life and Culture in the Old South* (New York, 1976), p. 195; Jones, *Labor of Love*, pp. 29–43.

to the activities of these healers as "doctoring." Compared to the antebellum male medical establishment, which rigidly excluded women, slave healers treated gender flexibly. Men as well as women demonstrated a general knowledge of common medicinal herbs, and both men and women, usually older ones, practiced as conjure doctors. Overall, the distribution of healing work among African American men and women suggests that in certain areas of healing—in particular conjuration, or hoodoo—claims to healing authority depended not so much on gender as on spiritual revelation, effectiveness, and training.

Despite the presence of male healers within slave communities, the laborious task of attending the sick on plantations devolved primarily upon enslaved women. Healers like Elsey accumulated their skills over a lifetime of labor. For example, a woman named Ellen Betts gained nursing experience as a girl by caring for the white and black children of a large Louisiana sugar plantation. Although the designation of "nurse" often meant child care, this task inevitably involved looking after sick children; and frequently, as in Ellen Betts' case, it led to other healing tasks. As a grown woman, Betts began nursing adults, and her work included dosing her patients with calomel, rhubarb, and ipecac left by the physician.[10] Another North Carolina woman, Sarah MacDonald, followed a similar path, beginning with wet-nursing and caring for children. She then moved to nursing the sick in white households, and to washing and shrouding their bodies before burial. In the course of this work, she developed her own practice as an herbalist and by the end of her life had established a reputation as a specialist in the cure of rheumatism.[11] While some women worked as healers for the plantation their entire life, planters assigned most women to nursing work only in youth and old age, reserving their strongest years for field work.[12] Many women took pride in their work, but the work took a heavy toll on their bodies. Ellen Betts summed up the fatigue of slave women's continuous heavy labor: "I don't do nothing all my days, but nurse, nurse, nurse."[13]

Sarah MacDonald's ability to develop skills as an herbalist while working as a sick nurse for white families points to a paradox within black women's healing. While masters and mistresses depended on slave women's healing work as a privilege of the planter class, slave women also used their healing skills as a basis for authority and leadership in their communities. The

10. B. A. Botkin, *Lay My Burden Down: A Folk History of Slavery* (Chicago, 1945; reprint, New York, 1994), pp. 132–37. Calomel, ipecac, and rhubarb were therapeutics used for purging and to produce vomiting.

11. Rawick, *The American Slave: A Composite Autobiography* (Westport, Conn., 1977), vol. 14, North Carolina, pp. 53–54.

12. Carole Shammas, "Black Women's Work and the Evolution of Plantation Society in Virginia," *Labor History* 26 (Winter 1985): 5–28.

13. Botkin, *Lay My Burden Down*, p. 133.

crucial role of black healers in the health of the slave quarters led scholar John Blassingame to suggest that the services of midwives, herbalists, and other healers elevated them in the social structure of slave communities.[14] One possible sign of the high status commanded by the doctoress Elsey appears in Alexander Telfair's records. In addition to Elsey the doctoress, Telfair's slave lists include a young woman and two small children named either Elsey or Elcy. Whether or not all these Elseys were related by blood is unclear. Although it was unusual for enslaved families to name daughters after mothers, they did sometimes name them after grandmothers. It is possible that the three younger Elseys were named for the midwife who attended their birth. Since enslaved African Americans used naming practices to remember an honored person, the recurrence of the name Elsey provides a glimpse into ways in which Thorn Island families may have recognized an older healer's respected position.[15]

Whereas the aging Elsey served the entire neighborhood, many enslaved women initially developed their skills within family circles. Among the memories that former slaves held of their mothers, recollections of home doctoring ranked high. Solomon Caldwell recalled his South Carolina childhood: "I' member my ma would take fever grass and boil it to tea and have us drink it to keep de fever away. She used branch elder twigs and dogwood berries for chills."[16] Many former slaves remembered their mothers dispensing a daily dose of preventative "bitters" (a mixture of whiskey and tree bark) or tying pungent asafetida bags around their necks to sustain health.[17] Others described more eclectic treatments. Ranson Sidney Taylor recalled, "My mother looked after most of us when we were sick. She used roots, herbs, and grease, and medicine the overseer got in town. When my mother got through rubbin' you, you would soon be well."[18]

Along with herb preparations, slave women attempted to preserve family well-being by teaching children the meaning of signs. Signs conveyed the threat of death, the meaning of dreams, and portents of future interactions with neighbors or enemies. Within slave community definitions of health, signs served as remedies against misfortune alongside herbal medicines. For

14. John W. Blassingame, "Status and Social Structure in the Slave Community: Evidence from New Sources," in *Perspectives and Irony in American Slavery*, ed. Harry P. Owens (Jackson, Miss., 1976), pp. 142–43.

15. "List of Negroes at Thorn Island," Account Book, 1837, Telfair Family Papers. On the significance of slave naming practices see Herbert G. Gutman, *The Black Family in Slavery and Freedom, 1750–1925* (New York, 1976), pp. 185–201; Cheryl Ann Cody, "There was no 'Absalom' on the Ball Plantation," *American Historical Review* 92 (June 1987): 563–96.

16. Rawick, *American Slave* 2, South Carolina, p. 171.

17. *Slave Narratives—A Folk History of Slavery in the United States*, vol. 12, Georgia Narratives (reprint, St. Clair Shores, Mich., 1976), pp. 19, 49, 134, 212.

18. Rawick, *American Slave* 15, North Carolina, p. 339.

example, Harriet Collins' mother taught her a host of "doctorin' things," including the use of white sassafras tea for rheumatism and horseradish poultices for headaches. She also instructed her in reading signs for good fortune and protection from enemies.[19] The knowledge of signs and of medicinal herbs and roots formed part of the slave woman's arsenal against the dangers of ill health and slaveholder violence. Watching over family health was thus a training ground for skills that some older women would later apply to entire communities.

Age played an important role in shaping the vulnerabilities and opportunities of slave women's healing work. Old age invested slave doctoresses with great authority that often extended beyond healing to broader community leadership.[20] In numerous reminiscences, former slaves recalled the work of elderly slave women with affection and respect. A woman named Polly Shine recalled "the best of care": "Maser would get us a Negro mama, and she doctored us from herbs she got out of the woods," for coughs and colds.[21] Children in slave communities grew up learning to behave respectfully toward the elderly and to honor the wisdom they had acquired by a long life. For many enslaved men and women, the "old folks" represented the closest link to the African past. As they approached the end of life, the spiritual potency of the elderly increased, since imminent death brought them closer to the world of ancestors and spirits.[22]

When sickness arose in the slave quarters, both slaves and slaveholders looked to older slave women's skills. Carrie Mason, born into slavery in Georgia, summed up the widespread reliance by both blacks and whites on elderly black women healers. Her twentieth-century interviewer recorded her words as follows: "Didn't nobody hardly have a doctor in dem days. De white folks used yarbs an' ole 'omans to he'p 'em at dat time."[23] Georgia

19. James Mellon, *Bullwhip Days: The Slaves Remember* (New York, 1988), p. 94. See also Rawick, *American Slave*, suppl. 1, vol. 4, Georgia, pp. 649–52, and suppl. 1, vol. 3, Georgia, p. 28; Newbell Niles Puckett, *Folk Beliefs of the Southern Negro* (Montclair, N.J, 1968), pp. 311–438.

20. Frances Anne Kemble, *Journal of a Residence on a Georgian Plantation in 1838–1839* (New York, 1863), p. 251. For a discussion of southern black midwives, their social authority, and their spiritual calling in the twentieth century, see Debra Anne Susie, *In the Way of Our Grandmothers: A Cultural View of Twentieth-Century Midwifery in Florida* (Athens, Ga., 1988).

21. Mellon, *Bullwhip Days*, p. 97.

22. For discussions of respect for the aged as part of African and African American culture, see Joyner, *Down by the Riverside*, pp. 64–65; Stuckey, *Slave Culture*, p. 31; John S. Mbiti, *African Religions and Philosophy* (New York, 1969), p. 81; Blassingame, "Status and Social Structure," p. 149; Wyatt Macgaffey, "The Eyes of Understanding: Kongo Minkisi," in *Astonishment and Power* (Washington, D.C., 1993), p. 59.

23. Rawick, *American Slave*, suppl. 1, vol. 4, Georgia, p. 421; Rawick, *American Slave 14*, North Carolina, p. 413. The Rawick series is a compilation of interviews with former slaves collected by WPA workers in the 1930s. Many of the WPA interviewers and editors attempted to represent the speech of elderly black men and women in "dialect." The dialect generally reflected more about the patronizing way that the writers perceived their

rice planter Richard J. Arnold instructed his overseer to rely on the experience of sixty-one-year-old Daphney and thirty-one-year-old Nan as the best nurses in case of a cholera epidemic. Daphney spent a good part of her time in domestic and nursing work, since she stayed to assist new mothers for a fortnight after their births.[24] Similarly, slave lists from a Virginia plantation in 1863 show a sixty-three-year-old woman named Malvina as "Doctress" for the Plantation.[25] A former slave from South Carolina, Gus Feaster, remembered older women would "take and study what to do fer de ailments of grown folks and lil' chilluns." Not only did these women know how to wean, feed, bathe, and protect the health of the babies, but Feaster also remembered them making pine rosin pills for the aching backs of men and women who worked in the fields.[26]

Older women left their legacy not only in their immediate healing work but in their role as teachers. Through what one North Carolina man called "fireside training," elderly healers passed along both their healing practices and their underlying views of illness to younger women.[27] When the doctoress Elsey left Thorn Island plantation to attend a birth, her daughter assumed Elsey's place as nurse for the slave children.[28] On another Georgia plantation, Susan, the plantation "hospital nurse," was the daughter of Sarah, designated as "Old Nurse" on a slave list.[29] Such evidence suggests that mothers found opportunities to teach their daughters healing skills and that plantation owners may have even expected these duties to pass from mothers to daughters. The transmission of healing knowledge, especially in the areas of healing and childbirth, continued into the post-emancipation generations. One woman in the South Carolina Sea Islands expressed her commitment to her mother's knowledge: "My moder taught me day way,

---

informants than about the informants' use of language. Quotations from the WPA collections appear in this study as they do in their original written form. Therefore, it is important for readers to keep in mind the biases represented in the appearance of these quotations.

24. J. R. Arnold to I. Swanston, 22 May 1837, Instructions to overseer, series 1.1, folders 2 and 3, Arnold and Screven Family Papers, Southern Historical Collection, Chapel Hill, N.C. I am indebted to Leigh Pruneau for directing me to this collection.

25. Plantation & Farm Record Inventory and Account Book, volume a3, 1863, Philip St. George Cocke Papers, Virginia Historical Society, Richmond, Virginia.

26. Rawick, *American Slave* 2, South Carolina, pp. 2, 55, 68. For other references to older women's primary role in healing see Rawick, *American Slave*, suppl. 1, vol. 3, Georgia, p. 239, and suppl. 1, vol. 4, Georgia, p. 421; Ophelia Settle Egypt, J. Masuaoka, and Charles S. Johnson, eds., *Unwritten History of Slavery: Autobiographical Account of Negro Ex-Slaves* (Nashville, 1945), p. 38; Harriet Jacobs, *Incidents in the Life of a Slave Girl*, edited by Jean Fagan Yellin (Cambridge, Mass., 1987), p. 98.

27. White, *Ar'n't I a Woman?*, p. 116. Rawick, *American Slave* 15, North Carolina, p. 3.

28. Thorn Island Rule and Direction Book, 11 June 1832, Telfair Family Papers.

29. Slave list from "The Refuge," 1859, Duncan Clinch Papers, Manuscripts Division, Library of Congress, Washington, D.C.

started me dat way, [I] keep up de way she started me."[30] Intergenerational continuity, as discussed below, was a central tenet of slave community spirituality.

Such a valuation of age and wisdom stands in stark contrast to the attitude of slaveholders, who in their ledgers recorded the depreciation of the bodies of older African Americans. From the slaveholder's viewpoint, a female slave too weak to work in the fields and too old for childbearing could still provide vital labor to the plantation through caring for the sick and looking after children. However, the age of these women—not their skills—determined their monetary value under chattel slavery. For example, slave lists from one Virginia plantation in 1854 valued Maria, aged fifty-three and listed as a "nurse," at $200. Nancy (no age recorded), a "nurse for sick," was valued at $250, while the same slaveholder assessed "prime" women field hands at $400.[31] Ironically, old age, the very factor which signaled authority in slave communities, devalued older women in the eyes of slaveholders. Compounding this devaluation of older women, as I shall discuss below, was a systematic condescension by the white male physicians who occasionally visited patients in the slave quarters.

Contrasting valuations of old age provide just one illustration of underlying tensions over gender, race, and authority in slave women's healing. Consigned to a position of subservience by white supremacist ideology, enslaved black women found their judgment and methods as healers frequently questioned by slaveholders, physicians, and overseers. The association of healing work with domestic labor also reinforced the racist conviction that slave women's function as nurses reflected their "natural" position of subservience. A divergent view emerged from enslaved communities, however, where healing connoted personal reputation, community position, and spiritual calling.

Spiritual Insight in Herbalism and Bedside Attendance

If enslaved women found their skills appropriated by slaveholders, many also viewed their healing work as a source of personal identity and spiritual growth. The language of spiritual empowerment served as the medium through which African American women claimed knowledge and explained their skills. Alabama midwife Lula Russeau used this language in looking back on her work and the work of her mother in slavery. In an interview with a Federal Writer's Project worker, Lula Russeau explained her ability to foretell the future and see spirits. Her mother, a slave woman with

30. Elsie Worthington Clews Parsons, *Folk-Lore of the Sea Islands, South Carolina* (New York, 1923), p. 197. See also Georgia Writers Project, *Drums and Shadows: Survival Studies among the Georgia Coastal Negroes* (Athens, Ga., 1940), pp. 131, 68.
31. "Inventory of Negroes," 1854, Philip St. George Cocke Papers.

Chickasaw heritage, had worked as a laundress, granny midwife, and spinner. She had made her own medicines from local plants and taught her daughter Lula everything she knew about herbs, charms, and birthing. In addition to the knowledge received from her mother, Lula Russeau also believed that she had a divine gift of healing. The caul covering her face at birth was a sign of her calling. "I was born one [a granny]," she declared, "God made me that way."[32]

Whether they worked primarily as midwives, herbalists, or nurses, many African American healers recounted similar experiences of spiritual revelation. Just as nineteenth-century white male physicians cited medical schools or reputable mentors to legitimate their practice, enslaved African American healers often pointed to divine insight as a legitimating source of their abilities. Healing knowledge came to them through dreams, signs, visions, guidance from God or "Doctor Jesus," and lessons passed on from previous generations. Many women healers, as well as some men, spoke in an explicitly Christian language of God working through them. The metaphor of serving as God's "instrument" enabled the healer to speak of her skills in terms of Christian humility while at the same time claiming her own authority and effectiveness.[33] Thus, a woman who had nursed numerous patients described herself as "an instrument in God's hand." She testified: "I always take Doctor Jesus with me and put him in front, and if there is any hope he lets me know."[34] Others referred to healing knowledge as a birthright. A Georgia woman explained: "Seems lak yuh jes' hab tuh be born wid duh knowledge. I jes allus seemed tuh know how tuh work cures and make medicines."[35] The assertion of confidence and capability in healing rested on a spiritual source of power that slaveholders could not undermine. These confident claims of slave women healers directly contradicted slaveholder images of the subservient, elderly nurse.

One of the healing traditions widely associated in the antebellum period with older African American women was that of herbalism. Preparations from local plants provided an extensive pharmacopeia, whether the remedy was pepper and dogwood tea for fever, snakeroot for stomachache, or a body wrap of cabbage or ginseng leaves.[36] Some of the medicinal plants

32. Lula Russeau interview, 1938, Federal Writer's Project, Microfiche Collection, Southern Historical Collection, Chapel Hill, N.C.

33. For a discussion of the language of female religious empowerment in a nineteenth-century context, see Jean McMahon Humez' introduction to *Gifts of Power: The Writings of Rebecca Jackson, Black Visionary, Shaker Eldress* (Amherst, Mass., 1981), pp. 1–50.

34. Johnson, *God Struck Me Dead*, pp. 97–98.

35. Rawick, *American Slave*, suppl. 1, vol. 4, Georgia, p. 584.

36. Rawick, *American Slave*, suppl. 1, vol. 3, Georgia, p. 27, Mellon, *Bullwhip Days*, p. 97; Rawick, *American Slave* 15, North Carolina, p. 134. Mention of medicinal plants is extensive in the WPA collections. For other descriptions of African American uses of botanical medicine, see Faith Mitchell, *Hoodoo Medicine: Sea Island Herbal Remedies* (Berkeley, 1978); William Ed Grimé, *Ethno-Botany of the Black Americans* (Algonac, Mich., 1979);

used on southern plantations were grown by black women in their small "patches" and in plantation fields. On a St. Helena Island plantation in the 1850s, a nurse and midwife named Judy laboriously ground and processed the plantation's arrowroot crop, which was used to nourish babies and invalids.[37] Another woman, Della Barksdale, remembered the patch of flagroot grown by her mother and grandmother during slavery in Virginia. As an adult, she continued to raise the tall grasslike plant, whose root was chewed or made into a tea for stomach ailments.[38]

Although selected herbs grew in gardens and fields, enslaved healers often had to leave the cultivated plantation lands in order to find medicinal plants growing wild. African American herbalists regarded the woods in particular as a space of divine insight. "Aunt Darkas," a blind woman known widely in Georgia as a healer, attributed her remarkable abilities with forest plants to God's guidance. A woman previously cured by "Aunt Darkas" described the healer's methods of herb gathering: "She wuz blind, but she could go ter the woods and pick out any kind of root or herb she wanted. She always said the Lord told her what roots to get, and always 'fore sunup, you would see her in the woods with a short-handled pick. She said she had ter pick 'em 'fore sunup."[39]

In the thick woods or marshy lowlands, one had to be able to find specific plants, such as black snakeroot, slippery elm, or wild sage. Besides distinguishing between poisonous and curative plants, the herbalist needed to know when a plant was ready to be picked, at what time of day or lunar cycle it would be most potent, and how to process it into medicine. Healing with herbs thus required a storehouse of knowledge about the southern landscape as well as human illnesses.[40]

The full significance of herbalism emerges only in its relationship to the spiritual life of slave healers. Seeking spiritual insight was an essential part of the process of healing with local plants, so much so that claims to

---

D. E. Cadwallader and F. J. Wilson, "Folklore Medicine among Georgia's Piedmont Negroes after the Civil War," *Georgia Historical Quarterly* 49 (1965): 217–27; Martia Graham Goodson, "Medical-Botanical Contributions of African Slave Women," pp. 198–203; Payne-Jackson and Lee, *Folk Wisdom and Mother Wit*, pp. 35–158.

37. Theodore Rosengarten, ed., *Tombee: Portrait of a Cotton Planter* (New York, 1986), pp. 477, 491, 512, 513, 590.

38. WPA Folklore Collection, 1941, box 2, folder 6, item 372. Steven Foster and James A. Duke, *A Field Guide to Medicinal Plants: Eastern and Central North America* (Boston, 1990), pp. 86, 312.

39. Mellon, *Bullwhip Days*, p. 95.

40. Rawick, *American Slave* 2, South Carolina, p. 24; Egypt, Masuoaka, and Johnson, *Unwritten History*, pp. 313, 38. Vennie Deas-Moore, "Home Remedies, Herb Doctors, and Granny Midwives," *The World and I: A Chronicle of Our Changing Era*, Jan. 1987, p. 480; Mitchell, *Hoodoo Medicine*, p. 27; Francis Peyre Porcher, *Resources of the Southern Fields and Forests* (Charleston, S.C., 1869), pp. 5–7.

spiritual revelation were often inseparable from discussions of skill and experience. Ethnobotanical studies of herbalism that employ a biomedical framework often focus exclusively on the botanical materials themselves as the efficacious agents in herbal healing.[41] Such an approach, however informative, fails to address the importance of the idea of God's guidance in the preparation and use of herbal medicines. Spiritual sources of knowledge played an important part in the gathering and administration of botanical medicines.

For many antebellum African Americans, knowledge of herbal medicine was rooted in a historical relationship between God, human beings, and nature. The theology of slave communities, anchored in the Exodus story, contained a strong theme of God's provision for a chosen people.[42] The provisioning extended to herbal medicines. Just as God had supplied manna in the wilderness to the Israelites, so too God provided divine sustenance for the sick and enslaved. Della Barksdale echoed the sentiments of many rural Southerners when she voiced her conviction that God had created roots and herbs for every imaginable illness.[43] Some leaders spoke of their knowledge as a "gift of understanding" that rivaled and even surpassed the wisdom of education through books.[44] Twentieth-century informants spoke of the knowledge of herbs as a "gift from God," granted under the particular circumstances of slavery. Janie Cameron Riley of North Carolina assessed the necessity of God-given knowledge: "They knowed what they was doing back in those days, people really did . . . I'm telling you right now, the black people had to have some kind of knowledge from God; they had to, "cause they didn't have nothing else to dwell on."[45] Some African Americans viewed this gift of understanding as a realm of power unavailable to white people. Silvia King, an accomplished herbalist, contrasted white folks' education with her own

41. A recent study which discusses an African American herbalist's spiritual calling as well detailing the pharmacological content of his medicines is Arvilla Payne-Jackson and John Lee, *Folk Wisdom and Mother Wit: John Lee—An African American Herbal Healer* (Westport, Conn., 1993).

42. Raboteau, *Slave Religion*, pp. 311–12; Mechal Sobel, *Trabelin' On: The Slave Journey to an Afro-Baptist Faith* (1979; reprint, Princeton, 1988), p. 125; Theophus H. Smith, *Conjuring Culture: Biblical Formations of Black America* (New York, 1994), pp. 67–69.

43. WPA Folklore Collection, box 2, folder 6, item 372, See also Charles L. Perdue, Jr., Thomas E. Barden, and Robert K. Phillips, *Weevils in the Wheat: Interviews with Virginia Ex-Slaves* (Charlottesville, Va., 1976), p. 310; Payne-Jackson and Lee, *Folk Wisdom and Mother Wit*, p. 19. For a discussion of twentieth-century African American beliefs about nature and gardening, see Richard Westmacott, *African-American Gardens and Yards in the Rural South* (Knoxville, 1992), pp. 87–100.

44. Rawick, *American Slave*, suppl. 1, vol. 11, South Carolina, pp. 68–72. Botkin, *Lay My Burden Down*, pp. 45–47.

45. Interview with Janie Cameron Riley & Moselle Cameron, June 6, 1975, Southern Oral History Program, Southern Historical Collection, Chapel Hill N.C.

knowledge when she remarked, "White folks just go through de woods and don't know nothin'."[46]

Healing knowledge for enslaved African Americans came not only from an individual's relationship to God but from an entire spiritual world. Dreams and visions were also an important source of insight. One elderly woman near Tuskegee described the encouragement she received when her sick baby granddaughter did not seem to be recovering. A dead friend came to her in a dream and reassured her that the child would not die. The dream restored her confidence in her treatments, and the child lived. "It sho' was a miracle sent from God," concluded the woman.[47] Justine Singleton, a Georgia woman, similarly described how her dead sister came to her with a remedy for her illness. Visions also warned of the impending death of a sick loved one.[48] Transmission of knowledge through such visitations revealed a cosmology in which the power to heal flowed from a community made up of living persons, ancestors, and God.

The nature of spiritual power in African American slave cosmology is captured in visual form by the image of the cosmogram. Art historian Robert Farris Thompson argues that the image of the Bakongo cosmogram and its trans-Atlantic variations inscribe the relationship of the world of the living to the world of spirits. The basic form of the cosmogram, $\oplus$, two intersecting lines within a circle, signified the structure of the universe with God above, the ancestors below, and the earth between. Drawn on the ground or represented in a forked stick or a crossroads, the cosmogram signified in African American lore the spiritual power that came from connections to one's ancestors.[49] In fact, it is possible that enslaved healers used this very symbol to fashion the clay bowls in which they processed their herbal medicines. Archaeologists of southern plantations have recovered many small bowls of a slave-made pottery called Colonoware. Carved into the base of each of these bowls is a basic cosmogram. Archaeologist Leland Ferguson has suggested that, although these vessels have been previously interpreted as food containers, they may instead have been medicine bowls for African American herbalists.[50] In its depiction of spiri-

46. Norman R. Yetman, ed. *Life Under the "Peculiar Institution": Selections from the Slave Narrative Collection* (New York, 1970), p. 201, quoted in Levine, *Black Culture and Black Consciousness*, p. 73.

47. Charles S. Johnson, *Shadow of the Plantation* (1934; reprint, New York, 1979), p. 195.

48. Georgia Writers Project, *Drums and Shadows*, p. 69; Alice Bacon, "A Trip through the South," *Southern Workman* 23 (May 1894): 81.

49. Robert Farris Thompson, "Kongo Influences on African American Artistic Culture," in *Africanisms in American Culture*, ed. Joseph E. Holloway (Bloomington, 1990), pp. 152-57; Robert Farris Thompson, *Flash of the Spirit: African and Afro-American Art and Philosophy* (New York, 1983), pp. 103-59.

50. Leland Ferguson, *Uncommon Ground: Archaeology and Early African America, 1650–1800* (Washington, D.C., 1992), pp. 110-113.

tual power infusing earthly life, the cosmogram in the medicine bowl illustrates the spiritual dimension of enslaved women's daily work. It serves as a reminder that the power of the spirit could be present in an older woman's remedies as well as in spirit possession and church meetings.

In addition to serving as a symbol of spiritual power, the cosmogram mapped out communal relationships that figured heavily in bedside attendance. Just as slave women were primarily responsible for making herbal remedies, they were also largely (but not exclusively) responsible for tending the sick. On the few very large plantations in the South, nurses worked in separate hospital buildings for the sick and injured. On most plantations, however, the sick received care within the slave quarters. The small size of one- and two-room slave houses with single hearths frequently brought the injured and the sick into the social life of evening gatherings. Especially when death seemed imminent, enslaved men and women placed great emphasis on surrounding the sick person with prayers and encouragement. Thus, gathering at the sickbed became an integral part of the healing process and underscored the connections between an individual and the larger community.[51]

An elderly freedman named Simon Brown emphasized the image of the community at the sickbed in his reminiscence of Virginia slavery. Recounting earlier days to young listeners, Brown explained that "if a slave became ill, he wasn't left alone to suffer unattended. . . . In time of illness or other trouble, fellow slaves would 'turn in and help out'." The support that men and women provided reflected the gendered division of labor within slave communities. Men cut firewood, and women came to the cabin to cook, tend children, and wash clothes. The spirit in which men and women performed these chores was important to Brown's story: "Women would come over jus' to sit a spell an' sing an' pray 'roun' the sickbed. Nobody was lef' to suffer alone. Sometimes a man or woman with a healin' touch would brew an herb tea, mix a poultice or apply peach tree leaves to a fevered brow, to help the sick get well. And all this lovin' care cheer' up the trouble' soul, whether he got well or died."[52] Brown's story paints a remarkable portrait of neighbors offering their presence as a healing balm to both the body and the "troubled soul." As I will argue below, this ideal of healing as a social process proved difficult to realize within the dangerous and unpredictable environment of the plantation.

Gathering around a sick or injured person became an important ritual in

51. Savitt, *Medicine and Slavery*, p. 162; John Michael Vlach, *Back of the Big House: The Architecture of Plantation Slavery* (Chapel Hill, 1993), pp. 18–32, 153–82; Margaret Washington Creel, *"A Peculiar People": Slave Religion and Community-Culture among the Gullahs* (New York, 1988), p. 311.

52. William J. Faulkner, *The Days When the Animals Talked: Black American Folktales and How They Came To Be* (Chicago, 1977), pp. 34–39. Also quoted in Stuckey, *Slave Culture*, p. 39.

the face of the violence of slavery. During the evening hours, slave women applied ointment to cuts and welts on the bodies of those who had been whipped and beaten during the day.[53] Solomon Northup's narrative of abduction from the North into slavery in the deep South describes the comfort of such care. After a day of abuse, Northup lay in his cabin bleeding and unable to move. As the workday ended, men and women came in from the fields and gathered around his bed. Two women boiled bacon, made him scorched-corn coffee, and tried to console him as they recounted the day's events. This was hardly an isolated occurrence in Northup's account of slavery. Several other passages in *Twelve Years a Slave* also described how fellow slaves "endeavored to assist and console" those who suffered from severe lashings and debilitating illness.[54]

In Northup's narrative, as in many slave narratives published in the antebellum years, slave efforts to attend the sick served as a strategic metaphor that heightened the humanity of enslaved women and men and underscored the lack of human compassion in the slaveholder. Mary Prince, who endured Caribbean slavery, repeatedly portrayed the empathy and assistance of fellow slaves in the face of cruel and indifferent slaveholders.[55] Other antebellum slave narratives emphasized the barbarity of slavery by highlighting the slaveholder's denial of Christian comforts, such as Bible reading, to dying slaves. Henry Bibb described sickness and death under slavery where "no special aid is afforded the suffering slave even in the last trying hour."[56] Set against this backdrop of callousness, simple acts such as feeding and bathing the sick became weighty evidence of the humanity and moral integrity of enslaved communities. In this way, slave narratives translated a central ritual of slave community healing into a powerful image in abolitionist literature.[57]

As both slave narratives and the testimony of former slaves demon-

53. Rawick, *American Slave* 14, North Carolina, p. 5, and vol. 15, North Carolina, p. 101; Johnson, *God Struck Me Dead*, p. 26; Moses Grandy, *Narrative of the Life of Moses Grandy, Late a Slave in the United States of America* (Boston, 1844), in *Five Slave Narratives: A Compendium* (New York, 1968), pp. 23, 32.

54. Solomon Northup, *Twelve Years a Slave: Narrative of Solomon Northup* (New York, 1853), in Gilbert Osofsky, ed., *Puttin On Ole Massa: The Slave Narratives of Henry Bibb, William Wells Brown, and Solomon Northup* (New York, 1969), pp. 288, 321, and 367. For a similar account see F. N. Boney, ed., *Slave Life in Georgia: A Narrative of the Life, Sufferings, and Escape of John Brown, A Fugitive Slave* (1855; reprint, Savannah, Ga., 1972), p. 27.

55. Mary Prince, *The History of Mary Prince, A West Indian Slave, Related by Herself* (London, 1831), in *Six Women's Slave Narratives*, ed. Henry Louis Gates Jr. (New York, 1988), pp. 8, 11, 14, 18–19.

56. Henry Bibb, *Narrative of the Life and Adventures of Henry Bibb, An American Slave, Written by Himself* (New York, 1849), in Osofsky, *Puttin On Ole Massa*, p. 122.

57. For an analysis of the transformative role of healing in Harriet Jacobs' narrative and the fiction of later African American women authors, see Athena Vrettos, "Curative Domains: Women, Healing, and History in Black Women's Narratives," *Women's Studies*, 16 (1989): 455–73. Elizabeth B. Clark argues that stories of suffering in antebellum slave

strated, spiritual power was vested not only in individual healers but in communal care. Through their presence at the pallet of a sick or injured person, African American women and men reaffirmed their collective relationship with God and acknowledged the bridge connecting life and death. Although bedside nursing practices can be analyzed in social terms alone, such an interpretation does not grasp the depth of meaning created by rituals of bedside attendance. The notion of spirituality in African American culture encompassed relations of kin and community, not just the dyad of God and an individual person. Thus, the custom of keeping the sick company, like the related practices of conjuration and divination, testified to the strength of the "sacred world" in which slave community activity was embedded. Prayer and song worked as medicine alongside the teas and poultices.[58]

Slave Women's Nursing in an Arena of Conflict

Simon Brown cherished a social and spiritual vision of healing, but the realities of plantation labor frequently denied the realization of such ideals. Enslaved black women forged their identities as healers in the midst of conflict. A Virginia midwife and nurse, Mildred Graves, made this point in her account of a bedside confrontation. Called to assist a white woman's birth complications, Graves arrived to find two white physicians already at the house. "I tol' dem I could bring her 'roun'," she recalled, "but dey laugh at me an' say, 'Get back darkie, we mean business an' don' [want] any witch doctors or hoodoo stuff.'"[59] Mildred Graves' memory of the event rings with the indignity of practicing midwifery in a society that regularly called upon yet frequently denigrated her skills. While this conflict was illustrative of a broader national conflict between physicians and midwives in the nineteenth century, it was also an important example of the particular obstacles that slave women faced as healers.[60] Slave women had to contend with a planter ideology that demanded subservient female labor and assumed the intellectual and spiritual inferiority of enslaved workers. It was Mildred Graves' identity as a slave woman, not just as a midwife, that

---

narratives had a transforming effect on the broader conception of individual rights. See Clark, "'The Sacred Rights of the Weak': Pain, Sympathy, and the Culture of Individual Rights in Antebellum America," *Journal of American History* 82 (Sept. 1995): 463–93.

58. Although informants generally describe the communal context of healing as supportive and harmonious, healing also had a conflictual side. This is seen in hoodoo, a system of harming and healing equally embedded in community relationships.

59. Perdue, Barden, and Phillips, *Weevils in the Wheat*, p. 120.

60. For a discussion of conflict between physicians and midwives during the early to mid nineteenth century see Judith Walzer Leavitt, *Brought to Bed: Childbearing in America, 1750–1950* (New York, 1986); Catherine M. Scholten, "'On the Importance of the Obstetrick Art': Changing Customs of Childbirth in America, 1760–1825," *William and Mary Quarterly* 34 (1977): 426–45; Richard W. Wertz and Dorothy C. Wertz, *Lying-In: A History of Childbirth in America* (New York, 1977).

caused the physicians to choose this particular insult. And it was by target-
ing her alleged spiritual beliefs that the physicians disparaged her medical
abilities. Their attack demonstrated a great degree of ambivalence in the
slaveholders' dependence on the healing labor of slave women.

The planters' view of slave women as plantation laborers often frustrated
these women's efforts to locate healing in community life. For women not
designated as plantation midwives or nurses, the ideal of healing within the
community was particularly elusive. Work schedules kept many slave mothers from providing their own families with a bedside presence and led them
to rely on "othermothers" in the quarters to provide the care they wished to
give.[61] Fannie Moore saw her grandmother, an experienced herbalist, come
to the aid of her mother, whose task of plowing the cotton fields of a South
Carolina plantation kept her from caring for her feverish son. Moore
recalled, "Granny she doctah him as bes' she could, evah time she git way
from de white folks kitchen. My mammy nevah git chance to see him, 'cept
when she git home in de evenin'." Labor demands probably did the most
to impede community care, but at times the isolation of sick or injured
slaves was deliberately enforced by slaveholders as a measure of "punishment." One man remembered how his grandmother died "wid nothin'
done fer her an' nobody wid her" after an overseer kicked her for resisting
a whipping. After the beating, the overseer had the woman taken to her
cabin and left abandoned until her death three days later.[62] Even the
provision of medical treatment by slaveholders at times interfered with this
collective vision of health, as when planters removed children and sick
adults on coastal plantations from their families to inland "pine lands"
considered to be healthier locations.[63]

In addition to denying community care, planter class ideology allowed
little room for black women to exercise medical authority through their
healing skills. Many southern planters, especially the wealthy owners of
large plantations, relied on older slave women to manage the daily health
concerns of the quarters. Charles Manigault, owner of several rice plantations
on the Savannah River, instructed his overseer to consult a slave woman
named Bina on matters of sickness. "The old Nurse Bina is a woman of the
highest character everybody has the highest opinion of her," he wrote.

61. Patricia Hill Collins argues that "othermothers, women who assist bloodmothers by
sharing mothering responsibilities, traditionally have been central to the institution of Black
motherhood." See Collins, "The Meaning of Motherhood in Black Culture and Black
Mother-Daughter Relationships," in *Double Stitch: Black Women Write about Mothers and
Daughters* (Boston, 1991), p. 47.

62. Rawick, *American Slave* 15, North Carolina, pp. 130–31, and vol. 14, North Carolina,
p. 395.

63. K. Washington Skinner to Charles Manigault, 29 October 1852 and 3 December 1852,
Manigault Family Papers, Special Collections Department, Duke University Library,
Durham, N.C. For an account of a black woman in Norfolk, Va., resisting the efforts of a
physician to remove her smallpox-afflicted son to the pest house, see Perdue, Barden, and
Phillips, *Weevils in the Wheat*, p. 262.

"Should a Negro come to you and say he is sick you should question him as to what ails him and then tell him to go to the Nurse Bina—when you will have time to decide what is best to be given him or her."[64] Several other references to Nurse Bina make it clear that she had far greater experience in the care of lowland illnesses and epidemics than did transient overseers. Yet, it was important to Manigault that treatment decisions—at least in appearance—rest with the overseer. Despite the dependence of planters and physicians on the healing work done by women within the slave quarters, these men viewed themselves as the appropriate final authorities on slave health.

The planters' assumption that slave women worked properly only under white authority obscured the spiritual dimensions of African American healing. When white observers did recognize the links between African American healing and religion, as in the story of Mildred Graves, many ridiculed the spiritual sources of legitimacy claimed by enslaved women healers. In nineteenth-century antebellum racial ideology, the elderly black woman came to represent the very embodiment of what slaveholders termed "superstition." Southern medical journals casually used the words "negroes" and "old women" as metonyms for "ignorance" in popular medicine. In so doing they underscored the centrality of gender and racial hierarchies to the construction of medical authority.[65] Despite a fervent national interest during this period in the relationship between mind and body, white slaveholders singled out slaves' beliefs as evidence of intellectual inferiority. Mesmerism and homeopathy, although marginalized, were experiments in science; black folk medicine was superstition.

Most slaveholders simply assumed that "superstition" and lack of knowledge impaired the ability of slave women to care independently for the sick. In their records, slaveholders frequently ascribed such characteristics as callousness, ignorance, and deceitfulness to slave women. Many planters reserved special hostility for African American mothers. William Massie responded to the death of a slave infant on his Virginia plantation in the 1840s by entering the notation: "Romulus died by waste caused by the unnatural neglect of his infamous mother."[66] Similarly, South Carolina planter Thomas Chaplin expressed exasperation over what he perceived as a slave woman's carelessness with her sick husband: "*Sept. 21st [1851].* Isaac had not the fever in the morning, but his precious wife [Amy] went off

64. "Hints for Mr. Papot," letters and papers 1840–1843 folder, Manigault Family Papers.
65. See, for example, E. M. Pendleton, "On the Comparative Fecundity of the Caucasian and African Races," *The Charleston Medical Journal and Review* 6 (1851): 355; James B. McCaw, "On the Present Condition of the Medical Profession in Virginia," *Virginia Medical and Surgical Journal* 3 (Oct. 1853): 45; "Medical Ethics in Virginia," *The Virginia Medical Journal* 7 (1856): 257; "Medical Cossacks," *Virginia Medical Journal* 11 (Oct. 1858): 355.
66. Entry of 3 April 1844, Account Book, 1836–1865, William Massie Slave Records, Virginia State Library, Richmond, p. 21.

to church instead of coming to me for quinine for him as she was directed, & consequently the fever came on again in the evening." As a devout Christian, Amy's concern over her husband's illness may very well have increased her desire to attend Sunday morning worship. Thomas Chaplin, focused as he was on the course of quinine treatments, could see Amy's actions only in terms of disobedience towards him and disregard for Isaac's health.[67]

The preoccupation of slaveholders with the issue of disobedience on the part of slave nurses points to a particular dilemma for African American women healers in the antebellum South. Professional writings by American physicians during the first half of the nineteenth century indicate that although physicians accepted white women as the primary household healers, they also worried that women were naturally inferior thinkers in matters of medicine and science.[68] Derogatory assumptions about slave women healers reflected an even sharper contradiction particular to African American women's position as enslaved female workers. While planters relied on the labor of black women as healers to sustain plantation slave populations, they simultaneously devalued the skills of black women and distrusted their claims to authority among kin and community. The contradictions of dependency and hostility in planter views of slave women healers are clear in the thesis of a South Carolina medical student, H. W. Moore, who wrote on slave nurses and "plantation hygiene."

> And here it might be well to state, in a few words, the propriety, and advantage of supplying plantations with suitable nurses. There are usually persons on every place who affect this title, but with little show of reason. With capable and willing nurses, the labors of the physician would be less burdensome and more efficacious. Among the educated, the Practitioner finds intelligence to comprehend his views, and willingness to assist him in carrying them out but among ignorant negroes, the case is far different. They are much given to malingering and deception. Reliable nurses should be at hand to see to the proper fulfillment of the directions of the physician.[69]

Moore's discussion reflected common themes in planter discourse on enslaved laborers—that they were duplicitous, unreliable, and lazy. The "suitable nurse" in Moore's eyes was a capable healer whose merits were judged not so much by the degree of her skill but by her alacrity in following orders.

67. Rosengarten, *Tombee*, pp. 542, 154.
68. The tensions between women's role as household healers and their supposed incompetence in matters of medical science emerged clearly in nineteenth-century domestic medicine manuals. Lamar Murphy argues that writers of medical manuals began in the late eighteenth century to devalue popular wisdom and insist that women submit to the guidance of physicians. See Lamar Riley Murphy, *Enter the Physician: The Transformation of Domestic Medicine, 1760–1860* (Tuscaloosa, Ala., 1991).
69. H. W. Moore, "A Thesis on Plantation Hygiene," Feb. 1856, Medical College of the State of South Carolina, Waring Historical Library, Charleston, p. 10.

When African American women claimed spiritual insight, divine calling, and communally derived authority, they clearly undermined slaveholder views of them as subservient assistants. Susan Juster, along with other contributors to this book, has pointed out the opportunities and limitations of women's claims to spiritual revelation in specific historical contexts. In the plantation South, a world hostile to black female authority, claims of divine guidance enabled elderly enslaved healers to assert their knowledge. Yet the position of these same women in the plantation labor scheme ensured that they would be embattled in their work. That slave healers exercised authority even in such highly contentious settings speaks to the power of healing work as a mode of resistance to an ideology that would reduce an enslaved woman's labor to a work of the hands alone.

Slave women's claims of spiritual empowerment also illuminate the work of healing as a pathway to female leadership in African American communities. Several scholars have described how black women in free and post-emancipation communities claimed a voice and exerted authority within church institutions that privileged formal male leadership.[70] Studies of the "invisible institution" of black Christians during slavery devote major emphasis to the role of male preachers but provide less insight into avenues to spiritual authority for enslaved women.[71] An exploration of healing reminds us that large areas of African American spiritual experience were not situated exclusively within the church or subject to formal male leadership. Moreover, the continuity of practices between specialists like the doctoress Elsey and the daily familial care by countless other slave women indicates a fluidity in healing that diverged from the institutional boundaries between Christian clergy and laity. To explore slave women's healing work is thus to delve more deeply into the gendered dimensions of the sacred worldview of slave communities.

Finally, this study of African American women's healing in slavery suggests the fruitfulness of exploring the juncture between labor and religion in daily female work. Clearly, relations of class and privilege insured much variation in work-based expressions of women's spirituality. For example, Luisah Teish, writing on voudou in New Orleans, describes how antebellum voudou practitioners facing persecution by local authorities "infused the most common household items and acts with spiritual power."[72] White

---

70. Evelyn Brooks Higginbotham, *Righteous Discontent: The Women's Movement in the Black Baptist Church, 1880–1920* (Cambridge, Mass., 1993); Cheryl Townsend Gilkes, " 'Together and in Harness': Women's Traditions in the Sanctified Church," *Signs* 10 (Summer 1985): 678–99; William L. Andrews, ed., *Sisters of the Spirit: Three Black Women's Autobiographies of the Nineteenth Century* (Bloomington, 1986), pp. 16–22.

71. Genovese, *Roll, Jordan, Roll*, pp. 255–79; Raboteau, *Slave Religion*, pp. 133–43, 231–39. Margaret Washington Creel mentions women as spiritual guides and prophets among antebellum Gullah communities in Creel, *Peculiar People*, pp. 284–86, 291.

72. Luisah Teish, *Jambalaya: The Natural Woman's Book of Personal Charms and Practical Rituals* (San Francisco, 1985), p. 7.

evangelical women in the antebellum South filtered the meaning of their daily household chores through the lens of domestic duty and tests of faith. Enslaved women such as Elsey, Lula Russeau, and Mildred Graves also entwined notions of spiritual power with the work of daily living. In the process of "working cures and making medicine" they exercised their faith and, to the extent possible, reclaimed the meaning of their labor. The work of enslaved healers thus provokes a revisioning of nineteenth-century women's religiosity as it extended past the church and into the complex conditions of daily work.

CHAPTER 9

Reading, Writing, and the Race of Mother Figures: Shakers Rebecca Cox Jackson and Alonzo Giles Hollister

ETTA MADDEN

In 1876 white male Shaker Alonzo Giles Hollister (1830–1911) received from Shaker leaders an autobiographical manuscript written by black female Shaker Rebecca Cox Jackson (1795–1871) and a blank book for transcribing the work. His response to this event, recorded in his own autobiographical manuscript, is remarkable: "I felt I had received a treasure. I greatly enjoyed the copying, evenings and mornings and sabbath days." Hollister's narrative, in this and the surrounding passages, reveals that Jackson, known to many Shakers as "Mother Rebecca," was an important spiritual figure for him. He wrote of her, for example, "I regard her as a true Prophet of Jehovah—and as a second and independent Witness to the Second Appearing of Christ."[1] The first witness to Christ's second appearing, according to Shaker tradition, had been "Mother" Ann Lee, who in the latter half of the eighteenth century founded the sect, ushering in their millennial vision and their practice of celibacy.

Why this fascination of a white male for a black female whom he had never met? Why this attempt to translate Jackson, as embodied in her text, to the status of Ann Lee, who by this point in Shaker history had become a symbolic icon?[2] In this chapter I will argue that as an African American mother figure, Jackson provided Hollister spiritual and emotional sustenance and wholeness during the years he was editing her text and writing about it in his "Reminiscences." He read Jackson, as depicted in her

---

1. Alonzo Giles Hollister, "Reminiscences, by a Soldier of the Cross" (Mt. Lebanon, N.Y., [ca. 1908]), pp. 189, 193, Collection of Western Reserve Historical Society (OCIWHi), X:B-31.

2. These questions have been instigated by Robert Stepto's study of the editorial framing devices and publications of slave narratives and by Jean Humez's and Diane Sasson's comments on Hollister's work with Jackson's manuscript (neither elaborates on the material that follows). Robert B. Stepto, "Narration, Authentication, and Authorial Control in Frederick Douglass's *Narrative of 1845*," in *Afro-American Literature: The Reconstruction of Instruction*, ed. Dexter Fisher and Robert Stepto (New York, 1979), pp. 178–91; Jean MacMahon Humez, ed., *Gifts of Power: The Writings of Rebecca Jackson, Black Visionary, Shaker Eldress* (Boston, 1981), pp. 65–68; Diane Sasson, *The Shaker Spiritual Narrative* (Knoxville, 1983), pp. 84–99.

spiritual narrative, as an "other," and creatively rewrote her into his own narrative. Her "otherness" for him, includes both her gendered experiences in the "female realm" and her racial experiences as an African American.[3]

Hollister's empowering reading of Rebecca Jackson as a mother figure is best understood in comparison with the significance of mother figures for Jackson. Another task of this chapter is to demonstrate that her narrative offers another view of spiritual empowerment through her readings of both white and black women. Both Jackson's and Hollister's uses of these mother figures are illuminated by what Robert Orsi and Carolyn Walker Bynum have underscored as the polysemic nature of religious symbols. The symbol—in this case, the mother figure—provides a creative space in which the imaginations of participants in a religious ritual operate.[4] Participants' imaginative work is shaped by their individual experiences, which include becoming gendered and learning their racially determined cultures. Hollister and Jackson, in the reading and writing of their spiritual narratives (a kind of religious ritual), reveal their use of the spaces offered by black and white mother figures.

Hollister's and Jackson's uses of mother figures offer interesting insights into their personal gender construction and its relation to the Shakers' gender-inclusive god imagery. In her recent analysis of female god imagery in Shakerism, Linda Mercadante had hoped to discover that having a female aspect to the deity greatly empowered female Believers. However, based on an examination of numerous personal written testimonies, she concluded that "Shaker believers' actual use of female imagery for God in their personal expressions of faith was uneven and sporadic. Many believers' religious experience does not seem to have been deeply affected by these images." Additionally, she learned that among those Believers affected by the imagery, "men were equally as likely as women to use female Christ imagery in describing their religious experience." Inviting further study of the topic, she asked, "Why were some believers more likely to be

---

3. I draw concepts such as "wholeness" and "otherness" from Lacanian pyschoanalytic and linguistic theory. See Jacques Lacan, Introduction in *Feminine Sexuality*, ed. Jacqueline Rose and Juliet Mitchell, trans. Jacqueline Rose (New York, 1985). Also, I slip quite facilely here between the terms "autobiographical manuscript" and "spiritual narrative." Hollister's and Jackson's are spiritual narratives in that each reconstructs and re-members the lives of the respective writers, and the primary concerns of those lives have been spiritual. For distinctions between the Shaker genres "testimony," "autobiography," and "spiritual narrative," see Sasson, *Shaker Spiritual*, pp. 67–83 and Linda A. Mercadante, *Gender, Doctrine, and God: The Shakers and Contemporary Theology* (Nashville, 1990), pp. 128, 192, n. 43.

4. Caroline Walker Bynum, Stevan Harrell, and Paula Richman, eds. *Gender and Religion: On the Complexity of Symbols* (Boston, 1986). Robert A. Orsi, "'He Keeps Me Going': Women's Devotion to Saint Jude Thaddeus and the Dialectics of Gender in American Catholicism, 1929–1965," in *Belief in History: Innovative Approaches to European and American Religion*, ed. Thomas Kselman (South Bend, 1991), pp. 137–69.

positively affected by female imagery than others? It would be interesting—possibly more from a psychological than a theological point of view—to find correlations between members' gender, background, time in the community, and their choice of imagery." In response to this invitation, my analysis of their uses of mother figures suggests that both Hollister and Jackson were positively affected by female imagery. However, due to "gender, background, [and] time in community," their apparent understandings of the imagery—and thus the ways in which their "selves" were empowered by it—differ radically.[5]

What follows is primarily an analysis of "narrative selves" rather than of "historical selves." I attempt to reconstruct reading subjects—Jackson and Hollister reading the mother figures—from what we know of them as writing subjects. Numerous works other than Hollister's "Reminiscences," written both by him and by other Shakers, contribute to the contours of his "historical" self and my reading of his narrative. In the case of Jackson, we have little other than her spiritual narrative.

Jackson's narrative has received attention previously from critics who have discussed it in the context of personal narratives by black women and in relation to other Shaker narratives. These critics have highlighted the impact of her race as she associated with the predominantly white Shakers.[6] They have commented on the spiritual visions that structure Jackson's

---

5. Mercadante, *Gender*, pp. 15, 16, 150–51, 143. To Mercadante's comment I add two glosses. First, the "background" of these two Believers includes their racial experiences; second, while Mercadante distinguishes a theological from a psychological perspective, I conjoin the two. The "spiritual lives" and the "experiences" I put forth are, of course, largely constructions of my own reading experience, drawn primarily from the writers' "narrative selves."

6. The most in-depth analysis of Jackson's life and writing as a mystic, an African American, a female, and a Shaker is Humez's Introduction to her *Gifts of Power*. All references to Jackson's writings refer to Humez's edition of her manuscripts. Joanne Braxton notes the fragmented form of Jackson's narrative and argues that through her visions and recording of them, Jackson distanced herself from her oppressive surroundings, thus carving a space in which she could "create" her "self." Nellie McKay emphasizes Jackson's female "supportive communities" and how she demonstrates her "connectedness" to "collective human experience" through the genre. Priscilla Brewer discusses Jackson's conflicts with Shaker authorities, noting her mystical power, her attempt to "exercise . . . executive authority," and her view of racial oppression within the predominantly white communities. Diane Sasson analyzes the text in the context of other Shaker works, suggesting that the pulpit rhetoric of the African Methodist Episcopal Church contributed to the lyrical and oral qualities of Jackson's prose. Joanne Braxton, *Black Women Writing Autobiography: A Tradition within a Tradition* (Philadelphia, 1989), pp. 51, 61; Nellie McKay, "Nineteenth-Century Black Women's Spiritual Autobiographies: Religious Faith and Self-Empowerment," in *Interpreting Women's Lives: Feminist Theory and Personal Narratives* (Bloomington, 1989), pp. 140, 150; Priscilla J. Brewer, "'Tho' of the Weaker Sex': A Reassessment of Gender Equality among the Shakers," *Signs* 17 (1992): 627–28; Sasson, *Shaker Spiritual*, pp. 158–88. See also William L. Andrews, *Sisters of the Spirit: Three Black Women's Autobiographies of the Nineteenth Century* (Bloomington, 1986), p. 3; Alice Walker, *In Search of Our Mothers' Gardens* (New York, 1983), pp. 71–82.

writings, the interpretations Jackson gave them, and her decisions to live according to the guidance they provided. These decisions tore her away from her involvement with the African Methodist Episcopal Church in Philadelphia in the 1830's; they caused her to practice celibacy and eventually leave her husband; they directed her to preach as an itinerant in Pennsylvania, New York, Connecticut, Rhode Island, New Jersey, and Massachusetts; and they brought her to live with Shakers at Watervliet, N.Y., and guided her to leave them to lead her own group of Shakers in Philadelphia. In comparison with comments about her spiritual visions, little has been written about how Shaker theology and mother imagery contributed to Jackson's empowerment.[7] Even less has been written about Hollister's empowerment through his narrative.[8] As a Shaker document the narrative is significant, for its author lived almost his entire life as a Believer and played a key role in publishing and preserving many of the Society's texts in the late nineteenth and early twentieth centuries. In addition to copying works by Shakers such as Jackson, Hollister was responsible for assisting in the compilation of the first bibliography of Shaker literature and what has come to be the largest collection of documentary materials by and about the Shakers. The narrative provides insights into the perceptions of a man steeped in both textual and Shaker traditions.

While my analysis of Jackson's and Hollister's reading and writing of mother figures appears primarily as a case study, noting elements of their spiritual narratives unique to the two writers, its significance goes beyond pointing to the spiritual empowerment of two nineteenth-century Shakers. Above all, Hollister's and Jackson's narratives problematize notions of race and gender—particularly hierarchical dichotomies like masculine/feminine—that underpin many analyses of Shakerism and nineteenth-century American religion. Both narratives reveal the blurred boundaries of the dichotomies that generally accompany the masculine/feminine opposition: culture/nature, reason/mysticism, intellectualism/spiritualism, literacy/ orality, and progress/tradition. In many ways Hollister and Jackson clearly fall into the gendered realms of "masculine" and "feminine," respectively. For example, their narratives may be said to adhere to patterns noted in studies of gender and spiritual narrative. Hollister's is more focused on "externals," is more "linear and chronological," and is less expressive of humility than Jackson's, which is more internally focused and "cyclical and associational." However, Hollister and Jackson are complex subjects and,

7. Humez suggests the significance of the images: "Shakerism was to provide a feminist theology, useful when she came to the decision to create and lead her own, predominantly black, Shaker sisterhood in Philadelphia." She gives no further details about Jackson's use of the "feminist theology," however (*Gifts*, p. 24).

8. The most extensive work with Hollister's narrative is Diane Sasson, "A 19th Century Case Study: Alonzo Giles Hollister (1830–1911)," *Shaker Quarterly* 17 (1989), pp. 154–72; 188–93.

as such, neither remains consistently fixed in the "appropriate" domain.[9] And what follows here also demonstrates that neither realm encourages greater "spirituality" or "progress." In addition to demonstrating how both Hollister and Jackson fulfill their spiritual needs by reading and writing mother figures, my analysis points to how both suggest progress and change while working within the confines of Shakerism and its traditions. This chapter thus illustrates how females and males of varied racial backgrounds, both in the past and the present, may read creatively for spiritual ends. Sometimes they may draw from cultural inscriptions of race and gender; at other times they may overwrite them. The study of Hollister's and Jackson's creative writing and reading should provide contemporary readers with examples of empowering ways of struggling with racial and gendered depictions of the deity.

Mother Figures in Shakerism

> Sing, O barren, thou (that) didst not bear; break forth into singing and cry aloud thou (that) didst not travail with child . . .
>
> Isaiah 54:1

The uses of mother figures in Alonzo Hollister's and Rebecca Jackson's narratives can be appreciated only if one has some understanding of the role of mother figures in Shakerism. The epigraph from Isaiah illustrates something of this role. The scripture appears as a proof text for a Shaker tract written by Hollister and entitled "Divine Motherhood" (1887). Based on the title and publication date alone, contemporary readers familiar with the nineteenth-century notion of "true womanhood," which emphasized that a woman's duties to society and to her Creator are partly fulfilled through mothering her natural offspring, might expect "Divine Motherhood" to center on woman's salvation through childbearing (see 1 Tim. 2:15). The tract, however, honors barrenness as the ideal for which women should strive. It also professes elements of Shaker theology and history that have led some scholars to believe that nineteenth-century Shakers aided in the campaign to move females from the realm of "true Women" to that of "new Women."[10]

9. With regard to Shaker narratives, Sasson notes that narratives of men tend to be concerned with externals, such as natural surroundings, and to be outwardly directed, while the writing of women tends to be more internally focused, personal, and directed primarily to the self (*Shaker Spiritual*, p. xii). Mercadante explains that Shaker women are "more self-abnegating and servile" in descriptions of their inadequacies than Shaker men (*Gender*, p. 136). See also Cheryl Glenn, "Author, Audience, and Autobiography: Rhetorical Technique in *The Book of Margery Kempe*," *College English* 54 (1992): 540–53.

10. Alonzo G. Hollister, *Divine Motherhood* (Mt. Lebanon, N.Y., 1887). On the "true woman" see Barbara Welter, "The Cult of True Womanhood, 1820–1840," *American Quarterly* 18 (1966). On the "new woman," see Carroll Smith-Rosenberg, "Discourses of

The Shakers' founding and early leadership by a woman, Ann Lee, their belief in a four-part godhead comprised of Father God, Holy Mother Wisdom, Jesus Christ, and his female parallel "Mother Ann," their ecclesiastical structure consisting of both male and female leaders, and their doctrine of celibacy and practice of communal living are all elements of Shakerism that have led some critics to suggest that the group offers a model for women's equality and empowerment in the embattled contemporary religious arena. Most recent studies of gender and Shakerism, however, have concluded that nineteenth-century Shakerism reinforced the image of the "true woman" more than that of the "new woman" by upholding the belief that men and women naturally inhabit separate spheres.[11] This ideology becomes obvious in the remainder of the passage from Isaiah, which is quoted in Hollister's "Divine Womanhood." According to Jehovah, "more are the children of the desolate, than the children of the married wife." While the Shaker woman will not travail in childbearing, she will travail in childrearing. Shaker women rejected "natural" motherhood to become figurative and spiritual mothers to Believers and to prospective converts by fulfilling traditional domestic responsiblities in their communities.

Motherhood, then, continued to be an important ideal for the sect in spite of the fact that female Believers did not conceive and give birth and that women who entered Shaker communities with children of their own gave them up to be raised by appointed caretakers. The ideal was conveyed orally and in writing through the symbols and exemplary models of the female Christ figure, Mother Ann Lee, the female counterpart to Father God, Holy Mother Wisdom, and female leaders such as Rebecca Jackson who were given the title "Mother" as a sign of authority, respect, and endearment.

The first and most important Shaker mother figure was Ann Lee. Ann Lee's ecstatic visionary experiences distinguished her from the group of Shaking Quakers she worshipped with in England in the mid-eighteenth

---

Sexuality and Subjectivity: The New Woman, 1870–1936," in *Hidden from History: Reclaiming the Gay and Lesbian Past*, ed. Martin Bauml Duberman, Martha Vicinus, and George Chauncey, Jr. (Markham, N.Y., 1989). See Brewer, "Weaker Sex," for a survey of those critics who have viewed Shakerism as a model for women's reform.

11. Louis J. Kern, *An Ordered Love: Sex Roles and Sexuality in Victorian Utopias—The Shakers, the Mormons, and the Oneida Community* (Chapel Hill, 1981), p. 124; Brewer, "Weaker Sex," p. 635; Jane F. Crosthwaite, "'A White and Seamless Robe': Celibacy and Equality in Shaker Art and Theology," *Colby Library Quarterly* 25 (September 1989), p. 189. See Marjorie Proctor-Smith on the similarities between nineteenth-century Shaker women and their "worldly" female counterparts. She points out that even a text written by a Shaker woman instructs women to possess virtues "fully consistent with the cult of domesticity" (Proctor-Smith, *Women in Shaker Community and Worship: A Feminist Analysis of the Uses of Religious Symbolism* [Lewiston, N.Y., 1985], pp. 204–5). See also Sally L. Kitch, *Chaste Liberation: Celibacy and Female Cultural Status* (Urbana, 1989).

century. As a result of her visions she began preaching and practicing
celibacy, even while living with her husband (eventually differences in
spiritual fervor separated them). From the earliest years of her mystical
experiences, she was subject to persecution, spending time in prison in
England and being beaten during mob violence in Revolutionary
New England, where she had brought a small band of followers in 1774. In
New England she was accused of being a witch and of being a man in
woman's clothing.[12] It seems likely that these accusations arose because she
posed a threat to male leadership in established churches and because her
social aggressiveness and departure from concerns of a "natural" family
made her appear masculine.

As Marjorie Proctor-Smith has noted, among Ann Lee's many titles—the
Elect Lady, the Bride of Christ, the Mother of all Believers, the woman
of the Apocalypse, and the King's daughter—"Mother" was the most
common. The image lent itself to a variety of usages. For example, one
Believer testified that on one occasion, in the face of persecutors, Mother
Ann described herself in feminine terms as "a poor, weak woman." In
addition to being described as "giving birth" to the society and to "nurturing" individual believers, however, Mother Ann was often depicted as
authoritative, aggressive, and powerful, traits that might be considered
"masculine."[13]

For the most part, though, among the Shakers as among their worldly
counterparts, "mother" was part of the "feminine" realm. Even though the
group encouraged female leadership, in the Shaker communal hierarchy
the "feminine" realm was primarily one of "orality," following the example
of illiterate Mother Ann Lee. Mother Ann was able to draw a large number
of followers in America due to her charisma and to her skills as a prophet
and preacher. As Shaker testimonies depict it, much of her interaction
with followers and would-be Believers occurred on an extremely personal
level. Her voice, her look, and her touch—rather than any "book learning"—were what affected the people she encountered.[14] Mother Ann's

12. Ann Lee left no written records of her life; tradition holds that she could neither read
nor write. These images of Lee are taken from the most extensive and earliest descriptions
by Shakers of her life. See *Testimonies Concerning the Life, Character, Revelations, and Doctrines
of our Ever Blessed Mother Ann Lee, and the Elders With Her* (Hancock, Mass., 1816), pp. 38,
95, 140, 142, 318.

13. Proctor-Smith, *Women*, pp. 105–7; see also pp. 139, 146–48; Mercadante, *Gender*, p.
138; *Testimonies* (1816), p. 139. For explanations for these ambivalent images, see Jean
MacMahon Humez, ed., *Mother's First-Born Daughters: Early Shaker Writings on Women and
Religion* (Bloomington, 1993), pp. 3–8.

14. This physicality of Ann Lee is most apparent in the *Testimonies Concerning the Char-
acter and Ministry of Mother Ann Lee and the First Witnesses of the Gospel of Christ's Second
Appearing* (Albany, 1827). See Jean MacMahon Humez, "'Ye Are My Epistles'": The
Construction of Ann Lee Imagery in Early Shaker Sacred Literature," *Journal of Feminist
Studies in Religion* 8 (1992): 92.

verbal power was transmitted only orally, to people who were in immediate social and physical contact with her. Thus in Shakerism mother imagery generally was not affiliated with "textual" literacy. Female Believers, following suit, were not heavily involved in the "textual" realm until near the end of the nineteenth century.[15] Adhering to this established pattern, Jackson's and Hollister's literacies were shaped by their experiences as a black woman and a white man during the periods they were involved with the sect. Their narratives reveal different valuations of "literacy," and these valuations, in turn, are intertwined with their understandings and uses of mother figures.

Rebecca Jackson: Literacy, Mothers, and Bodily Presence

Numerous references to mother figures appear in Rebecca Jackson's spiritual narrative. Shaker leader Mother Lucy Wright, Holy Mother Wisdom, Mother Ann Lee, and Shaker women in general all seem to have influenced Jackson spiritually as mother figures. Additionally, references to her "natural" mother and grandmother indicate how Jackson's interaction with her biological relatives and her own activities as a "mother" and "woman" prior to becoming a Shaker influenced her understanding of the sect's gender-inclusive theology. As Nellie McKay has observed, Jackson's writing indicates that she absorbed the culture of free African American women of the time. The mother figures in her early life in Philadelphia worked, earned money, and gained leadership roles in prayer circles. She learned from them the importance of spiritual community and relationship, even as she learned a kind of independence.[16]

Jackson was raised by her grandmother until "between three and four," when she returned to live with her newly remarried "natural" mother. She maintained a close relationship with this early mother figure, writing later that she "loved [her] very much." Her descriptions of two dreams about her grandmother demonstrate their mutual affection. One of these accounts also provides a glimpse of Jackson's relationship with her biological mother. Although her mother had threatened to whip her for relating a dream

15. Readers familiar with Shakerism may wish to suggest some exceptions. Mother Lucy Wright encouraged literacy during her leadership (1796–1821). Paulina Bates' *Divine Book of Holy and Eternal Wisdom* (Canterbury, N.H., 1849), appearing during the Era of Manifestations, was the first published text written by a Shaker woman. During this period some women wrote hymns, composed "spirit letters" and "spirit drawings" while under the influence of mediums, and wrote personal testimonies. However, what I wish to emphasize here is that women were not involved in writing the doctrinal treatises and apologias which predominated among Shaker publications until later in the century. For more on women's writing during early Shakerism, see Humez, *Mother's First-Born Daughters*.

16. Nellie McKay, "Nineteenth-Century Autobiographies." Jacqueline Jones (*Labor of Love, Labor of Sorrow: Black Women, Work, and the Family from Slavery to the Present* [New York, 1985]) also discusses the significance of work and family for black women of the nineteenth century.

predicting her step-father's death, Jackson wrote, "she was one of the best of mothers, and I bless the memory of her." Jackson's mother believed in the visionary gift her daughter displayed, which probably contributed to the daughter's respect.[17]

These two mother figures and Jackson's loss of them at a fairly young age (the grandmother died when Jackson was seven, the mother when she was 14) demonstrate her ability to relate to more than one female authority figure and suggest why she so easily moved into a "mothering" role. She had learned that one of a woman's responsibilities was to serve as a mother to any children that had the need. Jackson writes that even as a child she had assumed domestic responsibilities: "I always was faithful in work from my childhood, never inclined to play like the rest of my mother's children." Her domestic work most likely included caring for children.[18] This sense of responsibility as a "mother" appears again as Jackson describes her burden of work as an adult female in the 1830s and her desire to "get learning": "having the charge of my brother and his six children to see to, and my husband, and taking in sewing for a living, I saw no way that I could now get learning without my brother would give me one hour's lesson at night after supper or before he went to bed."[19]

Jackson's relationship with her biological mother is also displayed in a vision she received in 1849, after converting to Shakerism. In response to a prayer to her "Heavenly Parents" (Father God and Holy Mother Wisdom), expressing concern for her deceased and spiritually "lost" mother, Jackson sees her sleeping peacefully in the midst of a garden of "sweet flowers in full bloom." She also learns that her mother has become "a caretaker of children," a Shaker position. The implication is that her mother converted to Shakerism once she had passed to the spirit world, a belief quite common during this period of Shakerism. Jackson's concern and relief shows her continued care for this early mother figure. Post-Freudian readers may interpret Jackson's separation from her mother as a young child, her mother's three marriages, and her mother's early death as contributing to some hostility or at least ambivalence toward this woman that she was supposed to love. Similarly, Jackson's description of her mother's threat to whip her may be read as a sign of a latent fear or anger directed toward her mother. The daughter's dream of her mother's conversion to Shakerism and peaceful eternal sleep might be understood as a psychological resolution of guilt she experienced over ambivalent feelings toward her mother or over her own departure from her family to become an independent itinerant and Shaker.

17. Humez, *Gifts*, pp. 120, 240.
18. Ibid., pp. 85, 234.
19. Ibid., p. 107. This is the second complaint of this nature. See also p. 82.

Set against these references to mothering in her life prior to Shakerism, Jackson's lack of comments about fathering are obvious—she appears to have been raised in the absence of fathers. She refers once to her mother's second husband, a sailor who was probably often away. Jackson's only comments about him come in the description of the dream foretelling his death (which actually occurred soon after the dream) and his punishment in Hell. Her mother remarried, but we learn nothing of the new third "father." While this dream and the absence of other paternal references in descriptions of her pre-Shaker life may be read as manifestations of Jackson's desire to remain connected to her mother or to other women, Jackson does not seem to have a fear of or hatred for father figures. She eventually married, and she desired a relationship with a Father God. Moreover, she refers postively in her writing to a Shaker man having a "father's and brother's countenance."[20] What becomes clear through her writing is that her relationships with men were secondary to those with women. Even while desiring autonomy and separation, motivations that were manifest in relationships with men and father figures, Jackson maintained a sense of connectedness to mother figures and to other women.[21]

From the women she knew early in life she also learned that mystical, spiritual power was not to be overlooked, and even as a child she began to develop what I will call her spiritual literacy—the interpretation and application of spiritual voices and visions. Jackson's spiritual literacy led to her conversion and her sanctification experience (which included the receipt of the doctrine of celibacy) while she was affiliated with the African Methodist Episcopal Church. It brought about her textual literacy, for she claimed to have learned to read and write miraculously, by a gift of the spirit; and it led to her discovery of "God's people on earth"—the Shakers—and their gender-inclusive imagery.

In fact, Jackson's affiliation with the Shakers appears to be directly related to their openness to the "female" realm of mystical gifts. The Shakers viewed the Bible as only part of divine revelation; visions and spiritual voices in the present age directed them as well. Undoubtedly, in addition to the doctrine of celibacy, which Jackson had already received via spiritual vision, she was attracted to the Shaker doctrine of continual divine revelation, one that place doctrinal and other inspired texts and spiritual visions on an equal plane with the Bible. She came in contact with the Shakers in the 1840s, during a period of revival known as the "Era of Manifestations"

---

20. Ibid., p. 147.
21. For a discussion of historical contexts, cultural specificity, and an individual's gender identities in the light of psychoanalytic theory, see Nancy Chodorow, *Feminism and Psychoanalytic Theory* (New Haven, 1989), pp. 4–6.

or "Mother's Work."[22] Several kinds of ecstatic behavior, instigated by spirit possession, were manifested during the period. Some Believers spun like tops during meetings, others received prophetic utterances in English, or in "tongues," and shared them orally or in writing with others. Additionally, numerous spirits visited the Shakers during this period. Holy Mother Wisdom, deceased Shakers, national political heroes such as George Washington and Benjamin Franklin, and members of ethnic minorities such as Indians, Arabs, Africans, and Asians—all these and others made appearances in living Shaker mediums or "instruments." Famous and "exotic" spirits alike usually described their conversions to Shakerism while in the spirit world.[23]

I shall suggest the significance of these nonwhite converts for white Shakers later, when I undertake an analysis of Hollister's narrative. Here I want to argue that in addition to the mysticism of the period and the gender-inclusive imagery, the Shakers' explicit openness to ethnic minorities drew Jackson to the sect. One of the earliest written references to this evangelistic thrust is the 1816 *Testimonies Concerning the Life, Character, Revelations and Doctrines, of our Ever Blessed Mother Ann Lee*. According to these testimonies of her followers, Mother Ann visualized the conversion of "negroes."[24] Like the conversions of those in the spirit realm, conversions of ethnic minorities seem to have been instigated by these remembered words of Mother Ann. Although few minority persons lived within the Shaker communities at the time of Jackson's early contacts, her awareness of this voiced evangelistic thrust may have made the Shakers appealing to her.[25] Spiritual life in a supposedly interracial Shaker community would have been more tolerable than spiritual life in the late 1830s in the Philadelphia area—where no other religious community would accept her mystical powers and where persecution had erupted in racial riots.[26] Although she never makes this explicit in her narrative, Jackson's knowledge that Shakers were concerned about the salvation of these ethnic minorities appears to have

22. For a description and analysis of this period, see Stephen J. Stein, *The Shaker Experience in America: A History of the United Society of Believers* (New Haven, 1992), pt. 3.

23. Apparently Mother Ann established the pattern of conversions in the spirit world. She frequently refers to visions of conversions in the 1816 *Testimonies*. For descriptions of the deceased spirits who visited the Shakers during this period, see *A Return of Departed Spirits of the Highest Characters of Distinction, as well as the Indiscriminate of all Nations, into the Bodies of the "Shakers", or United Society of Believers in the Second Advent of the Messiah* (Philadelphia, 1843); *A Revelation of the Extraordinary Visitation of Departed Spirits of Distinguished Men and Women of All Nations* (Philadelphia, 1869).

24. *Testimonies* (1816), pp. 42–43.

25. Brewer ("Weaker Sex," p. 627) writes that "few blacks joined the sect" and that census records in 1840 demonstate that less than one percent of the total Shaker population was African-American.

26. For a description of the racial scene in Philadelphia, see Humez, *Gifts*, pp. 14–15.

drawn her to them. In Shakerism she could aspire to spiritual power, even though it might mean racial assimilation.

With regard to the appeal of gender-inclusive god imagery, Jackson specifically refers to the offer of a spiritual mother through Shakerism. During one of her early visits to a Shaker community, a female Believer asks her, "Don't you wish you had a mother?" She smiles in response. After receiving her first vision of "a Mother in the Deity" she comments, "Was I not glad when I found that I had a Mother!" On another occasion Jackson describes that she was "filled with love" and felt "like one moving in the waves of the sea" when she received a "Mother's look" during a Shaker meeting.[27] In addition to teachings of celibacy and ethnic salvation, the Shakers' openness to mystical gifts and the role of women as spiritual mothers fulfilled Jackson's needs.

Jackson understood these matters in light of the life and teachings of Ann Lee. Whether she learned of Lee by reading Shaker texts or by orally transmitted stories Shakers are known to have shared, she was drawn to Shakerism and empowered by her understanding of this white mother figure. As Jean Humez has written, "Jackson's career as a female religious leader presents some striking parallels with that of Ann Lee, as Jackson herself was aware."[28] Several implicit allusions to Lee within her life story demonstrate that Jackson saw herself or "read" and "wrote" her life according to the *topoi* of Mother Ann's biography. In general, her ecstatic visionary experiences and explications of them, her challenges to male-dominated religious institutions, her decision to practice and preach celibacy (which eventually led to separation from her husband), and her persecution by unbelievers mark areas where this black woman inscribes her life within the parameters of the Ann Lee story. More specifically, Jackson describes her abilities to heal people by the laying on of hands and by prayer, to see into a person's heart, and to inspire people to confess their sins. As for her suffering and persecution, she describes how she had been accused of being a witch, and at one point she makes an explicit connection between her suffering and that of Mother Ann and Jesus. And Jackson's vision of her biological mother in the spirit world echoes Mother Ann's vision of her deceased mother.[29]

Jackson's reading and writing of the traditions associated with the symbol of Mother Ann follows the pattern described by Robert Orsi in his analysis of female devotion to St. Jude:

Religious traditions must be understood as zones of improvisation and conflict. The idea of "tradition" itself is the site of struggle, and historically situated men

27. Humez, *Gifts*, pp. 162, 154, 168.
28. Ibid., p. 39.
29. Ibid., pp. 132, 164, 150, 164, 186, 160, 275–76; *Testimonies* (1816), p. 42.

and women build the traditions and counter-traditions they need or want as they live. Finding meaning in a tradition is a dialectical process: women worked with the form and structures available to them, and their imaginings were inevitably constrained by the materials they were working with. Still, through the power of their desire and need, and within the flexible perimeters of devotional practice, they were able to do much with what they inherited.[30]

Jackson's most powerful and creative reading of this kind occurs when she uses her visions to justify leaving the predominantly white community of Watervliet in 1851, without the blessing and authority of its leaders. Her call, she believes, is to help "her people" in Philadelphia rather than to remain within the cloistered Watervliet community. She may have drawn once again from the image of Mother Ann visualizing the receptivity of "negroes" to the gospel, creatively rereading the passage with herself as the evangelist rather than as one of the converted. She probably also draws from Mother Ann's itinerancy during the "opening of the gospel" in New England; she was an aggressive missionary who did not confine herself within the bounds of the Shaker commune.

In addition to these implicit allusions to Lee, other explicit references to mother figures reveal Jackson's creative, empowering readings. Diane Sasson has argued that the writings of the female visionary Shaker Minerva Hill have "a specificity of image, a concreteness of detail," that makes them "more akin to spiritual drawings than linear, written narratives. Shape and color predominate; the power of her visions is the power of dream images whose meanings cannot be fixed."[31] Similarly, early in her writings, Jackson's depictions are often visually dramatic. Describing one of her first Shaker meetings in 1842, for example, Jackson writes:

> I saw the head and wings of their blessed Mother in the center of the ceiling over their heads. She appeared in glorious color. Her face was round like a full moon, with the glory of the sun reflecting from it in streams which formed a glorious crown. And her face in the midst. And she was beautiful to look upon. Her wings was gold. She being in the center, she extended her golden wings across the room over the children, with her face toward me and said, "These are all mine," though she spoke not a word. And what a Mother's look she gave me. And at that look, my soul was filled with love and a motion was in my body, like one moving in the waves of the sea.[32]

The depiction of Holy Mother Wisdom with gathering, sheltering wings marks the passage as analogous to several references to Lee in the *Testimonies* and to biblical passages regarding Jesus and Jehovah (Matt. 23:37; Mal.

---

30. Orsi, "He Keeps Me Going," p. 160.
31. Diane Sasson, "Individual Experience, Community Control, and Gender: The Harvard Shaker Community During the Era of Manifestations," *Communal Societies* 13 (1993): 45–70.
32. Humez, *Gifts*, p. 168.

4:2), possible sources for Jackson's creative imagination.[33] The picture also suggests the physicality and specificity typical of these early visions. The physical, bodily image of Holy Mother Wisdom speaks without speaking: "she . . . said, 'These are all mine,' though she spoke not a word." Though not a complete portrait, the depiction recreates her bodily presence. This body, though a spiritual one, appears tangible; Holy Mother Wisdom, to Jackson, is not merely a "felt sense" or a metaphor for interior, mental peace. Perhaps reminiscent of Jackson's physical relationship with her mother, the images of sheltering wings and rocking in the waves impart a sense of comfort and physicality that goes beyond words.

Jackson later describes a vision of an unnamed woman, while "under the instruction of my heavenly Father and Mother": "I looked out in the elements and saw a woman in the air . . . She wore a white garment, and a crimson scarf which was brought over her right shoulder and loosely tied under her left arm, and the two ends hung down to near the bottom of her garment. She was bare headed, bare footed, and bare handed. Her hair was black, loosely falling over shoulders, and she was beautiful to look upon. She appeared pensive and looked upon this city like one bemoaning her only child."[34] Two images dominate this vision: the silent woman appearing to mourn her lost child (perhaps again reflecting Jackson's unresolved emotions in her mother/daughter relationship), and the woman's physical (if not erotic) beauty, evidence of the pictorial force of the narrative.

As her life progresses, however, Jackson's writing and the appearance of mother figures become less physical and more abstract. The women continue to offer instruction, but it is often only verbal; Jackson hears the Mother's instructive voice rather than sees her authoritative presence and comforting body. For example, she wrote on her fifty-seventh birthday: "I have spent the day in prayer and thanksgiving to my Heavenly Parents for their kind dealings with me, and in reading *Holy Mother Wisdom's Book*, from which I received understanding in the work of God, and in reading *The Sacred Roll*." And a year later, turning fifty-eight, she writes, "A day wherein my Heavenly Parents have looked upon and instructed me in mercy, concerning the two continents, the eastern and the western, which are a representation of two in the spirit world—one for those who are in the work of regeneration, and the other for souls that leave the body, wholly in a natural state."[35] This passage continues, heavily saturated with the language of Shaker doctrinal texts and lacking the physical description of earlier visions.

The shift from visual to verbal instruction is understandable—Jackson's reading has increased. She frequently refers to her reading of Shaker texts,

33. *Testimonies* (1816), pp. 213, 238; 241–42.
34. Humez, *Gifts*, p. 203.
35. Ibid., p. 232.

often accompanied by spiritual instruction. One reason for Jackson's increased reading is her new position of authority among the Philadelphia Shakers. When she eventually receives a blessing from the leaders at Watervliet in 1858 to oversee the Philadelphia community, she requests two doctrinal works. The request implies that she did not have personal copies before (which implies that her reading of them was limited) and that as an official leader she may sense a responsibility to do more "book learning," since in general the Shaker leaders, including women, during this period were allowed more reading time. Jackson's reading also increases, I believe, because she is growing old and her health is failing. Once extremely active but now less capable of physical activity, she has more time for books. One vision, which occurs during an illness in 1858 when Jackson was about 62, depicts Mother Ann comforting her by assuring her that in the spirit world she will be able to continue her physical and spiritual work of spreading salvation; thus she should not feel guilty for relinquishing some of her bodily tasks in this world.[36] As she reads more, and as she officially receives a greater leadership role, Jackson becomes more involved in the "masculine" world of texts. However, her reading may also be seen as an act of female piety, quite common and highly encouraged in the era, both within Shakerism and in "the world." But more important than trying to place her clearly in either a male or a female realm, or in the realms of African Americans or white Shakers, is recognizing her involvement in all, as her spiritual needs demand.

In spite of the increased influence that Shaker texts have on her and, consequently, on her depictions of mother figures, Jackson continues to rely upon her spiritual literacy, which allows her to cross culturally determined boundaries. This literacy appears in one of her last pieces of writing: "Being told that I should be instructed in it [a Shaker book] . . . meant that I should have the spiritual meaning of the letter revealed in my soul by the manifestation of God. This revelation, then being in Heaven, was the true book which must come to give us the true meaning of the letter—as 'the letter killeth, but the spirit maketh alive'."[37] Her explications of Shaker doctrine, derived from personal revelation, demonstrate that she continues to read creatively. These explications are filled with phrases common to Shaker doctrinal works, but they often include personal twists. Even with her increased textual literacy, Jackson continues to rely on "the spirit" to help her with "the letter" of the texts. As she puts it, the "true book," which comes from on high, is spiritual revelation. While Jackson's desire for literacy early in her life and her later desire for Shaker books could mark her as someone who, socially subordinate, aspires to power through assimila-

---

36. Ibid., p. 274.
37. Ibid., p. 290.

tion into the dominant group (white and male), her writings demonstrate that, for her, textual literacy remains subordinated to the realm of spiritual literacy, which includes bodily presence, mysticism, and orality. She follows the example of her mother figure Ann Lee.

Alonzo Hollister: Literacy, Mothers, and Bodily Absence

Alonzo Hollister's spiritual narrative, in relation to Rebecca Jackson's, is almost without mother figures. Hollister implicitly alludes to Mother Ann's life when he briefly comments on his temptations, his suffering, and his longing to know God's will for his life.[38] Less than a half-dozen explicit references to Lee appear in his hundred-page narrative, and none refer to Holy Mother Wisdom. A reading of these few references, coupled with an awareness of his numerous other writings and his experiences as a white male Shaker, suggest, first, that while Jackson most often reads herself in parallel relation to both black and white mother figures, Hollister's readings of mother figures stand in stark contrast to his own experiences; they are "others" he admires. Second, these passages reveal that his admiration increases as he redefines his place within Shakerism. Studies of Shaker demographics have noted a declining membership and a shift from a male-dominated to a female-dominated sect during the second half of the nineteenth century.[39] Both these changes influenced Hollister—the former producing a general feeling of loss and the latter altering his views of his masculinity; both contributed to a sense of powerlessness that the writing of his narrative could heal.

Hollister entered the Shaker lifestyle during the same period as Jackson—the Era of Manifestations—though in a different community and at a different period in his life. He came to the New Lebanon community with his family in 1838, just before his eighth birthday. The mystical activities, which reached their peak during the 1840's and included visitations by Holy Mother Wisdom, occurred while he had been separated from his biological mother and placed in the "Children's Order" under the guidance of a male caretaker.

Besides his entrance into Shakerism as a child and his near lifetime involvement with the sect, Hollister's narrative describes his physical labors within the community—working in the shoeshop, the garden, the herb industry, and the extract business (Jackson mainly describes her mystical experiences, paying little attention to details of her other work as a Shaker woman). He also continually refers to his work as a writer and editor, work he took upon himself "after hours" and initially without official recognition by Shaker leaders. In the narrative Hollister appears deeply ensconced in

38. Hollister, "Reminiscences," pp. 175–77.
39. Brewer, "Weaker Sex"; Stein, *Shaker Experience*, pt. 4.

the industries of the Shaker male realm, which is not surprising since from the beginning he was surrounded by masculine role models in caretakers such as Philemon Stewart. (He refers to Stewart with more space and emotion than he does his biological mother.)[40] Along a male-female axis, however, Hollister falls increasingly toward the feminine pole, especially when judged by worldly standards. He is a man of letters and a man of the cloth, characteristics that Ann Douglas's study of nineteenth-century masculinity has shown were sources of gender ambiguity, either as experienced in the self or as judged in others. Add to that his celibacy and a physical accident he sustained: in 1859 he lost the fingers of his left hand in an accident with a cutting machine.[41] While he includes no reference to this loss in his narrative, it appears to have influenced his work as a Shaker. Sasson proposes that the accident moved him from the herb shop into the extract business, and I suggest that it situated him more deeply in the realm of letters. Hollister's increasing "feminization" by the world's standards coincides with the increasing communal and institutional leadership among women within Shakerism, the numerical decline of Shakers, and the memories of the mystical fervor of his youth. In combination, they are aspects of his experience that influence his reading and writing of mother figures and our understanding of his spiritual narrative.

Hollister's two explicit references to Mother Ann in his "Reminiscences" (not counting where he associates her with Jackson) depict her as an authority figure rather than as a nurturing woman. First, in a recorded conversation with "Brother" Abram Whitney of the Shirley community, recipient of the Shaker's musical notation system (which differed from the usual one by using only the first eight letters of the alphabet rather than the standard symbols on a staff), Hollister notes that Whitney explained "that Mother Ann was the author of that system. He received it from her." In the second passage he glosses a discussion of the value of sermons directed to outsiders at Shaker meetings. One Shaker had explained that sermons help the sect's image by increasing outsiders' understanding of Shakerism. Hollister assents, borrowing Lee's words for support: "As Mother [Ann] said on this subject, 'I say it does good. If the living will not hear the word of God, the ded [sic] will. There is not a word of God lost, that ever was spoken.' When the Gospel is preacht in this world, it is heard in both worlds at once." Again, the image here is not one of a nurturing woman but of a

40. Rather than being raised in father-absent families like many of their male counterparts "in the world," Shaker boys had an abundance of father figures. This might lead them to repress their fascination with mother figures less than men outside Shakerism. Hollister appears to have transferred any repressed attraction for his mother to Shaker mother figures and to male caretakers rather than to a woman in a heterosexual relationship.

41. Sasson, "19th Century," p. 159.

wise instructor and authority figure.[42] It's possible that he doesn't refer to nurturing aspects of Mother Ann because he had the comfort of male caregivers as a child; as well, he needs her as an authority because leaders who knew her in the flesh have died and because other living Shakers are suggesting changes in doctrine and practice. As an authority figure Lee is an "other" for Hollister, for she possesses acknowledged power within the community, and he does not.

Hollister's other references to Mother Ann appear as he discusses Mother Rebecca, bringing the two together as significant mother figures for him. Why would Hollister make this connection? The passage above provides some initial insight. In addition to Mother Ann's authority, it demonstrates Hollister's belief in the spirit world. He believes, like Jackson and other Shakers, that the physically dead as well as the living may be converted. Given Hollister's strong belief in the spirit world, we should conclude, along with Humez, that when copying and editing Jackson's text Hollister "respected his author" and "believed absolutely in the authenticity of her visions."[43]

Among the characteristics embedded in Jackson's narrative, Hollister reiterates two intertwined ones—her race and her spiritual literacy. In the midst of his hundred-page manuscript, he devotes nine pages to Jackson's writing. Hollister first describes his trip in 1878 to visit the Philadelphia Shakers, where he reads his edition of Jackson's autobiography to them to have its accuracy confirmed. Next he perfunctorily gives her dates of birth and death. Then he turns to Jackson's literacy, noting that "she was taught by the spirit to read and write."[44] Though her writing and spelling are "of inferior grade," they are "intelligible," he explains. The two sections that follow are lengthy excerpts from her writing, describing her conversion and sanctification experiences. The first gives her description of being guided by two voices in the midst of a thunderstorm. She discerns the voice of God from the voice of Satan and follows the former's instruction to pray for deliverance rather than the latter's to run for safety. She is delivered.

The "sanctification" excerpt marks Jackson's understanding—through a spiritual vision—of sexual relationships as "works of the flesh" that must be left behind when living a regenerate life. In both passages Hollister highlights Jackson's reliance on the directions of the spiritual voice. This process

42. Hollister, "Reminiscences," pp. 164–65, 179–80. In neither of the two references does Hollister "see" Mother Ann. Her physicality seems to have been repressed; she has been translated into a bodiless "other," much more easily known and acceptably described by a celibate male Shaker than the physically beautiful woman Jackson described. Shaker women would be recognized for what they said—their words of wisdom—rather than their physical beauty. This lack of pictorial qualities also corresponds to the "masculine" nature of William Leonard's narrative, described by Sasson ("Individual Experience," p. 31).

43. Humez, *Gifts*, p. 67.

44. Hollister, "Reminiscences," p. 188.

continues. For example, he next explains her being "constrain'd *by the spirit* to go abroad and preach the gospel that was taught her *by the spirit*"; this itinerancy, of course, is what leads to her first contact with the Shakers and her receipt of a doctrinal book.[45] What is significant in these passages—for Jackson first and now for Hollister—is that she was preaching Shaker doctrine before she read the book; the doctrine came to be known extratextually, apart from the written word, beyond the sacred page. She was accused, by some who heard her during her itinerancy, of preaching from the Shaker text; she did not. "At least," Hollister notes, "such is the impression I retain from a recent reading of her story."[46] Her spiritual literacy, rather than any formal, ecclesiastical Christian hermeneutic, informed her doctrine, empowered her to cross racial boundaries, and empowers Hollister as he reads her text.

Hollister next summarizes Jackson's fragmented physical interaction with the community at Watervliet in a somewhat incoherent manner. The passage appears to be Hollister's validation of her life as a Shaker and the spiritual authority she possessed. Evidence of his desire to validate her spiritual literacy follows the passage, when he writes: "I regard her as a true Prophet of Jehovah—and as a second and independent Witness to the Second Appearing of Christ." He reinforces this statement by observing that she made her first appearance "on the 100th anniversary of Mother Ann's natural birth," a numerological reading of current events typical of millennialist groups' explanations or defenses of their faiths. He continues his association of Lee with Jackson, noting especially their alphabetic illiteracy and their keen spiritual literacy: "It is remarkable that both Mother Ann and Mother Rebecca, were destitute of book learning—& were educated in the common duties of life by practice & the Spirit of God. They were Divinely illuminated, and commissioned proficient in all the duties of life, and became Leaders and Teachers of Men, examples of Righteousness blameless in action, and wise in things spiritual, beyond all others in their day and generation."[47]

Hollister's narrative reveals no similar spiritual literacy in his own life. A description of a trip to communities in Maine depicts one of Hollister's few mystical experiences. Having traveled by train as far as Boston, where he is to catch a ferry to Portland, he finds himself amidst city chaos—large crowds gathered for a parade, blocked streets, and "idle" cars. Hollister feels insecure and trapped. He writes, "Feeling some uncertain[ty] as to my future chances, I exclaim'd in [thought] 'Thou O God can'st Deliver me out of this.'" The result, "soon after," is that "something seemed to say, 'Get out of here.'" He placed himself near a policeman, "of whom I might

45. Ibid., p. 192, emphasis mine.
46. Ibid., p. 193.
47. Ibid.

ask any question tending to relieve the situation." He recalls, "All at once I felt as tho help might come from there."[48] The phrasing here, "Something seemed to say" and "I felt as though" reveals his uncertainty about the source of his spiritual guidance; it is not specifically from Mother Ann, Holy Mother Wisdom or the Almighty Father, but from "something."

The other recorded mystical experience is a nightmare he has before a sales trip to Connecticut with Skeen's Biblical Chart. After an encounter with some "ruffons" who feigned interest in the chart and drew him into what may have been a bar or club, Hollister remembers a dream of wolves wanting to devour him. He writes of the humiliating and frightening situation, "I believe it was a Divine Power that saved me." As in the previous passage, his uncertainty about exactly what it was that saved him delineates him as different from Jackson in the area of spiritual literacy.[49]

In addition to Jackson's spiritual literacy, part of Hollister's fascination with Jackson as an "other" is racially oriented. This fascination emerges in his comments about her textual illiteracy. Hollister, like other nineteenth-century white Shakers, felt an affinity with African Americans and Native Americans as oppressed, marginal groups within mainstream American society. In spite of this vicarious shared suffering, though, Shakers were not unlike their mainstream counterparts in wanting to civilize these "savages" and assimilate them into their version of Christianity.[50] Hollister demonstrates this desire as he recalls in his narrative visitations of ethnic minorities during the Era of Manifestations:

> I was deeply interested in watching the strange acting of brethren and sisters under the influence of native Indian spirits, negroes and others, who came to us for a number of months in 1842. They exhibited some awkwardness and ignorance of the ways of white people, at first, but were soon and easily tamed and brot into a degree of order and conformity to our customs. . . . After they had learn'd their lesson, they exprest great thankfulness both in word and song for their privilege and the instruction that had been given them. . . . When one tribe had learn'd, it withdrew, and another came.

This attitude appears also in a passage describing the observation of a mystical experience at Watervliet, where an "Indian spirit" testifies that

48. Ibid., p. 200, emphasis mine.

49. Ibid., p. 243. As in the references to Mother Ann's authority, the experiences of spiritual guidance are heard and felt but not seen; they are primarily verbal, rather than visual like Jackson's.

50. At least one Shaker scholar has noted this tendency. Lawrence Foster writes, "That the Shakers shared much of the cultural baggage of their contemporaries is suggested by the fact that the figures from whom the Shakers received revelations were strikingly similar to the heroes and heroines of the school textbooks of the period, as described in Ruth Miller Elson's *Guardians of Tradition: American Schoolbooks of the Nineteenth Century*" (Lawrence Foster, *Women, Family, and Utopia: Communal Experiments of the Shakers, the Oneida Community, and the Mormons* [Syracuse, 1991], p. 257 n. 18).

Hollister is capable of "thinking work." He glosses the spirit's message: "Part was spoken in broken English, and part in deep seriousness and good proper English as any of *us* do."[51] His attitudes toward these native spirits may have been transferred to the "uneducated negro" Rebecca Jackson. She represents for him the possibility of the future of "the world" at large— "improvement" of uneducated ethnic minorities.

Additionally, as an African American convert Jackson represents the future of Shakerism—"conversion" of new members without physically aggressive missionary action. She found her way to Shakerism as a result of her spiritual literacy. Hollister would have been concerned with these issues—Jackson's race, her spiritual literacy, and her conversion without aggressive evangelism—during the time he was writing his "Reminiscences." His fascination with Jackson's spiritual literacy and the spirit world may be read as a reflection of his desire for a part of the female realm, associated with the mother from whom he had been detached since childhood. His narrative contains only one reference to his biological mother, a brief summary of his pre-Shaker life, although she continued to live at New Lebanon until her death in 1874. However, as mentioned previously, Hollister writes with high regard for Philemon Stewart, who cared for him during his first summer at New Lebanon. Known during this period as an inspired author (of *A Holy, Sacred, and Divine Roll and Book*, 1843), Stewart also may have served as a role model in later years, when Hollister was increasing his writing, editing, and interest in mystical activities of the past. Although the narrative suggests that Hollister was able to transfer his need for relationship to male caretakers or to female god imagery, it also reveals latent unresolved anxieties about his loss.

Loss, for Hollister at this point in his life, included more than a biological mother. Shaker writings from the Era of Manifestations and afterward note a concern over the loss of members who knew Mother Ann in the flesh, a concern with a loss of "true Shakerism" of the earlier periods. Discussions or debates over theological changes show Hollister to be a more conservative Shaker, as Sasson has noted.[52] Several of the doctrinal tracts Hollister wrote, which concern themselves with women's roles in the light of Shaker theology, appear "progressive" by title but are implicitly conservative. In addition to "Divine Womanhood," noted above, he wrote other works discussing Ann Lee as founder and exemplar of Shaker faith: "Heaven Annointed Woman" (1887), "The Free Woman" (1904), and "Brief Sketch of Ann Lee, the First Anointed, Emancipated, New Woman" (1905).[53]

---

51. Hollister, "Reminiscences," pp. 174, 187, emphasis mine.
52. Sasson, "19th Century," pp. 163–70.
53. "The Free Woman" is printed in Hollister's twenty-six-page collection entitled *Calvin's Confession* (1904). "Brief Sketch of Ann Lee" is one of his several subtitles for his *Prophesy Unseal'd* (Mt. Lebanon, N.Y., 1905).

These tracts testify to Hollister's fascination with this Shaker mother figure and his attempt to rekindle the Shakerism of the past by focusing on Ann Lee while appealing to readers "in the world"—possible converts—who are concerned with the changing status of women. His evangelism (if it may be called that) is nonaggressive and "feminized," in that it is carried out by means of texts rather than through face-to-face confrontation.

Other parts of Hollister's narrative confirm that both his personal sense of loss and the shift in the male-female balance within the Shaker sect influenced his attitude toward white and black mother figures. Two topics in particular—his literacy and his relation to his "home"—manifest the increasing isolation or "bodily absence" that surrounded him as numerous Shakers died, his anxieties over these losses, and his desire to maintain traditional Shaker values.

Hollister's concern for maintaining the traditions of Shakerism is manifested in his references to the crumbling sense of "home" in the Shaker communities. Of the period when a New Dwelling House was being built, he writes, "I felt the absence of a home feeling—that is, as if without home." Later on the same page he continues: "Reading the paragraf of the home feeling, reminds me that bringing hired men to board in our kitchen was a great detriment to the union of the family, and to the home feeling."[54] Post-Freudian readers may interpret these entries as expressing Hollister's subconscious desire for the comfort and stability associated with the mother, the womb, or death. The passage also demonstrates that Hollister favors a "closed circle," except for potential converts. Jackson, on the other hand, leaves "home" to open up the family even more. As a woman who has acquired an acute sense of mothering, Jackson carries her sense of home within herself, creating it wherever she is by building and nurturing relationships. Of course, one might say that Jackson's understanding has less to do with gender than with other aspects of her childhood, when she first became accustomed to moving and to building new relationships; Hollister, in contrast, lived almost his entire life in one Shaker community. However, Hollister writes in the opening of his narrative that in his childhood his family "moved so often that I think it gave me a roving disposition, so that when we came [to the New Lebanon Shaker community] I was ready and glad to move. It opened to me a new field of discovery.[55] He claims that he liked to move, travel, explore, and read maps. Indeed, his narrative substantiates this love of travel.

As in Jackson's account, references to trips punctuate the text. His travel descriptions are of two kinds—events he participates in at other Shaker communities, and observations of the world outside Shakerism. Unlike

54. Hollister, "Reminiscences," p. 181.
55. Ibid., p. 158.

Jackson's account, Hollister's follows the pattern of nineteenth-century travel narratives. As critics of travel and tourism have observed, only the different, the "other," is noteworthy to the writer.[56] Hollister depicts himself as a fragmented subject positing himself through his gaze, generally directed to the topography, vegetation, terrain, soil, and architecture. Jackson, in contrast, is numb to differences in physical surroundings as she travels; perhaps her concern for people and their spiritual conditions distract her from observing and recording her physical surroundings. In addition to describing his physical surroundings, Hollister records spiritual conversations both with people of the "world" and with fellow Shakers. These passages in Hollister's narrative are aptly captured in Dennis Porter's summary of travel writing: "in their writings travelers put their fantasies on display often in spite of themselves. In one way or another, they are always writing about lives they want or do not want to live, the lost objects of their desire or the phobias that threaten to disable them."[57]

Hollister twice refers to his interactions in other Shaker communities as "ecstasies," apparently for the fresh spiritual companionship and the intellectual discussion they provide. These interactions—not the contacts with outsiders—titillate him. The interactions with outsiders most often cause anxiety and fear. The mystical accounts in Boston and Connecticut described earlier, where the chaos of the city and the brutality of the bar overwhelm him, occur far from Shaker communities. For Hollister, unlike Jackson, accounts of these trips express not his active evangelism but his fears of "the world" beyond Shaker villages. He writes of another trip, "I don't know that I ever felt a more contented, happy, *satisfied* home feeling, than during a few weeks previous to this journey and after."[58]

Hollister's desire for a stable, continuing home is manifest, then, in his travel accounts—his "ecstasy" when in the surroundings of his extended "home" (other Shaker communities) and his fear when in the face of the "other"—and in his explicit references to a "home feeling." His fascination with his two mother figures, Mother Ann and Mother Rebecca Jackson, are

56. James Buzard, "A Continent of Pictures: Reflections on the 'Europe' of Nineteenth-Century Tourists," *PMLA* 108 (Jan. 1993): 30–44. Highlighting the desire for alterity common to travel writings, Buzard argues that the tourist is looking for the "peculiar"; he asks, "who goes abroad to encounter what is near at hand?" (pp. 30–31). John Urry (*The Tourist Gaze: Leisure and Travel in Contemporary Societies* [London, 1990]) also discusses the "difference" that necessarily attracts the tourist's gaze.

57. Dennis Porter, *Haunted Journeys: Desire and Transgression in European Travel Writing* (Princeton, 1991), p. 13. Describing a trip to Harvard, Shirley, and Enfield in 1872, Hollister writes, "Like the visit to Watervliet and Groveland, in 1857, it was one continued ecstasy. A feast of reason and flow of soul" ("Reminiscences," p. 183). He also describes a trip to Watervliet as "an exstacy," but gives no explicit reason.

58. Dean MacCannell's emphasis on the impact of sensory impressions upon travellers, including the disorienting rush of impressions upon travellers from rural areas in cities, is an apt description of what happens to Hollister in both these instances (*The Tourist: A New Theory of the Leisure Class* [New York, 1976], p. 45).

intertwined in his sense of a Shaker "home." These Shaker mother figures, for Hollister, came to replace his biological mother in a community where an explicit devotion to a divine mother figure—though never a physical relationship—was acceptable and encouraged. Mother Ann and, in her shadow, Mother Rebecca contributed to his security, stability, and sense of home.

Hollister's overt relationship with these figures is primarily textual and verbal rather than bodily or visual, his experiences being predominantly in a masculine and textual realm. His narrative also reveals the value of literacy for him. His writings exude the discourses of nineteenth-century physical sciences, social sciences, and travel literature; in one instance he casually refers to Ralph Waldo Emerson's birthday, exhibiting his familiarity with the philospher-theologian. Writing, as well as reading, is important to him. He opens his narrative with a preface explaining why he writes; he mentions receiving a blank book as a Shaker child; he refers to visits to bookstores during his travels and instructions from Shaker leaders not to buy more books; he describes his offense at being inappropriately edited by Shakers responsible for publishing his work in their periodicals; he lists the numbers of works he was written and published; he quotes from letters received as positive responses to his writing. Sasson has noted, and I echo, Hollister's role as a Shaker person-of-the-book. Examining his "redaction" of one Believer's autobiography, she notes Hollister wanted to correct the time sequence, clarify the point of view, and find an organizing metaphor. And of his narrative as a whole, she explains that it is drawn "from written sources rather than personal experience."[59] I would have said, however, that for Hollister personal experiences *are* largely the experiences of written sources. His personal experiences, expressed on paper late in his life, were shaped extensively by his textual literacy. While he values the spiritual literacy of Mother Ann and Mother Rebecca, their literacies differ from his own. With the numerical decline of Shakers in his and other communities, he finds himself more and more steeped in the isolated textual world rather than in the world of living and active bodies. No less spiritually empowered than Jackson, Hollister's empowerment arrives through his readings of the mother figures who fill the physical voids of the Shaker communities.

Race, Gender, Spirituality, and Change

Differences between Hollister's and Jackson's uses of mother figures emerge from the two writers' different valuations of textual literacy. While both are capable of reading and writing, Hollister is steeped in an isolated, textual—primarily white—world, while Jackson subordinates the text to her concern for flesh-and-blood connections, especially those among African Americans. Jackson's realm of orality was primarily the realm of the

59. Sasson, *Shaker Spiritual*, p. 85.

woman, one she learned of outside of Shakerism; Shakerism, however, reinforced it. For Hollister, the male realm that he learned in the Shaker world consisted of outdoor and text-centered work. Jackson's and Hollister's understanding of "woman" and thus of the mother figure was overtly shaped by their positions in their respective gendered and racial realms. Jackson's references to mother figures illustrate an apparent dissolution of boundaries between Self and Other, both in gender and in race, brought about by bodily experiences situated primarily in an oral and mystical realm. In contrast, Hollister's references to mother figures—primarily in nonpictorial and doctrine-based clichés—derive from his experiences in a predominantly textual and rational realm; they reveal his fragmentation and his desire for wholeness through merging with the female Other.

It is possible then, to emerge from a reading of these two narratives with the conclusion that Hollister and Jackson reinforce the categories and dichotomies of masculine/feminine, literate/oral, and traditional/progressive that other studies of gender, literacy, and spiritual narrative have described. In this light, Hollister's textuality makes him a repository of written Shaker tradition, while Jackson's visionary, visual sense allows her to see beyond the words of doctrinal works. Mercadante has written of the relation of personal experience to the traditions of doctrine: "Experience can be translated into new images and concepts only when the religious imagination is allowed to operate freely."[60] Less limited by textual thinking, Jackson possesses a more creative, freer religious imagination than Hollister, who is more text-bound. Whereas Jackson creates her own community and leads in the flesh, Hollister stays in community and leads only textually. The highly literate white male belonging to the realm of "writing," "reason," and "culture"—a realm often associated with "progress" and "improvement"—reveals himself to be clinging to tradition.

However, by preserving Shaker manuscripts such as Jackson's, Hollister does allow for change by depicting her as one who creatively reads her mother figures. The less literate black female, who abides in the female realm of "orality," "mysticism," and "nature," inadvertently allows for societal changes through the innovation of her religious imagination, which sets an example for Hollister and others reading her narrative. Both writers, then, through their gendered roles and their movements between "masculine" and "feminine" realms, their racial backgrounds and their willingness to sometimes write over them, and their textual and spiritual literacies, draw from their experiences to read mother figures and find, through them, spiritual fulfillment and sustenance. By doing so, they offer future readers a chance for the same.

60. Mercadante, *Gender*, p. 29.

CHAPTER 10

"When We Were No People, Then We Were a People": Evangelical Language and the Free Blacks of Philadelphia in the Early Republic

STEPHEN HUM

Pavel Svinin's description of a black Methodist church service in early nineteenth-century Philadelphia mingled fascination with repugnance.[1] He wrote as if he had witnessed the performance of an exorcism. Worshippers, he observed, "leapt and swayed in every direction and dashed themselves against the ground [and] gnashed their teeth." All this was done, he speculated, to demonstrate that evil spirits had been cast out from their bodies. "When the preacher ceased reading, all turned to the door, fell on their knees, bowed their heads and started howling and groaning with sad, heart-rending voices," he continued. Their hymn singing, which he appreciated as integral to the service, impressed him as singularly unattractive, "loud, shrill [and monotonous]." Svinin, secretary to the Russian consul in Philadelphia, had an understanding of religion that was heliocentric: Russian Orthodoxy was his sun, and all other religions were judged according to their distance from its light. In that schema, black Methodism in America was an outlying planet.

As a cultural observer, then, Svinin was a good bureaucrat. Still, stripped of its patina of exoticism, his observations have some value. Svinin identified the most important public institution of black life in post-Revolutionary Philadelphia, the evangelical churches. Moreover, his sense that hymn singing was central to the experience of the worshippers within was correct. This chapter begins where Svinin ended—with the psalms that even that stiff-necked diplomat knew to be so meaningful to the black Christians of Philadelphia. The aim is to make a close study of the first hymnal of the African Methodist Episcopal Church of Philadelphia. Published in 1801, it was used by the black Methodists until 1818, when it was discarded by their

---

1. Svinin was the secretary to the Russian consul in Philadelphia from 1811–1815, and an accomplished watercolorist. The descriptions above are drawn from Paul Svinin, *Picturesque United States of America, 1811, 1812, 1813, Being a Memoir of Paul Svinin, Russian Diplomatic Officer, Artist and Author* . . . trans. Avrahm Yarmolinsky (New York, 1929), pp. 20–22.

leaders and replaced with the standard hymnal of the white Methodist churches.

Specifically, I am concerned with the uses, and misuses, of evangelical language. I explore the ways in which an emerging elite within Philadelphia's free black population in the early republic developed a political language derived from the traditions of evangelical Protestantism that served to constitute free blacks as a self-conscious community. The language of evangelical piety possessed the power to raise a people from the dust. Russell Richey has identified an evangelical or pietist "vernacular," shared by all the churches of the revival, as the most salient aspect of Methodist expression. This pietist aspect was informed, Richey contends, by the "the vernacular of religious experience, a richly biblical and highly evocative language."[2] However, he maintains that it was an almost entirely oral medium, rarely incorporated into or used in published formal or doctrinal discourse. Erupting in the heated ecstasy of camp meetings, love feasts, and services, traces of the vernacular persist but elude capture by historians. When found in print, this "popular" voice is confined to private journals or letters. Richey acknowledges the capacity of this vernacular to "evoke the corporate life of the Christian community," but he argues that its métier was the expression of private emotions, and not the shaping of public experience.[3]

Yet, in Philadelphia, it was precisely the shaping of public experience through the evangelical vernacular that embodied the black Methodist church, and through it, a free black political identity. Gregory Schneider has argued that for white Methodists, the "way of the cross" led home in the nineteenth century. That is to say, Methodist religiosity was congruent with the rise of Victorian domestic ideology, defining a cultural space for the feminized private life—meant to complement and be subordinated to a masculine public sphere. However plausible this argument may have been for white Methodists, for black evangelicals, the way of the cross led elsewhere. The language of domesticity, and a preoccupation with respectability, that marked the taming of early Methodism was evident in black Methodism too, but it never acquired the same valence that it did for their white co-religionists.[4]

While a rising tide of racism, discrimination, and violence directed at free blacks in the city from the late 1790s onward is sufficient to explain the

2. Russell Richey, *Early American Methodism* (Bloomington, Ind., 1992), p. xvi.
3. Richey, *Early American Methodism*, p. 85.
4. A. Gregory Schneider, *The Way of the Cross Leads Home: The Domestication of American Methodism*, (Bloomington, Ind., 1993). Schneider writes that "it is not clear . . . what nineteenth-century blacks made of the trends toward domestication and respectability . . . Only . . . a study supported by long immersion in different sources [than Schneider's] can answer the question for the black Christians of America" (p. xxiii). This chapter may not be that study, but perhaps it can contribute to it.

drawing together of the local black population—for protection, if nothing else—it sheds relatively little light on how a community so constituted understood itself from within. Anti-black racism, powerful and well-documented as it was, ultimately fails to explain how free blacks were able to negotiate fissures of class and caste that divided them from each other. Hymns acquire an importance to historians concerned with this process of negotiation because they constitute the single most accessible point of entry into the emotional life of the black evangelical community. Journals and personal letters are in the final analysis, private. Parsing out the representative from the idiosyncratic in them, while not impossible, tells us less than we might want to know. Sermons are wholly "public," but fewer of them survive than we might wish. However, hymnals, printed in multiple copies, are comparatively easy to obtain and, like sermons, have a public aspect that journals and letters usually lack. Moreover, unlike sermons, which are written from a vantage of relative privilege—the office of the preacher—and delivered to a waiting flock, the singing of hymns was a shared experience between leaders and followers, and frequently informed the composition and delivery of the sermons themselves.[5] Thus, an attempt to understand the meaning of what it meant to be free and black in the early United States can only be helped by an examination of the vernacular of black Methodist experience.

White racism and violence were undoubtedly sufficient to bind together disparate elements of Philadelphia's heterogeneous black population on many issues. However, entirely too much tends to be assumed about the character and content of such binding ties. It is certainly true that the existence of, and the struggles against, racial slavery dominated and shaped the history of African Americans in the first half of the nineteenth century. But this does not mean that differences within the black population were insignificant. In the case of Philadelphia's free blacks, there were very real differences of class and caste dividing them. Class consciousness, especially among the black entrepreneurial elite, was unmistakable. In 1813, James Forten, a prominent sailmaker and perhaps the richest man in black Philadelphia, penned a series of articles denouncing a proposal before the Pennsylvania legislature that would have required the registration of all free blacks with the civil authorities. Forten feared that if enacted, the measure would have been used to detain free people caught without the proper

5. In her autobiography and journal, Jarena Lee, the first woman to work as a preacher in the African Methodist Episcopal Church, frequently refers to instances when lines from hymns, mixed with passages from the Bible, provided the inspiration and metaphoral 'signature' of sermons she or other black Methodist preachers and exhorters delivered. In effect, alongside the Bible itself, hymns supplied the metalanguage of Methodist preaching. See Jarena Lee, *Religious Experience and Journal of Mrs. Jarena Lee, Giving an Account of Her Call to Preach the Gospel*, reprinted in Susan Houchins, *Spiritual Narratives* (New York, 1988).

papers, and sell them into slavery. In his *Letters of a Man of Colour*, Forten took it upon himself to speak for all free blacks. Yet, he seemed almost as outraged by the failure of the legislation to distinguish between the "respectable" and lower class blacks as he was by the proposal itself. "Many of us are men of property," he maintained. "We grant that there are a number of worthless men belonging to our colour, but there are laws of sufficient rigor for their punishment . . . [There] are also men of merit among the African race, who are useful to society."[6] Men, of course, like himself.

He was not alone in his opinions. As Julie Winch has pointed out, many of the city's free black entrepreneurs, natives of Philadelphia, came to feel a stronger cultural affinity to the Haitian refugees, many of whom were mulattoes, who arrived in the 1790s following the slave revolution in their homeland, than they did with African American migrants from the Chesapeake.[7] It was remarkably easy for the West Indian newcomers to find acceptance. "In many cases," Winch writes, "they [simply] merged with the Philadelphia elite, which contained a disproportionate number of mulattoes."[8] On the other hand, migrants from the American countryside were often received with as much fear and contempt by the black natives of Philadelphia as they were by whites. The intense personal identification of Richard Allen, first bishop of the African Methodist Episcopal Church, with the oppressed was well documented. Yet, even he would have agreed with Forten's remarks about respectability and property. As much as he sympathized with the black poor, Allen was never able to understand why "frolicks," involving dressing up, drinking, and dancing, were so popular with them. The sober, hard-working pastor never missed an opportunity to

6. James Forten, *Letters of a Man of Colour* (Philadelphia, 1813).

7. As Gary Nash has detailed in *Forging Freedom: The Formation of Philadelphia's Free Black Community, 1720–1840* (Cambridge, Mass, 1988), Philadelphia was perceived by African Americans throughout the country (but especially in the slave states to the south) as the "city of refuge" (see particularly Nash's chap. 5). Between 1780 and 1820, the black population of the city grew at a rate faster than its nonblack population; blacks were 3.6 percent of the overall total in 1780, and nearly 11 percent in 1820—12,000 out of a population of 112,000 (pp. 142–45). Slavery, on the decline in the city since 1780, had disappeared by 1820. Of course, as the city's black population grew, it also changed dramatically. Black natives of the city shrank as a proportion of the free black population. Increasingly, Philadelphia blacks came to share the common recent history of slavery in the southern states. Many had only recently been freed in the upper Chesapeake. Lacking the capital to establish themselves there, many streamed into Philadelphia searching for a living and for safety from slave catchers, who were not particularly scrupulous about who they swept into their nets. Moreover, while many of these recent migrants were legally free, a considerable number were runaway slaves. Increasingly, even for the city's white philanthropists and abolitionists, "black" came to mean frightening, dark-skinned people with different speech patterns and few urban skills, very often suffering from the psychic disorientation of sudden manumission and migration.

8. Julie Winch, *Philadelphia's Black Elite: Activism, Accommodation, and the Struggle for Autonomy, 1787–1848* (Philadelphia, 1989), pp. 31–33.

hector his flock about the links binding their preferred leisure pursuits and mortal sin.

Yet despite the genuine significance of what divided them, a self-conscious free black community, composed of rich and poor, came into existence in the generation after the Revolution. More than anywhere else, this community was forged in the city's black church life. There, unlike anywhere else, it was possible for rich and poor, dark-skinned newcomer and light-skinned native, to meet on relatively equal social footing. Even if inequality was not transcended, it was at least momentarily obscured. The church was symbolically—if not functionally—class-neutral ground. And, it was there, in the language and ceremonial of the churches that a community of free blacks was most vividly dramatized. It was there that a free black society tried to come to terms with its ambiguous place in early American life; and it was there, that an elite asserted its leadership over the rest of the free black population. In doing so, what the free blacks created was less a community of institutions than a community of language. Standing at the center of black Philadelphia's religious life, the Methodists of Bethel church exemplified the means whereby the city's free blacks came to identify themselves as a well-defined community through their use of a distinctive political language and discourse. In the decades after American independence, converts, especially from the black laboring classes, flocked to the Methodist church established by Richard Allen. Bethel, founded in 1794, grew rapidly. In 1799 it had 211 members; by 1813 the congregation numbered 1,272, more than twice the size of the next largest black denomination.[9] In 1816 Bethel was at the forefront of the movement by blacks out of the Methodist Church, a departure that led to the African Methodist Episcopal Church—the first independent black denomination in the United States.

A close study of how the plain, emotionally transparent language of private piety drawn from the evangelical tradition came to be adopted as a public, political idiom might provide some insight into how this community was constituted. Evangelicalism furnished a usable language for politics in this early free black community. The possibilities and problems generated by this rhetorical transformation put into relief the circumference of African American life in the early republic. This evangelical-political hybrid was effective when it sought to articulate a vision of social order within the free black community. It could be affecting and eloquent when it spoke truth to power—when it staked claims to freedom and autonomy. Yet although this evangelical idiom was a powerful language of black community and identity, it was unable to establish itself as a language of American citizenship in a liberal society that countenanced slavery.

9. Nash, *Forging Freedom*, p. 193.

A Collection of Hymns and Spiritual Songs, published in Philadelphia in 1801, made an immediate impression upon the city's black Christians. Compiled and edited by Richard Allen, it was well received by his congregation and went through two printings that first year. The second edition added ten songs to the original text, at whose initiative it is uncertain. It was printed, at considerable personal expense to Allen, for the exclusive use of his own church, but other congregations possibly used it as well. Allen could easily have used the official Methodist hymnal rather than trouble himself with the compilation of a new version.[10] What is more, as Eileen Southern has pointed out, "as a good Methodist [Allen] should have [used the official hymnal]—instead he consciously set about to collect hymns that would have a special appeal to the members of his congregation."[11] Southern believes that Allen worried about the alienation of blacks, especially the laboring poor, from worship that emphasized cold intellectual ritual over the transparency of emotion.

Undoubtedly, the salvation of souls was Allen's most pressing concern, and to the extent that this concern was central, the hymnal should not be wholly abstracted from those essentially private moments of epiphany and personal redemption that it was meant to dramatize and illuminate. However, in its public aspects his hymnal took on exceptional importance. In terms of their cultural force, hymns, as Mary De Jong has suggested, were second in influence only to the Bible itself in nineteenth-century evangelical experience, for both black and white Christians. Evangelicals revered hymns, believing that they had an enormously beneficial influence on individuals. Some even credited the singing of hymns, or memories of lines or stanzas from them, for conversion experiences.[12] It has been argued that, for nineteenth-century evangelicals, hymns shaped identity with inestimable intensity. In the performance of hymns, singers were dramatizing the self in relation to the deity and their fellow Christians.[13]

In this conception of hymn singing, the act of performance both illumi-

10. Aside from his pastoral duties, Allen had to be concerned with the cold practicalities of getting by. His church could not provide a sufficient income for him, and Allen at various times was a teamster, a woodcutter, a brickyard worker and a day laborer—his time was severely taxed. See Richard Allen, *The Life Experience and Gospel Labors of the Rt. Rev. Richard Allen* (Nashville, 1960).

11. Eileen Southern, *African American Music* (New York, 1973), p. 90.

12. Jarena Lee dated the moment when her conversion began to an afternoon prayer meeting in 1804, in Philadelphia. "At the reading of the Psalms, a ray of renewed conviction darted into my soul. These were the words . . . 'Lord, I am vile, conceived in sin, / Born unholy and unclean. / Sprung from man, whose guilty fall, / Corrupts the race, and taints us all.' This description of my condition struck me to the heart," she remembered. this incident took place among Presbyterians, however; it is but one instance among many in her narrative where hymns play a pivotal role in moving events forward. Lee, *Religious Experience*, pp. 3–4.

13. This reading is indebted to Mary De Jong's ongoing work on gender and hymnody in nineteenth-century America. See her contribution in this volume, Chapter 6.

nated and dissolved the boundaries between singers and writer, between singers and God, and between the individual and the Christian community. By uniting poetry with music, hymns worked in concert with the values of personal piety and social order promoted by the evangelical denominations. By participating, psalm singers signaled their submission to the symbolic order dramatized in the poetry of the hymns. Thus, hymns stand as a peculiar form of literature. Arising out of essentially private religious experiences, they derive much of their emotional potency from their tremendous public significance. Like conversion, the fundamental drama of evangelical life, hymns required an audience well acquainted with their tropes to be truly complete.

The substance of what it meant to be a black Methodist was embodied in the hymnody of the church. Indeed, in a Christian community where literacy was not universal, and time to read in short supply in any case, the hymns, many committed to memory, probably superseded the Bible in cultural force. That said, the hymnal was neither dogma nor instructional manual. It was never meant to supplant the formal disciplines of the church, but rather to supplement and reinforce Methodist values and instruction. Black Methodists understood that while control of property and the establishment of hierarchy were essential, they were ultimately not the rock upon which to build a church. Richard Allen, for instance, always cherished his years spent with the brotherhood of Methodist circuit riders, with their informal but warm connections to one another. He retained an abiding mistrust of organization and system, fearing them to be the first steps to spiritual desiccation and error. In his autobiography, Allen recalled his ambivalent response to the establishment of the American Methodist Church in 1784. Even as he acknowledged the inevitability, even desirability, of the move, he was uneasy. "When [we—the Methodists] were no people, then [we] were a people; now [that we] have become a people [we are] no people," he felt.[14] The Allen hymnal was the true rock of the church—it served as the archives of black Methodist emotionality.

Thus, any examination of the place of the hymnal must begin with its fundamental Methodist character—how it dramatized sin, grace and salvation, the relationships between sinner and deity, and between sinners and saints. At the heart of black Methodist hymnody was the recurrent enactment of spiritual turmoil, despair, and the final release of conversion.

> How lost was my condition,
>   Till Jesus made me whole;
> There is but one physician
>   Can cure a sin sick soul:
> Next door to death he found me,

14. Allen, *Life Experience*, p. 22.

> And pluckt me from the grave;
> to tell all around me,
>   His wond'rous power to save!
>
> Of men great skill possessing,
>   I thought a cure to gain,
> But that prov'd more distressing,
>   And added to my pain:
> Some gave me up for lost,
>   Thus every refuge fail'd me,
> And all my hopes was cross'd
>
> At length this great physician
>   . . . undertook my cure;
> First gave me sight to view him,
>   For sin, my sight had seal'd,
> Then bid me look unto him,
>   I look'd and I was heal'd.[15]

The classic evangelical conversion narrative was thus distilled into three brief stanzas: the sinner's search for relief from life's pain, the ineffectual ministrations of worldly solutions, and finally the encounter with the divine power of grace, which eventually leads to salvation. The meeting of poetry with music was designed to carry singers through a spectrum of progressively more powerful emotional responses—despair, followed by hope, then ecstasy. The characterization of the redeemed saint's former life as a kind of illness was also a common conceit of both conversion narratives and their poetic analogues in hymns. Many other songs in the hymnal mimicked the architecture of "How Lost Was My Condition." Considered collectively, they captured the emotional textures and passions of the conversion experience. "Some gave me up for lost, / If I the next should be, / That crumble with the dust; / My soul what becomes of thee!" ran one lament. Doubtlessly, this expression of fear accentuated the sensations of relief and love captured elsewhere in the lyrics: "I'll slight thy love no more, / Dear Saviour now that the spirit send / Which I so griev'd before."[16]

In sermons and in prose, Methodist preachers continually "performed" the sinner's despair for the instruction of their flocks. Jarena Lee recalled that after her initial realization of her tainted "condition," so strongly did she feel the "weight of [her] sins, and sinful nature" that she was driven to desperation. "Not knowing how to run immediately to the Lord for help, I was driven of Satan, in the course of a few days, and tempted to destroy myself." She considered drowning herself in a deep brook near her home.

---

15. Richard Allen, ed., *"How Lost Was My Condition": A Collection of Hymns and Spiritual Songs* (Philadelphia, 1801), p. 6.
16. Allen, "A solemn march we make," in *Hymns*, p. 50.

Even though she fought off that impulse, she reported that she then fell ill, "so great was the labor of [her] spirit and the fearful oppressions of a judgement to come." Attended by a physician, she recovered physically but not spiritually. Not until she heard Richard Allen preach at Bethel did she truly become well, she told her readers. When her cure came, it was in a moment, like the sudden recovery of sight. "The text [of the sermon] was barely pronounced, which was 'I perceive thy heart is not right with God', when there appeared in my view [the path to salvation]."[17]

Richard Allen, the catalyst for Lee's salvation, recalled the spiritual turmoil preceding his deliverance from slavery in language exactly mimicking that of conversion narratives and hymns:

> The bands of bondage were so strong that no way appeared for my release; yet at times a hope arose in my heart that a way would open for it; and when my mind was mercifully visited with the feeling of the love of God, then these hope[s] increased, and a confidence arose that he would make for my enlargement; and as a patient waiting was necessary, I was sometimes favored with it, at other times I was impatient. Then the prospects of liberty almost vanished away, and I was in darkness and despair.[18]

Indeed, Lee's journal suggests that it would be difficult to determine the direction in which influences moved. However, whether the language of conversion narratives and sermons provided the templates for hymns, or whether hymnals provided the metalanguage of Christian narratives or sermons, may in the end be neither answerable nor pertinent. In the narratives of Lee and Allen, the poetry of hymns and the often-lush prose of preachers were so inextricably entangled that many black Methodists rarely distinguished one from the other.

However, the rhetoric of love, hope, and deliverance found in the hymnal was only one aspect of this Methodist metalanguage. Black Methodist hymnody portrayed a starkly cleaved universe: the family of Christ embraced in deadly combat with the kingdom of the serpent. "That great and awful day / Of parting soon will come," one of the Allen hymns warned, "When sinners must be hurl'd away; / and christians gather'd home!"[19] This same psalm, "Behold that Great and Awful Day," then proceeded to describe Judgement Day in excruciating detail: parents watch children "sink into endless flame," the condemned "gnash teeth, and crisp and fry," and devils gag the mouths of sinners, while "forc[ing] the fuel in."[20] "[Such] language," Jarena Lee remarked, "is too strong to be applied to any suffering in time. Were it to be thus applied, the reality could be no where found

17. All quotations in this passage are from Lee, *Religious Experience*, pp. 4–5.
18. Allen, *The Life Experience . . .* , p. 72.
19. Allen, "Behold that great and awful day," in *Hymns*, p. 11.
20. *Ibid.*

in human life ... [and would be] false testimony. But when made to apply to an endless state of perdition ... then this language is found not to exceed our views ..."[21] Such graphic and gruesome depictions of sin's consequences were theologically consistent with the mainstream Methodism from which the African Methodist Episcopal Church had evolved. They were certainly consistent with the disquiet with which the Methodist preachers, and the rest of the free black elite, viewed the lower classes of the black population in Philadelphia. It was black evangelicals such as Allen and his old friend Absalom Jones, a Baptist preacher, who united with respectable businessmen like James Forten to form the Society for the Suppression of Vice and Immorality in order to cultivate Christian virtues and sobriety among the city's lower-class blacks.[22] However, these themes, while they formed the heart of the black Methodist hymnody, ultimately fell within the confines of private experience, where, as Richey has suggested, the evangelical vernacular primarily existed. However, along with the passion for conversion and the preoccupation with sin and punishment so evident in the hymnal, there is persuasive evidence of the existence of a distinctly black Christianity, which reshaped the pietistic vernacular of Methodism to new ends.

Not slaves, but not citizens, the free blacks of the early republic lived lives of inherent contradiction, tension, and danger. Richard Allen was apparently once accosted by slave catchers who had recently arrived in Philadelphia and were trawling for victims. Picked up without papers, Allen was saved from a terrible fate only by his high profile and his many friends—black and, more importantly, white.[23] The fears that moved Forten to campaign against the proposed 1813 legislation, then, were certainly legitimate. The political radicalism, which had produced in Pennsylvania what was acknowledged as the most revolutionary state constitution anywhere during the War of Independence, and the gradual withering away of slavery there beginning the 1780s, first frayed significantly in the 1790s

21. Lee, *Religious Experience*, p. 7.
22. Gary Nash has suggested that in black Philadelphia, as in white society, the boundaries that existed between high and popular culture blurred the boundaries between lower class and "respectable" forms of cultural expression, particularly the modes of self-presentation and sociability, such as personal dress, music, and pageantry (Nash, *Forging Freedom*, pp. 219–24). Certainly, by the second third of the nineteenth century, white Philadelphians came to associate the street 'frolicks' of the black lower classes with the entire free black community. The very formation of an elite-sponsored anti-vice organization suggests just how determined the black entrepreneurial elite was to differentiate themselves from the majority of the black population, and to decisively assert their leadership over them.
23. Carol George recounts this incident in her study of the formation of the AME Church. Interestingly, Allen never mentioned this moment in his autobiography, and George, unfortunately, neglects to attribute it. See Carol George, "Introduction," in *Segregated Sabbaths* (New York, 1973).

and then began to disintegrate by the early nineteenth century. The reforming spirit that had led anti-slavery activists around the Atlantic to regard
Philadelphia as the site of a grand experiment—the possible incubator of
genuine interracial harmony in the United States—collapsed under the
weight of white fears generated by the demographic changes in the black
population and by the Haitian Revolution. The effects of developments in
the West Indies in the 1790s cannot be underestimated. The shadow of
black Jacobins and an apocalyptic race war haunted federalist America like
a malignant specter.[24] Slave revolt was not, of course, imminent in Pennsylvania; nonetheless, white Americans were consumed by fears and fantasies
of black violence and conspiracy in the 1790s. Arson and conspiracy rumors
involving resentful blacks were reported across the United States: in Albany, New York City, New Haven, Williamsburg, Charlotte, Norfolk,
Baltimore, and Philadelphia. Perhaps the most disturbing incident for white
Philadelphians occurred on 4–5 July 1804. Independence day celebrations
ended unpleasantly as youths from the heavily black Southwark neighborhood formed themselves into military-style brigades and marched through
the streets. Armed with swords and clubs, they roughed up whites who
crossed their paths, singling out well-known enemies of their race for special
attention.[25] This behavior, repeated the next day, panicked whites, who
immediately feared that the Haitian infection had reached their city. Even
earlier, in 1798, the Governor tried to prohibit the further landing of "any
French negroes" anywhere in his state.[26] Unmistakably, and in significant
ways, by the end of the first decade of the nineteenth century free blacks had
found their political and social room for manoeuvre increasingly constricted.

Yet, despite this bleak reality, a segment of the city's black population
began to assert itself. Legally free, yet clearly second-class in a slaveholding
white republic, free black entrepreneurs—despite the ambiguities of their
cramped status—did increasingly see themselves as the select leaders not
only of black Philadelphia but of all Americans of African descent. Yet
this would-be leadership had to find ways to define and affirm itself. Yet
doing so required the simultaneous fulfillment of two fundamentally
contradictory goals. First, in a country where all political institutions and
power rested with whites, they needed to secure at least occasional
acknowledgement and aid from whites to substantiate their assertions of
prominence and leadership. Second, they had to demonstrate conclusively
that they truly represented—and could influence—other free blacks. To
accomplish this second goal, however, they found that they had to follow
lower-class blacks—by anticipating their demands and aspirations—as

24. Nash, *Forging Freedom*, chap. 6. See also Sylvia R. Frey, *Water from a Rock: Black
Resistance in a Revolutionary Age* (Princeton, 1991), chap. 7.
25. Nash, *Forging Freedom*, pp. 175–76.
26. Nash, *Forging Freedom*, p. 176.

much as lead them. In order to secure their own legitimacy, this free black leadership class found that it had to satisfy the demands of two very different, and diametrically opposed, constituencies.

On the one hand, James Forten could go to great lengths—in a document ostensibly composed on behalf of all free blacks—to differentiate himself from the "worthless" sort among his own race. Effective as Forten may have been with influential whites (the legislation was ultimately defeated), his opinions, like the anti-vice activities of the evangelical preachers, would likely have met a cool reception from the black laboring poor.

However, in the socially neutral space of the churches Forten's class-biased pleas for civic recognition could be reformulated in a far more inclusive form, which derived credibility and resonance from its emotional force. Consider the lyrics of "What Poor Despised Company":

> What poor despised company
>   Of travellers are these
> That's walking yonder narrow way,
>   Along that rugged maze?
>
> Why they are of a royal line,
>   They're children of a King;
> Heirs of immortal Crown divine,
>   And loud for joy they sing.
>
> Why do they appear so mean,
>   And why so much despis'd?
> Because of the rich robes unseen
>   The World is not apprized.[27]

The emotional foundations of Forten's claim to the rights and protection available to white Americans can be found here, divorced from class consciousness and expressed in a rhetoric glorifying the humble and poor. The temper of this particular psalm, which seems to embrace social leveling and reversal, was typical of the 1801 hymnal. Indeed, it was indicative of the work performed by hymnody in the negotiation of class and caste differences within the heterogenous ranks of the African Methodist Episcopal Church and black Philadelphia at large. Generally, the hymns were emphatic in their repudiation of the social categories that structure life on earth. In the arms of the Lord, they promised, earthly privilege and acquisitions are of no importance. There would be no masters or slaves, employers or workers, no humiliating legislation—only the terrible, perfect justice of the "eternal judge"—as God is identified in a number of songs. If not in quotidian reality then in performance, the hymns effaced the existing class boundaries within Methodist congregations. In other words, the evan-

27. Allen, "What poor despised company," *Hymns*, p. 17.

gelical vernacular of the hymns contradicted the lived experiences of the singers.

The hymns of the 1801 collection provided their performers with a particular African American critique of American society, including the religion that they had embraced. Black Christians never conceded the contemptuous opinions that many of their white co-religionists held about them. Black evangelicals denied that Christianity could ever justify slavery and subjugation—in essence, that Christianity was ultimately a "white man's" religion. The 1801 hymnal contained an implicit grievance against the hypocrisy of their white co-religionists. As a collection, the songs emphasized the demands of conscience, warning of impending judgement for those who had heard God's word without heeding it: "Who e'ver thou art, / If here on earth thou hast thy heart, / However large thy share may be / Eternal wants remain for thee."[28] Continual references are made to a "pharaoh" throughout the collection. Although his identity is never made explicit, among the catalogue of his many sins was that of hypocrisy— hearing the word without acting upon its demands. This attention to hypocrisy could not be aimed strictly at white Christians, however; the theology dramatized in Methodist hymnody also implicitly ratified the belief that fortunate blacks had to adopt their weaker brethren's cause as their own.

Negotiating social differences within the free black population, hymnody made its most striking contribution when it evoked one of evangelicalism's most compelling themes: the promise of the Christian community. The notion of a sacred community standing apart from the profane world, so much a part of evangelical religion's psychological appeal, emerged with particular force within the black evangelical churches. Intimately acquainted with equality's compromised realities, black congregations embraced and elaborated upon the Biblical epic of the exodus from Egyptian slavery by the Israelites. "What Poor Despised Company" employed imagery and turns of phrase derived from the drama of the Exodus. The travelers, who suffer the contempt of the mighty, are revealed as the chosen of an almighty force. This force, the hymn promises, would lead them to "happy ground," and would ensure that they would be "with hidden Manna fed"—as were former slaves of Egypt. Another hymn, "O Don't You Hear the Alarm," draws upon the Exodus explicitly. "Let us well remember," it goes, "How Israel was freed, / When from the hand of Pharaoh, / By Moses they were led . . . No doubt we shall win the day, / If we but trust in God."[29] This imagery identified freedom from servitude with freedom from personal sin, a link that preachers constantly made in their

28. Allen, "Think worldling, think,' *Hymns*, pp. 28–9.
29. Allen, "O don't you hear the alarm," *Hymns*, p. 54.

sermons and writings. Within autonomous black institutions, the spontane-
ous expression of Methodist emotionality could easily evolve into the language of a self-conscious people divided from, and often antagonistic to,
whites. In using the pietistic vernacular as the language of a social as well as
a sacred community, Methodist hymnody, having symbolically separated
black evangelicals from the world around them, had still to convince the
poor and the dark-skinned that they had more in common with privileged
families such as the Fortens, Allens, and Joneses than either their own life
experiences or the Society for the Suppression of Vice might have suggested. This it did, but in ways that effaced one type of social boundary by,
implicitly, illuminating another.

One of the most striking things about the 1801 hymnal is the clear tension
between the language and imagery of passivity, preoccupied with submission and love, and the language and imagery of struggle, preoccupied with
warfare and confrontation. The interpenetration of amatory and martial
language was common in evangelical hymnody, but the way it operated
within communities like free blacks warrants thought. Acceptance of passivity is a pervasive theme in black Methodist hymns concerned with the
conversion experience. Only sinners are agents—they "slight," "flee" from,
and "fight" Christ. They revel in sinfulness. Submission to grace, which
heralds their assimilation into the Christian community, is the final act of
free agency. Judgement for sinners and hypocrites is assured, although
punishment is always the prerogative of the almighty, and in the next world
not the present one. Even the epic story of the Israelites depicted God's
work and his people's endurance. In essence, the message was given that it
was God's office to act, and humanity's to tremble and pray.

Yet, as striking as the hymnal's language of passivity is, it was considerably more complex than might be supposed. Its functions are indicated by
the contexts where it would occur. Frequently it was embedded in imagery
that could be broadly described as amatory: "Almighty love inspire / My
heart with sacred fire / and animate desire, / My soul to renew. / My tender
hearted Jesus, / thy love my soul amazes . . . No Seraph could redeem us, /
No angel could retrieve us, / No arm could relieve us, / But Jesus alone."[30]
Evocations of the saviour are replete with a lush, passionate romanticism:
the hymns alternately characterized Jesus as friend, "divine lover," and
bridegroom, the singer of the hymn being the bride. Passivity is thus
dramatized as submission not to earthly power but rather to the love of
God, and as entry into an embracing Christian community. The hymns'
most frequent metaphor of entry into this community was a "melting"
together of souls. "Melting" had a powerful emotional—even erotic—
resonance for Methodists, black and white. It was central to their under-

30. Allen, "Almighty love inspire," *Hymns*, p. 59.

standing of piety and worship. Love feasts, camp meetings, and prayer groups were often characterized in private letters and journals as meltings of individuals into a single unity.

It is important, then, to understand the frequent appearance of passive, amatory imagery in terms of its meanings within the black population itself, rather than in the context of white power and black powerlessness. The imagery of submission, of free agency exchanged for union, was entangled in a specific discourse of community relations among the free blacks of Philadelphia. Richard Allen spent his career trying to drive a single point home in his sermons and prose writings: that the community of Christ and the community of African Americans were one. The rhetoric with which preachers like Allen argued this owed much to the "melting" language of the hymns:

> In thee we now together come,
>   In singleness of heart . . .
> We part in body, but not in mind:
>   Our minds continue one;
> And each to each in Jesus join'd,
>   We hand to hand go on.
>
> Subsist as in us all one soul;
>   No pow'r can make us twain:
> Tho' mountains rise and oceans roll,
>   To sever us in vain.
> Present we still in spirit are,
>   and intimately nigh;
> While on the wings of faith and pray'r
>   We each to other fly.[31]

Juxtaposed to and often intertwined with this sort of imagery was a far harsher, bloodier type of language. "No rose can learn to blush like this, / Nor lilly look so fair" appears in a hymn about girding oneself in armor for spiritual battle.[32] Submission is thus transfigured; love becomes defiance. Warfare is the second recurring trope in the hymnal. "Am I a Soldier of the Cross" and "O! Don't You Hear the Alarm" are typical titles of this repertoire of martial songs. In them Jesus, the lover and bridegroom, becomes a mighty war leader. "Come let us go together," typical lyrics read, "For Jesus is our captain . . . Come like a valiant soldier, / And cast away your fears . . . His armor on you take . . . Then let us go together, / With weapons in our hand, / Let us begin the battle, / Like David and his sling!"[33] At their most transparent level, such lyrics succeed as apt dramatizations of

---

31. Allen, "In thee we now come together," *Hymns*, pp. 18–19.
32. Allen, "Drest uniform the soldiers are," *Hymns*, p. 51.
33. Allen, "O! don't you hear the alarm," *Hymns*, pp. 52–53.

the personal, interior struggles waged by the sinner to achieve conversion, or saints seeking to gird themselves against backsliding—images of steel, armor, and blood evoking spiritual battles.

However, this type of language must be understood as having the potential to subsume emotional strife within the church and project it outward, into the public life of the white republic. This was made possible by the ways performance was able to resolve the inherent tension and contradictions between the language of love and that of war. Throughout the hymnal, and ultimately uniting these seemingly opposing emotional responses, was the recurring metaphor of family. Just as a reworking of the Exodus served to affiliate sacred history with the daily lives of the performers, so the earthly imagery of "family" was reshaped and affiliated with the sacred life to come. God as father and Jesus as a sacrificing brother, lover, or bridegroom were embedded in a rhetoric that consciously conceived of the Christian community as an immense extended family—"children of the light," as one hymn put it. The heroes of biblical times were posthumously adopted into this family (thus strengthening analogies made between contemporary Christians and ancient Israel). Heaven was characterized as "my happy home"—a home that, like the awful torments Jarena Lee said were reserved for sinners, was from a time where "congregations ne'er break up, / And sabbaths never end." For the saved, the life to come is envisaged as a majestic homecoming: "there we shall meet and never part again."[34] The dramatization of Christian life as familial was then extended backward into the present life, and the unity shaped by love, and attained by submission, was put to use in this world. "Firm united let us be, / In the bonds of charity; / As a band of brothers join'd"—this was the indispensable imperative of evangelical fellowship.[35] A community based upon such terms was more easily captured for public purposes, and this fact demonstrated one of evangelical Christianity's essential features in the nineteenth century. It had the capacity to paper over the cracks in the edifice of conventional politics and economic life. It has always been Christianity's promise (or opiate, depending on one's opinion) to the poor and oppressed: there are no social classes in heaven. In Methodism, black and white, this promise was redeemed in part, if not in whole, in the language of "democracy and sentiment," which served to demarcate the moments "out of time" in Methodist life from the profane world—love feasts, camp meetings, services in church and class meetings.[36]

---

34. Allen, "Jerusalem is my happy home," *Hymns*, p. 13. See also Mechal Sobel, *The World They Made Together* (Princeton, 1987), pp. 109–10, 127, 130, 214–15 for an intriguing discussion about the African roots of the familiar conception of the afterlife and its assimilation (Sobel argues) into the religious sensibility of American evangelicalism.

35. Allen, "Firm united," *Hymns*, p. 74.

36. Schneider, *Way of the Cross*, pp. xvi–xxvii.

The Methodist vernacular, so lush and warm, stands as a demonstration of why the metaphor of family has been one of the most potent in the rhetorical arsenal of group identity, and of what Michael Ignatieff has termed "blood nationalism." It is in the family that we experience some of our most unequal social relationships, yet it is precisely within our family lives that power relations are most often, and effectively, obscured. This metaphor acquires its potency through the imagination, and performance, of what in essence is a waking dream—nation constituted as family. The black Methodist preachers, and the rest of the free black elite, never used religious discourse cynically, simply to impose their political will and material interests upon the naive lower classes. Rather, figures such as Allen and Lee held their religious convictions, which mingled spirituality and nationality, sincerely. Moreover, the emerging churches were the single social space where a discourse could emerge and flourish unhindered among African Americans about their place in the larger American society. The evangelical vernacular shaped and reshaped political identity, but autonomous black institutions provided the stage upon which an ongoing dramatization of community was acted out.

If the uses of evangelical language for an oppressed community are clear, its limits are perhaps less obvious; but they can be located in the nexus connecting language to institutions and practice. Evangelical language served to efface class and caste differences within a population in which this might have been a greater problem otherwise. Yet, it effaced class by, in effect, reifying gender distinctions within the church. If the nation called into being by the black church was mediated through evangelical language, then the tension between the amatory and martial imagery of Methodist hymnody takes on a significance beyond that of class politics. To suggest that black Methodist hymnody's amatory imagery—"love," "my love," and "bride"—was understood as feminine, and its martial imagery—"armor," "steel," and "battle"—as masculine by performers may risk reifying the two categories. Certainly, the language of sentiment and that of confrontation were, in black Methodist terms, mutually dependent. Harmony in their Christian family was, by necessity, understood on both their terms: love for Christ, and one another required submission from all—male and female, rich and poor. Courage and a fighting spirit served love, and the injunction to love and struggle applied to all Christians. Moreover, even if the Methodist language of sentiment was congruent with the demarcation of male public, and female private spheres in nineteenth-century American life, this congruence was—Schneider suggests—more applicable to white than black Christians.

However, the career of Jarena Lee is instructive. Moved by the preaching of Richard Allen, and haunted by the words remembered from hymns, she converted to Methodism in 1804. A few years afterward, Lee came to feel a call to preach the gospel, and went to see Allen to get his blessing to proceed. Allen offered her the chance to act as an exhorter, or leader, at class meetings. Methodism's smallest unit of social cohesion—and control—was the class meeting. Organized by groups of twelve, classes were required to meet at least once a week. There Methodists sang, prayed together, and confessed to one another. Tears flowed freely at these affairs, and they were the mechanism that substantiated Methodist community through the enforcement of discipline. Yet, as important to the community as they were, class meetings were ultimately an instance of the sort of private piety that Richey identifies as the truest home of the evangelical vernacular. As for public preaching, Allen discouraged Lee. Allen told her, she reported, that "as to women preaching . . . our discipline knew nothing at all about it—that it did not call for women preachers." Lee submitted to Allen's ruling, initially with relief—"because it removed the fear of the cross." But soon her relief turned to resentment: "I found," she said, "that a love of souls had in measure departed from me [when she was refused]; that a holy energy which burned within me, as a fire, began to be smothered. This I soon perceived."[37] Years later, when she wrote her narrative, the memory still rankled; she argued with her readers, telling them that even if the image of a woman preaching was unseemly to them, "nothing is impossible with God." With the Methodist community, though, some things apparently were impossible.

Lee was allowed to preach at prayer and class meetings, even at love feast and camp meetings, but always under the aegis of Allen or another "certified" male preacher. If her story was typical, then we have a particularly instructive example of how the language of domesticity and sentiment, when it intersected with institutions, shaped black Methodist life in ways that distinguished it from white Methodism. Black Christian community, understood through the gendered language of the Methodist hymns, did not draw a sharp distinction between a feminine domestic sphere and a masculine public domain, as white Methodists began to do. Yet, the distinction existed nonetheless, and was meaningful. The dramatization of sentiment was open to male and female Christians: Jesus as friend, as parent, or even as bridegroom was perhaps an identifiably "feminine" image; but the metaphor of family love—and submission to it—did not specifically exclude men; quite the opposite. However, the imagery of warfare and struggle, that is the Methodist language of democracy, often explicitly excluded women: "like David with his sling," and "Firm united let us be . . . As a band of brothers join'd." Jarena Lee was permitted, even encouraged, to witness—an informal role with authority derived from earthly sources—but never to preach—a formal role sanctioned by heavenly

37. Lee, *Religious Experience*, p. 11.

authority. Excluded, then, from the "band of brothers," Lee Lived a "semi-public" life; through the agency of the church, she acquired a public role, but one in which she was clearly meant to be subordinate to the earthly "fathers" of the Christian family. In his account of the African Methodist Episcopal service, Svivin provides intriguing evidence that the gendered language of the hymns was meant to be substantiated through performance. With regard to the singing, he noted that "all rose and began chanting psalms in chorus, the men and women alternating."[38]

Even so, the languages of the hymns had a remarkable capacity to function as the political idiom of an earthly community. What is not certain is the extent to which its potential uses were realized. With the hymnal, I would argue, we have a window into the political language of certain free blacks—black Methodists, particularly those of the economically privileged elite. But, the hymnal, as distinct from the songs themselves, were ultimately, a sample of preachers' culture. Traces of "popular" religiosity in Bethel, or in any of the other black churches in the early republic, are difficult to find. Many of the songs in the 1801 hymnal were drawn from an older popular evangelical tradition; Allen apparently chose songs that he knew to be already popular with lower-class members of his congregation. While the provenance of some of the hymns can be traced to prominent white Methodist figures—John Wesley himself, or Isaac Watts—many more were truly "popular," anonymous, and retrieved by Allen from an orally preserved repertoire established by black worshippers. These were hymns that he likely encountered during his early years as an exhorter and circuit preacher.

Both Svivin and Lee write that preachers often announced at the beginning of their sermons what hymns would be used that particuiar day. So preachers had enormous power to shape interpretations of the dramas enacted in the hymnal. The very acceptance of the pietistic vernacular as the proper idiom of worship by the congregations empowered the ministers. These men could claim, with considerable justice, to have superior knowledge of scripture and doctrine, if not necessarily superior access to salvation. Moreover, the immense personal charisma that many of them possessed was ensured by their mastery of evangelical dramaturgy, continually reasserted by each successful, stirring sermon. Charisma, in turn, gave them the legitimacy to shape the interpretation of the hymnal's lyrics. The hymns used words with precision and passion, yet the prescriptions they offered were ultimately ambiguous. Hymns had the potential to mobilize without rigidly dictating what must be done. In fact, ambiguity was the source of their power; vagueness conferred a timelessness upon them. Being "out of time," as Jarena Lee put it, their testimony was

38. Svinin, *Picturesque United States*, p. 22.

"true"; and rendered the hymns fit to bear the sacred narratives of a community.

It is likely that among black Christians in the first two decades of the nineteenth century, the dramatization of community identity, if not necessarily the determination o community interests, was dialogical—that is, a shared creation of rich and poor, male and female, on terms more equal than after the formal establishment of the African Methodist Episcopal Church in 1816. In the first decades after the Revolution, hierarchy and cultural forms were more fluid and unstable, and the black elites, seeking to establish their positions, remained mindful of their often precarious relations with the free black poor. So long as the hymnal was comprised of songs that resonated strongly with the popular traditions closest to the poor, the elites' control over the hymns' meanings and their grip on the rituals and institutions of church life remained uncertain. It was significant that in 1818 the African Methodist Episcopal Church replaced the 1801 hymnal with a new expanded hymnal, one that closely followed the hymnbook of the white Methodist Church, from which they had just recently separated. Only about a dozen of the original hymns were retained. In the following decades, black Methodism in the North evolved significantly. It gained in political purpose, social respectability, and organizational sophistication, playing an important role in the struggle waged against slavery. However, when its missionaries went south after the Civil War to preach to freed slaves, this was less a family reunion than it was an encounter of two very different, sometimes even mutually hostile, African American cultures. Allen perhaps was right: when they were "no people," they had been a people; later, they—the free black Methodists—were a people, yet, they were "no people," at least not a firmly united one.

The "performance" of nationhood in black Philadelphia was located in specific times and places, at church services or camp meetings. But, even as worship itself took place "out of time," daily reality stood impatiently at the doors of the church. The evangelical vernacular had greater potential as a political language within the black population, than as a political language of African American citizenship in the republic. The Revolution had a profound effect on the aspirations and expectations of black Americans. Many took seriously the revolutionary rhetoric of rights, freedom, and dignity that filled the air. Yet, from the beginning it was obvious that the political language of the Revolution, and then the republic, were not particularly open to use by blacks.

The political discourse of the Revolution and the early republic resists easy characterization. The rhetoric of classical republicanism, comprised of imagery embedded in an imagined classical European history, and the language of commercial liberalism, which privileged property, opportunity, and majority rule, came together in a constantly shifting amalgam of lights and shadows. Free blacks demonstrated in petitions, and in the street festivals that marked the "Negro election days" (coinciding with white elections), that they had mastered and could articulate, and even subvert the language of republican democracy. Yet, ultimately, neither republican nor liberal political discourse was receptive to the aspirations of free blacks for personal protection, or more importantly, civic recognition.

In every one of the important dichotomies that clarified the essence of republican discourse—independence versus dependency, masculine virtue versus feminized corruption, simplicity versus luxury, public versus private—blacks, slave and free, were firmly located by whites in the latter, damning categories. A 1799 petition sponsored by Allen, Jones, and other members of the Philadelphia free black community called upon Congress to end the slave trade. But no greater a son of republican liberty than James Madison declared that a petition from blacks had no claim on the affairs of the nation. The "republican" politics of white artisans and laborers admitted no blacks into the company of workers either. In Philadelphia in the late eighteenth century, changing attitudes in the upper classes were matched by those of lower-class whites, who lived and worked in closer proximity to free blacks and increasingly feared them as labor competition. The evolution of July the Fourth into a "workingman's" festival of liberty and equality, cherished by the lower classes and scorned by the wealthy, has been well documented. Yet, if upper-class whites freely evacuated this holiday, free blacks—most of the them laborers and artisans—were violently driven from it. As early as 1805, hostile whites made it clear that public spaces in cities like Philadelphia were dangerous for blacks on the Fourth. Anti-black rioting became a distressingly frequent part of white working-class "celebrations" in the eastern cities of the United States by the 1830s.[39]

The idiom of liberal opportunity and equal treatment was somewhat more receptive to blacks as free men—not the least because it was congruent with the evangelical vernacular. Liberal and evangelical "virtuecrats" agreed on the benefits of sobriety, continence, and respectability. To a remarkable extent, the morality of black evangelicalism found its analogue in what David Brion Davis has argued was the essential foundation of Quaker antislavery. Nascent capitalism opposed slavery first and foremost because it obtained by the lash what it preferred to be bred in the bone. In capitalism's schema, freedom was purchased at the cost of a new type of spiritual slavery—the slavery of the timeclock and the work ethic.[40] That at least some black laborers realized this was reflected in the continual resort

39. Nash, *Forging Freedom*, chap. 6 and 7; Paul Gilje, *The Road to Mobocracy* (Chapel Hill, 1987). For two quite different perspectives on the emergence of white working-class consciousness—one almost relentlessly celebratory and the other deeply pessimistic—see, R. Sean Wilentz, *Chants Democratic* (New York, 1987), and David Roediger, *The Wages of Whiteness: Race and the Making of the American Working Class* (New York, 1991).

40. David Brion Davis, *The Problem of Slavery in the Age of Revolution* (Ithaca, 1974), pp. 297–305.

of black preachers to edifying lectures to their skeptical flocks about the virtues of industry and sobriety.

However, in crucial ways, the political discourse of American liberalism was hostile to the participation of free blacks in a slave republic. In a recent and very rich study, *Multiculturalism and "the Politics of Recognition,"* Charles Taylor has argued that the United States was the seedbed of a type of liberal discourse—and an institutional regime—that has gradually achieved hegemonic status over much of the contemporary world.[41] The species of liberal discourse and practice that Taylor identifies with the United States is "procedural" liberalism. Discursively, this liberalism is preoccupied with articulating a social and political order that emphasizes "a commitment to deal fairly and equally" with all citizens and to permit disagreements about the "ends of life"; institutionally, it assumes and defends the existence of a neutral state. The foundational assumptions of such a liberal discourse are the existence of individualized citizens of equal legal standing, whose personal dignity and opportunities to pursue the "good life" are protected by the state. With the fusion of this discourse to the institutional mechanisms of property and the commercial marketplace, the basic contours of early American (and, Taylor would add, contemporary American) society become visible.

As Taylor observes, however, critics have argued that "procedural" liberal discourse has never been neutral or "equal"; rather, it has always been the discourse of the majority—one hostile to the dignity and interests of minorities, even to the point of denying that minority rights or dignity might exist. For free blacks in what was essentially a slave society, this point could not have been more applicable. Even though James Forten articulated the language of respectability and property, uncomfortable tensions had to arise from his use of it. In the final analysis, what were the meanings of "opportunity," of "property," and of "equality" inside the free black community? For a people who could just as easily *be* property as possess it, there was an inherent and unavoidable danger in assuming the voice of American liberalism. Moreover, within the free black population, an elite that spoke exclusively in the language of the market would have reopened the class fissures that the evangelical vernacular had negotiated and even effaced with such force. Finally, the contemptuous dismissal of the petitions of black men, even respectable ones, by the white leaders of the country harshly illuminated the boundaries of this liberalism: "equal opportunity" did not apply to black people.

Given this, could attempts by free blacks to lay claim to citizenship amount to much? On the most obvious levels, free black political agitation

41. Charles Taylor, *Multiculturalism and "the Politics of Recognition"* (Princeton, 1992), pp. 25–73.

yielded only ambiguous, even paltry, returns in the first part of the nineteenth century. In every part of the country, north as well as south, the lives of the free black minority became, by virtually every meaningful measure, more precarious, constricted, and dangerous as the century wore on. The evangelical vernacular, so effective within the black population, was most potent outside of it when it articulated the cause of antislavery.[42] Beyond abolition, the political discourse of free blacks left an ambiguous, but potentially important residue.

To "procedural" liberal discourse Taylor juxtaposes an alternative form of liberalism, one which he argues might—in a contemporary world where diverse cultures live inextricably together—ultimately represent the future of liberal practice. Accepting the argument that one of the foundational mechanisms of oppression and domination is the capacity of the oppressor to project a demeaning representation of inferior value and worth onto the dominated, and to ensure that the dominated accept this representation, Taylor then proposes that "procedural" liberal discourse provides no remedy to this oppression. This form of domination, rooted in deliberate misrepresentation of an individual's or group's sense of its won "authentic" self, Taylor suggests, can only be lifted by the commitment of society and the state to a civic recognition of that personal or cultural authenticity.

"Procedural" liberal discourse fails, Taylor argues, because it does not recognize the "substantive" claims of distinct communities, the most basic of which is group survival. Moreover, it is survival, continuance beyond the present generation into future ones, that depends above all on civic recognition. In other words, a recognition of, even agreement about, the "ends of life" is sometimes required of liberal societies and states. This is, Taylor argues, a form of liberal discourse uniquely open to use by minorities and politically marginalized groups. Taylor leaves open the question of whether this "substantive" liberal discourse—one which in practice acknowledges groups as well as individuals—has arisen historically but become submerged, or is yet to be born. I am suggesting that the evangelical vernacular of private piety, and its transformation by free blacks into a usable if flawed public political language, might provide a test of whether Taylor's notion of a substantive liberal discourse can be established in time—taken out of the realm of philosophical disputation and located in the realm of historical struggle.

In adopting, and adapting, the language of evangelical piety to politics, black Methodists used a rhetoric that was already richly conditioned by the experience of group identity—the sacred Christian family. In applying a rhetoric so intrinsic to the experience of sacred community to the political

---

42. The relationship of this evangelical vernacular with the politics of free black abolitionism deserves a separate study, and cannot be pursued here.

life of the republic, black Methodists would have made something truly new. In any case, theirs was not a stance of either simple assimilation into the "proceduralist" norms of American liberalism, or of defiant separation. As others have suggested, the black preachers who initiated the split with white Methodists in 1816 were reluctant revolutionaries. The establishment of the African Methodist Episcopalian Church had been sparked by the unremitting attempts of white Methodist bishops, many originally from the slave states of the South, to establish rigorous control over the institutional life of black congregations. More generally, the gradual betrayal of earlier antislavery positions by white Methodists at the beginning of the century had probably made some kind of secession movement by black Methodists inevitable. Yet nothing in either their experience or in their evangelical language prepared black Methodists to wish for, or accept, a permanent separation from their co-religionists. Even when they used the vernacular to constitute a racial fellowship, they never sought to use the language of Christian experience to exclude white Christians from the family of Christ.

Nor, unless they were prepared to consider emigration, would black Methodists have been able to disentangle themselves from American life—which they did not wish to do. Instead the free black elite drew on the discourses of republican democracy, liberal opportunity, and evangelical community to seek civic recognition. They sought a form of liberal citizenship that would accord them rights and protection equal to that of any white American, but it was an equality that was ultimately contingent upon the proper recognition of their dignity as a racial group. This was no intellectual game: recognition—and the risks of misrecognition—has serious consequences. The story about the middle-aged Richard Allen—who was very nearly scooped up by slave hunters in the streets of Philadelphia (misrecognition at its most basic and deadly) and was saved only by his white friends—may have been apocryphal. It has a powerful emotional credibility nonetheless. This emotional truth constitutes a compelling reason for historians to examine ever more closely the tensions and contradictions of free black people in a slave republic.

CHAPTER 11

The Governing Spirit:
African American Writers
in the Antebellum City on a Hill

JOHN ERNEST

In his 1859 essay "The Education of the Colored People," the Reverend Amos Gerry Beman of New Haven presents a remarkable appropriation of American cultural mythology, asserting that "The colored race is an element of power in the earth, 'like a city set upon a hill it cannot be hid.' Thanks to our friends—and to our foes—and to the providence of God."[1] As Sacvan Bercovitch has explained, the identification of New England initially and the United States eventually as a "city on a hill" was part of a larger American tendency to "give the kingdom of God a local habitation and a name."[2] Part of a general tendency to "impose metaphor on reality," Bercovitch argues, the vision of America as a city on a hill provided those looking to define the special mission of the American Puritans with "a prophetic view that unites sacred and secular history," an "overarching plan which explained the social pattern of their lives, and so allowed them to fuse the particular, the social, and the cosmic."[3] Bercovitch has traced the development of this prophetic view from colony to nation, in the course of which the "Yankee heirs" of the Puritans "substituted a regional for a biblical past, consecrated the American present as a movement from promise to fulfillment, and translated fulfillment from its meaning within the closed system of sacred history into a metaphor for limitless secular improvement."[4] The United States thus could be viewed as a nation blessed by God, a nation with a mission—the place where providential intentions would be realized in human actions.

To note that this vision of a favored nation was at best an achievement of rhetoric is to understand the grounds of its complex power, transforming

1. Amos Gerry Beman, "The Education of the Colored People," in *The Anglo-African Magazine, Volume I 1859,* ed. William Loren Katz (New York, 1968), p. 337.
2. Sacvan Bercovitch, *The American Jeremiad* (Madison, 1978), p. 40.
3. Ibid., pp. 40, 42.
4. Ibid., pp. 93–94.

God into a divine author working through human hands to establish a model city on a purely metaphorical hill.[5] That is, this mythology makes of history something like a text to be read, a text brought into focus in the nation's literature. This is the vision of national history one encounters, for example, in George Bancroft's *History of the United States from the Discovery of the American Continent*, a ten-volume work that ends with the American Revolution, moving Henry Adams to remark to Francis Parkman in 1884 that Bancroft had "written the History of the United States in a dozen volumes without reaching his subject."[6] Bancroft argues, though, that the geographical nation is only the particular manifestation of the ideological nation, a nation that stretches back through human history and gestures forward to a millennial future. And it is a nation that required new conceptions of authorship and literature. As Walt Whitman, one of the most prominent citizens of the ideological nation, asserts in the original edition of *Leaves of Grass*, priests in this nation will be displaced by "gangs of kosmos and prophets en masse" who "shall arise in America and be responded to from the remainder of the earth." These new "prophets en masse," Whitman asserts, "shall not deign to defend immortality or God or the perfection of things or liberty or the exquisite beauty and reality of the soul."[7] Representing these prophets in print, it would be enough for the poet simply to give voice to the self-evident soul of the people. Whitman and Bancroft might well quibble over whether these prophets will speak through the poet or the historian, but both find in the United States a socioreligious mythology ready to be developed and applied in the fields of literature.

In presenting the "colored race" as "a city set upon a hill," Beman both accepts and extends the implicit logic of this national myth, arguing that Blacks in America must themselves have an assigned role in the overarching plan. His envisioned city does not exist on some other hill, facing the nation in stern opposition; rather, Beman makes of the colored race, in effect, a

5. The metaphor of a city on a hill is one of many metaphors for a transcendent nation. As Gregory S. Jay notes in *America the Scrivener: Deconstruction and the Subject of Literary History* (Ithaca, N.Y., 1990), "the history of the United States has promoted a tradition in which writers and theorists have sought to identify—and identify with—a totalizing Subject of History. One thinks of the notions of the American Dream, the Errand into the Wilderness, the Virgin Land, the Representative Man, or the American Adam" (p. 142). As Jay's examples suggest, these notions are grounded in the representations of the nation in its literature.

6. *The Letters of Henry Adams*, vol. 2, ed. J. C. Levenson, Ernest Samuels, Charles Vandersee, and Viola Hopkins Winner (Cambridge, Mass., 1982), pp. 562–63. To the original ten volumes of Bancroft's *History of the United States* Adams adds Bancroft's two-volume *History of the Formation of the Constitution of the United States of America* (New York, 1882), which Bancroft later incorporated into his final revision of the six-volume edition of the work.

7. Walt Whitman, *Walt Whitman's Leaves of Grass: The First (1855) Edition*, ed. Malcolm Cowley (1959; New York, 1986), p. 22.

city *within* a city on a hill—or, as Martin R. Delany put it in 1852, "a nation within a nation."[8] In fact, Beman suggests that the role of the "colored race" is not only to "contribute their full share to the world's renovation and progress" but also to make visible the moral transgressions and failures of those who resist or restrict this progress.[9] Beman was not alone in following this line of argument; as Clarence E. Walker has noted, many nineteenth-century Black writers and speakers believed with their White counterparts that "history was progressive and that God was history's prime mover," and they seized upon this "interpretive framework" to argue that "God in his mysterious way was using the Negro for beneficial ends."[10] But these writers emphasized also that those who journey along this mysterious way must recognize their own responsibilities in the process. As J. W. C. Pennington puts it in the same issue of the *Anglo-African Magazine* in which Beman's article appears, "the issues involved in our cause are by far the greatest that now occupy the attention of God or man." "They are issues," Pennington contends, "that must be met, or God is dishonored and man is disgraced; they are issues that involve the integrity of God's moral government, and man's best happiness."[11] In his emphasis on God's ruling integrity, Pennington follows Beman in arguing that practical concerns of governance and social practice can be addressed only by reexamining the relation between secular practice and the sacred order.

I begin with this vision of a symbol contained by a symbol—a city within a city—to suggest a framework for understanding the intricate struggles that African American writers necessarily faced in the fields of literature and language. In their struggles for moral reform, African American writers could not promote moral insight without confronting the larger problem of establishing the authority of that insight, for their problem was not that they were *un*represented in the national symbolic city but that in fact they had been scrupulously *mis*represented. As Black editor Thomas Hamilton put it in his introductory "apology" to the first issue of the *Anglo-African Magazine*, "The wealth, the intellect, the Legislation, (State and Federal,) the pulpit, and the science of America, have concentrated on no one point so heartily as in the endeavor to write down the negro as something less than a man."[12] Similarly, in *The Conditon, Elevation, Emigration, and Destiny of*

8. Martin Robison Delany, *The Condition, Elevation, Emigration, and Destiny of the Colored People of the United States* (1852; reprint, New York, 1968), p. 209.

9. Beman, "Education," p. 338.

10. Clarence E. Walker, *Deromanticizing Black History: Critical Essays and Reappraisals* (Knoxville, 1991), p. 91.

11. In Katz, *Magazine*, p. 344.

12. In Katz, *Magazine*, p. 1. Consider, for example, works informed by theories of polygenesis, such as John Campbell, *Negro-Mania: Being an Examination of the Falsely Assumed Equality of the Various Races of Man . . .* (Philadelphia, 1851); or Josiah Clark Nott and George R. Gliddon, *Types of Mankind: or, Ethnological Researches, Based upon the Ancient*

the Colored People of the United States, Martin R. Delany notes the considerable power that White Americans gain by their "literary attainments," and complains about White authority and about Black submission to and endorsement of that authority, noting that "In religion—because they are both *translators* and *commentators*, we must believe nothing, however absurd, but what our oppressors tell us."[13] Barred from the avenues by which cultural authority could be acquired, African Americans could not talk their way out of their predetermined position by giving voice to the truth, for their voices were unauthorized and their truths, accordingly, unrecognized. African American writers who believed in and drew from a Christian framework needed to question the language of Christianity even while relying on it; they needed to establish their authority over the Word that would seem to deny them authority.

The task, in effect, was to follow the roads in the antebellum city on a hill to the governing center—the spiritual foundation upon which all structures of Christian thought were supposedly constructed. Having followed those roads, African American writers were able to point to structural weaknesses in American Christian institutions. Hamilton, for example, looks beyond White America's apparent "triumph" to its "unaccountable consciousness," its "aching dread," that "this great black sluggard, is somehow endowed with forces which are felt rather than seen," forces capable of shaking the national foundation.[14] That force, that ominous self-consciousness that Hamilton posits in the mind of White Americans, is powerful because it cannot in fact be adequately expressed. It speaks of the realm of repressed conscience and gestures towards Christian mystery, the realm of a governing spirit whose laws ultimately cannot be ignored. In other words, beyond the power of texts to "write down the negro as something less than a man" lies the power to suggest a force that is felt rather than seen. I am interested, then, in the power of literature—its power both to express and to resist expression; its power both to contain a symbol and to appropriate or invert the symbols of others.

What follows is a survey of the antebellum city on a hill as constructed in the texts of four African American writers, none of whom would look for literary power at the expense of moral duty, and none of whom would

---

Monuments, Paintings, Sculptures, and Crania of Races, and upon Their Natural Geographical, Philological, and Biblical History . . . (Philadelphia, 1854). Concerning biblical arguments in support of slavery and White supremacy, see, for example, Thornton Stringfellow, *Scriptural and Statistical Views in Favor of Slavery* (Richmond, 1856).

13. Delany, *Condition*, p. 191.

14. In Katz, *Magazine*, p. 1. The subject of White conceptions of and projections upon the Black "race" is attracting increasing critical attention—inspired in part by Toni Morrison's *Playing in the Dark: Whiteness and the Literary Imagination* (New York, 1992); see also George M. Fredrickson, *The Black Image in the White Mind: The Debate on Afro-American Character and Destiny, 1817–1914* (New York, 1971).

recognize any conception of literary power that didn't also account for what they considered the truth and power of Christianity. I begin with a consideration of what I call the moral hermeneutics of William Wells Brown's fictive narrative *Clotel; or, The President's Daughter: A Narrative of Slave Life in the United States* (1853). Using Brown's interpretive framework to negotiate the journey from modes of reading to modes of being, I turn to the concept of divinely authored selfhood as developed in two antebellum spiritual autobiographies: Jarena Lee's *The Life and Religious Experience of Jarena Lee, A Coloured Lady, Giving an Account of Her Call to Preach the Gospel* (1836) and Zilpha Elaw's *Memoirs of the Life, Religious Experience, Ministerial Travels, and Labours of Mrs. Elaw, An American Female of Color* (1846). Each of these autobiographies involves a search for a pure language, a language uncorrupted and incorruptible by human motivations. And this search takes us, finally, to the revolutionary spiritual silence we encounter in Harriet Jacobs's *Incidents in the Life of a Slave Girl* (1861). In this survey of the city on a hill, then, I argue that Brown indicates the means by which one can imagine a moral realm; Lee and Elaw demonstrate the terms of citizenship in that realm; and Jacobs discovers by way of that citizenship both community and revolutionary responsibilities.

Each of these writers seizes upon the ideology of a divinely favored nation to suggest that the community formed by oppression is itself the culmination of a providential plan, that oppression is the means of its formation, and that justice and renewed spiritual awareness are the ends to be attained by the community's agency. For example, throughout *The Life and Religious Experience of Jarena Lee*, Lee emphasizes her cultural position by presenting herself as a "poor colored female instrument," and she concludes by explaining her own understanding of her ability to hear and answer the call:

> It is known that the blind have the sense of hearing in a manner much more acute than those who can see: also their sense of feeling is exceedingly fine, and is found to detect any roughness on the smoothest surface, where those who can see can find none. So it may be with such as [I] am, who has never had more than three months schooling; and wishing to know much of the way and law of God, have therefore watched the more closely the operations of the Spirit, and have in consequence been led thereby.[15]

Like Zilpha Elaw, who emphasizes her own cultural position as a Black woman and vigorously supports the biblical vision of a hierarchy of gender, Lee views her position as a cultural outsider as significant not because it

---

15. Jarena Lee, *The Life and Religious Experience of Jarena Lee, A Coloured Lady, Giving An Account of Her Call to Preach the Gospel, Revised and Corrected from the Original Manuscript, Written By Herself*, in *Sisters of the Spirit: Three Black Women's Autobiographies of the Nineteenth Century*, ed. William L. Andrews (Bloomington, Ind., 1986), p. 48. Hereafter, page references are given in the text.

presents her with obstacles in the journey towards spiritual understanding but rather because it provides her with a disturbing advantage. Excluded from any recognized conception of cultural authority and power, Lee argues that such power can only limit and distort one's moral understanding. Similarly, in each of these texts, the divinely inspired lives of those beyond the pale of cultural authority become emblematic of a *force* that has no name, and emblematic as well of the failure of the larger community. The terms of citizenship are inverted: the inspired individual becomes as a city on a hill, and the nation itself becomes the unregenerate citizen of that community, a corrupting inhabitant in the lives of those close to the spiritual center of power. Each of these authors presents the literary text not as a repository of meaning but as an entrance into an ongoing process by which the world can be reenvisioned and moral understanding reinvigorated.

Brown's Moral Hermeneutics

The significant disjunction between the historical and the philosophical state informs Brown's *Clotel*, in which Brown follows Frederick Douglass in distinguishing between the "Christianity of this land" and the "Christianity of Christ."[16] The Christianity of the land is an institution, including methods and language for giving voice to moral understanding; the Christianity of Christ is that from which religion pretends to draw its authority, an ideal of understanding and experience. *Clotel* is addressed, in effect, to those torn by this dual and contradictory allegiance to the human institution and the divine intent. A complex amalgamation of historical documents, cultural myths, borrowed stories and poems, and interweaving narrative lines, *Clotel* relates "various incidents and scenes . . . founded in truth,"[17] as if to question whether the multifarious incidents and attitudes to be found in the United States add up to a unified and coherent cultural whole. Capitalizing upon persistent rumors, Brown presents the title character as the daughter of Thomas Jefferson, and he quotes liberally from Jefferson's writing as Clotel's tragic experiences progress from her position of mistress to her White purchaser Horatio Green to her eventual suicide to escape reenslavement. In his handling of the stories of Clotel's mother, sister, and daughter, Brown covers a broad range of regional and cultural issues relating to the slave system—among them, the efforts of the White woman Georgiana Peck, the Northern educated daughter of a slaveholder, to present a moral argument against enslavement that amounts to a

16. Frederick Douglass, *Narrative of the Life of Frederick Douglass, An American Slave, Written by Himself* (New York: Penguin Classics, 1986), p. 153.

17. William Wells Brown, *Clotel; or, The President's Daughter: A Narrative of Slave Life in the United States* (1853; reprint, New York, 1989), p. 245. Hereafter, page references are given in the text.

mode of interpreting the relation between human actions and divine intentions.

Georgiana stands as the most prominent mouthpiece of Christianity. Through her, Brown presents Christianity not as a religious institution but rather as a way of reading the world. Responding to both her slaveholding father's Christian defense of slavery and the views of the antislavery Mr. Carlton, who "had drunk too deeply of the bitter waters of infidelity" (p. 94), Georgiana begins with a general view of ethical principle and consequence. "We must try the character of slavery," she contends, "and our duty in regard to it, as we should try any other question of character and duty. To judge justly of the character of anything, we must know what it does. That which is good does good, and that which is evil does evil" (p. 95). The problem, of course, is that this judgment will take place in an insular world; as Douglass notes of the Maryland plantation of his youth, it was "a little nation by itself, having its own language, its own rules, regulations, and customs."[18] In such a world, good or bad actions will be determined according to a culture's definitions and necessities.

Georgiana, though, reaches beyond this insular world by referring to its own reliance on a larger sphere of authority, the design that encloses the design—the same sphere that her father looks to when he asserts in frustration, "The Bible is older than the Declaration of Independence, and there I take my stand" (p. 93). There, too, Georgiana takes her stand, but unlike her father she does not pretend that from that vantage point one can see beyond human actions into the broader sphere of an unknowable God. Instead, she speaks of duties, including the duty of reading carefully the *text* of human experience:

> "And as to duty, God's designs indicate his claims. That which accomplishes the manifest design of God is right; that which counteracts it, wrong. Whatever, in its proper tendency and general effect, produces, secures, or extends human welfare, is according to the will of God, and is good; and our duty is to favour and promote, according to our power, that which God favours and promotes by the general law of his providence. On the other hand, whatever in its proper tendency and general effect destroys, abridges, or renders insecure, human welfare, is opposed to God's will, and is evil. And as whatever accords with the will of God, in any manifestation of it should be done and persisted in, so whatever opposes that will should not be done, and if done, should be abandoned." (p. 95)

This is a mode of interpretation that looks for incongruity, disruptions, and incoherence, a way of reading the world that Douglass, for one, indicates when he defines American religion as "that which is revealed in the words, deeds, and actions, of those bodies, north and south, calling themselves

18. Frederick Douglass, *My Bondage and My Freedom* (New York, 1969), p. 64.

Christian churches, and yet in union with slaveholders."[19] As if transforming Douglass's charge of hypocrisy into an interpretive method, Georgiana
suggests that enlightenment comes not by looking into the light but rather
by attending to the significantly ominous shadows created by the obstruc-
tive cultural practices that keep the nation from fulfilling its moral duty. In
effect, Georgiana argues, one cannot see the light, one cannot envision the
Christianity of Christ with the certainty that Douglass brings to the task;
one can see only its negation. Viewing the world not from the sacred history
of an imagined theological perspective but rather from the secular history
and multiple perspectives suggested by daily events—by words, deeds, and
actions—Georgiana presents an interpretive method capable of exposing
the actual nation beneath the theological and ideological veneer.

Of course, it is also an interpretive method in and of a world that depends
upon that cultural veneer; the problem of communal self-justification
threatens to resume in other guises as long as human authority drives the
interpretive task. Accordingly, like so many nineteenth-century fictional
representatives of Christian virtue, Georgiana dies, and is thereby transformed into a spiritual presence both of and beyond this world. Having
fought for and "obtained the Christian's victory," Georgiana soon "wears
the crown" (p. 192). And as she attains that crown, she attains also the
office of representative of the ideal American republic, the redeemer who
provides an accessible perspective from beyond the cognitive and discursive
boundaries of the cultural realm. Deflecting our vision from the familiar
realm, she provides the lens by which the interpretive mode she argued for
can be maintained. For "if it were that departed spirits are permitted to note
the occurrences of this world," the narrator notes, "with what a frown of
disapprobation would hers view the effort being made in the United States
to retard the work of emancipation for which she laboured and so wished to
see brought about" (pp. 192–93).

What one can see from this perspective is the divinely authored sacred
history of the nation, the narrative of the land that God writes for those who
know how to read. Georgiana's life and death, that is, provide the contex-
tual and perspectival framework through which to view the most famous
episode in the narrative, Brown's adaptation of the story behind Grace
Greenwood's poem "The Leap from the Long Bridge: An Incident at
Washington."[20] Brown's story of Clotel's death focuses not on her heroic,
Christian life, but rather on the frustration of what could have been a
successful heroic story. Clotel is within range of attaining her freedom,
needing only to cross the bridge, "But God by his Providence had otherwise

19. Douglass, *Narrative*, p. 157.
20. Brown reprints Greenwood's poem (without noting the source), and adds a final
stanza (pp. 220–22; see William Edward Farrison's explanation in *Clotel*, p. 254n).

determined" (p. 219). And as we read this tragic conclusion to Clotel's life, Brown emphasizes the hand of God in the scene, working as a symbolic artist to comment on the corruption of the national mission: "He had determined that an appalling tragedy should be enacted that night, within plain sight of the President's house and the capitol of the Union, which should be an evidence wherever it should be known, of the unconquerable love of liberty the heart may inherit; as well as a fresh admonition to the slave dealer, of the cruelty and enormity of his crimes" (p. 219). And "thus," we are told as Brown emphasizes once again her representative function in this narrative, "died Clotel, the daughter of Thomas Jefferson, a president of the United States; a man distinguished as the author of the Declaration of American Independence, and one of the first statesmen of that country" (pp. 219–20).

That the death of Clotel is used again as a commentary on Jeffersonian political ideals only emphasizes the larger death in this scene, the death of American political ideals within sight of American political institutions.[21] Those who live and carry the burden of the failed national mission must either learn to read anew or suffer the consequences of the duplicity all but required by a form of Christianity that Douglass called "the climax of all misnomers."[22]

A Pure Language

When Clotel dies within sight of the Capitol, she is transformed from a slave in the United States to a citizen of a city on a hill; and in Lee's and Elaw's spiritual autobiographies, we see two attempts to establish moral citizenship in this world as well as the next. Lee and Elaw, that is, present what might be called narratives of sacred national selfhood, ways of reconceptualizing the relation between sacred and secular life, national and individual life. I can best explain what I mean by this by referring to one of the most prominent representations of national selfhood, the figure of George Washington that we encounter in volume 7 of Bancroft's *History of the United States*. Bancroft's Washington is a model of the representative American; indeed, Bancroft presents him as one whose "faculties were so well balanced and combined, that his constitution, free from excess, was tempered evenly with all the elements of activity, and his mind resembled a well ordered commonwealth."[23] A perfect example of a just correspondence between individual mind and nation, Washington becomes—in the

---

21. In 1846, Frederick Douglass made similar symbolic use of the same scene. See his "Reception Speech," reprinted in Douglass, *My Bondage*, p. 413.

22. Douglass, *Narrative*, p. 153.

23. George Bancroft, *History of the United States from the Discovery of the American Continent* (Boston, 1872–1874), pp. 396–97. Bancroft published the separate volumes of the history over a forty year period beginning in 1834; volume VII appeared in 1858.

pages of Bancroft's *History*—an embodiment of the principle *e pluribus unum* and the site for national balance: "Combining the centripetal and centrifugal forces in their utmost strength and in perfect relations, with creative grandeur of instinct he held ruin in check, and renewed and perfected the institutions of his country. Finding the colonies disconnected and dependent, he left them such a united and well ordered commonwealth as no visionary had believed to be possible."[24] Bancroft's message, here and throughout his *History*, is that ideological conflict is necessary, for only through conflict can limited and partial perspectives be combined and balanced to create a new mode of understanding. But the conflict requires a mind attuned to the directives of providence, directives no one—not even the visionaries Bancroft refers to here—can know with certainty.

And because this intellectual balance must be communicated to others, Washington's voice is as important as his mind. This is, after all, a history in which the narrator at one point bursts forth in a Whitmanesque rhapsody, "Go forth, then, language of Milton and Hampden, language of my country, take possession of the North American continent!"[25] Viewed in this light, Washington becomes representative in his ability to combine and balance not only political forces but discursive ones as well. What we see in Bancroft's presentation of Washington is, in fact, strikingly similar to Mikhail Bakhtin's conception of the complex world of social language. Social language, Bakhtin reminds us, is actually a world of many languages—for example, those of different social stratifications and professions, or those of specialized fields of knowledge—indicating different experiences of and perspectives on life. When one speaks, as Bakhtin argues, one participates in this complex world, to the extent that "Every concrete utterance of a speaking subject serves as a point where centrifugal as well as centripetal forces are brought to bear." "The processes of centralization and decentralization, of unification and disunification," Bakhtin argues, "intersect in the utterance."[26] Understanding thus becomes a communal process, something formed when different ways of speaking about the world work with and against each other. In this way, the mythologized Washington that we encounter in the nationalist fantasy of Bancroft's *History* becomes a model not only of leadership but also of judicious speech, balancing the warring factions of the rising nation in a "well ordered commonwealth" of careful utterances.[27]

24. Ibid., p. 400. In using the words "centripetal" and "centrifugal," Bancroft draws from a tradition of using Newtonian physics to explain the United States form of government.

25. Bancroft *History*, 4:456.

26. Mikhail Bakhtin, *The Dialogic Imagination*, trans. Caryl Emerson and Michael Holquist, ed. Michael Holquist (Austin, 1981), p. 272.

27. On the concept of a representative republican language, capable of bonding the government, the people, and the nation's founding principle, see Thomas Gustafson, *Representative Words: Politics, Literature, and the American Language, 1776–1865* (Cambridge, 1992). See especially chap. 10, "Corrupt Language and a Corrupt Body Politic, or the

I say this not in spite of but because of the fact that Bancroft very carefully avoids presenting Washington as a man who lives by and through words. "Washington," Bancroft asserts, "was a man of action, and not of theory or words; his creed appears in his life, not in his professions, which burst from him very rarely, and only at those great moments of crisis in the fortunes of his country, when earth and heaven seemed actually to meet, and his emotions became too intense for suppression; but his whole being was one continued act of faith in the eternal, intelligent, moral order of the universe."[28] One might say that as the central representative of governing order in the midst of what Washington Irving would later call the American "logocracy or *government of words*,"[29] George Washington must be a master of discourse. A man of few words, Washington becomes a man of meaningful silences. And when Bancroft's Washington speaks, his voice rises from the intersection of providential and human history, and his utterances embody and transcend conflicting historical and social forces in a new union of national identity.

If we attend to the underlying cultural logic of Bancroft's representation of Washington, then we can follow that logic beyond Bancroft's implicit boundaries and see a correspondence between this father of the country and those whom William Andrews terms "sisters of the spirit." In the autobiographies of Jarena Lee and Zilpha Elaw, one encounters a version of representative selfhood that speaks with the moral authority arising from but transcending the conflicting forces of human understanding. In these autobiographies the well-constituted Christian is the truly representative self— a self claiming citizenship in both earthly and providential cities; and in these works, one's fundamental allegiances are revealed by one's language. When attending the death of her sister, for example, Elaw witnesses her sister's crisis of faith—"I am going to hell," her sister announces from her deathbed—and Elaw witnesses as well her sister's subsequent vision of salvation that rises from this conflict. Commenting on this spiritual victory, Elaw speaks of the "antagonizing conflicts of Christian faith," conflicts that constitute "the natural cause and effect of exercise of Christian faith, in collision with forces asserted by the gospel to be engaged in hostile action to it."[30] Noting the universality of this experience, Elaw speaks of Christian

Disunion of Words and Things." On nineteenth-century concepts of and debates over the role of language, see Kenneth Cmiel, *Democratic Eloquence: The Fight over Popular Speech in Nineteenth-Century America* (New York, 1990); Daniel T. Rodgers, *Contested Truths: Keywords in American Politics Since Independence* (New York, 1987); and David Simpson, *The Politics of American English, 1776–1850* (New York, 1986).

28. Bancroft, *History* 7:398.

29. Quoted in Gustafson, *Representative Words*, p. 6.

30. Zilpha Elaw, *Memoirs of the Life, Religious Experience, Ministerial Travels and Labours of Mrs. Zilpha Elaw, an American Female of Colour; Together with Some Account of the Great Religious Revivals in America*, in Andrews, *Sisters of the Spirit*, pp. 72–73. Hereafter, page references are given in the text.

conflict and triumph as a "uniformity, like that of the human constitution, admitting of the greatest variety of individual features, yet all governed by the same laws" (p. 73). Like Bancroft's representative of republican selfhood, the Christian self Elaw here describes embodies the complex and conflicted forces of this world and speaks of a possible commonwealth of faith. And out of the spiritual struggle comes a new understanding and a new discourse, for although Elaw's sister was momentarily "to all appearance dead," she revives again, and sings in a language, Elaw reports, "too wonderful for me"; "I could not understand it." She then addresses her sister and informs Elaw that she "must preach the gospel" (pp. 72–73).

While we should recognize that Elaw believes that this possible commonwealth of faith cannot be held within geographical boundaries, it is still important to note her emphasis of its most productive earthly location—for Elaw, like so many others, finds providence blossoming most fully in the fields of America. Just as many early celebrants of the United States viewed the nation not geographically but ideologically, anticipating the day when all the world would be America, so Elaw, who believes in the universality of the Christian faith, believes that America is the ideal site for its development—and for largely the same reasons as did such literary nationalists as Whitman and Bancroft. "Human nature must be in every country radically the same," Elaw asserts, for "God is the same"; yet, she argues, "the word preached is generally attended in America with far more powerful and converting results than in Britain" (144). And although she declines to fully "account for the cause," she speculates that "the population of the United States have not been so extensively vitiated by the infidelity and sedition of the press; and being more thinly spread over an immense territorial space, there is less of contamination than in the more condensed masses of English society; and they perhaps possess more honest simplicity of character, and less of the self-sufficiency of a licentious intellectuality and worldly wisdom" (p. 144). This is a largely familiar vision of America as a garden of republican virtues thus far relatively uncorrupted by the temptations of the centralized power and entrenched authority that come with the earthly city.[31] The expansiveness of the garden itself becomes providential in Elaw's vision, forestalling intellectual and moral contamination simply by making the promotion of worldly wisdom more difficult.

In this vision of the American city on a hill, as in Bancroft's, the struggle for faith becomes a battle of conflicting discourses. It is not for nothing that

31. I am thinking of the vision of an American republican tradition influenced heavily by the libertarian thought of English commonwealthmen, of the kind presented in Bernard Bailyn, *The Ideological Origins of the American Revolution* (Cambridge, Mass., 1967); J. G. A. Pocock, *The Machiavellian Moment: Florentine Political Thought and the Atlantic Republican Tradition* (Cambridge, 1975); and Gordon S. Wood, *The Creation of the American Republic, 1776–1787* (New York, 1972).

Elaw warns her readers, "Take heed what you read," and presents the press as "a tree of knowledge, both of good and evil"—for the press, she warns, is capable of disrupting and even inverting the relation between words and their referents, "putting darkness for light, and light for darkness" (p. 52). The press, Elaw warns, can be "the scavenger of slander, and the harlequin of character; the masquerade of morals, and the burlesque of religion; the proteus of sentiment, and the dictionary of licentiousness; the seminary of libertines, and the hot-bed of sedition" (p. 52). It can so distort moral discourse that the individual subject of discourse can find herself or himself wandering down a path that diverges from the Providential course. "It is to be deplored," Elaw laments late in her *Memoirs*, "that there are so many Christians . . . who are of the world; [who] speak in accordance with its principles and sentiments, and walk according to its course" (p. 141). Presenting in print her case against the press, Elaw enters into a struggle not only against those who walk according to the world's course, but also against the sense of the source of the misunderstandings that encourage such worldly walkers—the misuse of the press and of language itself.

Like Bancroft's Washington, that is, Lee and Elaw suggest that the representative self must represent discursive governance—a morally-driven system of checks and balances capable of transforming limited human utterances into a language capable of speaking transcendent truths. In Lee's and Elaw's spiritual autobiographics, moral self-discovery is not simply a matter of learning one's moral lessons; rather, moral self-discovery is the process of learning how to align the human word with the divine intention. Lee, for example, begins her autobiography and her spiritual journey with a lie; she soon finds herself with a Roman Catholic family that presents her with a novel when she wants to read the Bible; and when she aligns her own words and deeds, once her "heart had believed" and her "tongue had made confession unto salvation," the "first words uttered," she reports, were "a part of that song, which shall fill eternity with its sound": "*glory to God*" (p. 29). From the teller of a lie to a voice in a larger chorus, Lee enters into a moral commonwealth, where language itself is transformed. With sanctification comes her entrance into a new spiritual realm that is also a new realm of discourse: "So great was my joy," she reports, "that it is past description. There is no language that can describe it, except that which was heard by St. Paul, when he was caught up to the third heaven, and heard words which it was not lawful to utter" (p. 34).

These autobiographies point to this realm past description and a discourse "not lawful to utter," but they exist to serve a world governed by other discursive laws; and Lee and Elaw both work to reconstitute the discourse of this world under the governing spirit of the divine realm. They work towards what Elaw calls "a pure language"—and as she explains this concept, it becomes clear that a pure language exists in distinction to human discourse. "A pure language," Elaw explains, "unalloyed by the fulsome compliment, the hyperbole, the tautology and circumlocution, the insinuation, double meaning and vagueness, the weakness and poverty, the impurity, bombast, and other defects, with which all human languages are clogged, seems to be essential for the associations of glorified spirits" (p. 74). The language Elaw imagines is, as I have said, *distinct* from human discourse, but it is not *separated* from it; indeed, this pure language rises from the confused mix of social languages. It cannot be known positively, and so must be discerned in negatives, by recognizing "the defects, with which all human languages are clogged." One cannot unclog human language, but if one can recognize the limitations of various forms of human discourse, as Elaw demonstrates here, and recognize also the conflicting varieties of the languages we speak, then one can at least apprehend another language, one expressive of a communal understanding that is something more than the sum of the individual human parts. As Washington's silences spoke eloquently of "one continued act of faith in the eternal, intelligent, moral order of the universe," so Elaw's attention to the noisy defects of human speech point to other possible modes of understanding.

The limitations of language, Elaw suggests, themselves reveal a world of truths just beyond human understanding; to know one's limits is to maintain an awareness of that which lies beyond those limits. Similarly, Jarena Lee looks to such limitations to establish specifically linguistic evidence in support of her vision of hell. Alluding to the biblical descriptions of hell, Lee argues that

> This language is too strong and expressive to be applied to any state of suffering in *time*. Were it to be thus applied, the reality could no where be found in human life; the consequence would be, that *this* scripture would be found a false testimony. But when made to apply to an endless state of perdition, in eternity, beyond the bounds of human life, then this language is found not to exceed our views of a state of eternal damnation. (p. 31)

Essentially, Lee here measures the inadequacy of any available referents for the biblical signifiers. Descriptions of fire "which burneth with brimstone" and of a "bottomless pit" speak of an unaccountable reality, and its very inapplicability in this world serves as evidence for the existence of another, terrible reality beyond the limits of human understanding and conventional credulity.

In this way, skepticism becomes part of the constitution of faith, for skepticism stands as evidence of the human inability to fully comprehend a reality that Lee and Elaw assert is evident in their lives. Skepticism, that is, identifies the conceptual boundaries of human discourse, a discourse that itself can only promote partial and contested perspectives. And the divine author, working to make those boundaries clear in order to draw humanity to a nearer apprehension of the workings of providence, finds the best vehicles to be those who will inspire the most skepticism: Lee, who called herself a "poor colored female instrument," and Elaw, "an American female of colour." These instruments of divine authorship are uniquely suited to the task of exposing those whose investment in this world keeps them from recognizing the presence of another. As Elaw notes, "There are many sceptical persons who conceitedly, rashly, and idly scoff at the idea of apparitions and angelic appearances; but they ignorantly do it in the face of the most extensive experience, instinct, belief, and credible testimony of persons of every nation, and of all ages, as well as the inspired statements of the Scriptures" (p. 77). Speaking from the conceptual world of scriptural statements, Elaw sees a world of "facts"—evidence of "the separate existence of the soul after death"—far more powerful and universal than those upon which human governance relies (p. 77). Throughout their spiritual autobiographies, Lee and Elaw anticipate and even count on the reader's resistance and skeptical response, and build that response into their texts, there to take part in the ongoing conflicts of human languages.

Lee's and Elaw's culturally assigned positions—in sharp contrast to their experience and verbal achievements (they have, after all, become known for their ability to transform others by words alone)—emphasize that the voice being resisted is not that of the "poor colored female instrument" but rather that which sounds through the instrument. As Elaw puts it at the beginning of her *Memoirs*, she offers in this book "a representation, not, indeed, of the features of my outward person, drawn and coloured by the skill of the pencilling artist, but of the lineaments of my inward man, as inscribed by the Holy Ghost" (p. 51). But throughout her spiritual autobiography as throughout Lee's, Elaw clearly addresses the world that has "drawn and coloured" her outward person in its own group portrait of the world. Shaping their narratives to emphasize the presence of a greater artist working through their lives, and speaking to that world of pencilling artists, Lee and Elaw draw together the various conceptual worlds they encounter into a single system of discursive governance. By so doing they make it possible to see the ways in which, as Lee puts it, "our by-laws of church government and discipline" can "bring into disrepute even the word of life" (p. 36). And they make it possible, as well, to reconceive as "matters of fact" (Elaw, p. 77) what might seem "fanciful speculations"—namely, a world of revelatory fact and a governing spirit that dominates human life but that human governance has not yet learned to see.

Linda Brent's Visionary Silence

Revelatory facts indicating a governing spirit are at the heart of Harriet Jacobs's *Incidents in the Life of a Slave Girl*, as is the task of learning to interpret those facts and learning one's duty to the spirit. Indeed, one might say that Harriet Jacobs works to heighten the eloquent silence to which Clotel surrenders herself, and that the story of Linda Brent, the pseudonymous narrator of *Incidents*, is the story of learning to read anew the divinely authored text of the human spirit. This autobiography is striking in a number of respects, but particularly in its vivid presentation of the sexual crimes committed within the self-justifying institution of slavery. Jacobs tells of the aggressive sexual advances of her enslaver, Dr. Flint; of her decision to take a White lover, Mr. Sands; of her avoidance of Flint's advances; of the children she has through her relations with Mr. Sands; and of her long journey—taken largely to protect her children's future—to the relative freedom of the North. This narrative, which begins with an appeal to "the blessing of God," ends with Brent in the North and legally "free," but still without a home of her own—for, she notes, "God so orders circumstance as to keep me with my friend [and employer] Mrs. Bruce."[32] The central question, then, of *Incidents* concerns the relation between Linda Brent's story of moral struggle and the providential narrative—the divinely ordered circumstance—that she invokes at the end.

The paradox of Brent's existence—as voice for the moral code that she herself has been forced to transgress—is represented at the very beginning of the narrative, on the title page itself. The reader encounters there two epigraphs: a testament, by "a woman of North Carolina," to the degradation inflicted and enforced by the slave system; and a verse from Isaiah (32:9): "Rise up, ye women that are at ease! Hear my voice, ye careless daughters! Give ear unto my speech." These epigraphs identify two spheres of existence—Northerners who are ignorant and women who are morally "at ease"—each capable of a culturally empowered response to its condition. The subject of the book, Linda Brent herself, is excluded from both spheres; they mark the points of a moral journey that she cannot make. Brent's story exists not in one sphere or the other but rather in a world of experience distant from both.[33]

Indeed, Linda Brent's experiences lead her to wonder, even as she identifies herself within the moral sphere, how exactly, by what providential design, her identity and experience as a slave can be possible. She finds herself torn between a paternal model of divinity and a conception of the Divine realm that offers otherworldly echoes of politics as usual: "Sometimes I thought God was a compassionate Father, who would forgive my

32. Harriet Jacobs, *Incidents in the Life of a Slave Girl, Written by Herself*, ed. Jean Fagan Yellin (Cambridge, Mass., 1987), p. 210. Hereafter, page references are given in the text.

33. On Brent's transgressions, see William L. Andrews, *To Tell a Free Story: The First Century of Afro-American Autobiography, 1760–1865* (Urbana, Ill., 1986), pp. 247ff.; on Jacobs's call for a careful readership, see Frances Smith Foster, "Harriet Jacobs's *Incidents* and the 'Careless Daughters' (and Sons) Who Read It," in *The (Other) American Traditions: Nineteenth-Century Women Writers*, ed. Joyce W. Warren (New Brunswick, N.J., 1993), pp. 92–107.

sins for the sake of my sufferings. At other times, it seemed to me there was no justice or mercy in the divine government." "These things," she tells the reader, referring to the existence and perpetuation of "the curse of slavery," "took the shape of mystery, which is to this day not so clear to my soul as I trust it will be hereafter" (p. 123). Lost in the contradictions of the "forms" of human culture, Jacobs sees not a science revealing the great movement of history but rather an inscrutable mystery.

The hope for a renewed awareness of the motive "idea" that informs human history—the means by which Providence finds its human agency—is restricted by the very "forms" used to give shape and meaning to hope. The model for understanding and maintaining the correspondence between human and divine history is neither the father nor government, for both paradigms ultimately invert the relation between the national structure and its putative foundation. The best model, in effect, would be no model at all—for all paradigms of the inexpressible are all too human, too eminently expressible. Like many other African American writers, Jacobs holds determinedly to the theology of Christian mystery as the hermeneutical key to biblical law. Mystery signifies that which lies beyond human understanding, and which therefore calls for scrupulous attention to the "forms" of human history and self-government that obscure the mystery by projecting it on ideological screens. Mystery signifies as well a mode of understanding and of communication, an inspired *speaking* not in tongues but rather in the understanding that comes of suspended uncertainty and incomprehension in the face of revelation—a speaking of that which lies beyond what one can know, and a speaking that acknowledges the limits of one's rational understanding.

Essentially, Brent's struggle is to rediscover the community of mystery from a disenfranchasized but therefore morally privileged position. She begins the struggle for a renewed community when she recognizes that she must engage in it alone, at the turning point in the narrative, when she refuses Dr. Flint's "offer" to establish her in a cottage as his mistress. Dr. Flint makes perfectly clear the restricted terms of this offer: "there are," he notes rather unnecessarily, "two sides to my proposition; if you reject the bright side, you will be obliged to take the dark one" (p. 84). The "bright" side, of course, refers to Flint's attempt to reposition Brent as a woman (from the site of deferred desire to the site for sexual exchange) by manipulating her identity as a mother (offering a "better" life for her children). Adapting Flint's terminology, Brent begins her struggle as a determined and self-determining woman and mother: "I had my secret hopes; but I must fight my battle alone. I had a woman's pride, and a mother's love for my children; and I resolved that out of the darkness of this hour a brighter dawn should rise for them. My master had power and law on his side; I had a determined will. There is might in each" (p. 85). This battle is an ideological Civil War, a battle between the power and law that claims to both support and depend upon womanhood and motherhood, and the will of one who is determined to embody the virtues associated with womanhood and motherhood. It is a battle between human and divine law—between human history and Providence—a battle that can be fought only by one who is a product of both.[34]

In this struggle lies the hope of a renewed community, the development of an invisible family of the oppressed. For Brent's task is to save her children by first seeming to abandon them, and to place her hopes in the reunion of her family in the far dream of self-liberation. Separated physically, the bonds of this family can be experienced only spiritually, and the experience strengthens Brent's resolve and heightens her spiritual awareness. She begins the struggle against "the doom that awaited my fair baby in slavery" by going to the graves of her parents to vow to save her children "or perish in the attempt" (p. 90). Noting that her mother's deathbed blessing had been a continuing comfort, she tells the reader that "in many an hour of tribulation I had seemed to hear her voice, sometimes chiding me, sometimes whispering loving words into my wounded heart."[35] While this might seem the conventional voice of motherhood speaking through the heart of memory, a staple of sentimental discourse, Jacobs increasingly makes it clear that she is speaking of a distinctively African American experience of the spirit, of visions and prophecy.[36]

As Brent hears other voices and discovers other bonds, she indicates the revolutionary subtext of the narrative, the threatening presence of the oppressed community endorsed and protected by God. At the graveyard, Brent is reminded of the voice of her mother; as she leaves, she *hears* the voice of her father—significantly, while passing a place associated with either the threat or promise (depending on one's reading of sacred history) of Black insurrection: "As I passed the wreck of the old meeting house, where, before Nat Turner's time, the slaves had been allowed to meet for worship, I seemed to hear my father's voice come from it, bidding me not to tarry till I reached freedom or the grave. I rushed on with renovated

34. On the terms and significance of Brent's struggle with Flint, see Dana D. Nelson, *The Word in Black and White: Reading "Race" in American Literature, 1638–1867* (New York, 1993), chap. 7.

35. Jacobs, *Incidents*, p. 90. It is important to remember that Jacobs worries about her own presence as mother for her children, for they "cannot remember me with such entire satisfaction as I remembered my mother" (p. 90). Like her mother, though, Jacobs hopes to give them a voice to remember.

36. Houston A. Baker, Jr., argues that "a primary component of what might be termed 'classical' Afro-American discourse is 'soul'. In more sacral dimensions, this component is labeled 'spirit'. Soul motivates; spirit moves. The generative source of style in Afro-America is soul; the impetus for salvation is spirit" (*Workings of the Spirit: The Poetics of Afro-American Women's Writing* [Chicago, 1991], p. 75). I would suggest that Jacobs here makes a point of writing from the soul in the name of the spirit.

hopes. My trust in God had been strengthened by that prayer among the graves" (p. 91). The voice signifies the intersection of Providential and human history, the manifest sign of one's election as an agent of God.[37] Only when most alone is Jacobs able to enter into this increasingly visible and immanent community—and the community is increased and strengthened by the threat of oppression that makes it dangerous to acknowledge a common struggle. The bonds of community are forced into literally unspeakable realms, imagined but not known, experienced but not discussed. Referring to her friend Fanny's own seclusion, Jacobs notes the "similar burden[s] of anxiety and fear" experienced by Fanny's mother Aggie and Brent's grandmother—"dangerous secrets [that] deepened the sympathy between the two old persecuted mothers" (p. 149). Similarly, Brent eventually rediscovers her own brother William in one of those coincidences that support the belief in a transcendent, overruling order. Noting that William's "old feelings of affection for me and Ellen were as lively as ever," Brent speaks of the community formed of similar burdens and dangerous secrets when she adds, "There are no bonds so strong as those which are formed by suffering together" (p. 170).

At the beginning of her own long seclusion, Brent has yet another vision, and she emphasizes that this is not to be taken as sentimental figuration but rather as a distinctively spiritual experience:

> And now I will tell you something that happened to me; though you will, perhaps, think it illustrates the superstition of slaves. . . . A band of serenaders were under the window, playing "Home, sweet home." I listened till the sounds did not seem like music, but like the moaning of children. It seemed as if my heart would burst. I rose from my sitting posture, and knelt. A streak of moonlight was on the floor before me, and in the midst of it appeared the forms of my two children. They vanished; but I had seen them distinctly. Some will call it a dream, others a vision. I know not how to account for it, but it made a strong impression on my mind, and I felt certain something had happened to my little ones. (pp. 107–8)

In this remarkable account, the evocation of the domestic sphere leads Brent not merely to an instinctual awareness of her children but to a manifest vision. We miss an important dimension of Brent's narrative—and of Jacobs's broader accounting of her world—when we pass by this lightly or try to account for it in ways that Brent herself cannot, for the motive power of a new mode of envisioning lies in the dynamics of individual belief, the unquestioning acceptance of mystifying experience. The point is not to

---

37. Nat Turner's presence here is, of course, significant. Indeed, Turner was a prominent presence in nineteenth-century African-American publications. See Eric J. Sundquist, *To Wake the Nations: Race in the Making of American Literature* (Cambridge, Mass., 1993), chap. 1.

understand it, but rather to acknowledge that which lies beyond understanding, and thereby to identify the limitations of culturally authorized ways of knowing. This vision, like the voices of her parents, signals Brent's transition from the labyrinths of the self-contradictory American ideological realm to a defiantly mysterious realm beyond, where the citizens of the moral realm speak beyond what culturally trained ears can hear.

In this way, Jacobs accounts for and capitalizes upon her own lack of cultural authority—not only as a woman but as a Black woman. Through her representative Linda Brent, Jacobs can speak of the presence in her life of something absent from her world. The "dream of [her] life . . . not yet realized," and lacking "a hearthstone of [her] own, however humble" (p. 201), Linda Brent embodies the disjunction of the sacred and the secular, which can be rejoined only by realigning human practices with a providential design threatening in its inscrutability. The silence of the mystery that informs Linda Brent's journey to relative freedom and that unifies the community of the oppressed is significant precisely because there seem to be no words capable of giving it adequate expression.

Linda's hearthstone, one suspects, awaits in an as-yet-unrealized city on a hill. Joining the spirit of Nat Turner to the promise of a gathering community, Jacobs begins the long struggle to build that spiritual city. And as oppression brings that community together, Jacobs suggests, the envisioned city's citizens will be better prepared for the struggle against the worldly cities of the United States, meeting power and law with a collectively determined will. The national mythology having failed them, African Americans appropriated symbols for imagining a blessed community— symbols through which those at the cultural margins could claim the moral center. And as these symbolic terms were brought to focus on the struggle to join the sacred and the profane within the individual, this vision of a spiritual community enabled women to claim active moral leadership. As one representative of Black female leadership, Frances E. W. Harper, puts it in her post-reconstruction novel *Iola Leroy*, "There is a field of Christian endeavor which lies between the school-house and the pulpit, which needs the hand of a woman more in private than in public."[38] And in those fields women would need to counter the inevitable corruptions of schoolhouse and pulpit, education and religion, working against what Harper elsewhere calls the "architects of destruction" to fulfill the "grandly constructive" mission of Black Americans.[39] Noting the need to build "above the wastes of war, more stately temples of thought and action," Harper in *Iola Leroy*

38. Frances E. W. Harper, *Iola Leroy, or Shadows Uplifted* (New York, 1988), p. 254.

39. Harper, *Trial and Triumph*, in *Minnie's Sacrifice, Sowing and Reaping, Trial and Triumph: Three Rediscovered Novels by Frances E. W. Harper*, ed. Frances Smith Foster (Boston, 1994), p. 241.

addresses directly the role of literature in this ongoing reconstruction of the national symbolic city.[40] In her closing note, she calls for those "upon whose brows God has poured the chrism of [a] new era to . . . use every power God has given them . . . to add their quota of good citizenship to the best welfare of the nation." And they can do that, she suggests, by gathering the scattered stories of Black experience and introducing them "into the literature of the country . . . and thus add to the solution of our unsolved American problem."[41] Symbols contained by symbols, solutions to problems defined by others, Harper's readers are encouraged to become writers, as is the novel's protagonist—because literature can redeem and because it can destroy, and because the cities we create are influenced by those we imagine.

40. Harper, *Iola Leroy*, p. 236.
41. Ibid., p. 282.

Notes on Contributors

Barbara Bair is the author of *Though Justice Sleeps: African Americans 1880–1900*, in progress for Oxford University Press, and the associate editor of *The Marcus Garvey and Universal Negro Improvement Association Papers* vols. 6 and 7, published by the University of California Press in 1989 and 1990.

Gail Bederman is Assistant Professor of History at the University of Notre Dame. She is the author of *Manliness and Civilization: A Cultural History of Gender and Race in the United States, 1880–1917*, which was published by the University of Chicago Press in 1995.

Yvonne Chireau is Assistant Professor of Religion at Swarthmore College. She has written on African American religion, black women, and folk traditions. She is currently completing a book titled *Black Magic: Dimensions of the Supernatural in African American Religion.*

Patricia Cline Cohen is Professor of History and Women's Studies at the University of California, Santa Barbara. She is currently completing a book tentatively titled, *The Murder of Helen Jewett: Gender and Sexuality in Jacksonian America.*

Mary De Jong is Associate Professor of English and Women's Studies at Pennsylvania State University, Altoona. She has published extensively on women writers and on women and religion. She is currently at work on a study of gender and hymnody in nineteenth-century America.

John Ernest is Assistant Professor of English and Director of the African American Studies minor at the University of New Hampshire. He is the author of *Resistance and Reformation in Nineteenth-Century African-American Literature: Brown, Wilson, Jacobs, Delany, Douglass, and Harper* (University Press of Mississippi, 1995). He is currently working on a study of nineteenth-century African American historians.

Sharla Fett is Assistant Professor of History at the University of Arizona and is currently conducting postdoctoral research at the Center for African American Studies at UCLA. She is working on a book on African American healing in nineteenth-century slave communities.

Stephen Hum is a doctoral candidate in History at the University of Michigan. He is writing a dissertation on triracial social interactions in Charleston, South Carolina, in the eighteenth and nineteenth centuries.

Susan Juster is a member of the History Department at the University of Michigan. Her book, *Disorderly Women: Sexual Politics and Evangelicalism in Revolutionary New England*, was published by Cornell University Press in 1994, and she is currently working on a comparative study of female prophecy and preaching in Britain, America, and Canada in the period 1780 to 1815.

Lisa MacFarlane is Associate Professor of English and Director of the American Studies minor at the University of New Hampshire. She has published on American women writers and on the construction of masculinity in nineteenth-century American fiction. Her current work explores the convention of the feminized minister in American letters.

Etta Madden is Assistant Professor of English at Southwest Missouri State University. She works on literacy and literature among religious communities in American culture prior to 1900, and has published on Puritan funeral sermons.

Index